GUMBALLS

BY: ERIN NATIONS

GUMBALLS © 2018 Erin Nations.

ISBN: 978-1-60309-431-3   21 20 19 18   1 2 3 4

Published by Top Shelf Productions, PO Box 1282, Marietta, GA 30061-1282, USA. Top Shelf Productions is an imprint of IDW Publishing, a division of Idea and Design Works, LLC. Offices: 2765 Truxtun Road, San Diego, CA 92106. Top Shelf Productions®, the Top Shelf logo, Idea and Design Works®, and the IDW logo are registered trademarks of Idea and Design Works, LLC. All Rights Reserved. With the exception of small excerpts of artwork used for review purposes, none of the contents of this publication may be reprinted without the permission of IDW Publishing. IDW Publishing does not read or accept unsolicited submissions of ideas, stories, or artwork.

Printed in Korea.

Editor-in-Chief: Chris Staros.
Edited by Brett Warnock & Leigh Walton.

Visit our online catalog at www.topshelfcomix.com.

TABLE of CONTENTS

THIS COMIC BOOK FEATURES AN ASSORTMENT OF SHORT COMICS, ILLUSTRATIONS, AND SERIALIZED WORK. COLORS ARE USED TO CATEGORIZE THEM. THE COLORFUL DOT NEXT TO EACH TITLE REPRESENTS THE FEATURE IT'S ASSOCIATED WITH. FOR EXAMPLE, THE COLOR PINK REPRESENTS COMICS ABOUT TOBIAS, SO THE TITLE "FIRST KISS" HAS A PINK DOT NEXT TO IT.

COLOR KEY

- TWINS-TRIPLET
- PLEASANT PEOPLE
- TALES OF BEING TRANS
- ILLUSTRATION

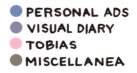

- PERSONAL ADS
- VISUAL DIARY
- TOBIAS
- MISCELLANEA

HAPPINESS COMES IN THREES

A LAP FULL - DONNA AND HUSBAND ERIC NATIONS OF OVERLAND, MO., ARE THE PARENTS OF TRIPLET DAUGHTERS BORN AT ST. JOHN'S MERCY HOSPITAL ON FRIDAY, AUGUST 20 TH. THEY ARE LAUREN WEIGHING 4 LBS. 2 OZ. AND 17 IN. LONG; ERIN WEIGHING 3 LBS. 11 OZ. AND 16 IN. LONG AND ABBY WEIGHING 4 LBS. 7 OZ. AND 18¼ IN. LONG, THE 3 GIRLS MAKING THEIR ARRIVALS AT 8:02, 8:03 AND 8:04 AM. IT IS REPORTED THAT ALL ARE DOING WELL AND THAT ABBY WHO NOW WEIGHS 4 LBS. 15 OZ. HAS GONE HOME. THEY ARE THE FIRST CHILDREN BORN TO THE NATIONS. **SUBMITTED PHOTO.**

STAND BY ME

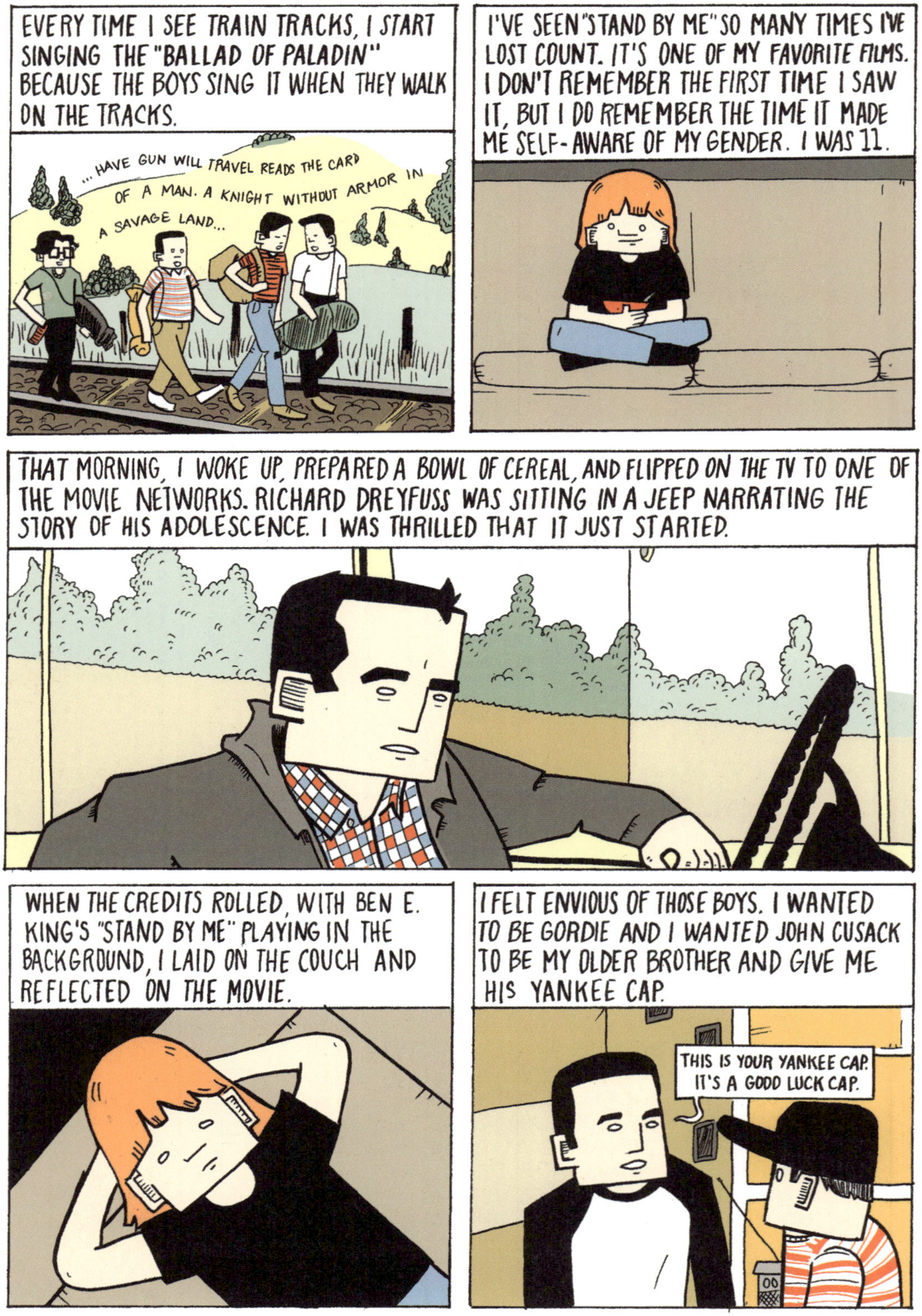
EVERY TIME I SEE TRAIN TRACKS, I START SINGING THE "BALLAD OF PALADIN" BECAUSE THE BOYS SING IT WHEN THEY WALK ON THE TRACKS.
... HAVE GUN WILL TRAVEL READS THE CARD OF A MAN. A KNIGHT WITHOUT ARMOR IN A SAVAGE LAND...
I'VE SEEN "STAND BY ME" SO MANY TIMES I'VE LOST COUNT. IT'S ONE OF MY FAVORITE FILMS. I DON'T REMEMBER THE FIRST TIME I SAW IT, BUT I DO REMEMBER THE TIME IT MADE ME SELF-AWARE OF MY GENDER. I WAS 11.
THAT MORNING, I WOKE UP, PREPARED A BOWL OF CEREAL, AND FLIPPED ON THE TV TO ONE OF THE MOVIE NETWORKS. RICHARD DREYFUSS WAS SITTING IN A JEEP NARRATING THE STORY OF HIS ADOLESCENCE. I WAS THRILLED THAT IT JUST STARTED.
WHEN THE CREDITS ROLLED, WITH BEN E. KING'S "STAND BY ME" PLAYING IN THE BACKGROUND, I LAID ON THE COUCH AND REFLECTED ON THE MOVIE.
I FELT ENVIOUS OF THOSE BOYS. I WANTED TO BE GORDIE AND I WANTED JOHN CUSACK TO BE MY OLDER BROTHER AND GIVE ME HIS YANKEE CAP.
THIS IS YOUR YANKEE CAP. IT'S A GOOD LUCK CAP.

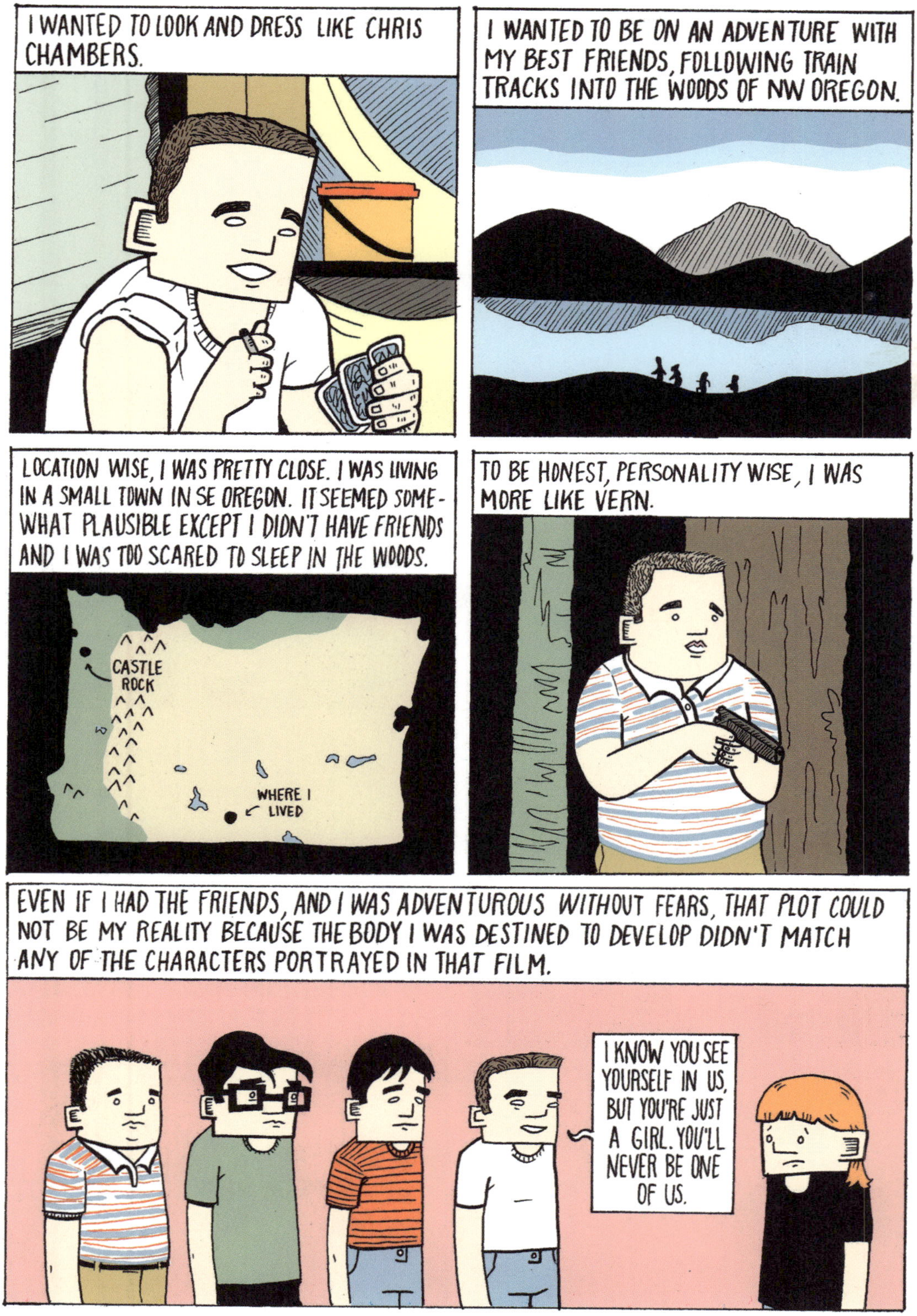
I WANTED TO LOOK AND DRESS LIKE CHRIS CHAMBERS.
I WANTED TO BE ON AN ADVENTURE WITH MY BEST FRIENDS, FOLLOWING TRAIN TRACKS INTO THE WOODS OF NW OREGON.
LOCATION WISE, I WAS PRETTY CLOSE. I WAS LIVING IN A SMALL TOWN IN SE OREGON. IT SEEMED SOME-WHAT PLAUSIBLE EXCEPT I DIDN'T HAVE FRIENDS AND I WAS TOO SCARED TO SLEEP IN THE WOODS.
CASTLE ROCK
WHERE I LIVED
TO BE HONEST, PERSONALITY WISE, I WAS MORE LIKE VERN.
EVEN IF I HAD THE FRIENDS, AND I WAS ADVENTUROUS WITHOUT FEARS, THAT PLOT COULD NOT BE MY REALITY BECAUSE THE BODY I WAS DESTINED TO DEVELOP DIDN'T MATCH ANY OF THE CHARACTERS PORTRAYED IN THAT FILM.
I KNOW YOU SEE YOURSELF IN US, BUT YOU'RE JUST A GIRL. YOU'LL NEVER BE ONE OF US.

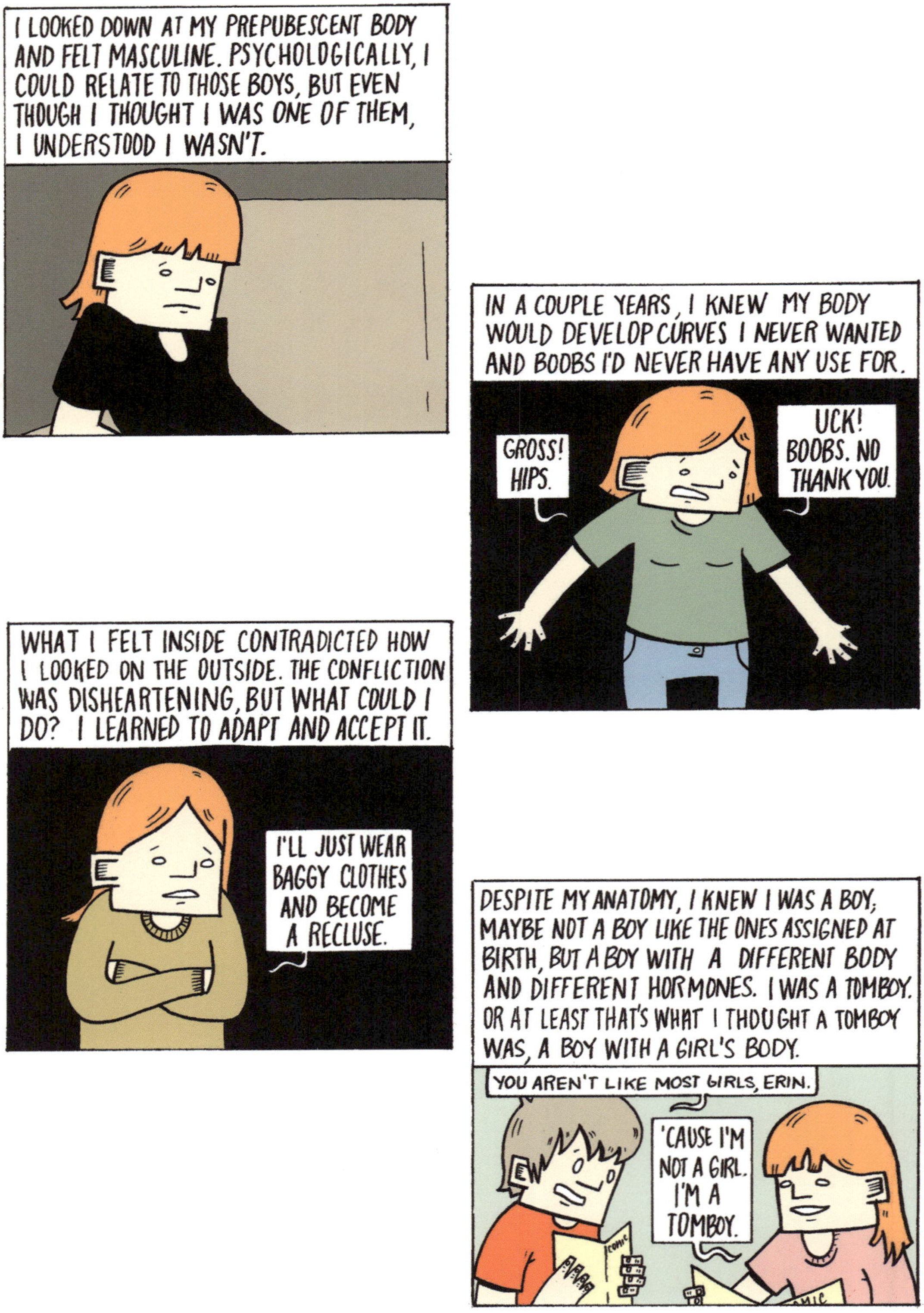
I LOOKED DOWN AT MY PREPUBESCENT BODY AND FELT MASCULINE. PSYCHOLOGICALLY, I COULD RELATE TO THOSE BOYS, BUT EVEN THOUGH I THOUGHT I WAS ONE OF THEM, I UNDERSTOOD I WASN'T.
IN A COUPLE YEARS, I KNEW MY BODY WOULD DEVELOP CURVES I NEVER WANTED AND BOOBS I'D NEVER HAVE ANY USE FOR.
GROSS! HIPS.
UCK! BOOBS. NO THANK YOU.
WHAT I FELT INSIDE CONTRADICTED HOW I LOOKED ON THE OUTSIDE. THE CONFLICTION WAS DISHEARTENING, BUT WHAT COULD I DO? I LEARNED TO ADAPT AND ACCEPT IT.
I'LL JUST WEAR BAGGY CLOTHES AND BECOME A RECLUSE.
DESPITE MY ANATOMY, I KNEW I WAS A BOY; MAYBE NOT A BOY LIKE THE ONES ASSIGNED AT BIRTH, BUT A BOY WITH A DIFFERENT BODY AND DIFFERENT HORMONES. I WAS A TOMBOY. OR AT LEAST THAT'S WHAT I THOUGHT A TOMBOY WAS, A BOY WITH A GIRL'S BODY.
YOU AREN'T LIKE MOST GIRLS, ERIN.
'CAUSE I'M NOT A GIRL. I'M A TOMBOY.

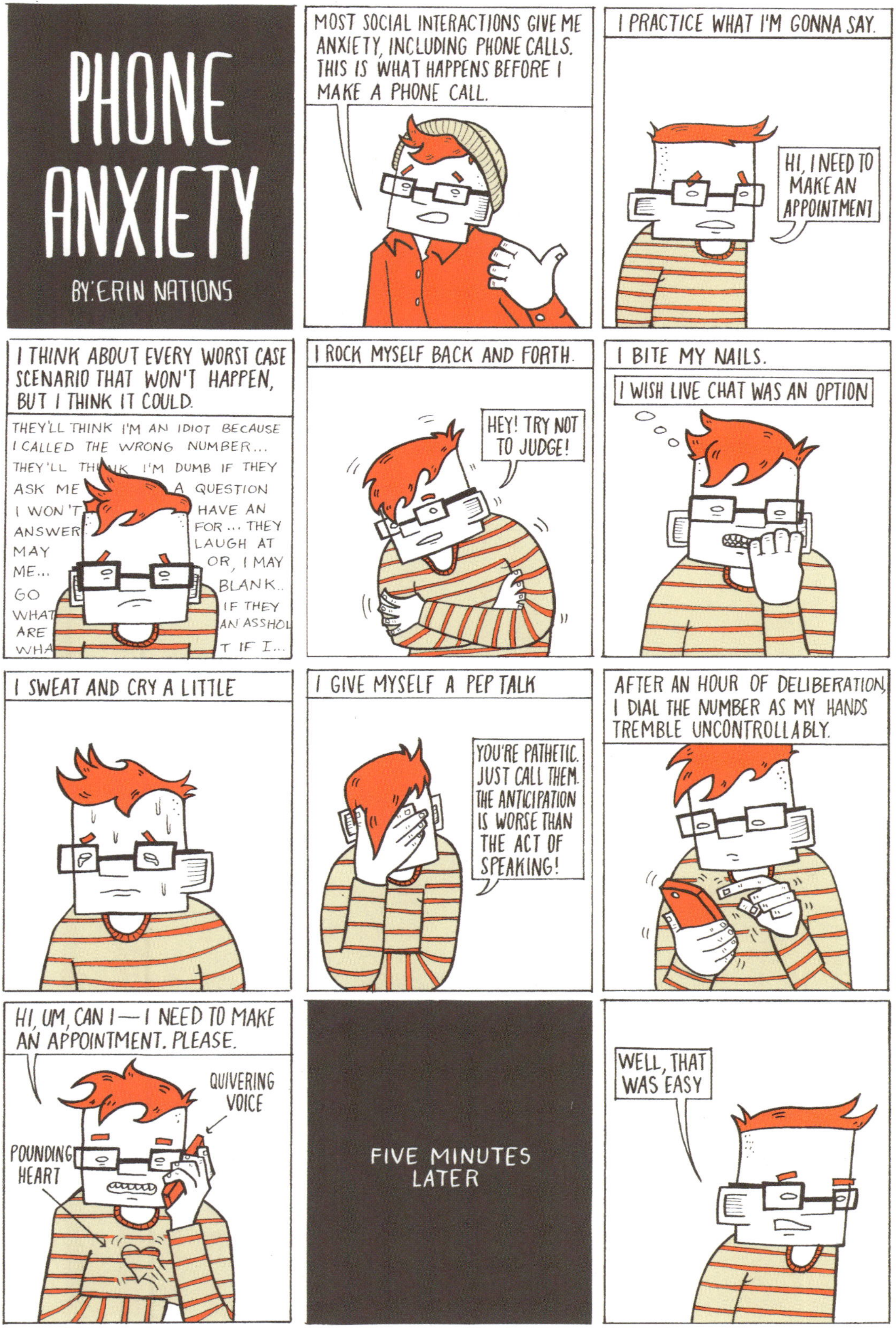
PHONE ANXIETY
BY: ERIN NATIONS
MOST SOCIAL INTERACTIONS GIVE ME ANXIETY, INCLUDING PHONE CALLS. THIS IS WHAT HAPPENS BEFORE I MAKE A PHONE CALL.
I PRACTICE WHAT I'M GONNA SAY.
HI, I NEED TO MAKE AN APPOINTMENT
I THINK ABOUT EVERY WORST CASE SCENARIO THAT WON'T HAPPEN, BUT I THINK IT COULD.
THEY'LL THINK I'M AN IDIOT BECAUSE I CALLED THE WRONG NUMBER... THEY'LL TH INK I'M DUMB IF THEY ASK ME A QUESTION I WON'T HAVE AN ANSWER FOR... THEY MAY LAUGH AT ME... OR, I MAY GO BLANK.. WHAT IF THEY ARE AN ASSHOL WHA T IF I...
I ROCK MYSELF BACK AND FORTH.
HEY! TRY NOT TO JUDGE!
I BITE MY NAILS.
I WISH LIVE CHAT WAS AN OPTION
I SWEAT AND CRY A LITTLE
I GIVE MYSELF A PEP TALK
YOU'RE PATHETIC. JUST CALL THEM. THE ANTICIPATION IS WORSE THAN THE ACT OF SPEAKING!
AFTER AN HOUR OF DELIBERATION, I DIAL THE NUMBER AS MY HANDS TREMBLE UNCONTROLLABLY.
HI, UM, CAN I—I NEED TO MAKE AN APPOINTMENT. PLEASE.
QUIVERING VOICE
POUNDING HEART
FIVE MINUTES LATER
WELL, THAT WAS EASY

PHILLIP

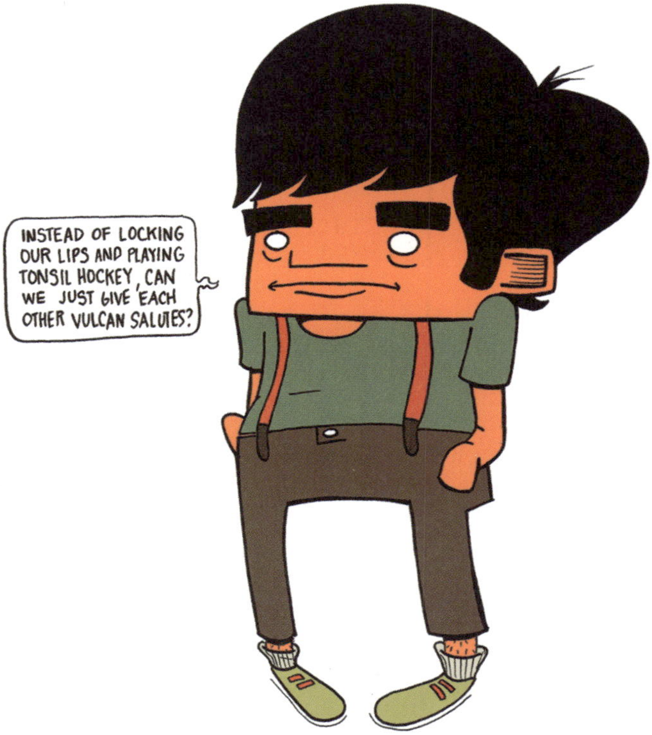
INSTEAD OF LOCKING OUR LIPS AND PLAYING TONSIL HOCKEY, CAN WE JUST GIVE EACH OTHER VULCAN SALUTES?

HELLO. I'M SEEKING A BEAUTIFUL DAMSEL. ARE YOU HER?
IF I COULD HAVE ONE SUPER POWER, IT WOULD BE TO JOIN MY TWO INDEX FINGERS TOGETHER AND STOP TIME LIKE EVIE DID IN THE TELEVISED SERIES "OUT OF THIS WORLD."
I HAVE FOUR FAVORITE FOODS. MY FOUR FAVORITE FOODS ARE BEEF JERKY, BIG LEAGUE CHEW, SLOPPY JOE, AND ONION RINGS.
I WISH I COULD BE A DRAGONWORM SLAYER, BUT FOR NOW I'M CONTENT WITH MY JOB AS A WEDDING VIDEOGRAPHER.
WHEN I'M NOT PRETENDING TO BATTLE INVERTEBRATES THAT SPEW FIRE AND TERRORIZE VILLAGES, I'M FIDDLING WITH MY RUBIK'S CUBE, READING "THE HITCHHIKER'S GUIDE TO THE GALAXY" FOR THE TENTH MILLIONTH TIME, AND PROBABLY WORKING ON MY NOVEL ABOUT DINOSAUROIDS TAKING OVER THE UNIVERSE.
I HOPE YOU RESPOND. FOR A FIRST DATE, I WAS THINKING A PANCAKE DINNER AND WATCHING MY "QUANTUM LEAP" DVD COLLECTION.

THINGS THAT SCARED THE SHIT OUT OF ME WHEN I WAS A KID.

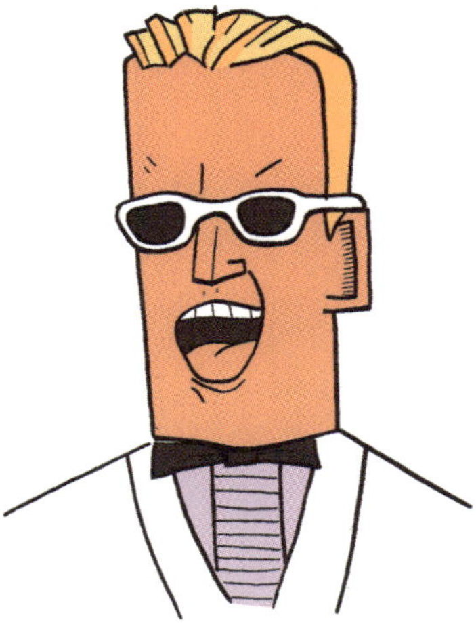

MAX HEADROOM

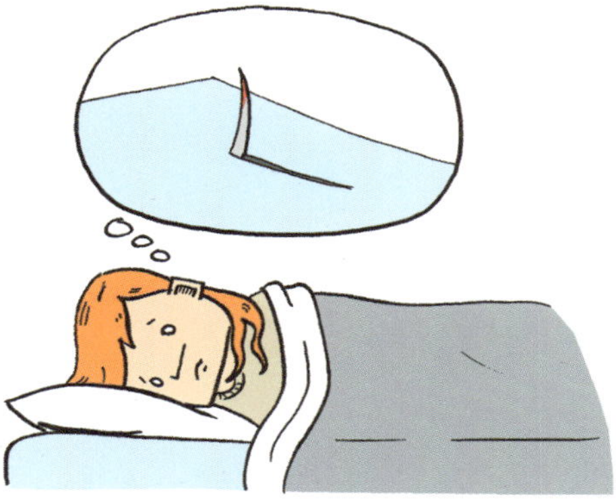

FREDDY KRUEGER'S CLAW HAND POPPING OUT OF MY MATTRESS AND SLICING MY ABDOMEN IN HALF.

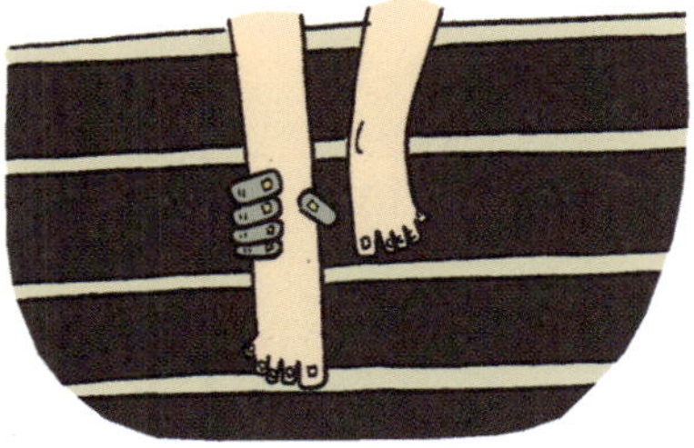

STAIRCASES WITH OPEN SLATS
BECAUSE SOMETHING MIGHT GRAB MY ANKLES

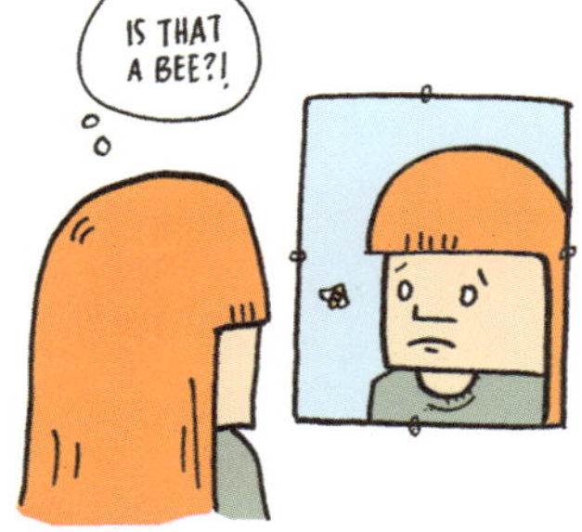
IS THAT A BEE?!

MIRRORS AND THE TEMPTATION TO SAY "CANDYMAN" 5 TIMES

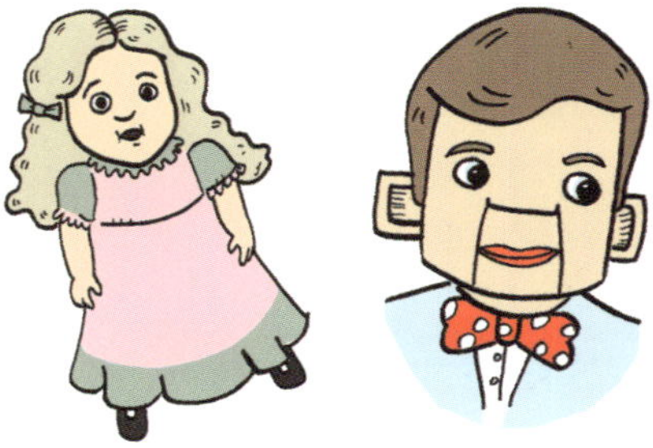

OLD PORCELAIN DOLLS + DUMMIES

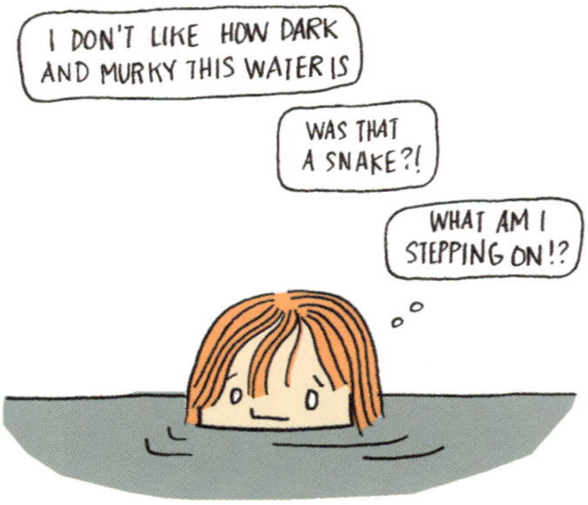
I DON'T LIKE HOW DARK AND MURKY THIS WATER IS
WAS THAT A SNAKE?!
WHAT AM I STEPPING ON!?

LAKES

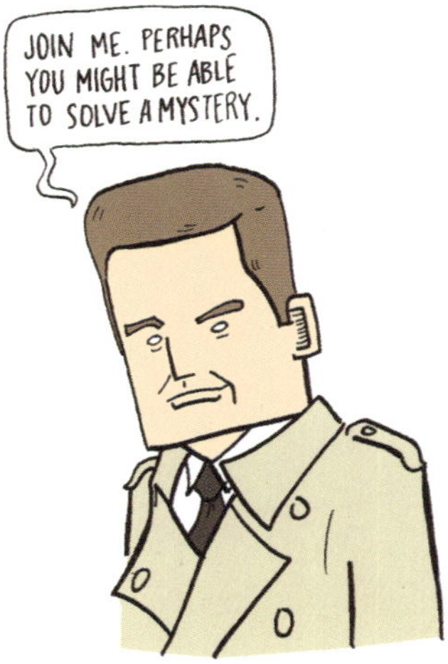
JOIN ME. PERHAPS YOU MIGHT BE ABLE TO SOLVE A MYSTERY.

ROBERT STACK'S VOICE
AND THE THEME SONG TO
UNSOLVED MYSTERIES

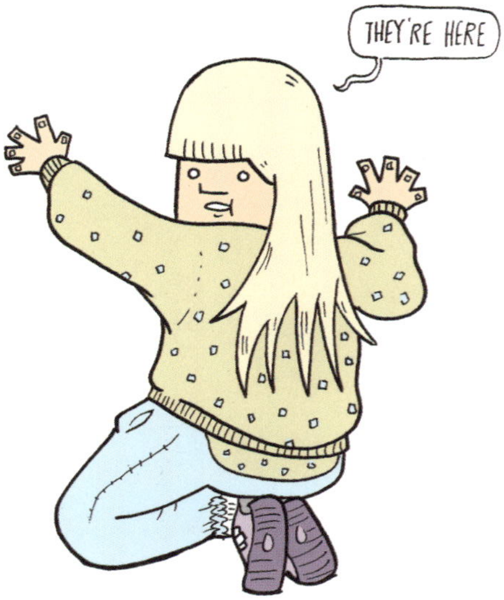
THEY'RE HERE

CAROL ANNE

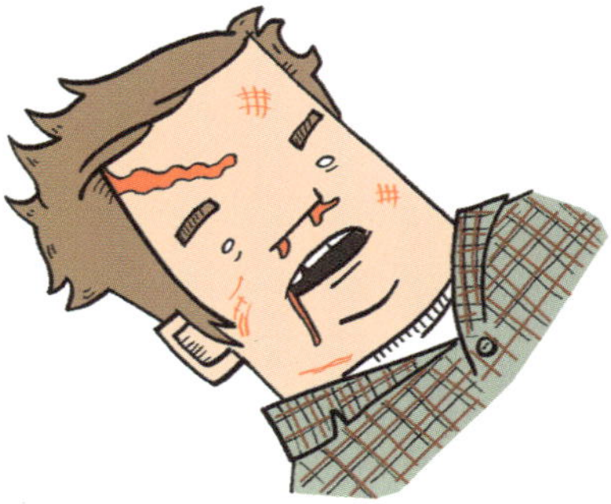

RAY BROWER'S DEAD FACE
IN THE MOVIE STAND BY ME

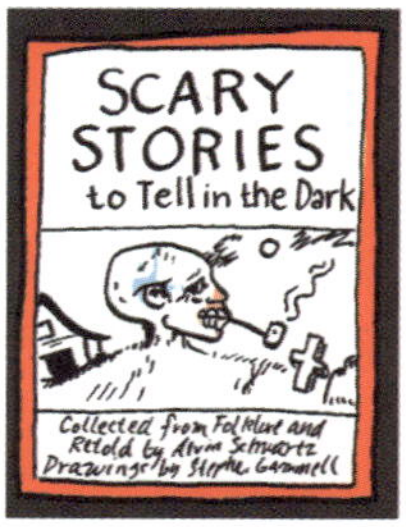
SCARY STORIES to Tell in the Dark

STEPHEN GAMMELL'S
ILLUSTRATIONS FOR SCARY
STORIES TO TELL IN THE DARK

BEDWETTER

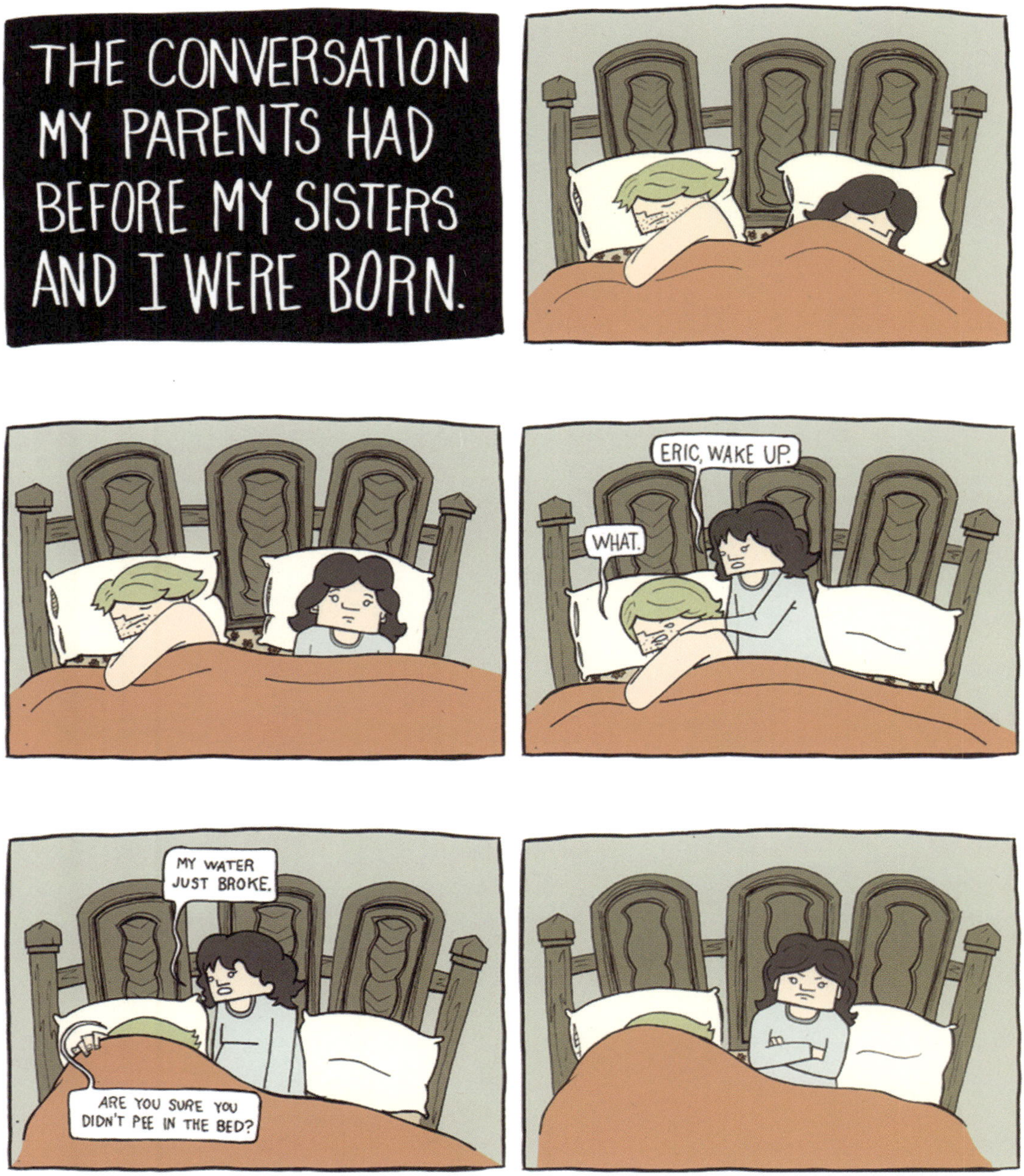
THE CONVERSATION MY PARENTS HAD BEFORE MY SISTERS AND I WERE BORN.
ERIC, WAKE UP.
WHAT.
MY WATER JUST BROKE.
ARE YOU SURE YOU DIDN'T PEE IN THE BED?

DOWNHILL

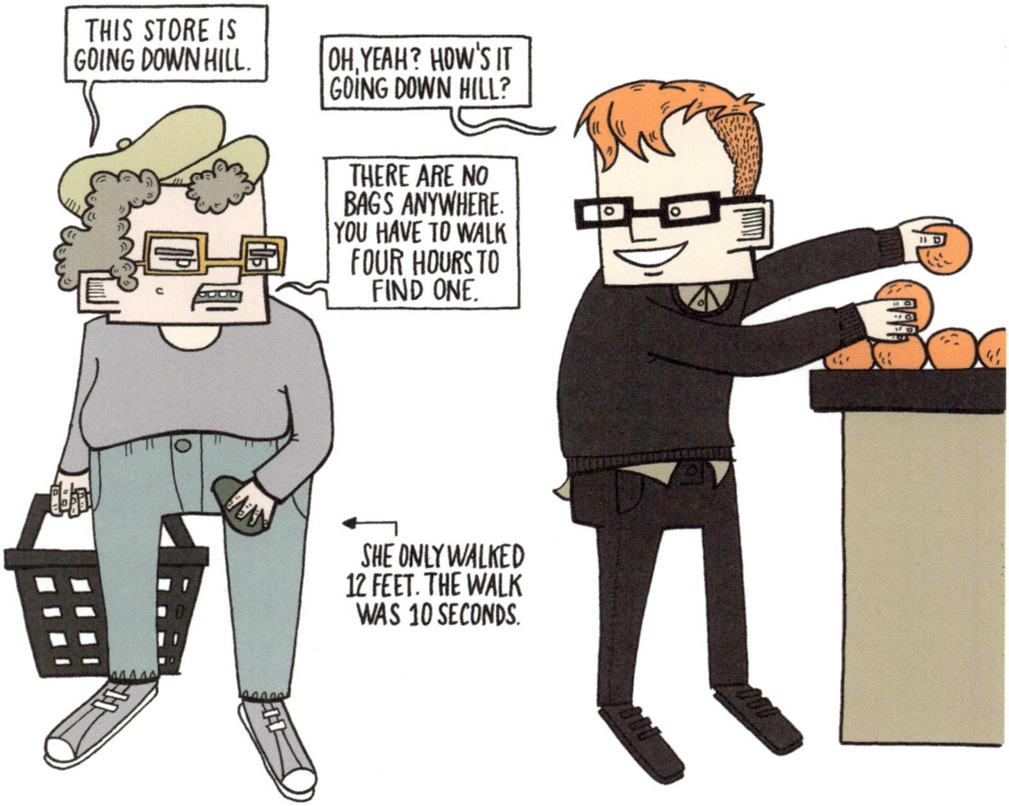
THIS STORE IS GOING DOWNHILL.
OH, YEAH? HOW'S IT GOING DOWN HILL?
THERE ARE NO BAGS ANYWHERE. YOU HAVE TO WALK FOUR HOURS TO FIND ONE.
SHE ONLY WALKED 12 FEET. THE WALK WAS 10 SECONDS.

A LITTLE BIT COUNTRY

I RODE MY BIKE TO WORK TODAY AT 4:30 AM. WHILE WAITING FOR THE STOP LIGHT TO TURN GREEN, I HEARD A MAN SHOUT AT ME.

YOU'RE GOOD LOOKIN'!
ON THE BIKE!
AW, BOY. GOOD LOOKIN'!
YOU A BOY OR A GIRL?

A DIFFERENT MAN SAID THE SAME THING TO ME A MONTH AGO. I'M NOT SURE WHAT TO SAY, SO I PRACTICE DIFFERENT RESPONSES IN MY HEAD.

I'M A LITTLE BIT COUNTRY AND A LITTLE BIT ROCK 'N ROLL... ...WELL, MOSTLY ROCK 'N ROLL, BUT I'M SOME WHERE IN THE MIDDLE.

VALENTINE'S DAY FOR THE SOCIALLY INEPT

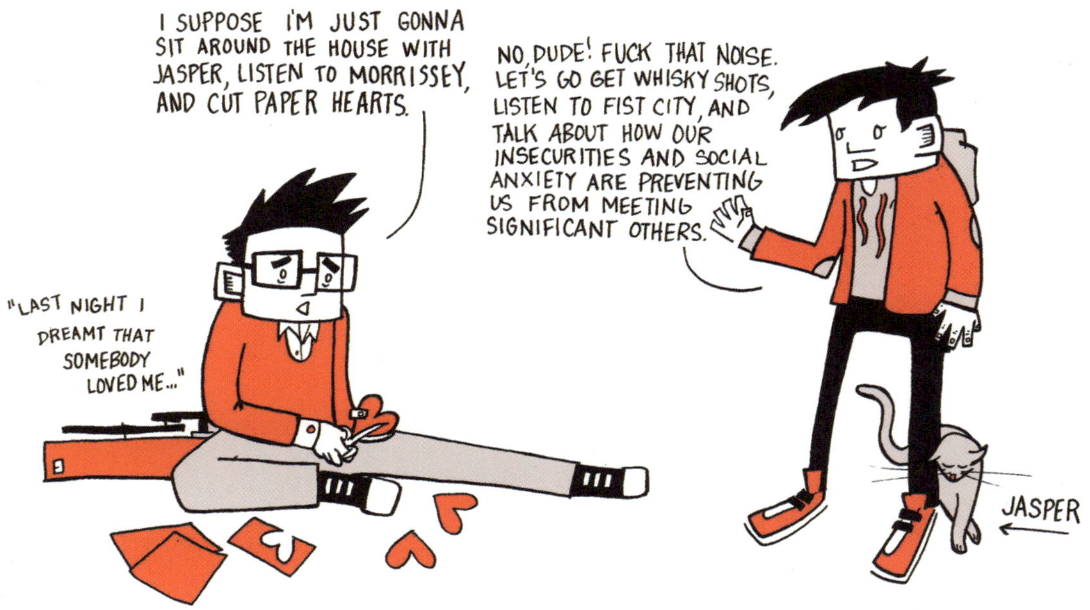

I SUPPOSE I'M JUST GONNA SIT AROUND THE HOUSE WITH JASPER, LISTEN TO MORRISSEY, AND CUT PAPER HEARTS.
NO, DUDE! FUCK THAT NOISE. LET'S GO GET WHISKY SHOTS, LISTEN TO FIST CITY, AND TALK ABOUT HOW OUR INSECURITIES AND SOCIAL ANXIETY ARE PREVENTING US FROM MEETING SIGNIFICANT OTHERS.
"LAST NIGHT I DREAMT THAT SOMEBODY LOVED ME..."
JASPER

FIRST KISS

UNFORTUNATELY, TOBIAS' FIRST KISS WAS NOT A SUCCESS.

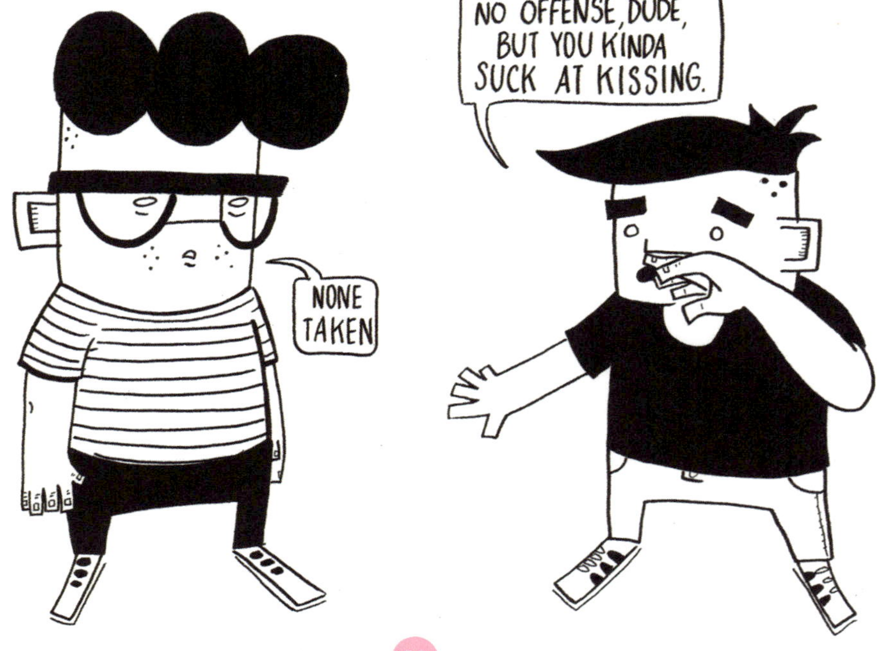

NO OFFENSE, DUDE, BUT YOU KINDA SUCK AT KISSING.
NONE TAKEN

DEPRESSION

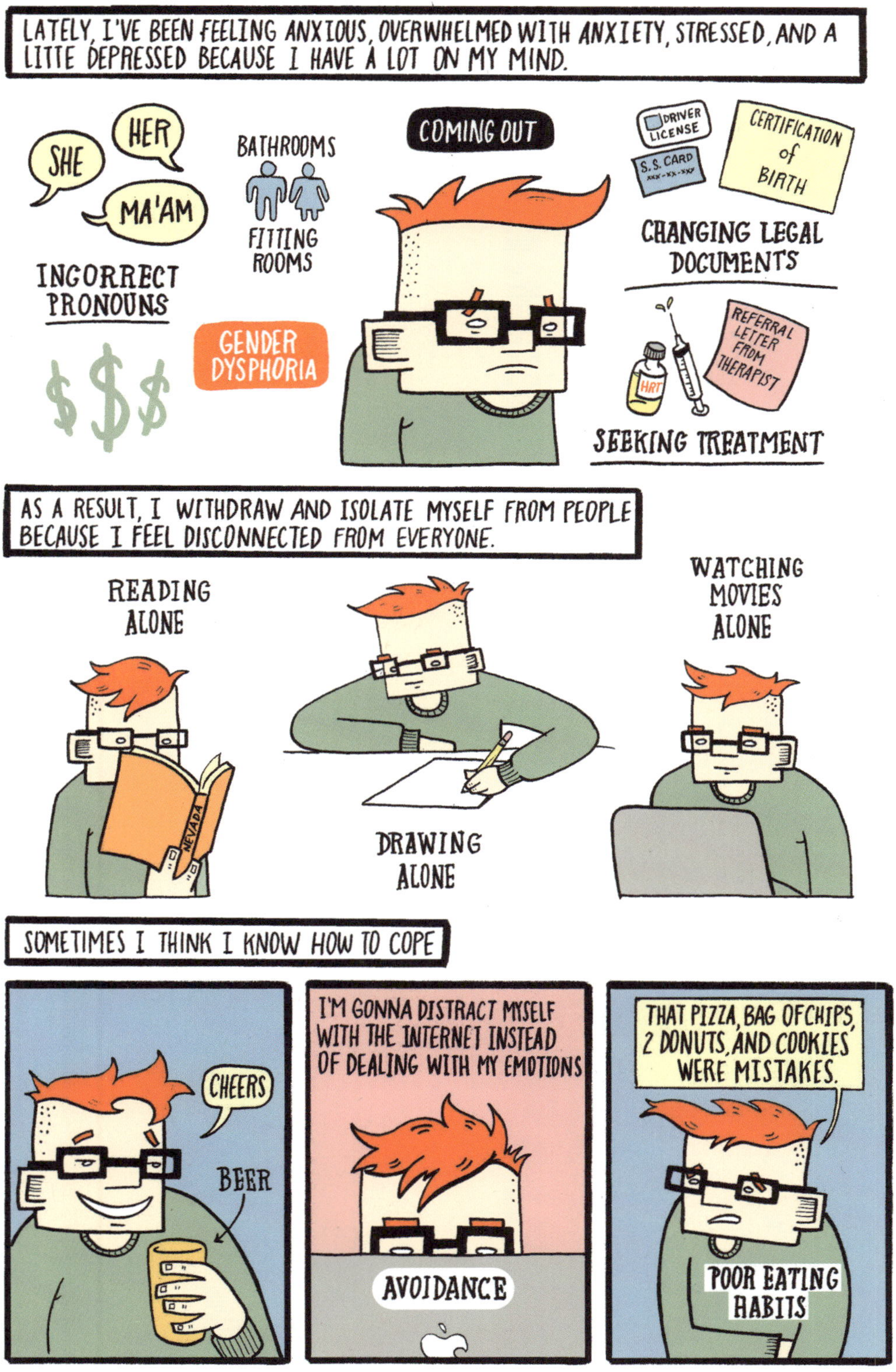

LATELY, I'VE BEEN FEELING ANXIOUS, OVERWHELMED WITH ANXIETY, STRESSED, AND A LITTE DEPRESSED BECAUSE I HAVE A LOT ON MY MIND.
SHE
HER
MA'AM
INCORRECT PRONOUNS
BATHROOMS
FITTING ROOMS
GENDER DYSPHORIA
$$$
COMING OUT
DRIVER LICENSE
S.S. CARD
CERTIFICATION of BIRTH
CHANGING LEGAL DOCUMENTS
HRT
REFERRAL LETTER FROM THERAPIST
SEEKING TREATMENT
AS A RESULT, I WITHDRAW AND ISOLATE MYSELF FROM PEOPLE BECAUSE I FEEL DISCONNECTED FROM EVERYONE.
READING ALONE
NEVADA
DRAWING ALONE
WATCHING MOVIES ALONE
SOMETIMES I THINK I KNOW HOW TO COPE
CHEERS
BEER
I'M GONNA DISTRACT MYSELF WITH THE INTERNET INSTEAD OF DEALING WITH MY EMOTIONS
AVOIDANCE
THAT PIZZA, BAG OF CHIPS, 2 DONUTS, AND COOKIES WERE MISTAKES.
POOR EATING HABITS

LUCKILY, I'M QUICK TO REALIZE THOSE ARE NOT SOLUTIONS. MOST DAYS AREN'T SO BAD BECAUSE I'VE FOUND WAYS TO MAKE MYSELF HAPPIER.

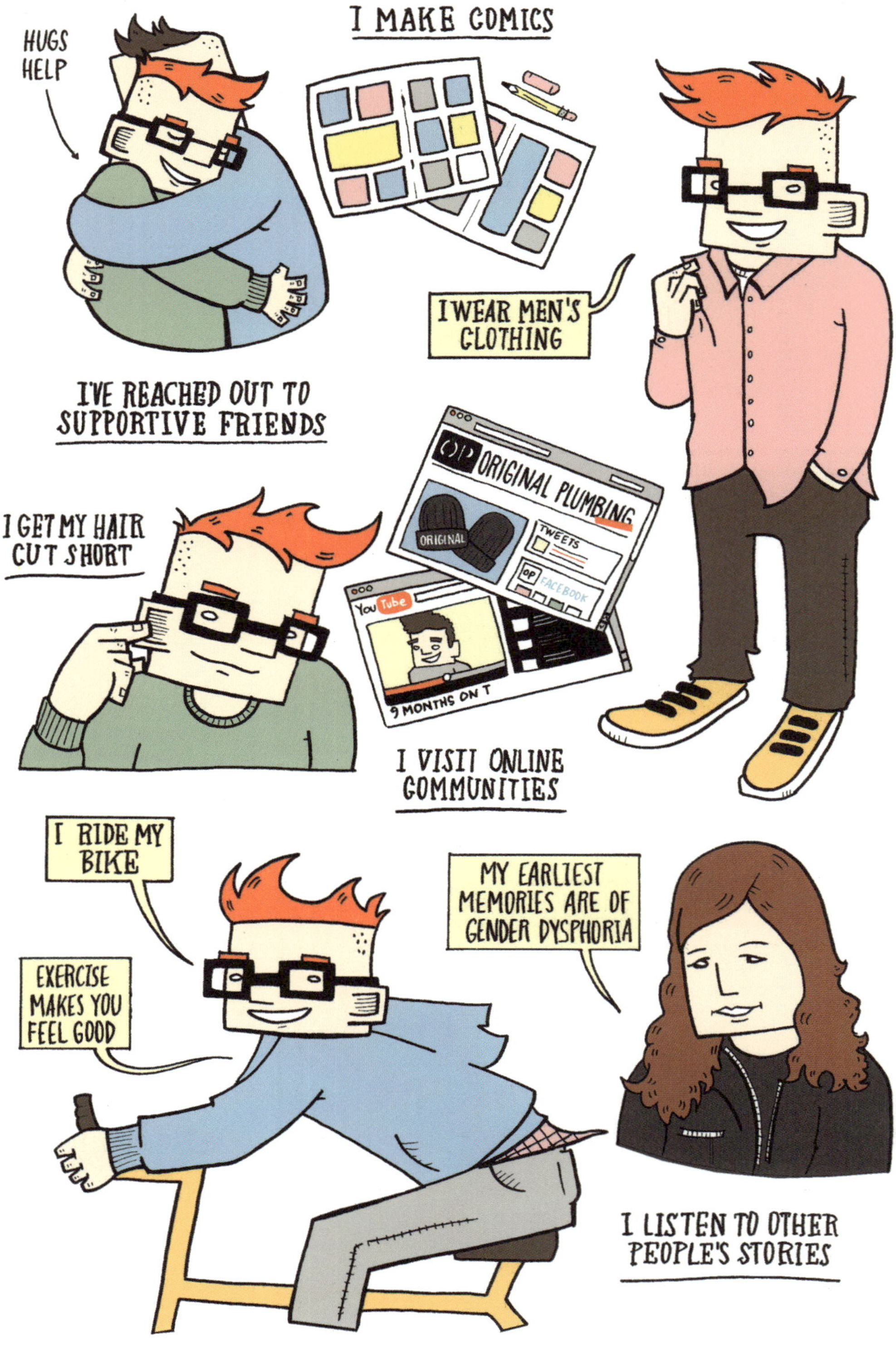
HUGS HELP
I'VE REACHED OUT TO SUPPORTIVE FRIENDS
I MAKE COMICS
I WEAR MEN'S CLOTHING
I GET MY HAIR CUT SHORT
ORIGINAL PLUMBING
ORIGINAL
TWEETS
OP
FACEBOOK
YouTube
9 MONTHS ON T
I VISIT ONLINE COMMUNITIES
I RIDE MY BIKE
EXERCISE MAKES YOU FEEL GOOD
MY EARLIEST MEMORIES ARE OF GENDER DYSPHORIA
I LISTEN TO OTHER PEOPLE'S STORIES

MEET TOBIAS

MY NAME IS TOBIAS DELANY. I'VE NEVER HAD A BOYFRIEND BECAUSE I LIVE IN A SMALL TOWN WHERE MY OPTIONS ARE LIMITED. I DON'T KNOW HOW TO WRITE A PERSONAL AD, SO I THOUGHT I'D ANSWER THIS QUESTIONNAIRE I FOUND ON deviantART.

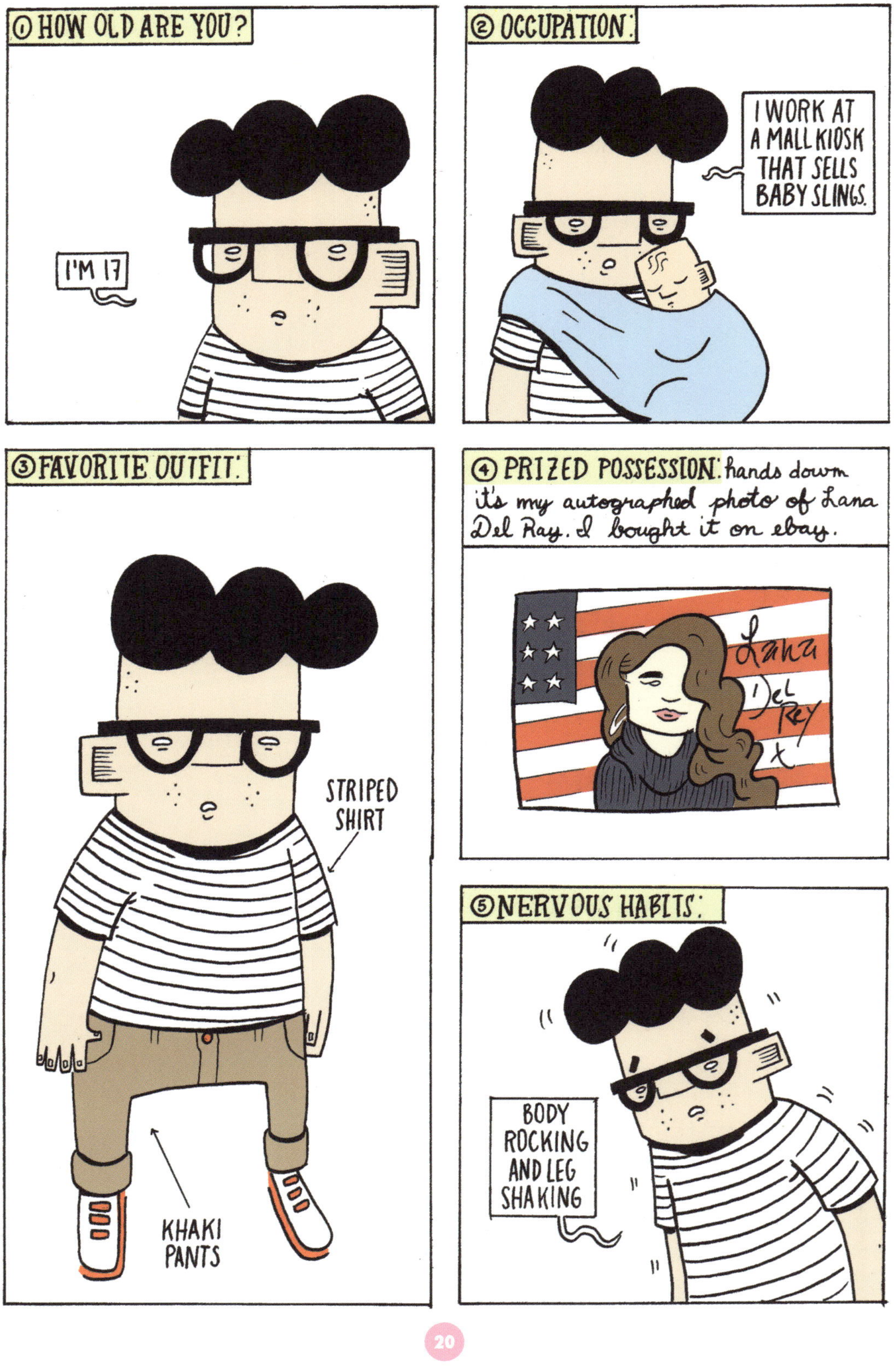
① HOW OLD ARE YOU?
I'M 17
② OCCUPATION:
I WORK AT A MALL KIOSK THAT SELLS BABY SLINGS.
③ FAVORITE OUTFIT:
STRIPED SHIRT
KHAKI PANTS
④ PRIZED POSSESSION: hands down it's my autographed photo of Lana Del Ray. I bought it on ebay.
Lana Del Rey x
⑤ NERVOUS HABITS:
BODY ROCKING AND LEG SHAKING

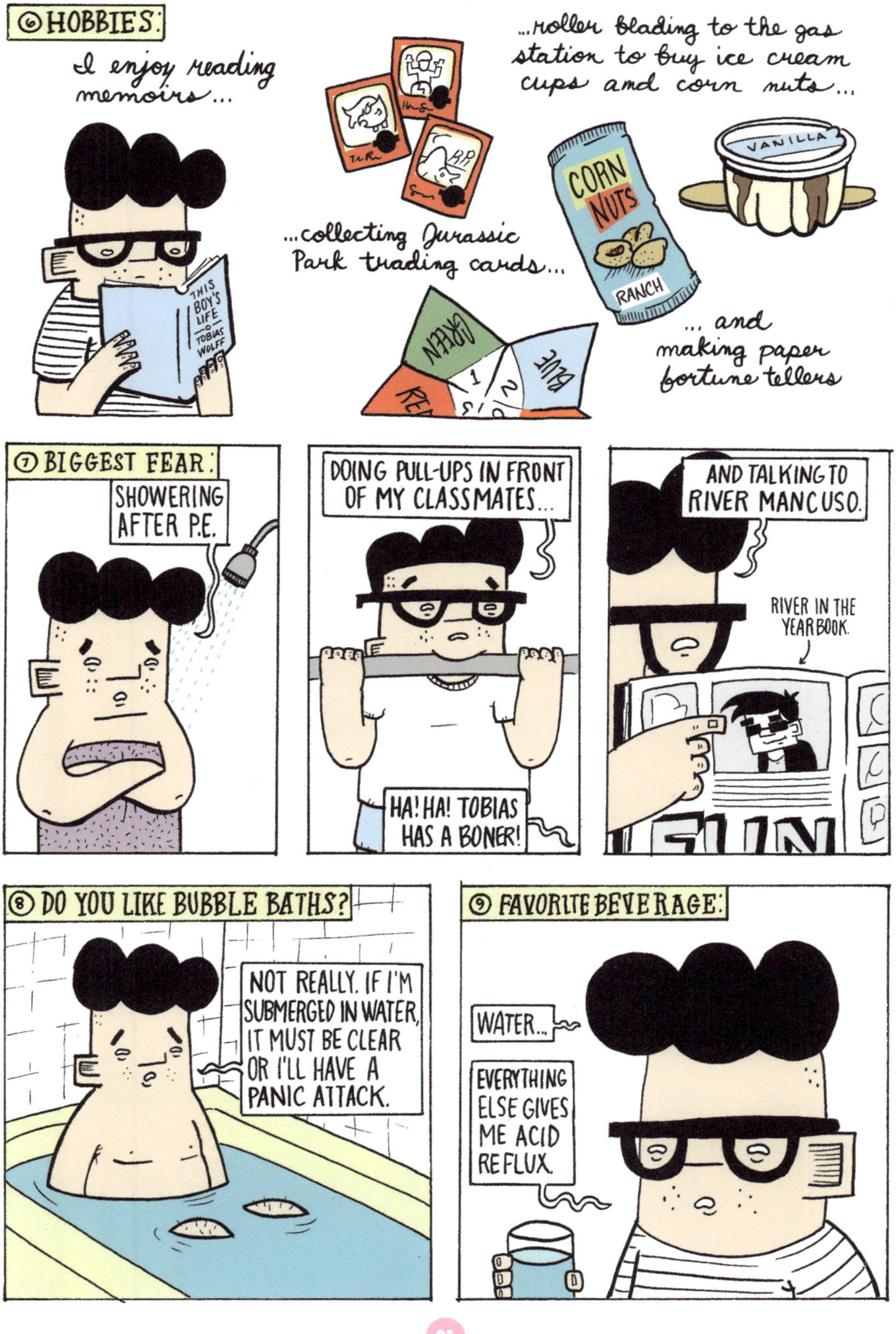

6 HOBBIES:
I enjoy reading memoirs...
THIS BOY'S LIFE
TOBIAS WOLFF
...collecting Jurassic Park trading cards...
...roller blading to the gas station to buy ice cream cups and corn nuts...
CORN NUTS
RANCH
VANILLA
GREEN
BLUE
... and making paper fortune tellers
7 BIGGEST FEAR:
SHOWERING AFTER P.E.
DOING PULL-UPS IN FRONT OF MY CLASSMATES...
HA! HA! TOBIAS HAS A BONER!
AND TALKING TO RIVER MANCUSO.
RIVER IN THE YEARBOOK.
8 DO YOU LIKE BUBBLE BATHS?
NOT REALLY. IF I'M SUBMERGED IN WATER, IT MUST BE CLEAR OR I'LL HAVE A PANIC ATTACK.
9 FAVORITE BEVERAGE:
WATER...
EVERYTHING ELSE GIVES ME ACID REFLUX.

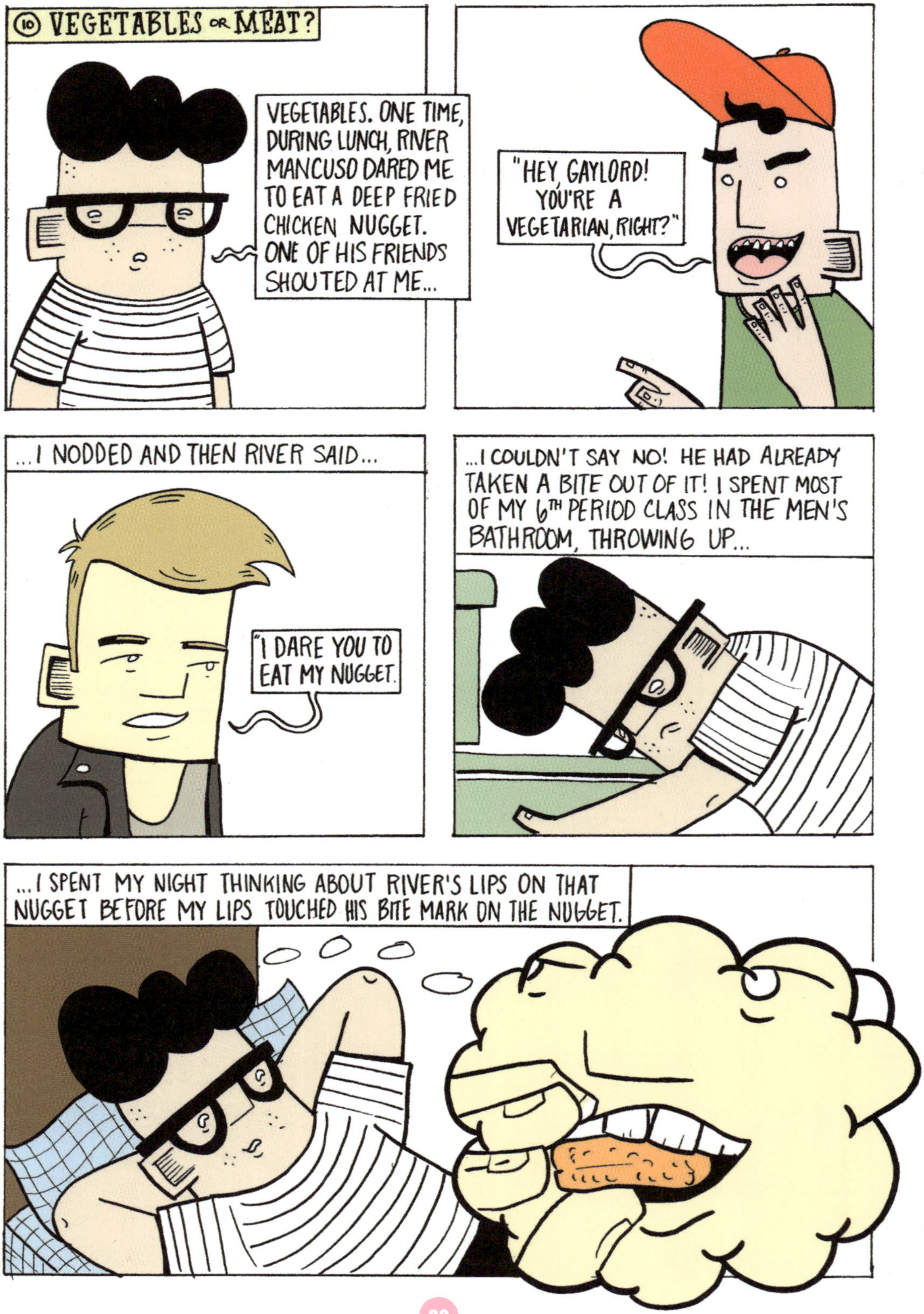
⑩ VEGETABLES OR MEAT?
VEGETABLES. ONE TIME, DURING LUNCH, RIVER MANCUSO DARED ME TO EAT A DEEP FRIED CHICKEN NUGGET. ONE OF HIS FRIENDS SHOUTED AT ME...
"HEY, GAYLORD! YOU'RE A VEGETARIAN, RIGHT?"
...I NODDED AND THEN RIVER SAID...
"I DARE YOU TO EAT MY NUGGET.
...I COULDN'T SAY NO! HE HAD ALREADY TAKEN A BITE OUT OF IT! I SPENT MOST OF MY 6TH PERIOD CLASS IN THE MEN'S BATHROOM, THROWING UP...
...I SPENT MY NIGHT THINKING ABOUT RIVER'S LIPS ON THAT NUGGET BEFORE MY LIPS TOUCHED HIS BITE MARK ON THE NUGGET.

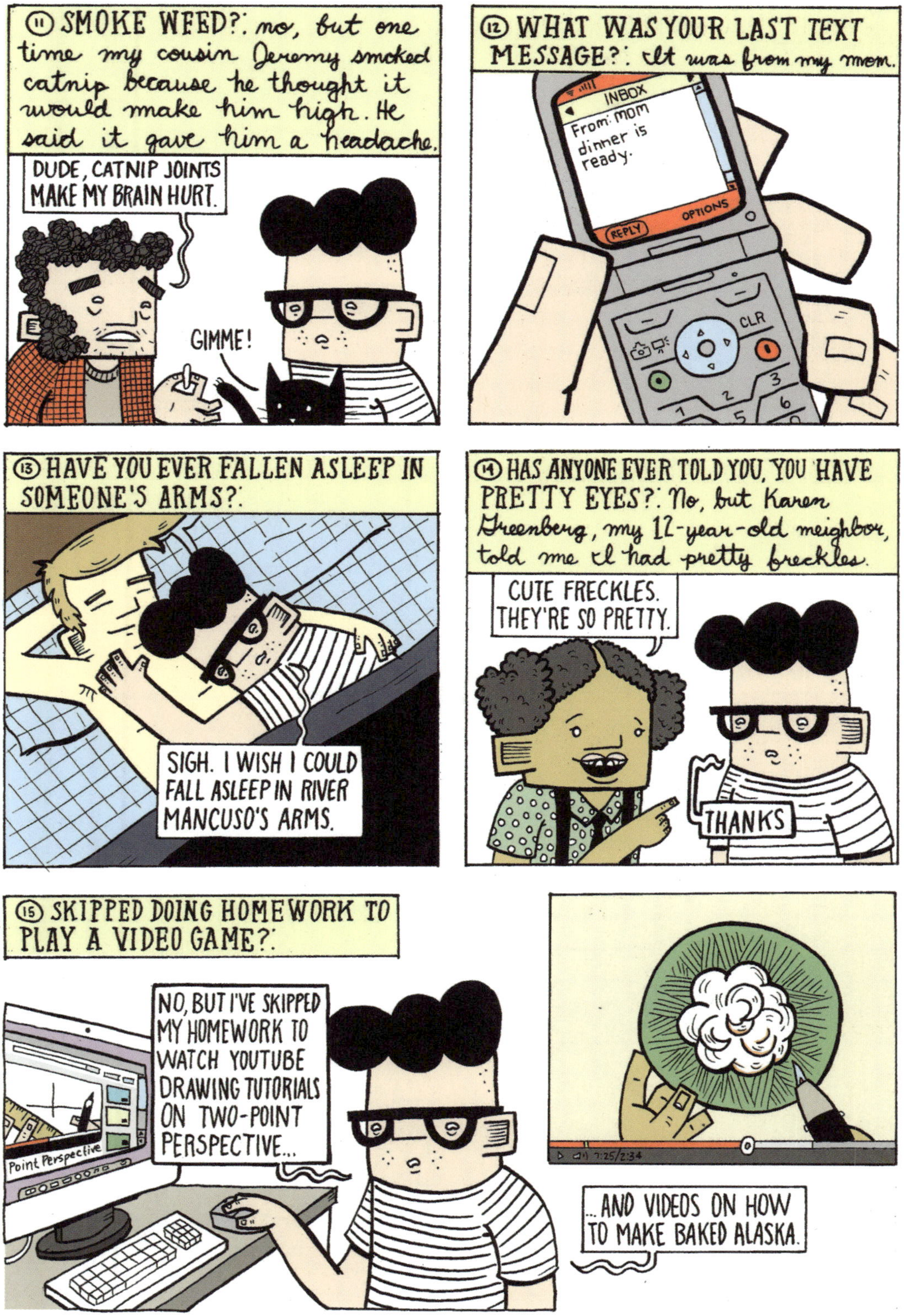

⑪ SMOKE WEED?: no, but one time my cousin Jeremy smoked catnip because he thought it would make him high. He said it gave him a headache.
DUDE, CATNIP JOINTS MAKE MY BRAIN HURT.
GIMME!
⑫ WHAT WAS YOUR LAST TEXT MESSAGE?: It was from my mom.
INBOX
From: mom
dinner is ready.
REPLY
OPTIONS
CLR
⑬ HAVE YOU EVER FALLEN ASLEEP IN SOMEONE'S ARMS?:
SIGH. I WISH I COULD FALL ASLEEP IN RIVER MANCUSO'S ARMS.
⑭ HAS ANYONE EVER TOLD YOU, YOU HAVE PRETTY EYES?: No, but Karen Greenberg, my 12-year-old neighbor, told me I had pretty freckles.
CUTE FRECKLES. THEY'RE SO PRETTY.
THANKS
⑮ SKIPPED DOING HOMEWORK TO PLAY A VIDEO GAME?:
NO, BUT I'VE SKIPPED MY HOMEWORK TO WATCH YOUTUBE DRAWING TUTORIALS ON TWO-POINT PERSPECTIVE...
Point Perspective
1:25/2:34
...AND VIDEOS ON HOW TO MAKE BAKED ALASKA.

16 FIRST THING YOU NOTICE ON A GUY/GIRL?: a cute butt.

BABY GOT BACK.

17 DO YOU SING IN THE SHOWER?: Yes. My shower jam is Pat Benatar's "Invincible".

"THIS SHATTERED DREAM YOU CANNOT JUSTIFY. WE'RE GONNA SCREAM UNTIL WE'RE SATISFIED. WHAT ARE WE RUNNING FOR? WE'VE GOT THE RIGHT TO BE ANGRY."

18 DO YOU DANCE IN THE CAR?: I can't help myself.

DANCING TO NO MUSIC

19 SOMETHING YOU'VE NEVER TOLD ANYONE:

WHEN I FOUND OUT MR. ANDERSON, MY TAI CHI INSTRUCTOR, WAS ENGAGED, I WAS SO SAD THAT I ATE A PINT OF ICE CREAM AND BINGE-WATCHED ALL 2 SEASONS OF "THE TORKELSONS."

I FEEL STRONGER WHEN DOROTHY JANE TALKS TO THE MAN IN THE MOON.

COFFEE-TOFFEE CRUNCH

DEBATE

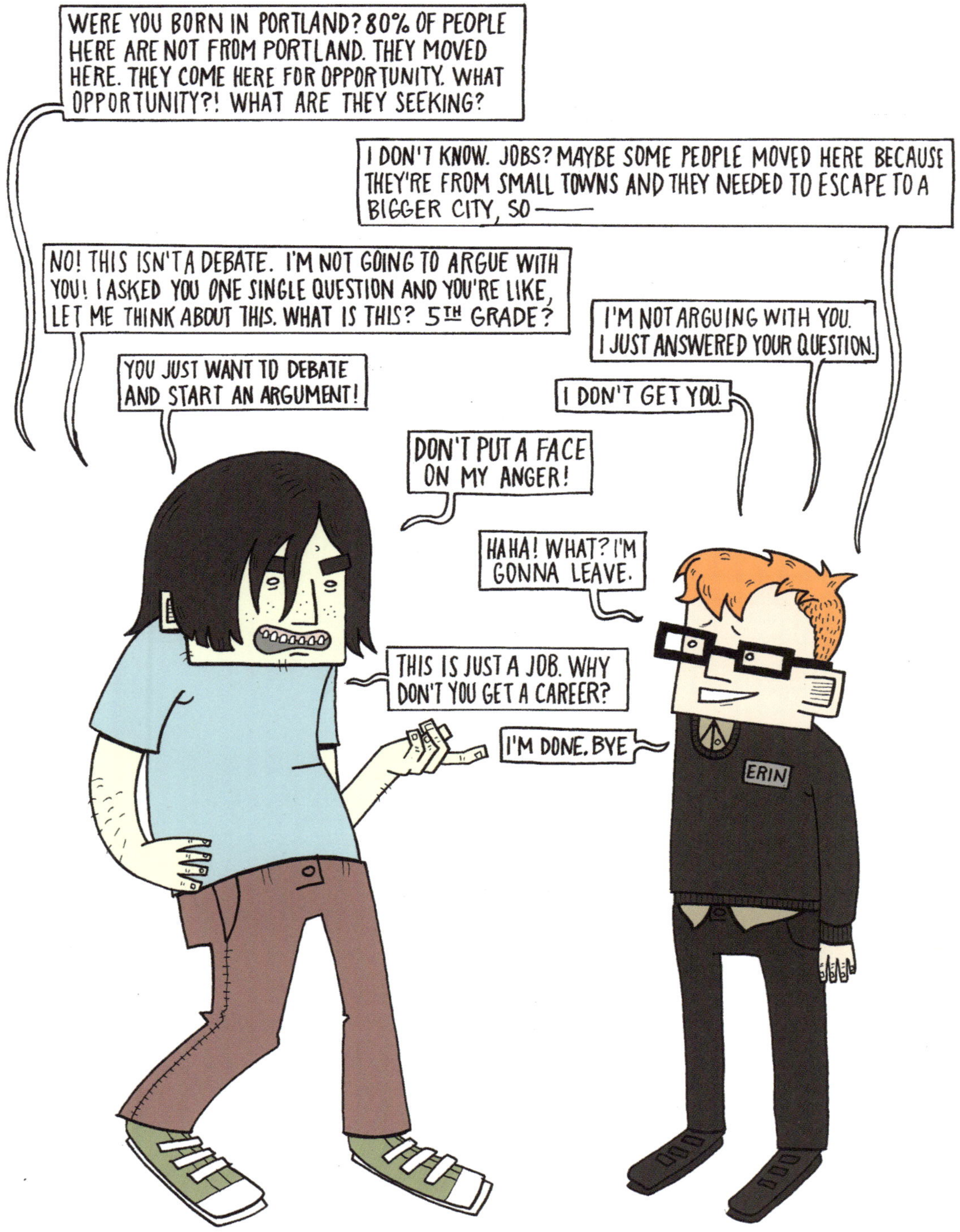
WERE YOU BORN IN PORTLAND? 80% OF PEOPLE HERE ARE NOT FROM PORTLAND. THEY MOVED HERE. THEY COME HERE FOR OPPORTUNITY. WHAT OPPORTUNITY?! WHAT ARE THEY SEEKING?
I DON'T KNOW. JOBS? MAYBE SOME PEOPLE MOVED HERE BECAUSE THEY'RE FROM SMALL TOWNS AND THEY NEEDED TO ESCAPE TO A BIGGER CITY, SO—
NO! THIS ISN'T A DEBATE. I'M NOT GOING TO ARGUE WITH YOU! I ASKED YOU ONE SINGLE QUESTION AND YOU'RE LIKE, LET ME THINK ABOUT THIS. WHAT IS THIS? 5TH GRADE?
I'M NOT ARGUING WITH YOU. I JUST ANSWERED YOUR QUESTION.
YOU JUST WANT TO DEBATE AND START AN ARGUMENT!
I DON'T GET YOU.
DON'T PUT A FACE ON MY ANGER!
HAHA! WHAT? I'M GONNA LEAVE.
THIS IS JUST A JOB. WHY DON'T YOU GET A CAREER?
I'M DONE. BYE
ERIN

7/29/14

TODAY I WOKE UP AT 5AM & BIKED 10 MILES
FROM NORTH PORTLAND TO SOUTHEAST PORTLAND.

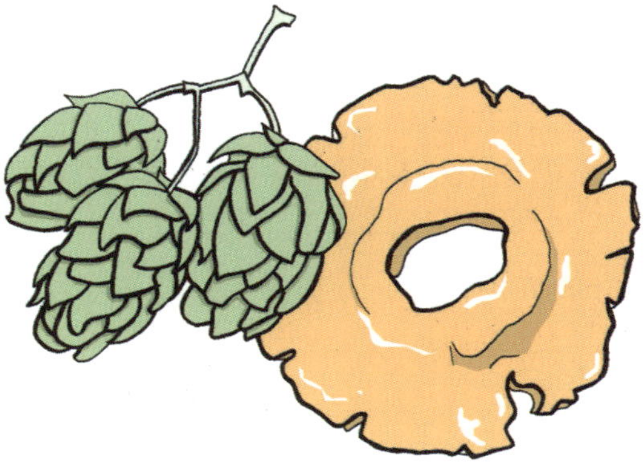

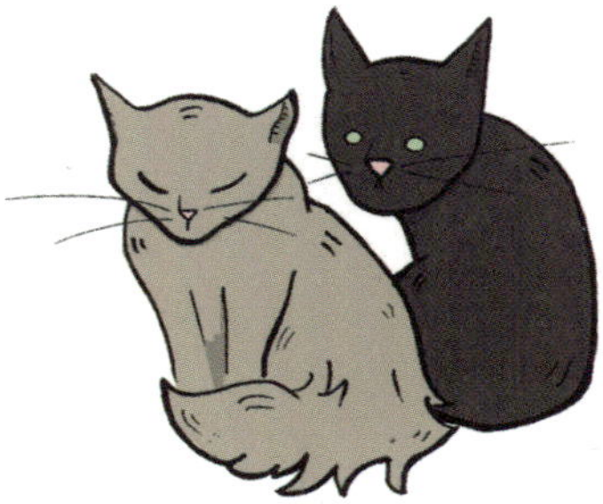

I PASSED 9 BRIDGES,
MET 5 CATS,
AND WATCHED ROWERS ROW
NEAR THE HAWTHORNE BRIDGE

TRIVIAL FACT: PORTLAND SMELLS LIKE MUSTY BEER HOPS & DONUTS IN THE EARLY HOURS OF MORNING

ALONG THE SPRINGWATER CORRIDOR, UNDER THE ROSS ISLAND BRIDGE, I CLIMBED BELOW TO CHECK OUT SOME GRAFFITI PIECES. THERE'S A SLEW OF HOMELESS CAMPS ALONG THE SHORELINE OF THE WILLAMETTE (BELOW THE TRAIL). TENTS AND LITTER LINE THE BANK. PARANOID I'D WAKE A SLEEPING RIVER DWELLER, I CLIMBED BACK UP THE HILL AND CONTINUED SOUTH.

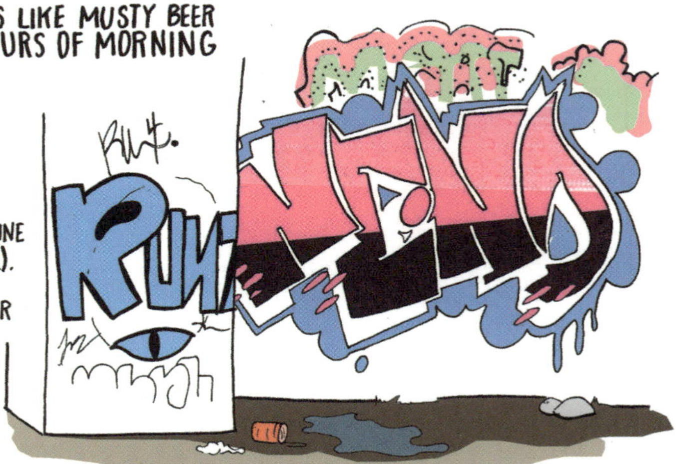

I STOPPED IN GRAND CENTRAL BAKERY, IN SELLWOOD, AND HAD A BREAKFAST SANDWICH.

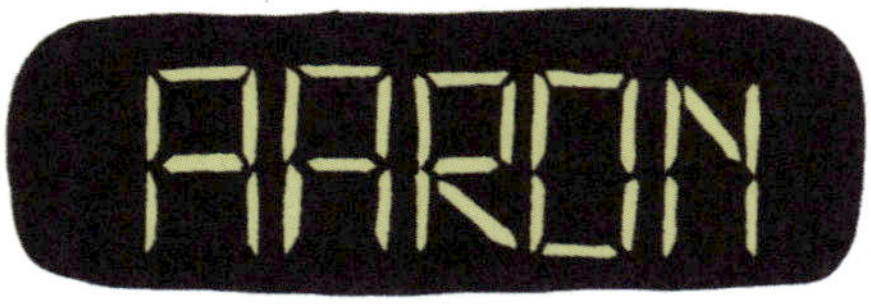
AARON

THE CASHIER TOOK MY NAME WHEN I PLACED MY ORDER. LATELY, PEOPLE SPELL MY NAME USING THE MALE VERSION. I DON'T CORRECT THEM.

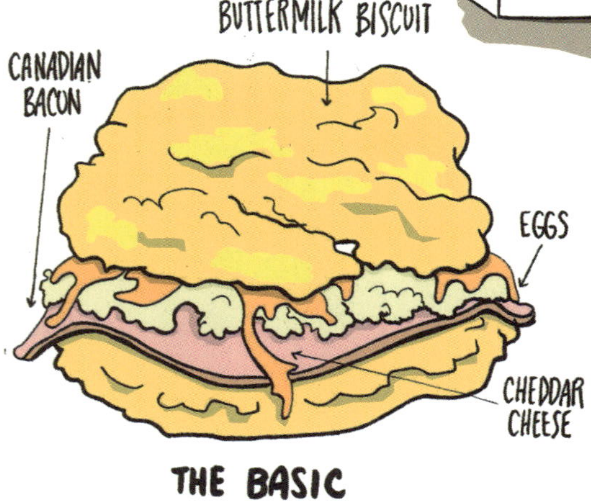
BUTTERMILK BISCUIT
CANADIAN BACON
EGGS
CHEDDAR CHEESE

THE BASIC

AFTER BREAKFAST, I WALKED ALONG SE 13TH.
EVERYTHING (MOSTLY ANTIQUE SHOPS) WAS CLOSED.

ANTIQUES

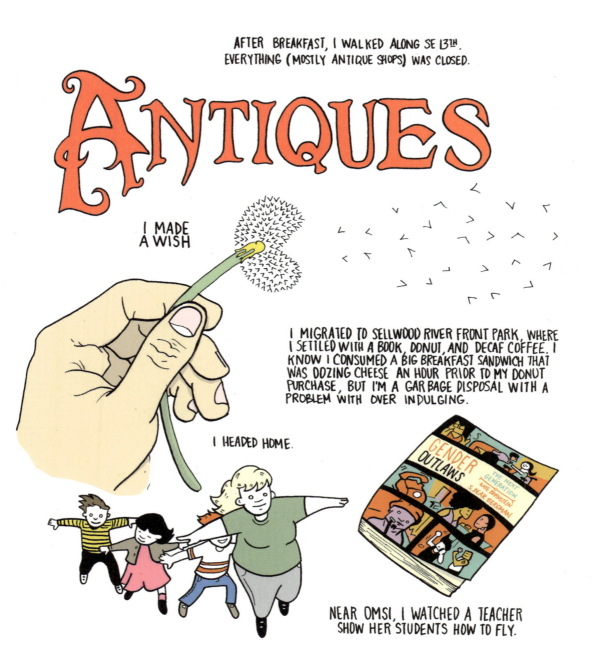

I MADE A WISH

I MIGRATED TO SELLWOOD RIVER FRONT PARK, WHERE I SETTLED WITH A BOOK, DONUT, AND DECAF COFFEE. I KNOW I CONSUMED A BIG BREAKFAST SANDWICH THAT WAS OOZING CHEESE AN HOUR PRIOR TO MY DONUT PURCHASE, BUT I'M A GARBAGE DISPOSAL WITH A PROBLEM WITH OVER INDULGING.

GENDER OUTLAWS
THE NEXT GENERATION
KATE BORNSTEIN
S. BEAR BERGMAN

I HEADED HOME.

NEAR OMSI, I WATCHED A TEACHER SHOW HER STUDENTS HOW TO FLY.

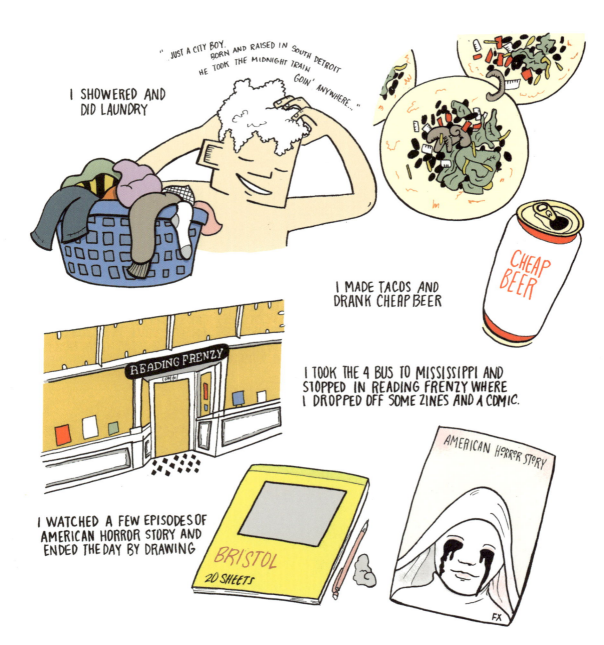

I SHOWERED AND DID LAUNDRY

" ..JUST A CITY BOY. BORN AND RAISED IN SOUTH DETROIT HE TOOK THE MIDNIGHT TRAIN GOIN' ANYWHERE.."

I MADE TACOS AND DRANK CHEAP BEER

CHEAP BEER

I TOOK THE 4 BUS TO MISSISSIPPI AND STOPPED IN READING FRENZY WHERE I DROPPED OFF SOME ZINES AND A COMIC.

READING FRENZY

OPEN

I WATCHED A FEW EPISODES OF AMERICAN HORROR STORY AND ENDED THE DAY BY DRAWING

BRISTOL 20 SHEETS

AMERICAN HORROR STORY

FX

EZRA

WANNA HELP ME ALPHABETIZE MY VINYL COLLECTION? OR WE COULD ORGANIZE MY FASHION ACCESSORIES BY COLOR?

SALUTATIONS, MY NAME IS EZRA AND I WORK AT ONE OF THOSE GRAPHIC DESIGN FIRMS THAT USE FITNESS BALLS INSTEAD OF CHAIRS AND THAT PLAY WITH PLAY-GROUND PARACHUTES WHEN BRAINSTORMING CREATIVE IDEAS. I LIKE LIVING MY LIFE IN ROUTINE. FOR THE PAST 7 YEARS, I'VE HAD THE SAME THING FOR BREAK-FAST: FRESHLY JUICED FENNEL AND CUCUMBER, HALF A CUP OF GLUTEN FREE OATS, GOJI BERRIES, RAW ALMONDS, CHIA SEEDS, AND 3 TABLESPOONS OF GOAT MILK KEFIR. I ONLY LISTEN TO BANDS THAT ARE PRAISED BY PITCHFORK. THE ONLY MOVIES I ENJOY ARE WES ANDERSON FILMS. HOARDING GIVES ME ANXIETY AND PUTTING KETCHUP ON MY EGGS IS A GUILTY PLEASURE. IF YOU HAVE A PREOCCUPATION WITH EXTREME PERFECTIONISM, AND YOU HAVE A HARD TIME RELAXING, MAYBE WE WOULD MAKE A SUPERB DUO.

NEW YEAR'S EVE 2014

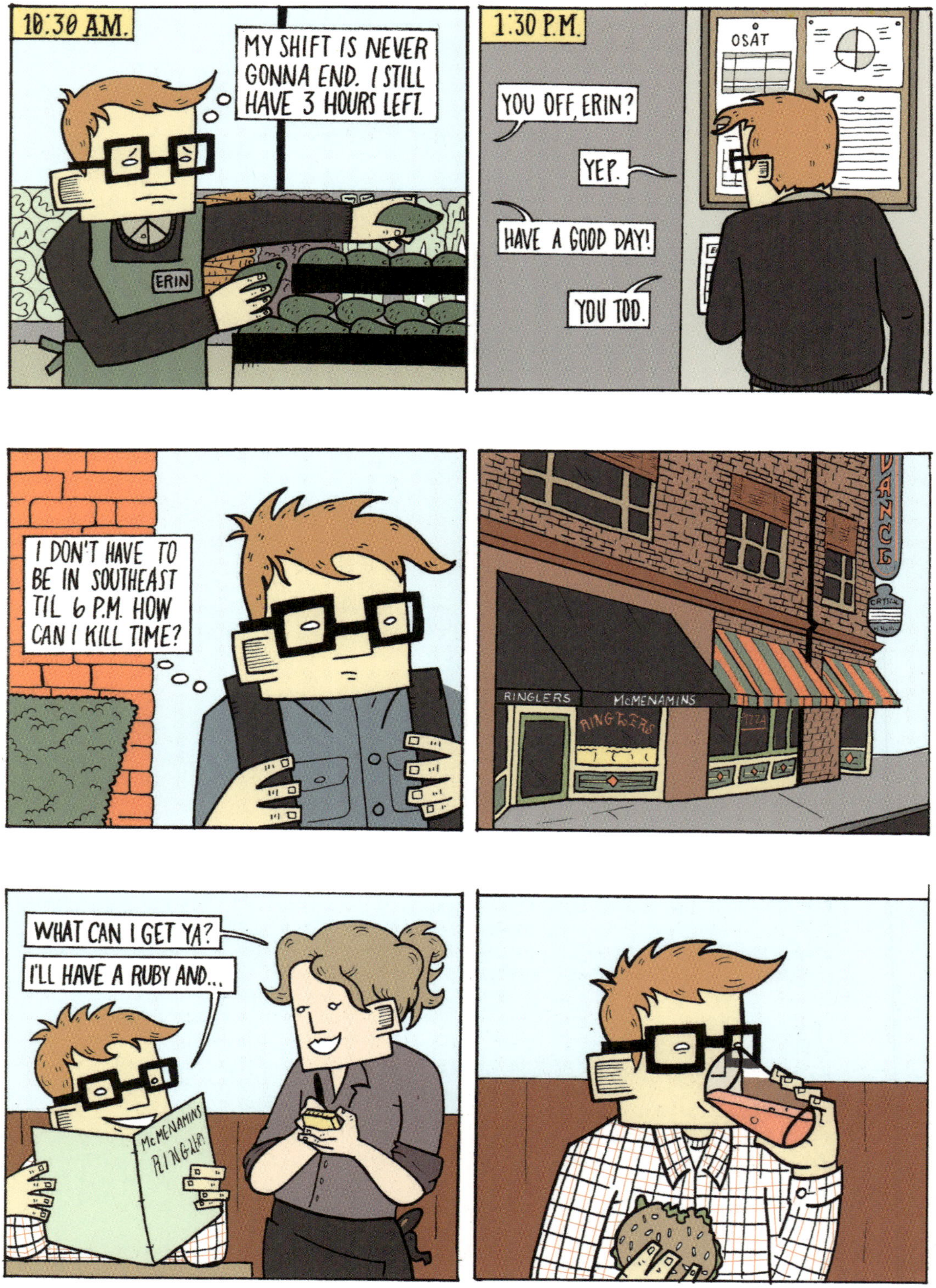

10:30 AM.
MY SHIFT IS NEVER GONNA END. I STILL HAVE 3 HOURS LEFT.
ERIN
1:30 P.M.
OSAT
YOU OFF, ERIN?
YEP.
HAVE A GOOD DAY!
YOU TOO.
I DON'T HAVE TO BE IN SOUTHEAST TIL 6 P.M. HOW CAN I KILL TIME?
DANCE
RINGLERS
McMENAMINS
WHAT CAN I GET YA?
I'LL HAVE A RUBY AND...
McMENAMINS

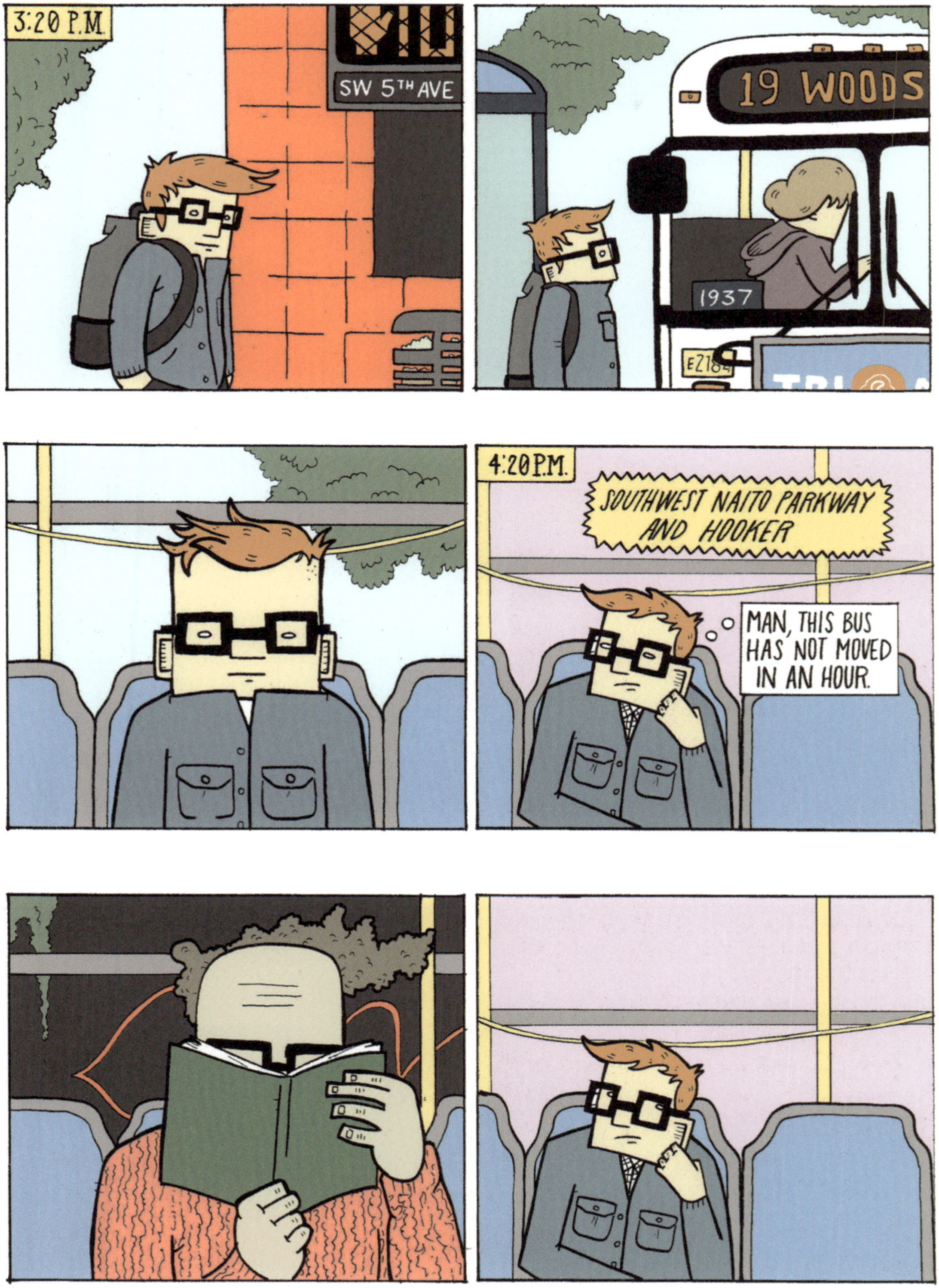
3:20 P.M.
SW 5TH AVE
19 WOODS
1937
4:20 P.M.
SOUTHWEST NAITO PARKWAY AND HOOKER
MAN, THIS BUS HAS NOT MOVED IN AN HOUR.

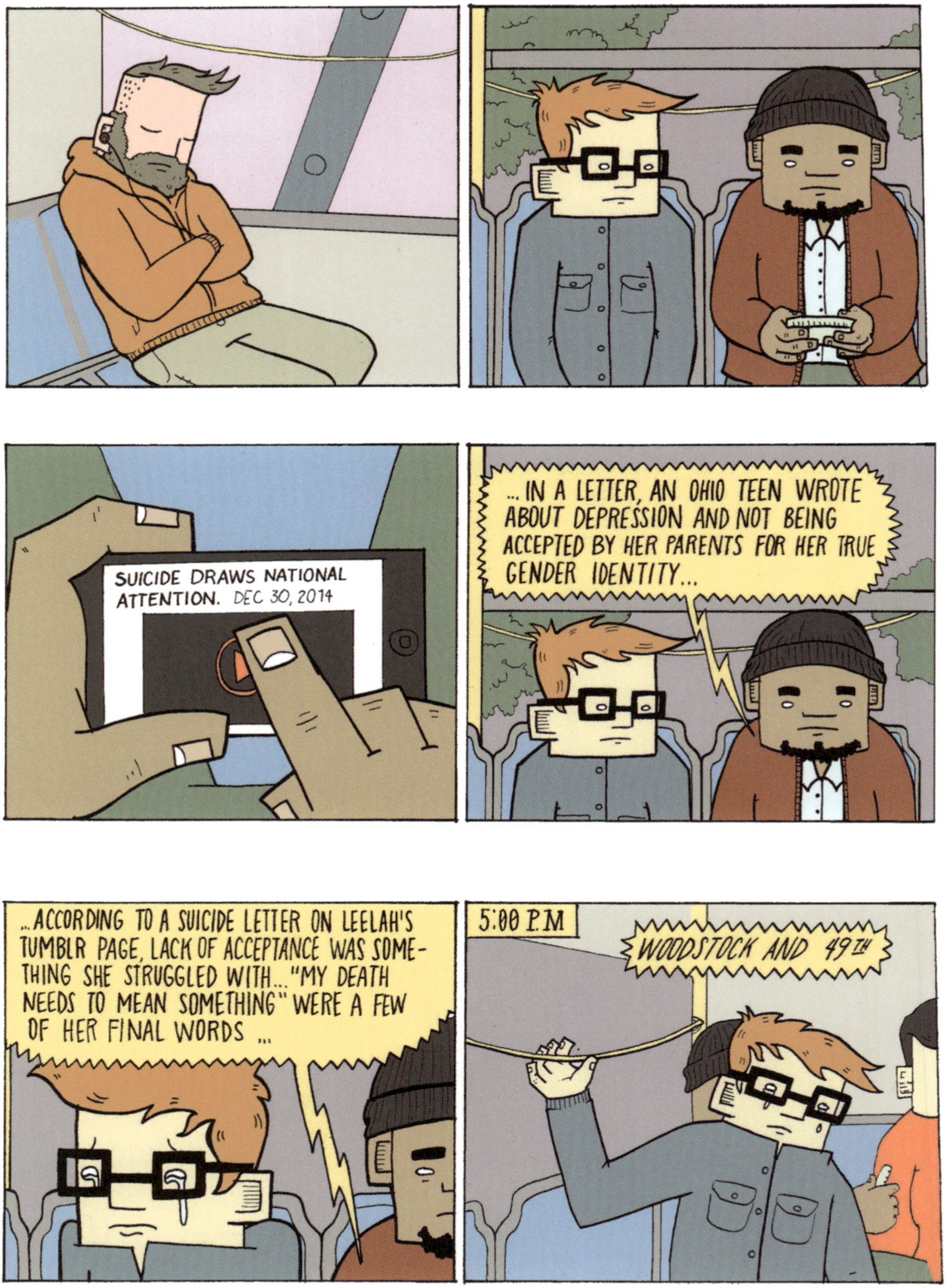
SUICIDE DRAWS NATIONAL ATTENTION. DEC 30, 2014
... IN A LETTER, AN OHIO TEEN WROTE ABOUT DEPRESSION AND NOT BEING ACCEPTED BY HER PARENTS FOR HER TRUE GENDER IDENTITY...
... ACCORDING TO A SUICIDE LETTER ON LEELAH'S TUMBLR PAGE, LACK OF ACCEPTANCE WAS SOMETHING SHE STRUGGLED WITH... "MY DEATH NEEDS TO MEAN SOMETHING" WERE A FEW OF HER FINAL WORDS ...
5:00 P.M
WOODSTOCK AND 49TH

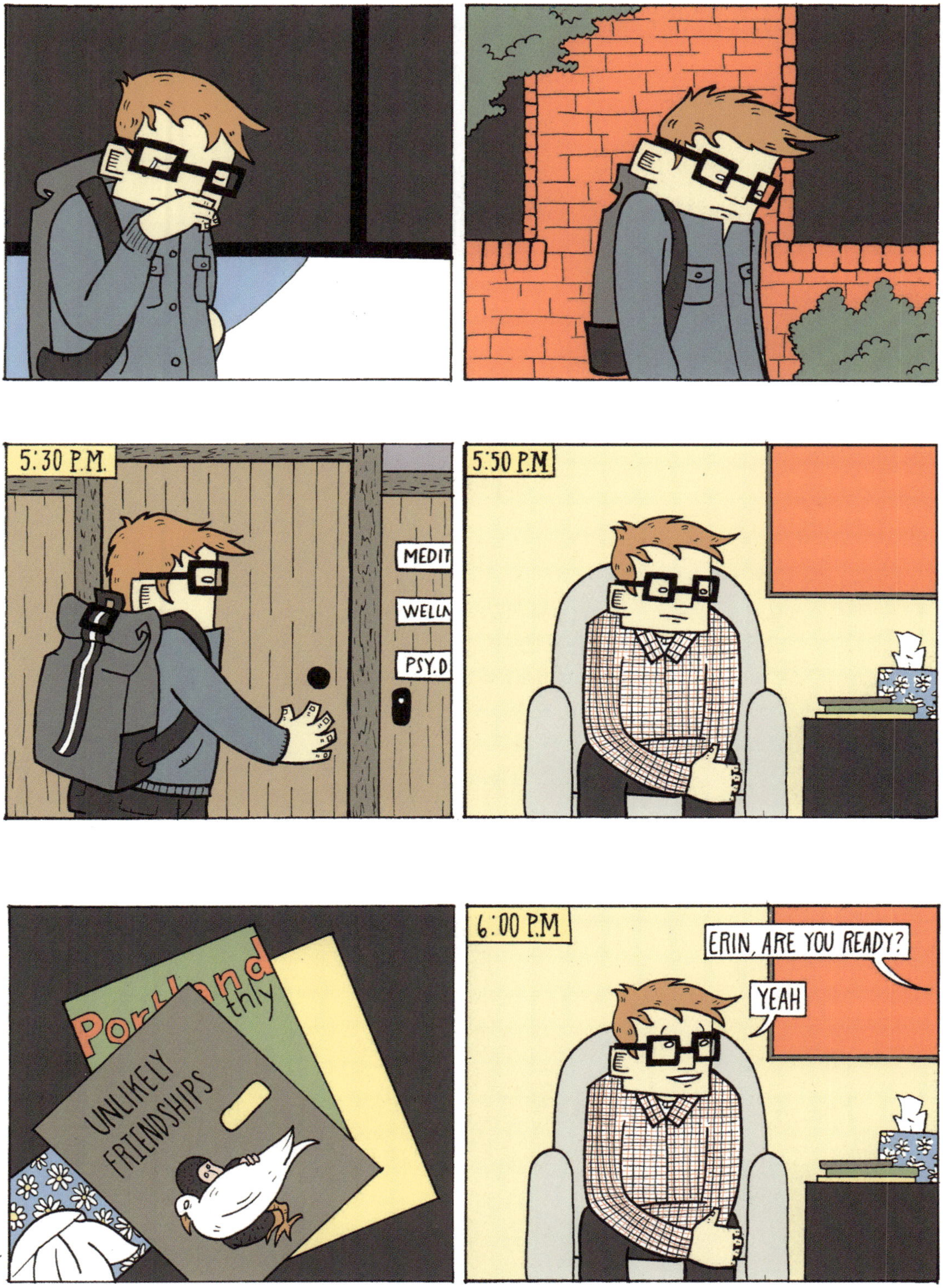
5:30 P.M.
MEDIT
WELLN
PSY.D
5:50 P.M
Portland
thly
UNLIKELY FRIENDSHIPS
6:00 P.M
ERIN, ARE YOU READY?
YEAH

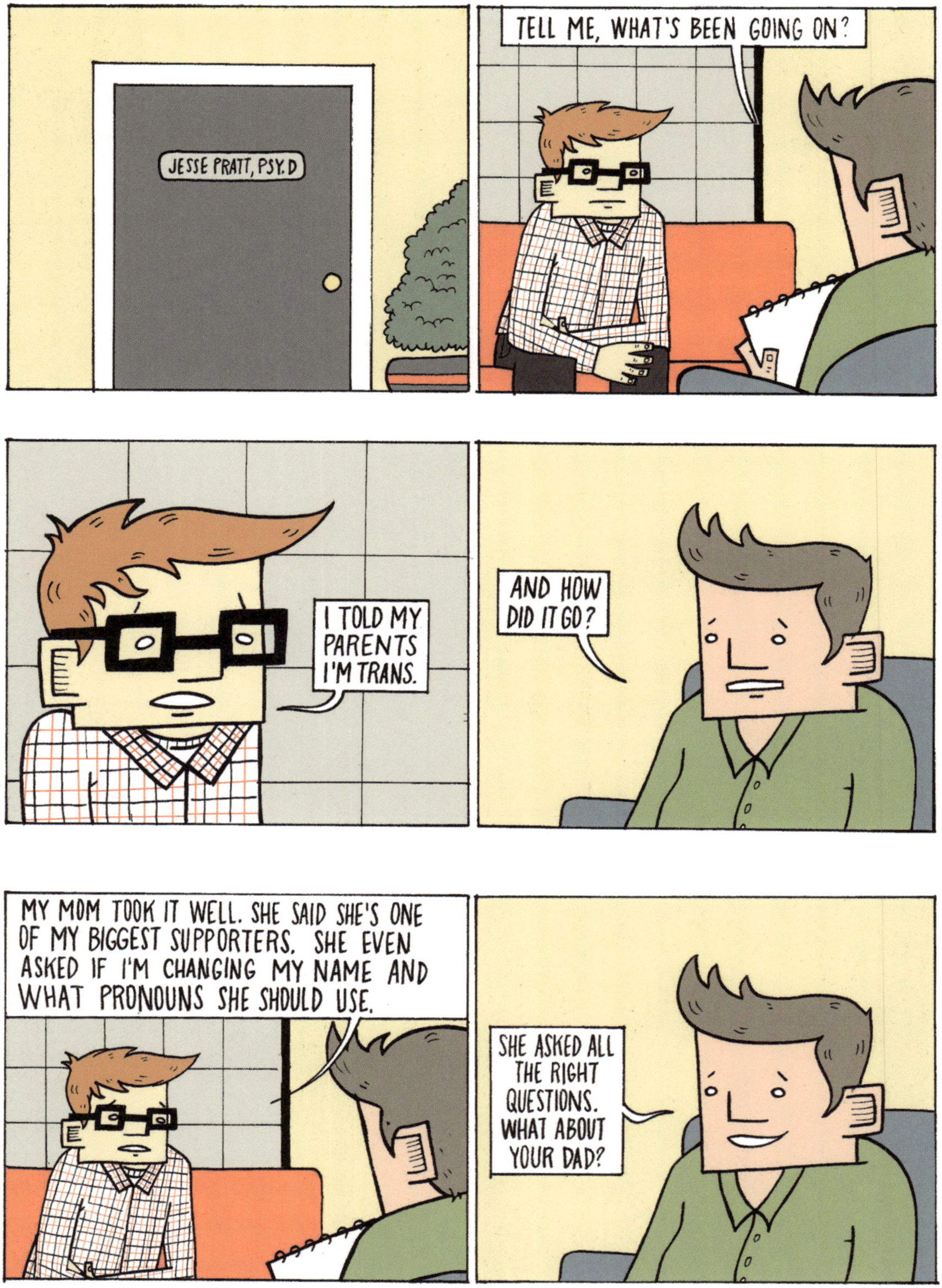

JESSE PRATT, PSY.D
TELL ME, WHAT'S BEEN GOING ON?
I TOLD MY PARENTS I'M TRANS.
AND HOW DID IT GO?
MY MOM TOOK IT WELL. SHE SAID SHE'S ONE OF MY BIGGEST SUPPORTERS. SHE EVEN ASKED IF I'M CHANGING MY NAME AND WHAT PRONOUNS SHE SHOULD USE.
SHE ASKED ALL THE RIGHT QUESTIONS. WHAT ABOUT YOUR DAD?

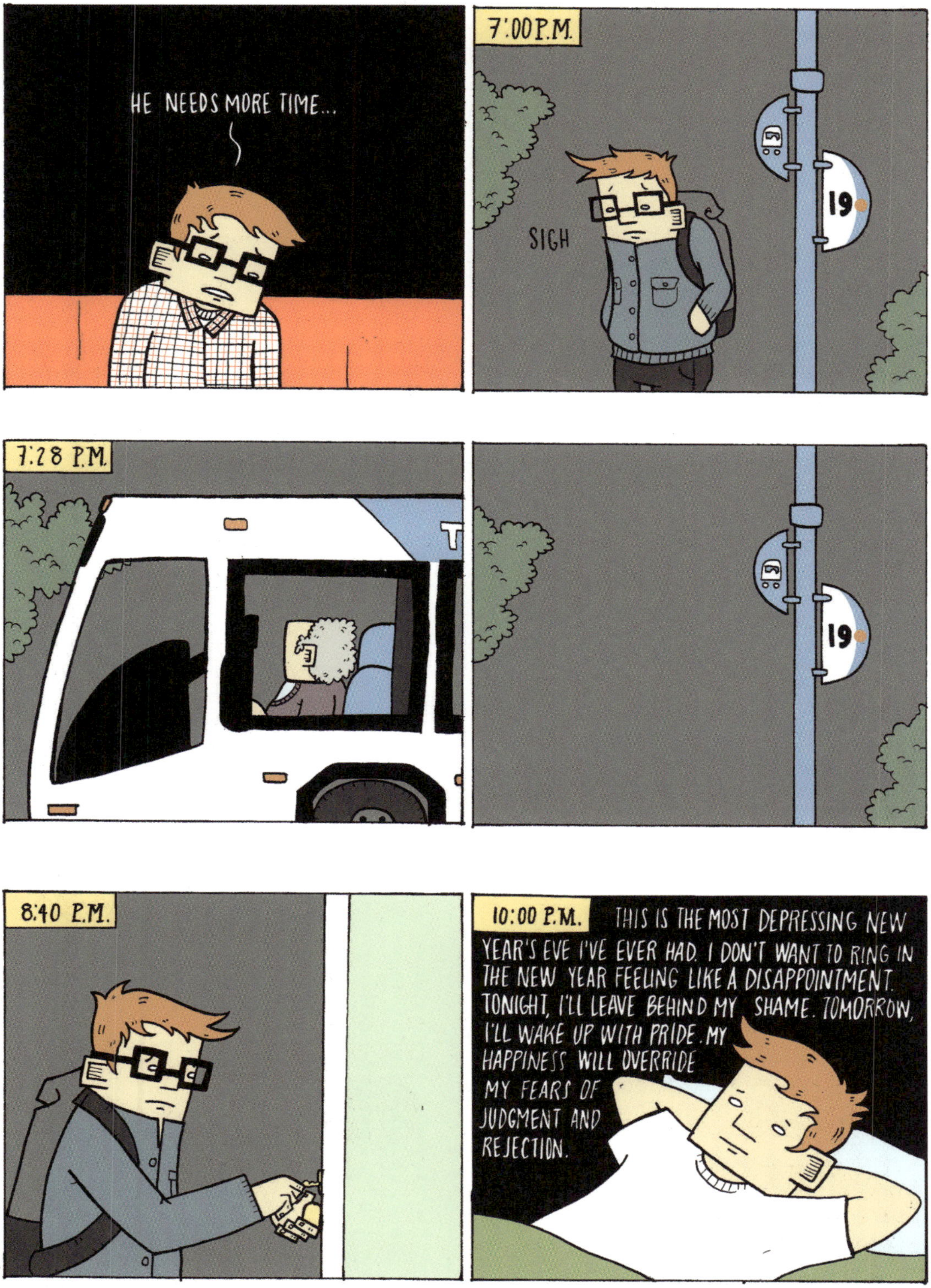
HE NEEDS MORE TIME...
7:00 P.M.
SIGH
19
7:28 P.M.
T
19
8:40 P.M.
10:00 P.M.
THIS IS THE MOST DEPRESSING NEW YEAR'S EVE I'VE EVER HAD. I DON'T WANT TO RING IN THE NEW YEAR FEELING LIKE A DISAPPOINTMENT. TONIGHT, I'LL LEAVE BEHIND MY SHAME. TOMORROW, I'LL WAKE UP WITH PRIDE. MY HAPPINESS WILL OVERRIDE MY FEARS OF JUDGMENT AND REJECTION.

TRUTH OR DARE

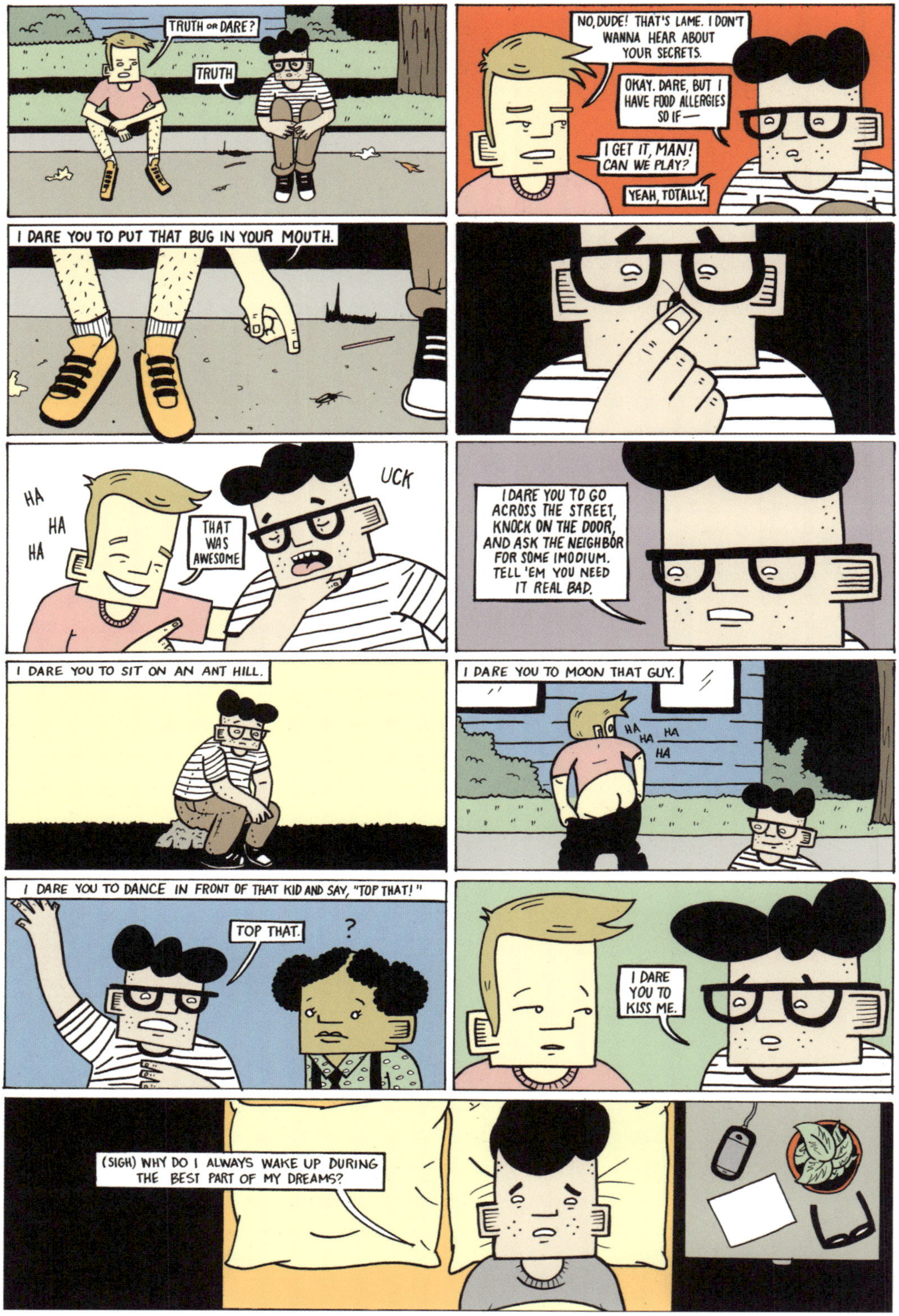

TRUTH OR DARE?
TRUTH
NO, DUDE! THAT'S LAME. I DON'T WANNA HEAR ABOUT YOUR SECRETS.
OKAY. DARE, BUT I HAVE FOOD ALLERGIES SO IF—
I GET IT, MAN! CAN WE PLAY?
YEAH, TOTALLY.
I DARE YOU TO PUT THAT BUG IN YOUR MOUTH.
HA HA HA
THAT WAS AWESOME
UCK
I DARE YOU TO GO ACROSS THE STREET, KNOCK ON THE DOOR, AND ASK THE NEIGHBOR FOR SOME IMODIUM. TELL 'EM YOU NEED IT REAL BAD.
I DARE YOU TO SIT ON AN ANT HILL.
I DARE YOU TO MOON THAT GUY.
HA HA HA HA
I DARE YOU TO DANCE IN FRONT OF THAT KID AND SAY, "TOP THAT!"
TOP THAT.
?
I DARE YOU TO KISS ME.
(SIGH) WHY DO I ALWAYS WAKE UP DURING THE BEST PART OF MY DREAMS?

BIRTH ORDER

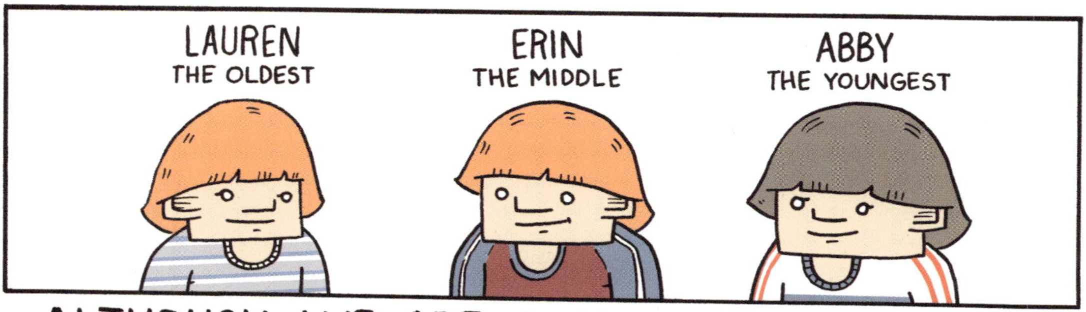
LAUREN
THE OLDEST
ERIN
THE MIDDLE
ABBY
THE YOUNGEST

ALTHOUGH WE ARE A MINUTE APART, BIRTH ORDER TRAITS ARE STILL PREVALENT AMÓNG US.

LAUREN
BOSSY

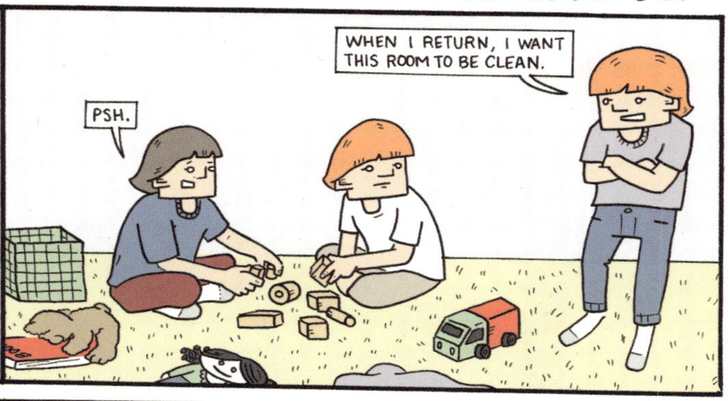
WHEN I RETURN, I WANT THIS ROOM TO BE CLEAN.
PSH.

ABBY
SOCIAL + OUTGOING

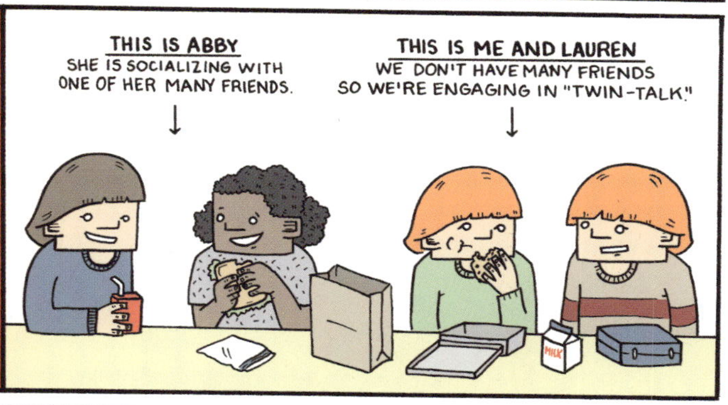
THIS IS ABBY
SHE IS SOCIALIZING WITH ONE OF HER MANY FRIENDS.
THIS IS ME AND LAUREN
WE DON'T HAVE MANY FRIENDS SO WE'RE ENGAGING IN "TWIN-TALK."
MILK

ERIN
INTROVERTED

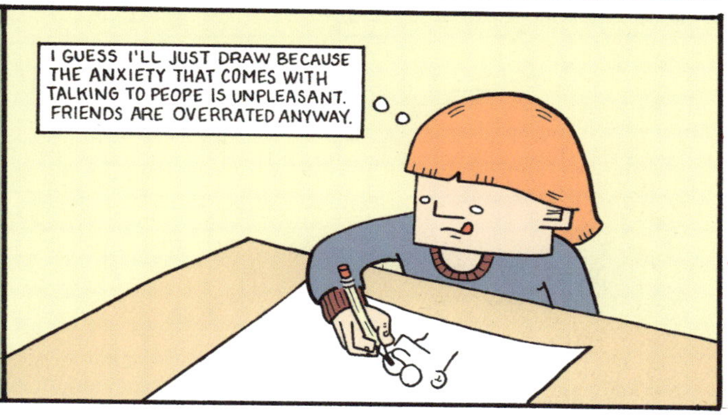
I GUESS I'LL JUST DRAW BECAUSE THE ANXIETY THAT COMES WITH TALKING TO PEOPE IS UNPLEASANT. FRIENDS ARE OVERRATED ANYWAY.

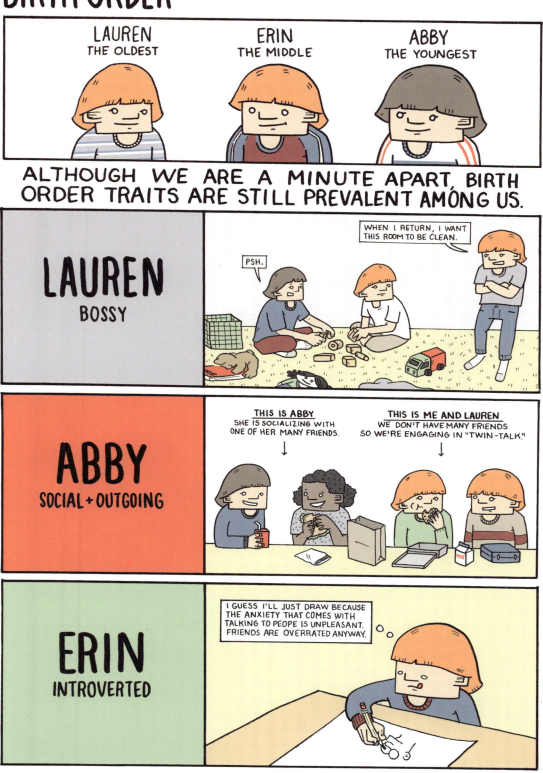

BIRTHDAY PARTIES

THIS IS WHAT HAPPENS AT BIRTHDAY PARTIES WITH TRIPLETS:

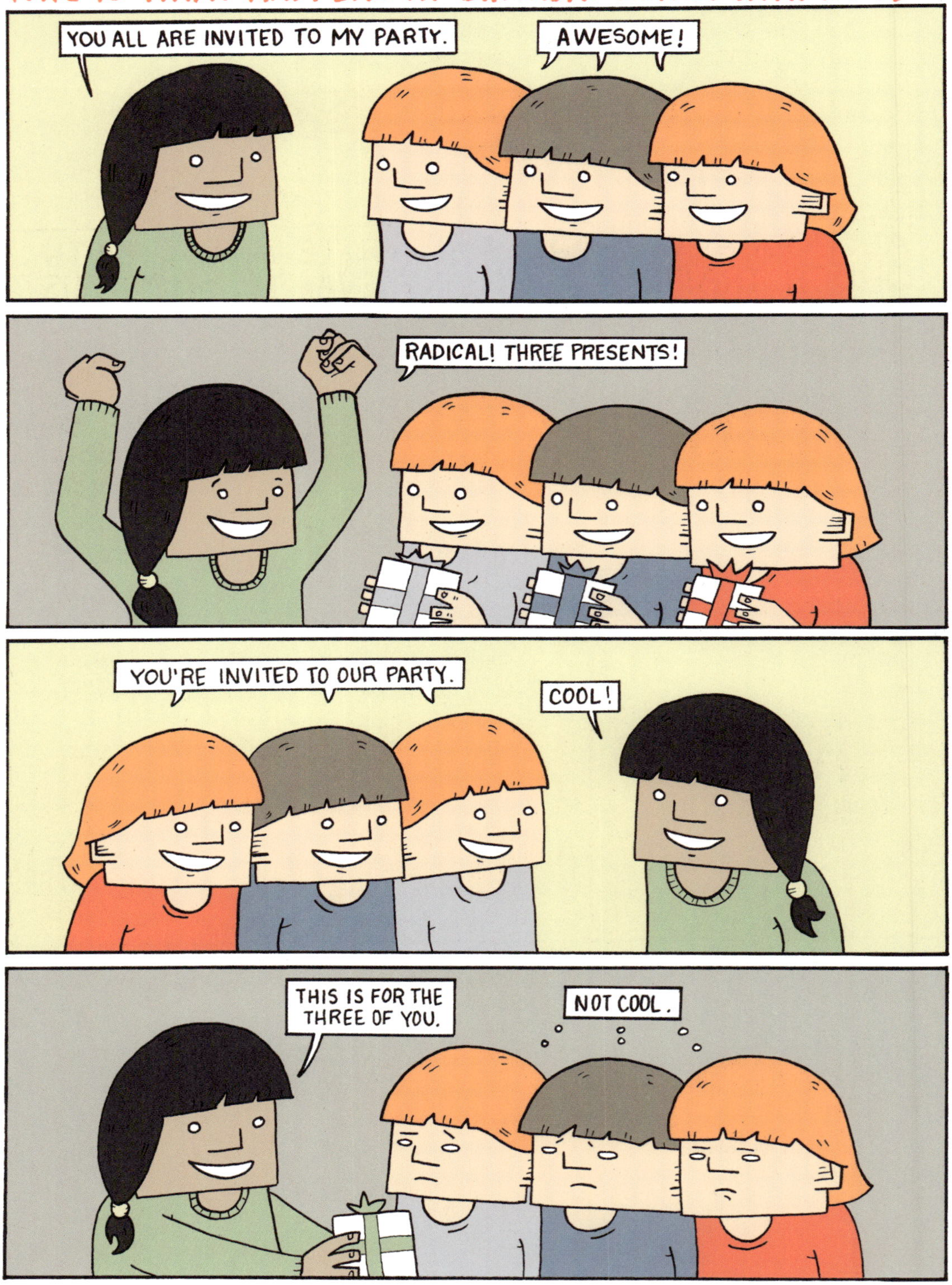

YOU ALL ARE INVITED TO MY PARTY.
AWESOME!
RADICAL! THREE PRESENTS!
YOU'RE INVITED TO OUR PARTY.
COOL!
THIS IS FOR THE THREE OF YOU.
NOT COOL.

FIRST CRUSH

DIVE BAR

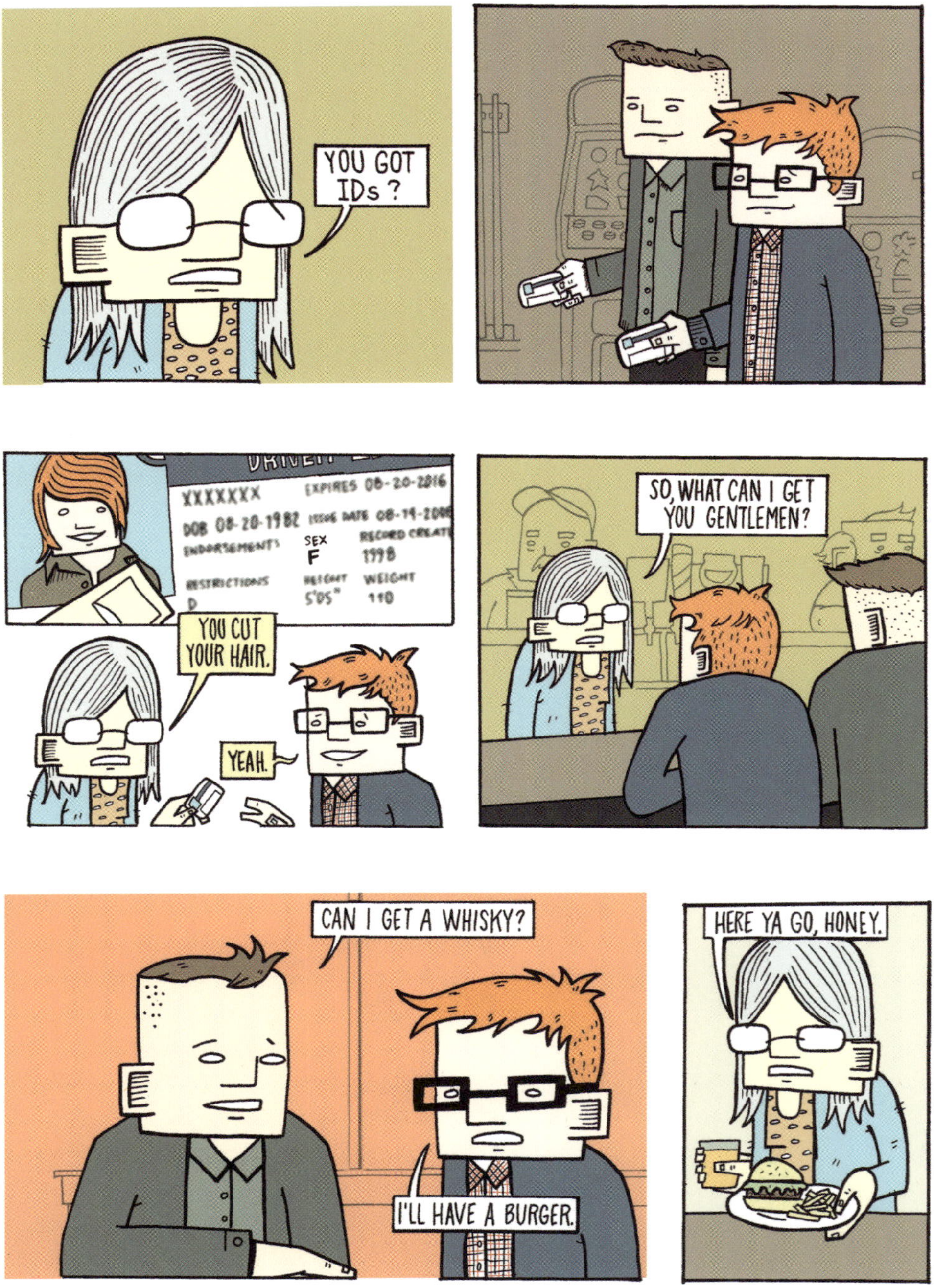
YOU GOT IDs?
XXXXXXX
EXPIRES 08-20-2016
DOB 08-20-1982
ENDORSEMENTS
SEX
F
RESTRICTIONS
HEIGHT
5'05"
WEIGHT
110
YOU CUT YOUR HAIR.
YEAH.
SO, WHAT CAN I GET YOU GENTLEMEN?
CAN I GET A WHISKY?
I'LL HAVE A BURGER.
HERE YA GO, HONEY.

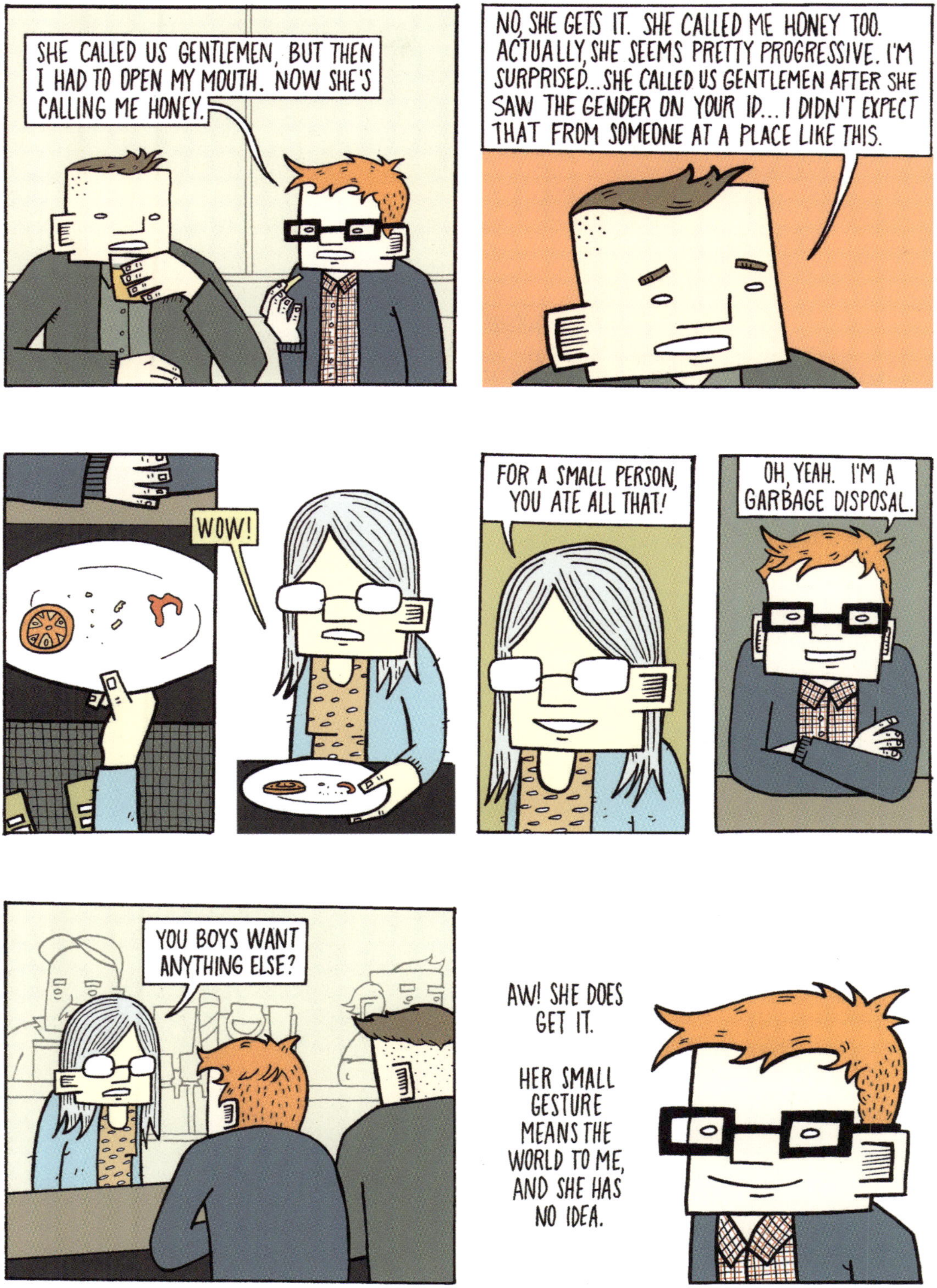
SHE CALLED US GENTLEMEN, BUT THEN I HAD TO OPEN MY MOUTH. NOW SHE'S CALLING ME HONEY.
NO, SHE GETS IT. SHE CALLED ME HONEY TOO. ACTUALLY, SHE SEEMS PRETTY PROGRESSIVE. I'M SURPRISED... SHE CALLED US GENTLEMEN AFTER SHE SAW THE GENDER ON YOUR ID... I DIDN'T EXPECT THAT FROM SOMEONE AT A PLACE LIKE THIS.
WOW!
FOR A SMALL PERSON, YOU ATE ALL THAT!
OH, YEAH. I'M A GARBAGE DISPOSAL.
YOU BOYS WANT ANYTHING ELSE?
AW! SHE DOES GET IT.
HER SMALL GESTURE MEANS THE WORLD TO ME, AND SHE HAS NO IDEA.

THE DEVIL

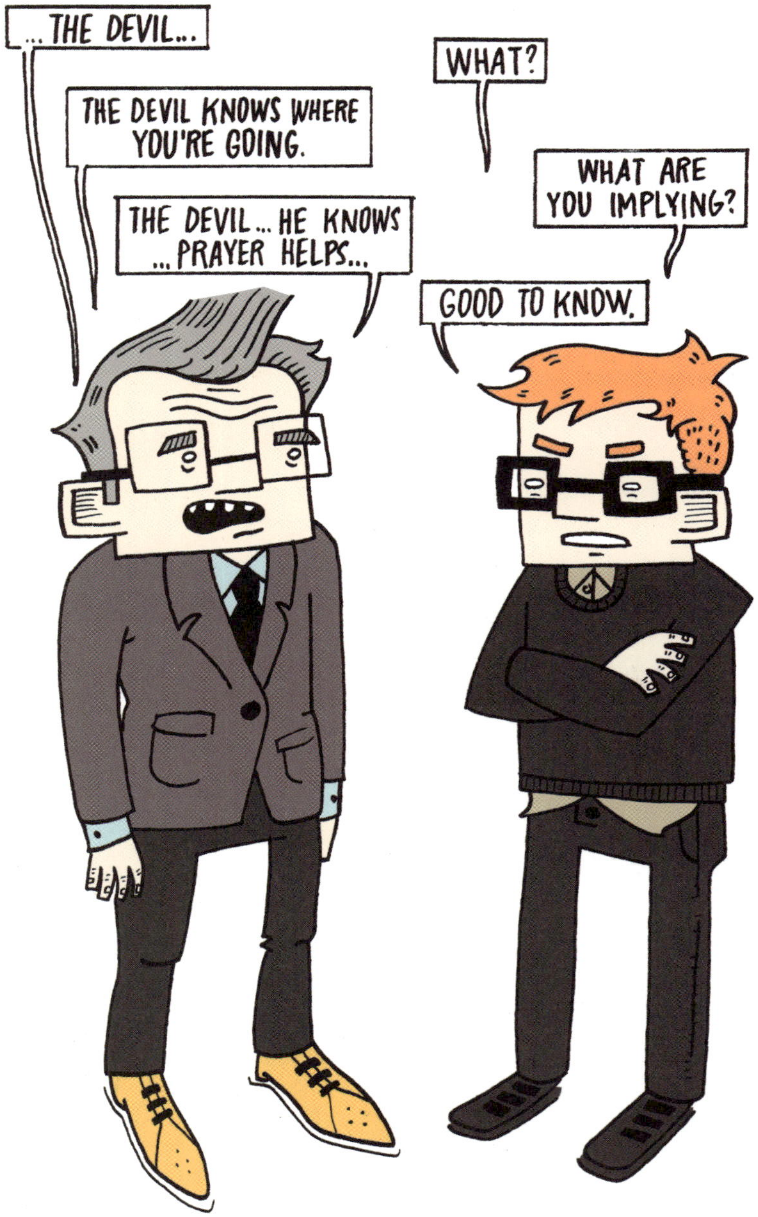
...THE DEVIL...
THE DEVIL KNOWS WHERE YOU'RE GOING.
THE DEVIL... HE KNOWS ...PRAYER HELPS...
WHAT?
WHAT ARE YOU IMPLYING?
GOOD TO KNOW.

CANDACE

WANNA CHECK OUT MY BOARD GAME COLLECTION?

I'M CANDACE. I'M 44 AND AN ELECTRICAL ENGINEER. I WAS BORN AND RAISED IN DES MOINES, BUT I'VE CALLED THE PACIFIC NORTH-WEST MY HOME FOR THE PAST TWELVE YEARS.
I LOVE TO COOK VEGETARIAN DISHES. ROASTED ROMANESCO IS MY FAVORITE. MY MEDICINE CABINET IS FULL OF VITAMINS AND SUPPLEMENTS. ONE OF MY KITCHEN CUPBOARDS IS DEVOTED TO HERBAL TEAS, SUCH AS WOMAN'S MOON CYCLE. MY HOBBIES INCLUDE: READING SCIENCE FICTION NOVELS, URBAN GARDENING, CAMPING, AND BOARD GAMES. I HAVE TWO CATS. THEY FIGHT A LOT. THEIR NAMES ARE TESLA AND EDISON.
MY IDEAL DATE WOULD TAKE PLACE AT MY HOUSE. I'D INVITE MY LOVER TO SNACK ON VEGETABLES FROM MY GARDEN AS WE SPOKE PASSIONATELY ABOUT OUR FAVORITE CAT BREEDS. THEN, WE'D TAKE A BIKE RIDE TO THE CO-OP AND BUY SOME LOCAL, ORGANIC, ARTISAN FOOD. NEXT, WE'D OPEN UP A BOTTLE OF PINOT NOIR, COOK DINNER TOGETHER, AND DANCE TO THE *REALITY BITES* SOUNDTRACK. AFTER ENJOYING AN INTIMATE PICNIC ON MY LIVING ROOM FLOOR, WE'D RETIRE TO THE BED-ROOM. WE'D SPEND THE ENTIRE NIGHT LYING NAKED ON A BED OF PILLOWS, PROCESSING OUR FEELINGS AS OUR MINDS COURSE WITH CARNAL DESIRE.
WANNA PLAY *SETTLERS OF CATAN*? DROP ME A LINE!

BREAKROOM

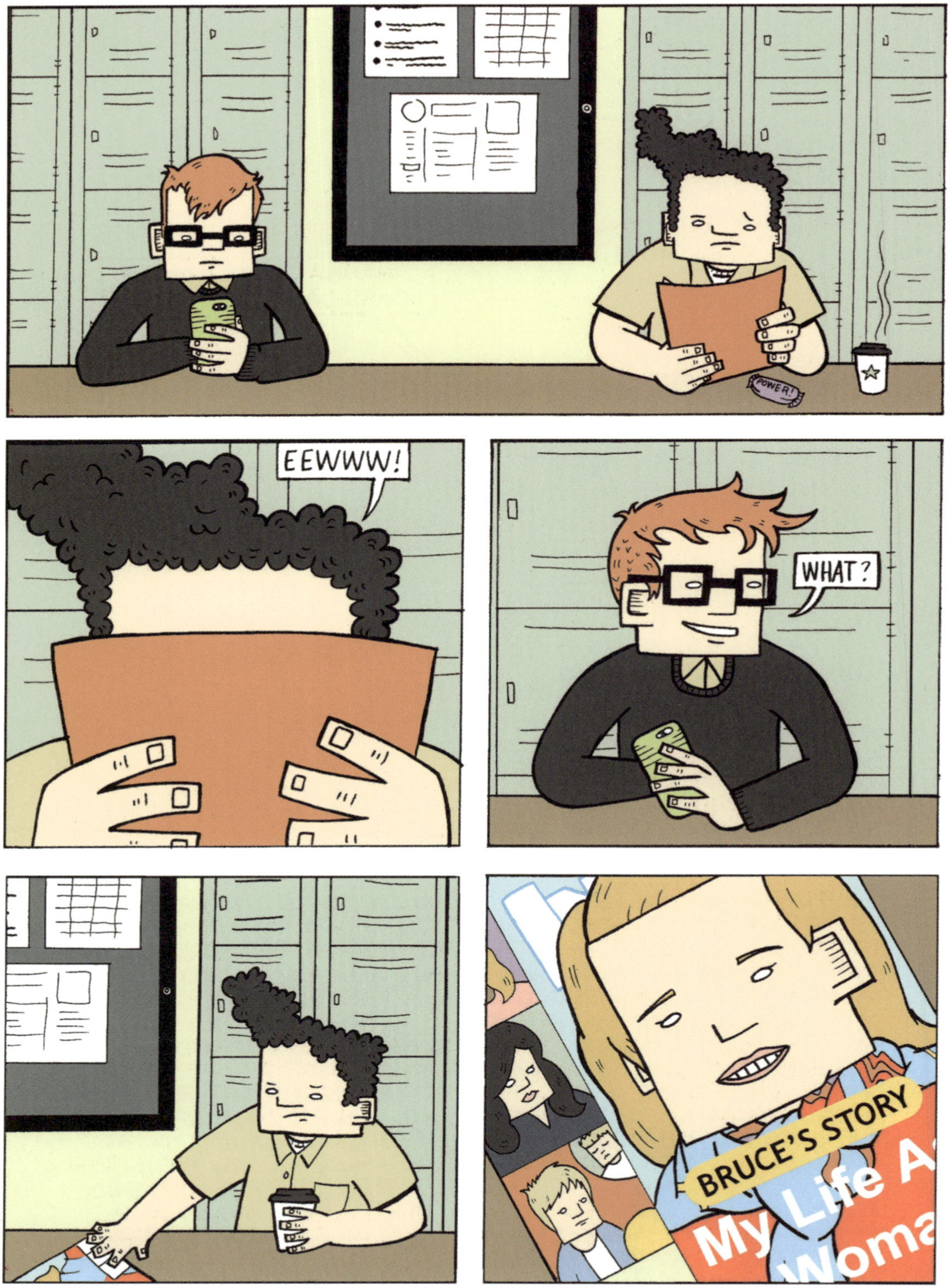
POWER!
EEWWW!
WHAT?
BRUCE'S STORY
My Life

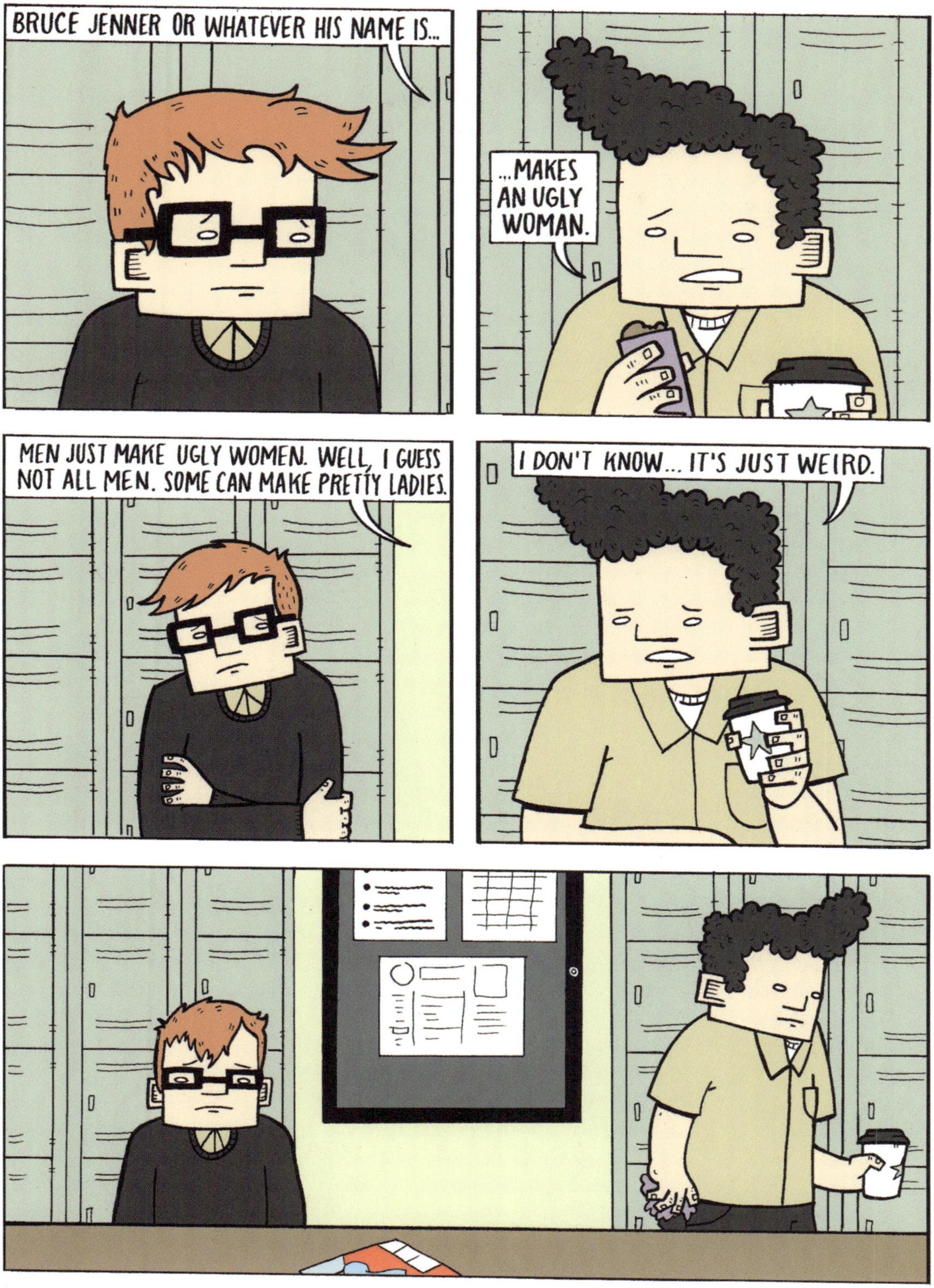

BRUCE JENNER OR WHATEVER HIS NAME IS...
...MAKES AN UGLY WOMAN.
MEN JUST MAKE UGLY WOMEN. WELL, I GUESS NOT ALL MEN. SOME CAN MAKE PRETTY LADIES.
I DON'T KNOW... IT'S JUST WEIRD.

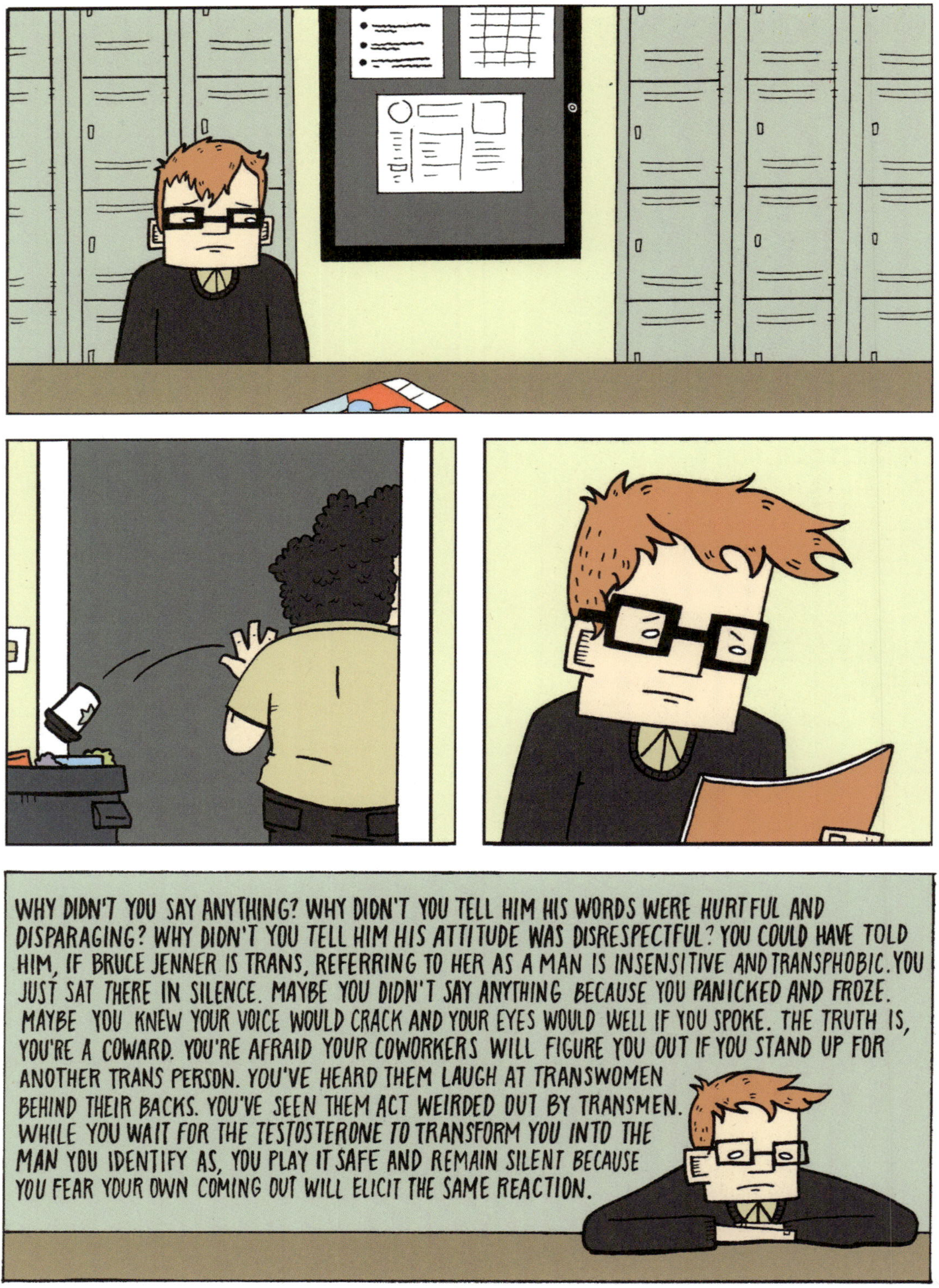
WHY DIDN'T YOU SAY ANYTHING? WHY DIDN'T YOU TELL HIM HIS WORDS WERE HURTFUL AND DISPARAGING? WHY DIDN'T YOU TELL HIM HIS ATTITUDE WAS DISRESPECTFUL? YOU COULD HAVE TOLD HIM, IF BRUCE JENNER IS TRANS, REFERRING TO HER AS A MAN IS INSENSITIVE AND TRANSPHOBIC. YOU JUST SAT THERE IN SILENCE. MAYBE YOU DIDN'T SAY ANYTHING BECAUSE YOU PANICKED AND FROZE. MAYBE YOU KNEW YOUR VOICE WOULD CRACK AND YOUR EYES WOULD WELL IF YOU SPOKE. THE TRUTH IS, YOU'RE A COWARD. YOU'RE AFRAID YOUR COWORKERS WILL FIGURE YOU OUT IF YOU STAND UP FOR ANOTHER TRANS PERSON. YOU'VE HEARD THEM LAUGH AT TRANSWOMEN BEHIND THEIR BACKS. YOU'VE SEEN THEM ACT WEIRDED OUT BY TRANSMEN. WHILE YOU WAIT FOR THE TESTOSTERONE TO TRANSFORM YOU INTO THE MAN YOU IDENTIFY AS, YOU PLAY IT SAFE AND REMAIN SILENT BECAUSE YOU FEAR YOUR OWN COMING OUT WILL ELICIT THE SAME REACTION.

FLOWER ESSENCES

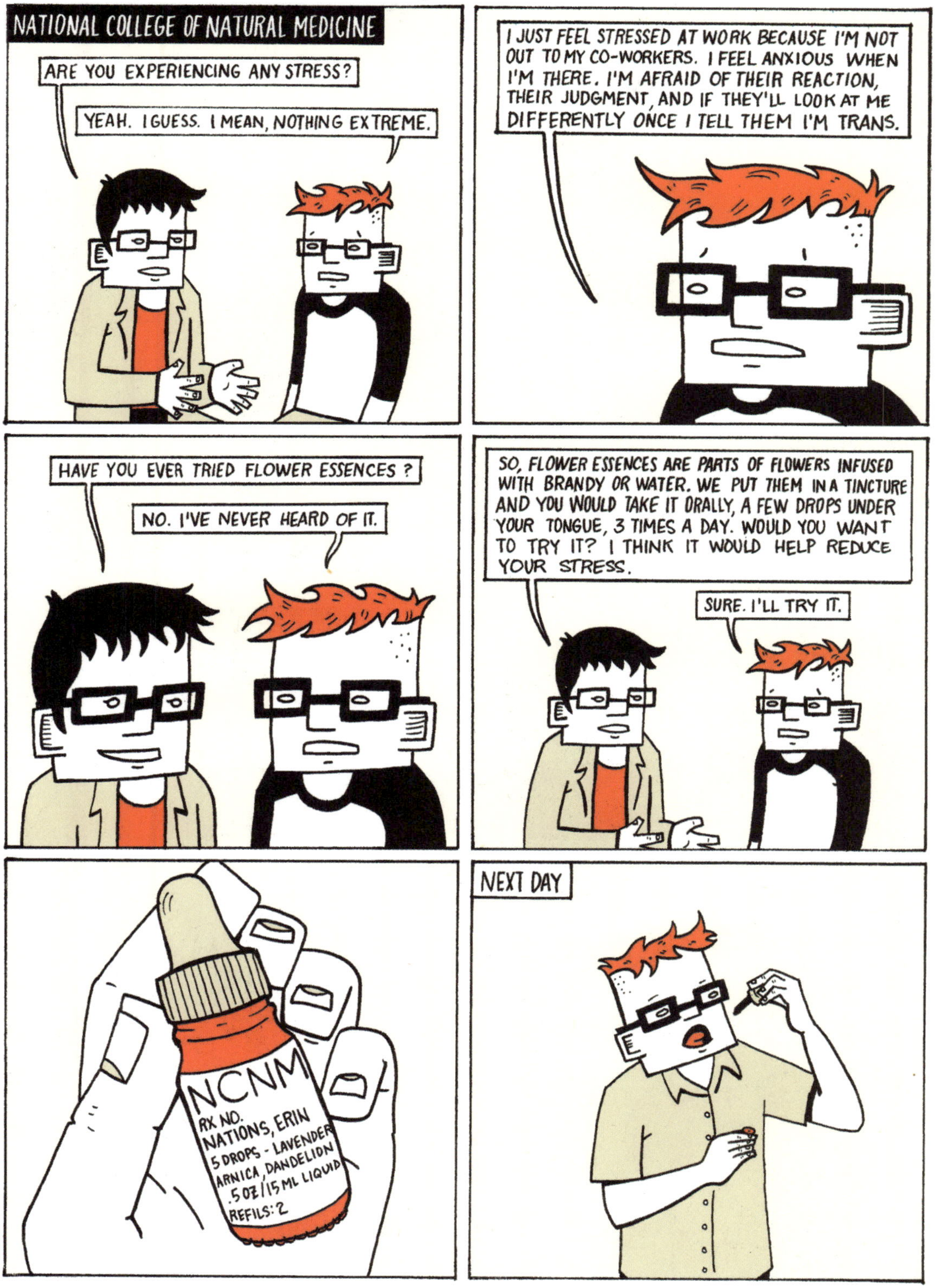

NATIONAL COLLEGE OF NATURAL MEDICINE
ARE YOU EXPERIENCING ANY STRESS?
YEAH. I GUESS. I MEAN, NOTHING EXTREME.
I JUST FEEL STRESSED AT WORK BECAUSE I'M NOT OUT TO MY CO-WORKERS. I FEEL ANXIOUS WHEN I'M THERE. I'M AFRAID OF THEIR REACTION, THEIR JUDGMENT, AND IF THEY'LL LOOK AT ME DIFFERENTLY ONCE I TELL THEM I'M TRANS.
HAVE YOU EVER TRIED FLOWER ESSENCES?
NO. I'VE NEVER HEARD OF IT.
SO, FLOWER ESSENCES ARE PARTS OF FLOWERS INFUSED WITH BRANDY OR WATER. WE PUT THEM IN A TINCTURE AND YOU WOULD TAKE IT ORALLY, A FEW DROPS UNDER YOUR TONGUE, 3 TIMES A DAY. WOULD YOU WANT TO TRY IT? I THINK IT WOULD HELP REDUCE YOUR STRESS.
SURE. I'LL TRY IT.
NCNM
RX NO.
NATIONS, ERIN
5 DROPS - LAVENDER
ARNICA, DANDELION
.5 OZ/15 ML LIQUID
REFILS: 2
NEXT DAY

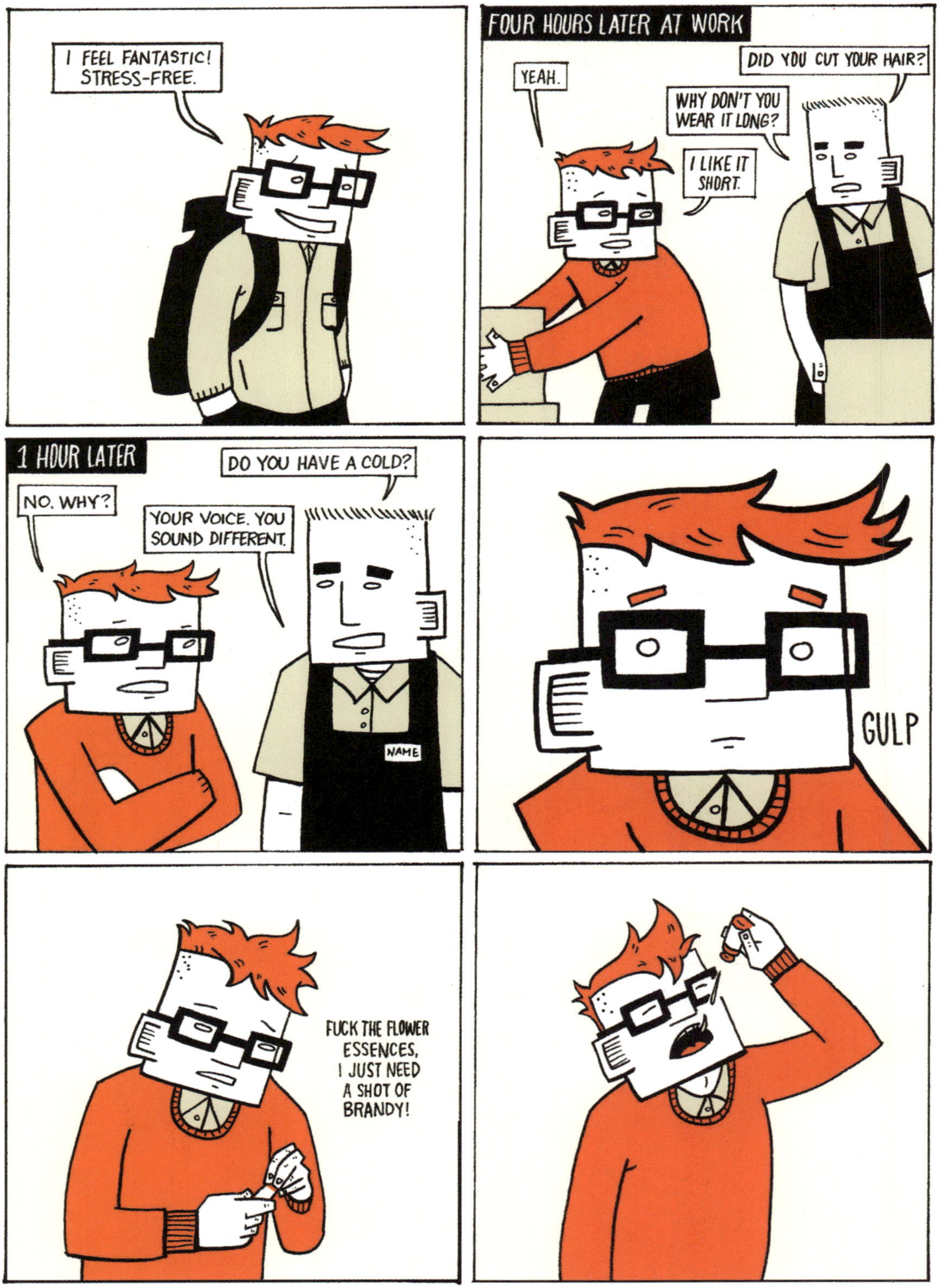

I FEEL FANTASTIC! STRESS-FREE.
FOUR HOURS LATER AT WORK
DID YOU CUT YOUR HAIR?
YEAH.
WHY DON'T YOU WEAR IT LONG?
I LIKE IT SHORT.
1 HOUR LATER
DO YOU HAVE A COLD?
NO. WHY?
YOUR VOICE. YOU SOUND DIFFERENT.
NAME
GULP
FUCK THE FLOWER ESSENCES, I JUST NEED A SHOT OF BRANDY!

DITCH IT

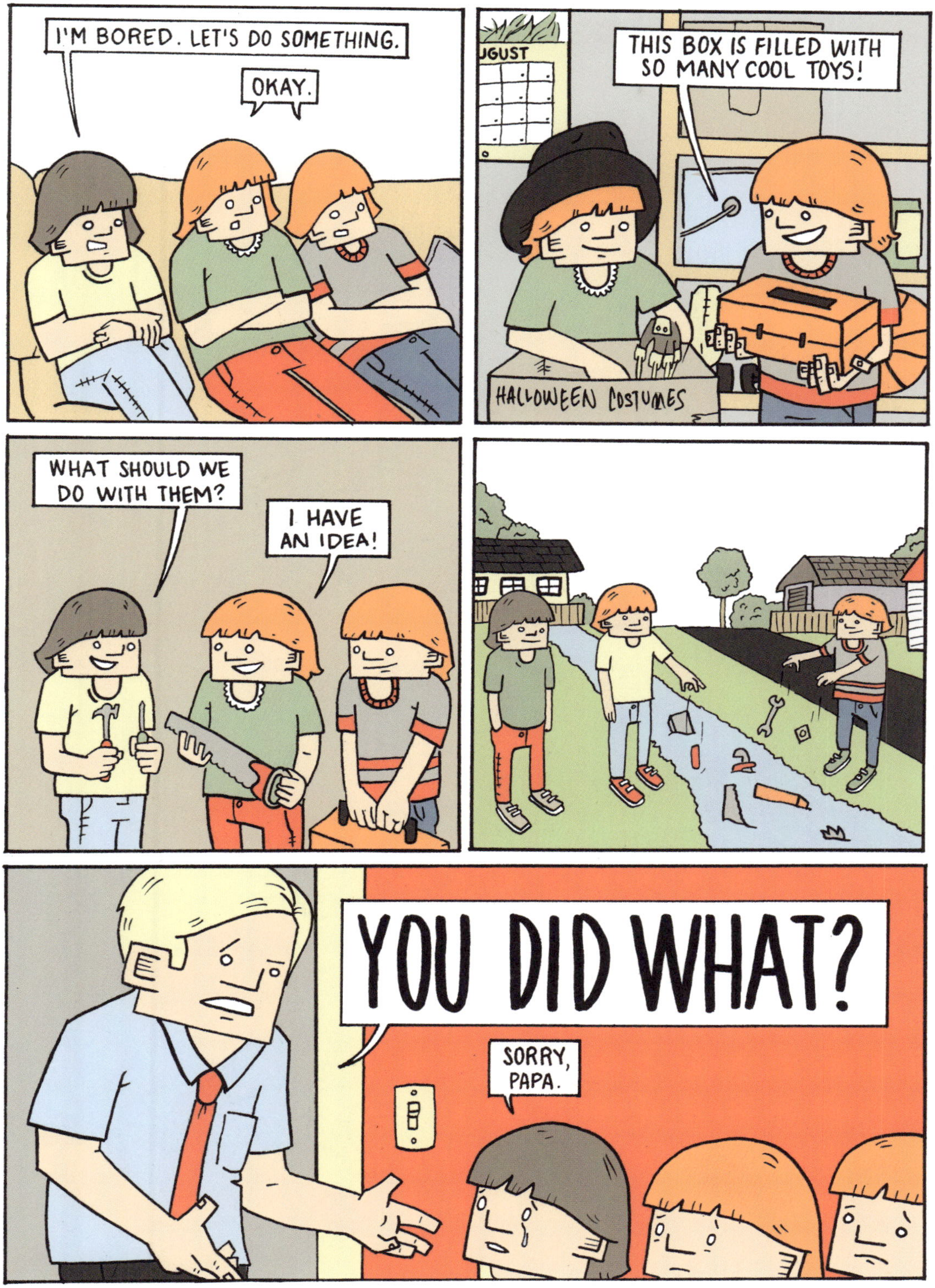

I'M BORED. LET'S DO SOMETHING.
OKAY.
AUGUST
THIS BOX IS FILLED WITH SO MANY COOL TOYS!
HALLOWEEN COSTUMES
WHAT SHOULD WE DO WITH THEM?
I HAVE AN IDEA!
YOU DID WHAT?
SORRY, PAPA.

THE INDECISIVE CAT

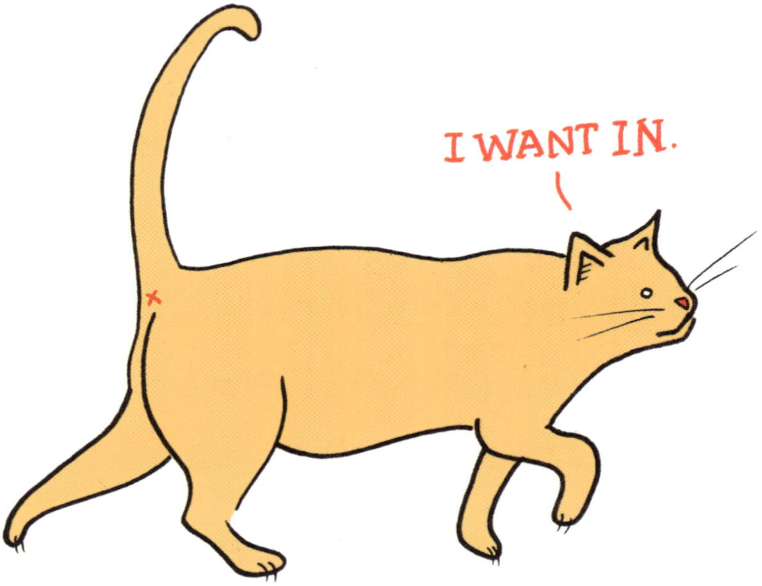
I WANT IN.

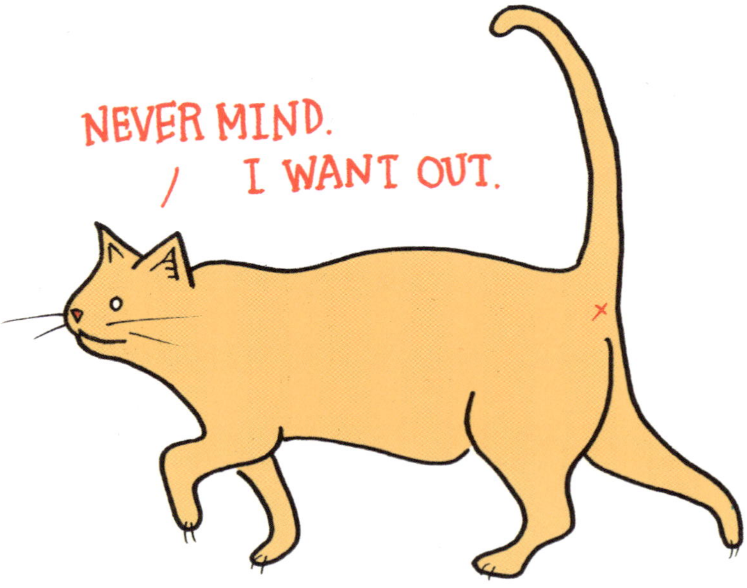
NEVER MIND.
I WANT OUT.

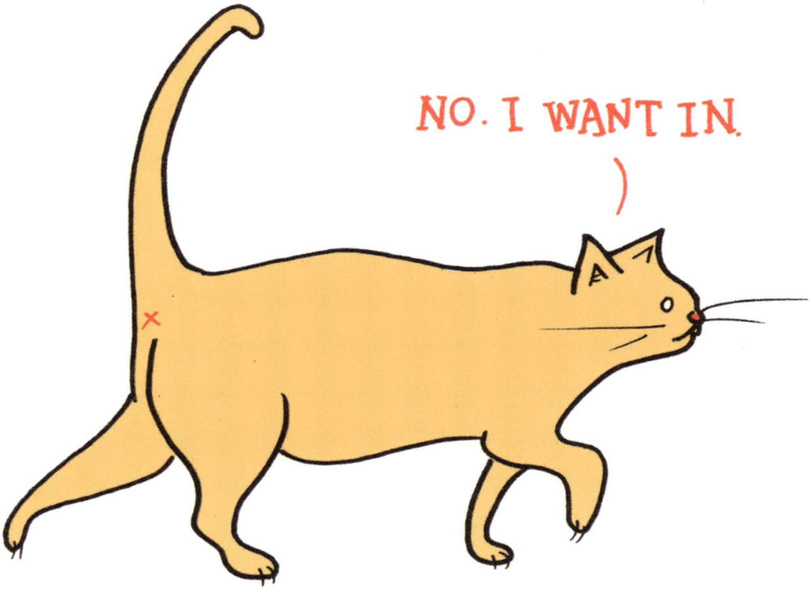
NO. I WANT IN.

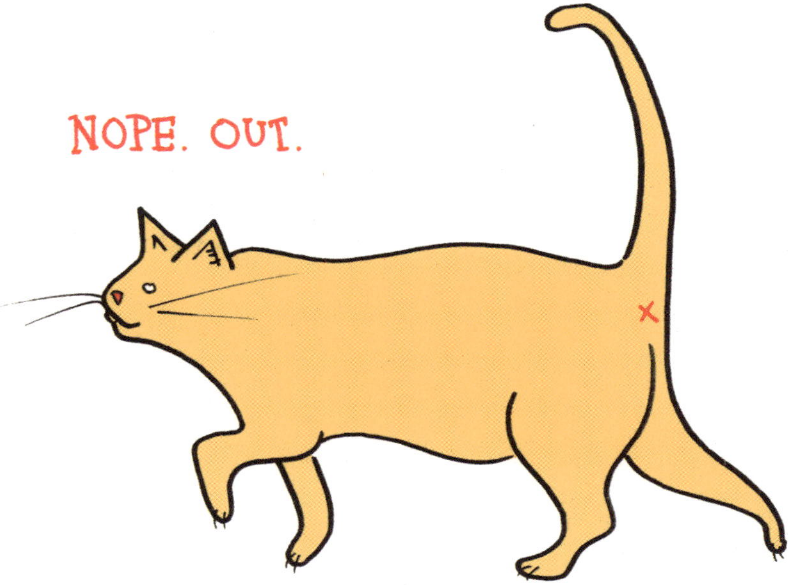
NOPE. OUT.

DWAYNE

HI. MY NAME IS DWAYNE. I'M A MODEST MAN. HOWEVER, I'M ALWAYS UP FOR AN ADVENTURE.
CURRENTLY, I'M TAKING SOME HOME LEARNING COURSES IN HOTEL/RESTAURANT MANAGEMENT THROUGH AN ONLINE CORRESPONDENCE SCHOOL. I ALSO WORK AS A RECEIVING CLERK AT A GROCERY STORE. DON'T WORRY! I'M NOT ALWAYS WORKING. I LOVE TO PLAY!
THE FOLLOWING ARE SOME FUN DATE IDEAS I CAME UP WITH: (1) TAKE A WALK ON A TRAIL SOMEWHERE PRETTY. ALSO, I LOVE DOGS, SO FIDO CAN JOIN US! (2) LET'S SPEND A DAY AT THE BEACH. LET'S WALK BAREFOOT ON THE BEACH AND COLLECT BROKEN SAND DOLLARS. WE'LL WATCH THE SUNSET. I'M A BIG ROMANTIC! I ENJOY TREATING WOMEN TO FANCY MEALS AT OLIVE GARDEN. LET'S SHARE A PLATE OF SPAGHETTI NOODLES. I PROMISE I'LL NUDGE THE LAST MEATBALL TOWARDS YOU. (3) HAVE A RELAXING SPA EXPERIENCE AT MY APARTMENT. I HAVE MOOD LIGHTS IN EVERY ROOM. I'M GREAT AT GIVING BACK RUBS AND FEET MASSAGES. I ALWAYS KEEP A SMALL BOTTLE OF ALMOND OIL IN MY FANNY PACK FOR THE OCCASION. AFTER THE MASSAGE, I'LL GRAB THE BATH BEADS SO WE CAN ENJOY A BUBBLE BATH TOGETHER. I'LL LET YOU SHARE MY LOOFAH!

DWAYNE'S FANNY PACK

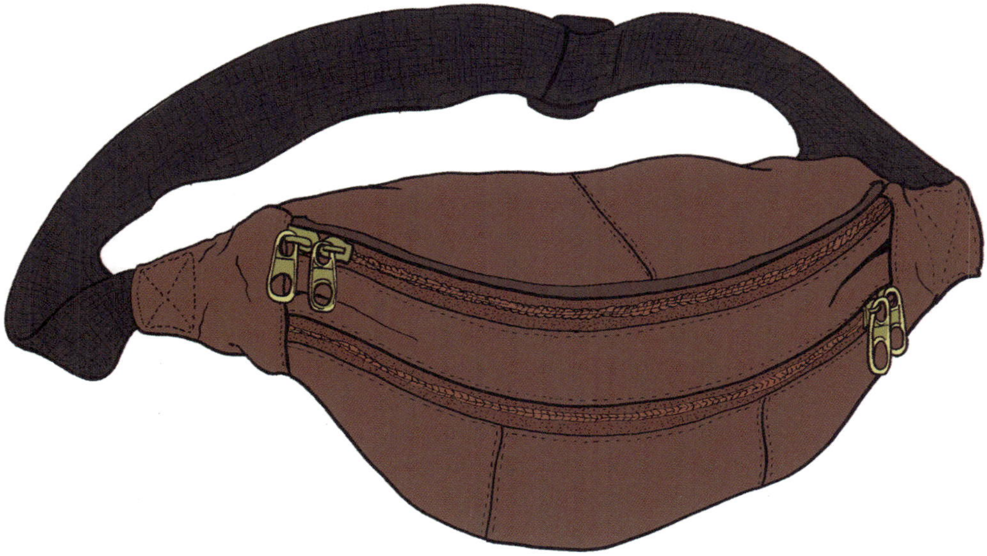

THE STUFF INSIDE DWAYNE'S PACK

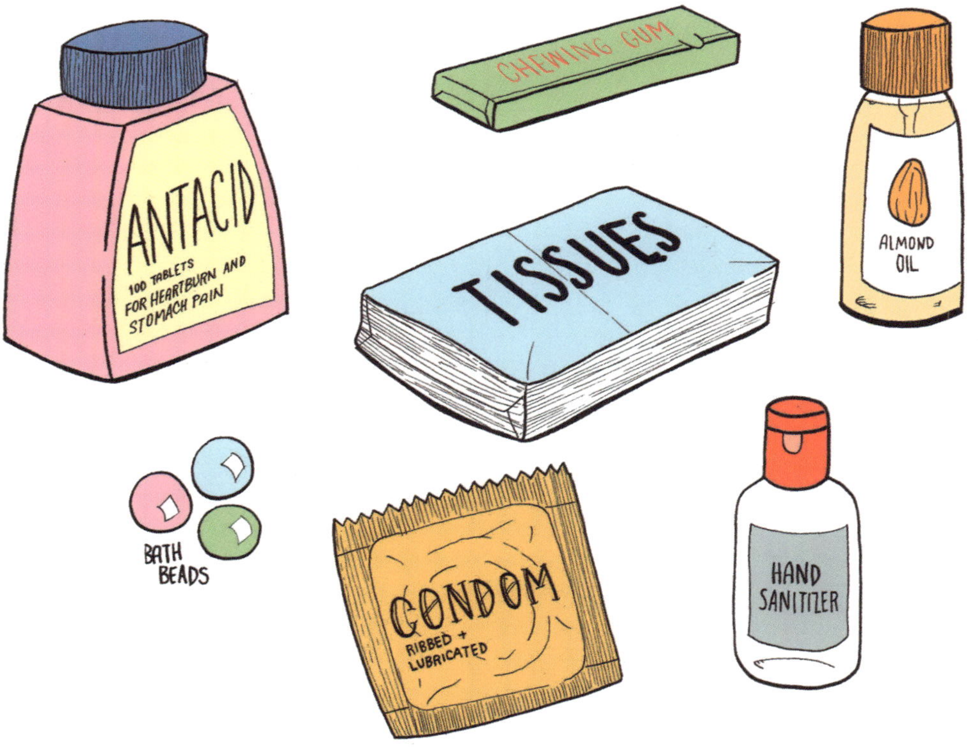
ANTACID
100 TABLETS FOR HEARTBURN AND STOMACH PAIN
CHEWING GUM
TISSUES
ALMOND OIL
BATH BEADS
CONDOM
RIBBED + LUBRICATED
HAND SANITIZER

TESTOSTERONE

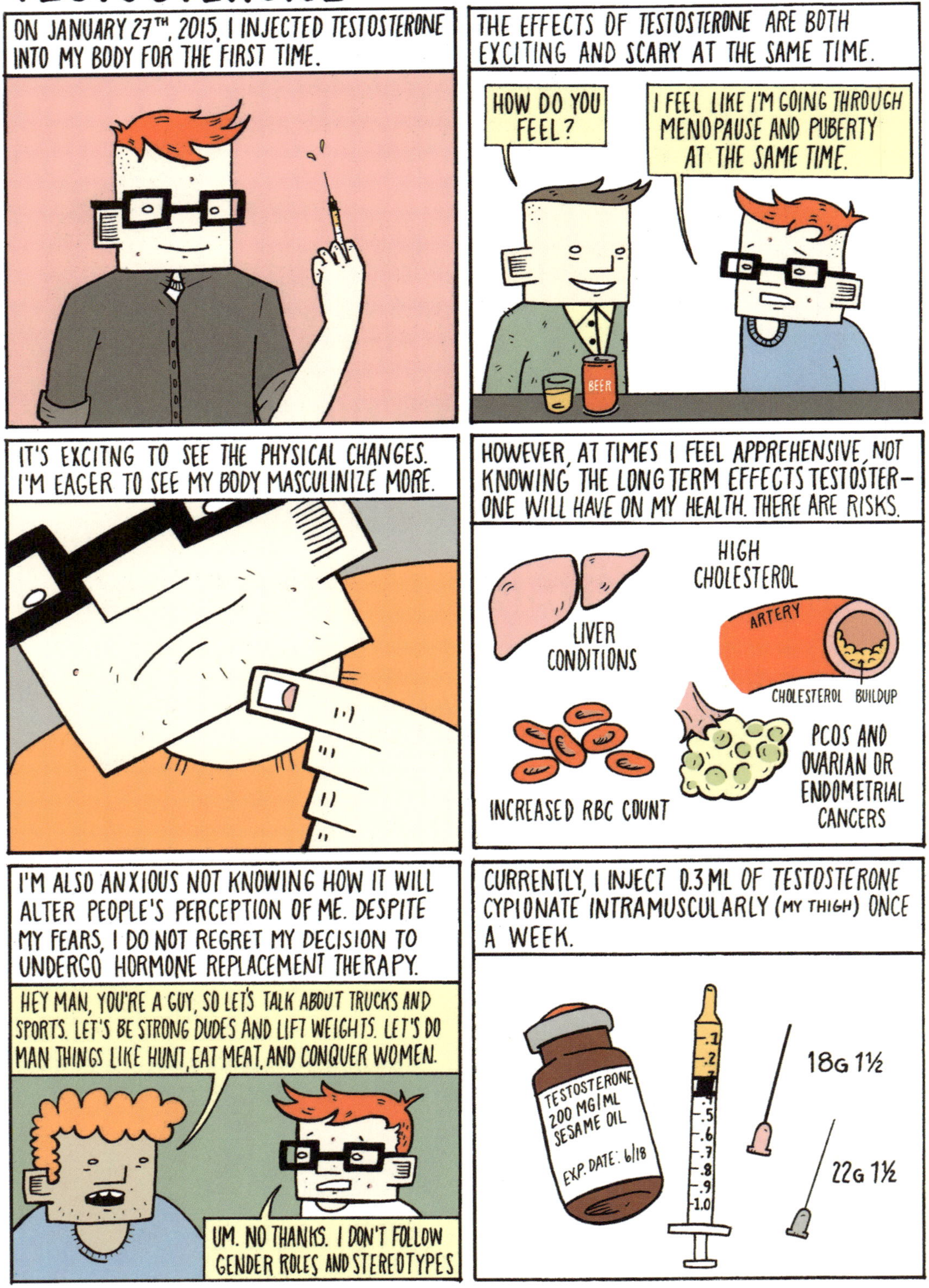

ON JANUARY 27TH, 2015, I INJECTED TESTOSTERONE INTO MY BODY FOR THE FIRST TIME.
THE EFFECTS OF TESTOSTERONE ARE BOTH EXCITING AND SCARY AT THE SAME TIME.
HOW DO YOU FEEL?
I FEEL LIKE I'M GOING THROUGH MENOPAUSE AND PUBERTY AT THE SAME TIME.
BEER
IT'S EXCITNG TO SEE THE PHYSICAL CHANGES. I'M EAGER TO SEE MY BODY MASCULINIZE MORE.
HOWEVER, AT TIMES I FEEL APPREHENSIVE, NOT KNOWING THE LONG TERM EFFECTS TESTOSTERONE WILL HAVE ON MY HEALTH. THERE ARE RISKS.
LIVER CONDITIONS
HIGH CHOLESTEROL
ARTERY
CHOLESTEROL BUILDUP
INCREASED RBC COUNT
PCOS AND OVARIAN OR ENDOMETRIAL CANCERS
I'M ALSO ANXIOUS NOT KNOWING HOW IT WILL ALTER PEOPLE'S PERCEPTION OF ME. DESPITE MY FEARS, I DO NOT REGRET MY DECISION TO UNDERGO HORMONE REPLACEMENT THERAPY.
HEY MAN, YOU'RE A GUY, SO LET'S TALK ABOUT TRUCKS AND SPORTS. LET'S BE STRONG DUDES AND LIFT WEIGHTS. LET'S DO MAN THINGS LIKE HUNT, EAT MEAT, AND CONQUER WOMEN.
UM. NO THANKS. I DON'T FOLLOW GENDER ROLES AND STEREOTYPES
CURRENTLY, I INJECT 0.3 ML OF TESTOSTERONE CYPIONATE INTRAMUSCULARLY (MY THIGH) ONCE A WEEK.
TESTOSTERONE 200 MG/ML SESAME OIL
EXP. DATE: 6/18
.1
.2
.5
.6
.7
.8
.9
1.0
18G 1½
22G 1½

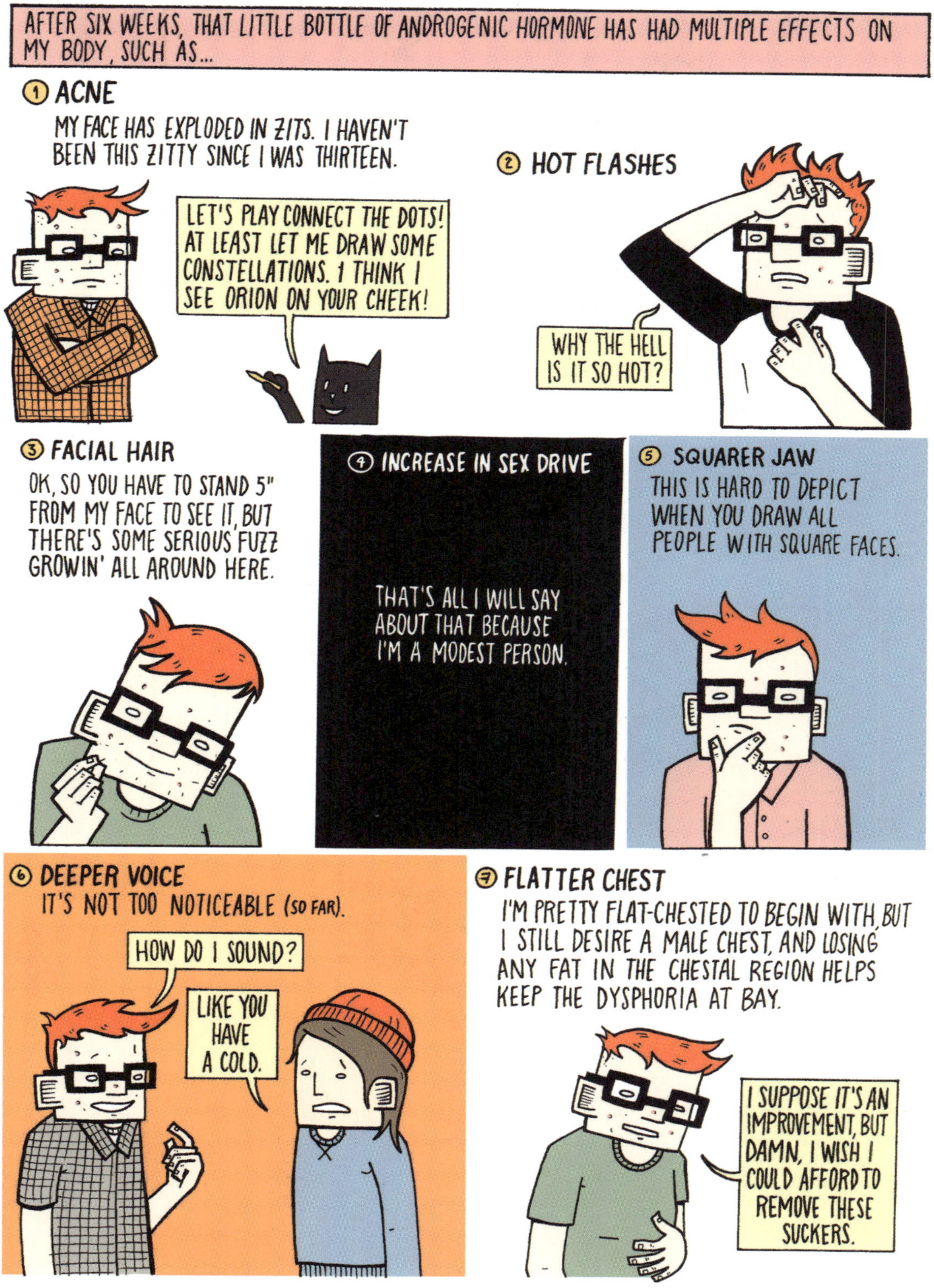

AFTER SIX WEEKS, THAT LITTLE BOTTLE OF ANDROGENIC HORMONE HAS HAD MULTIPLE EFFECTS ON MY BODY, SUCH AS...
① ACNE
MY FACE HAS EXPLODED IN ZITS. I HAVEN'T BEEN THIS ZITTY SINCE I WAS THIRTEEN.
LET'S PLAY CONNECT THE DOTS! AT LEAST LET ME DRAW SOME CONSTELLATIONS. I THINK I SEE ORION ON YOUR CHEEK!
② HOT FLASHES
WHY THE HELL IS IT SO HOT?
③ FACIAL HAIR
OK, SO YOU HAVE TO STAND 5" FROM MY FACE TO SEE IT, BUT THERE'S SOME SERIOUS FUZZ GROWIN' ALL AROUND HERE.
④ INCREASE IN SEX DRIVE
THAT'S ALL I WILL SAY ABOUT THAT BECAUSE I'M A MODEST PERSON.
⑤ SQUARER JAW
THIS IS HARD TO DEPICT WHEN YOU DRAW ALL PEOPLE WITH SQUARE FACES.
⑥ DEEPER VOICE
IT'S NOT TOO NOTICEABLE (SO FAR).
HOW DO I SOUND?
LIKE YOU HAVE A COLD.
⑦ FLATTER CHEST
I'M PRETTY FLAT-CHESTED TO BEGIN WITH, BUT I STILL DESIRE A MALE CHEST, AND LOSING ANY FAT IN THE CHESTAL REGION HELPS KEEP THE DYSPHORIA AT BAY.
I SUPPOSE IT'S AN IMPROVEMENT, BUT DAMN, I WISH I COULD AFFORD TO REMOVE THESE SUCKERS.

⑧ **BODY ODOR**

YEP, THAT CHANGES TOO, AND NOT FOR THE BETTER.

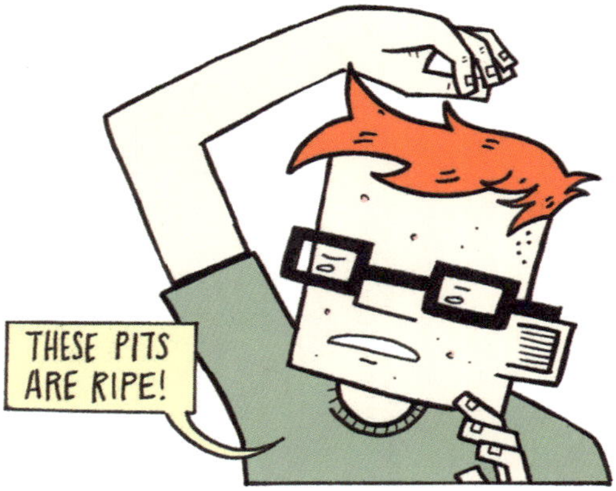
THESE PITS ARE RIPE!

⑨ **BOOST IN ENERGY**

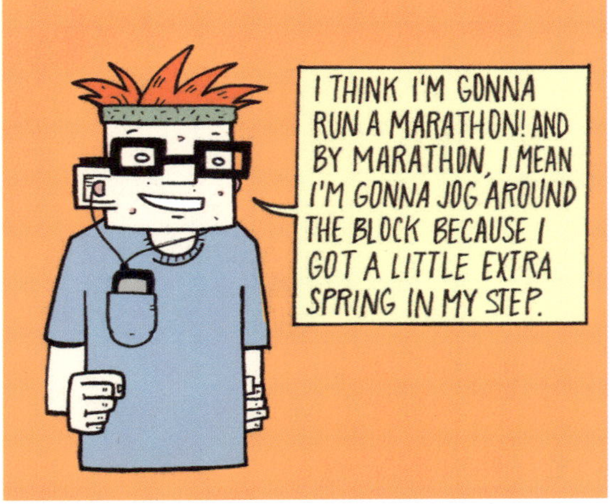
I THINK I'M GONNA RUN A MARATHON! AND BY MARATHON, I MEAN I'M GONNA JOG AROUND THE BLOCK BECAUSE I GOT A LITTLE EXTRA SPRING IN MY STEP.

⑩ **MOOD SWINGS**

ON A FEW OCCASIONS, TOWARDS THE END OF MY 7 DAY CYCLE, I'VE BEEN HELLA CRANKY. IF SOMETHING ANNOYS ME, I GET PISSY. I'LL BE UPSET WITHOUT A REASON.

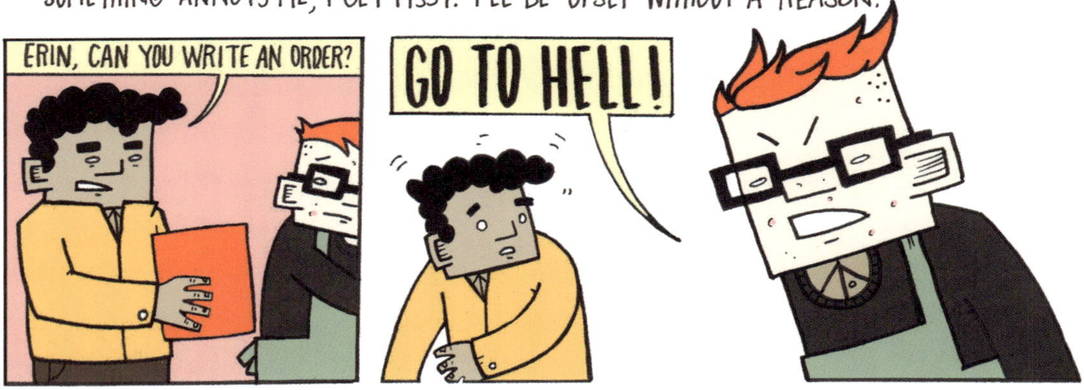
ERIN, CAN YOU WRITE AN ORDER?
GO TO HELL!

⑪ **CONFIDENCE**

I'VE BEEN TOLD I'M MORE CONFIDENT AND I STAND TALLER NOW.

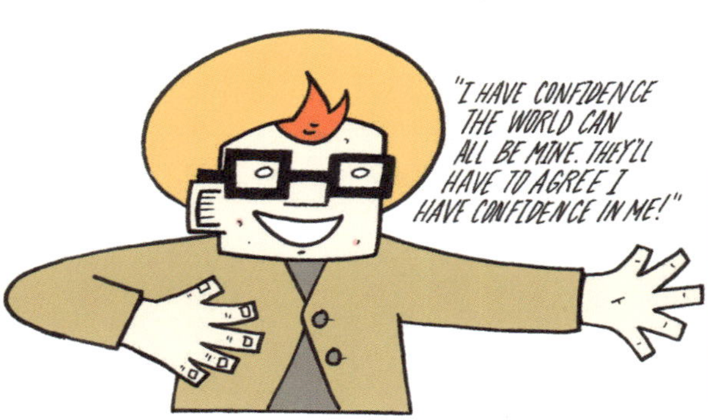
"I HAVE CONFIDENCE THE WORLD CAN ALL BE MINE. THEY'LL HAVE TO AGREE I HAVE CONFIDENCE IN ME!"

⑫ **CESSATION OF MENSES**

I CRINGE AT THE WORD PERIOD AND DESPISE ANY DISCUSSION REGARDING IT, BUT IT'S TRUE, **T** STOPS IT FROM RETURNING. IT'S FABULOUS! I USED TO PLAN MY VACATIONS AROUND IT BECAUSE IF I'M GONNA TRAVEL, I WANT TO ENJOY MYSELF WITHOUT ANY INTERRUPTIONS FROM MY UTERUS.

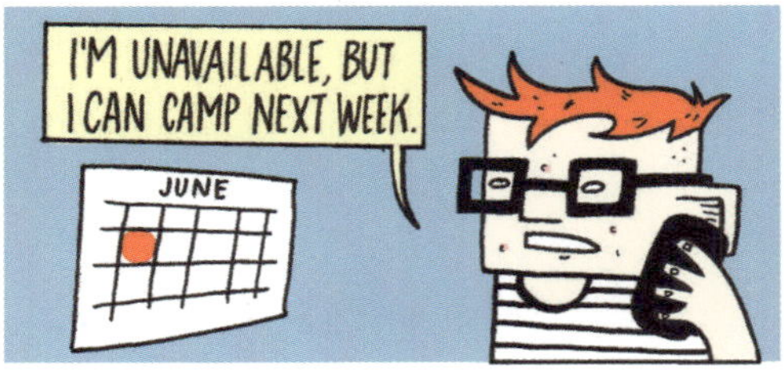
I'M UNAVAILABLE, BUT I CAN CAMP NEXT WEEK.
JUNE

CHILLAXIN'

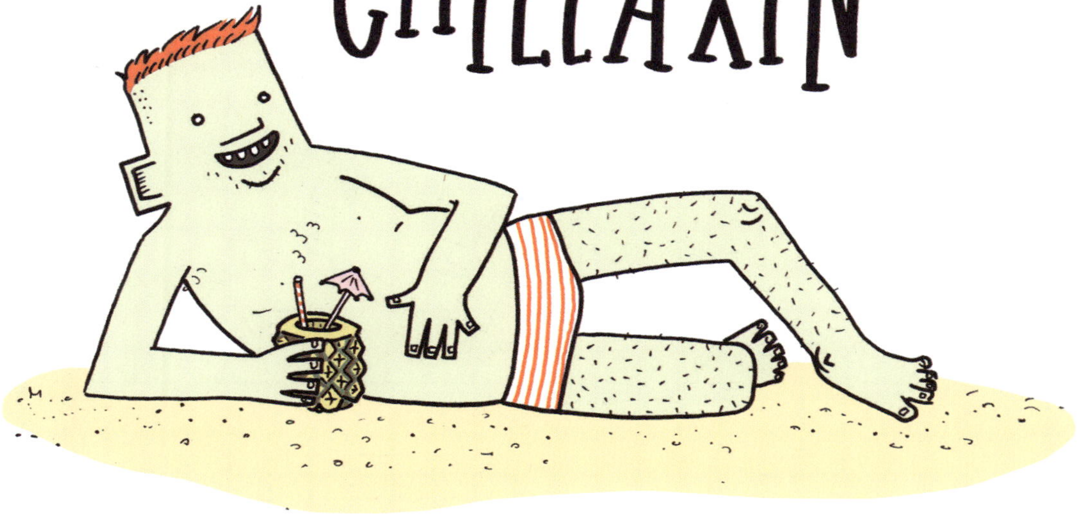

SNIFF

SOMETIMES HUMANS HAVE THE SAME THOUGHTS AS DOGS.
THEY JUST HAVE A HARD TIME VERBALIZING IT.

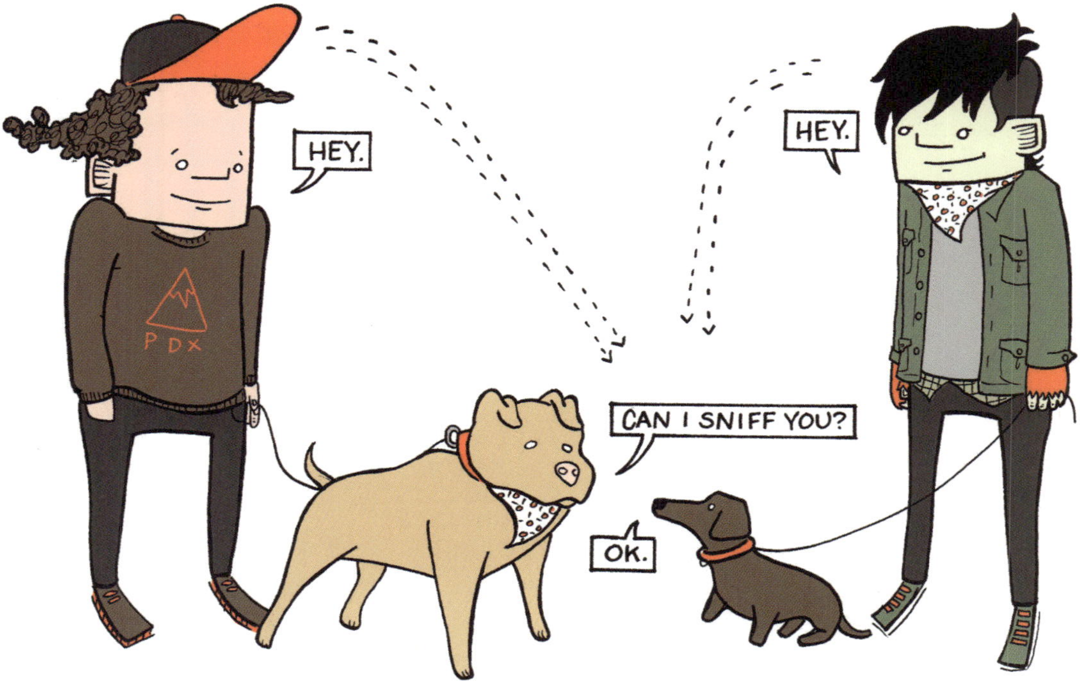
HEY.
HEY.
PDX
CAN I SNIFF YOU?
OK.

CHILDHOOD INFATUATION

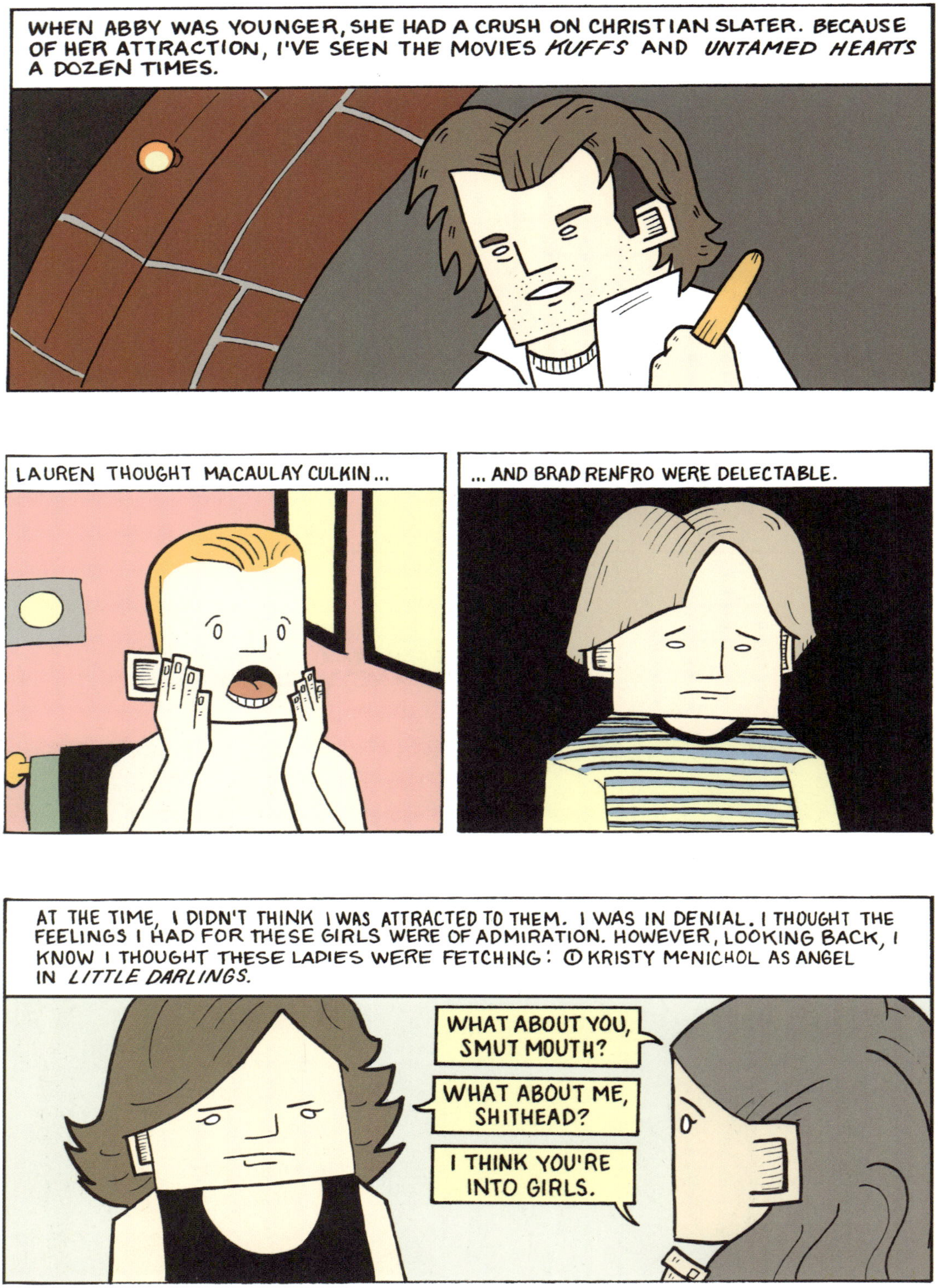
WHEN ABBY WAS YOUNGER, SHE HAD A CRUSH ON CHRISTIAN SLATER. BECAUSE OF HER ATTRACTION, I'VE SEEN THE MOVIES *KUFFS* AND *UNTAMED HEARTS* A DOZEN TIMES.
LAUREN THOUGHT MACAULAY CULKIN...
... AND BRAD RENFRO WERE DELECTABLE.
AT THE TIME, I DIDN'T THINK I WAS ATTRACTED TO THEM. I WAS IN DENIAL. I THOUGHT THE FEELINGS I HAD FOR THESE GIRLS WERE OF ADMIRATION. HOWEVER, LOOKING BACK, I KNOW I THOUGHT THESE LADIES WERE FETCHING: ① KRISTY McNICHOL AS ANGEL IN *LITTLE DARLINGS*.
WHAT ABOUT YOU, SMUT MOUTH?
WHAT ABOUT ME, SHITHEAD?
I THINK YOU'RE INTO GIRLS.

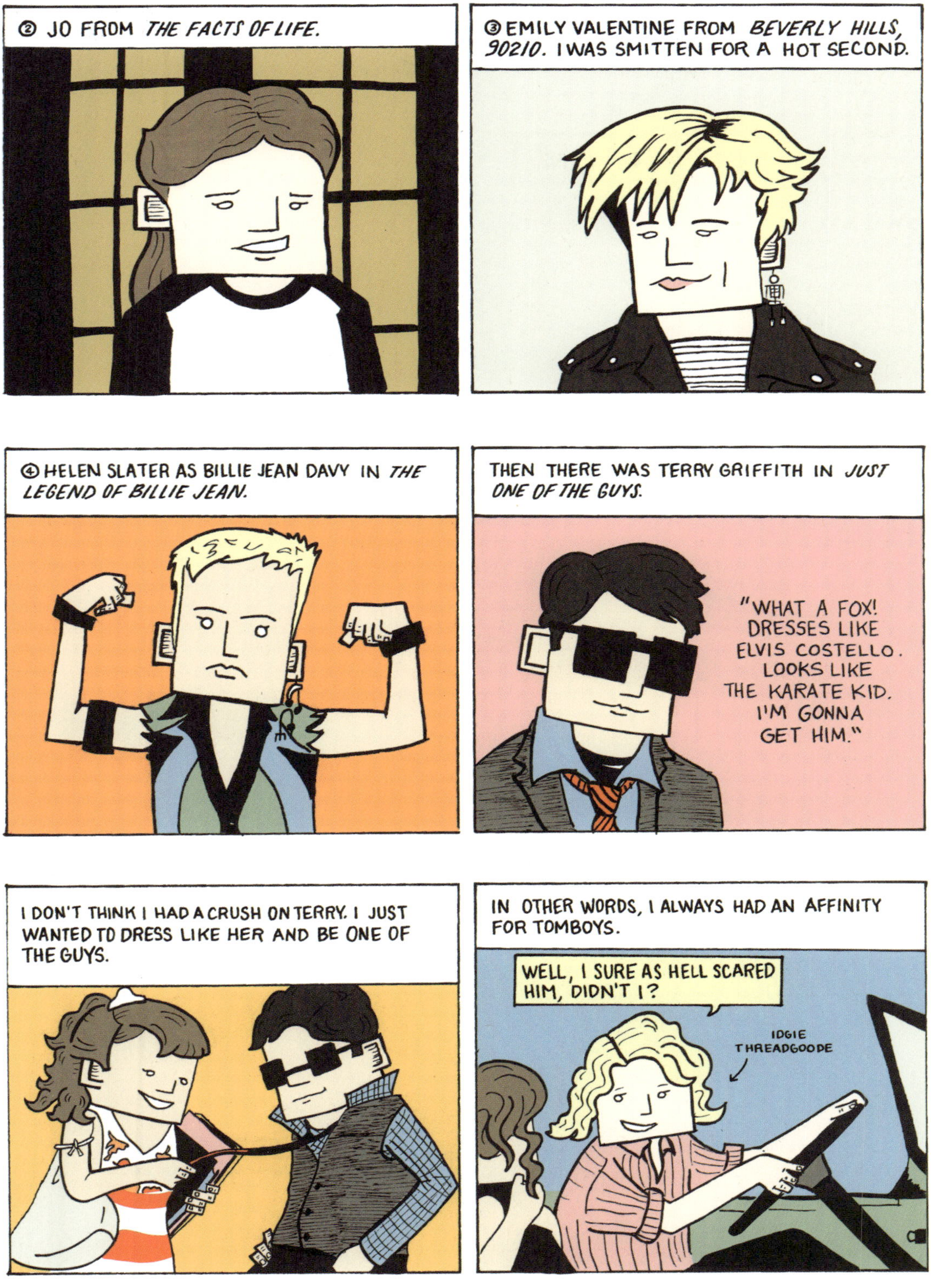
② JO FROM *THE FACTS OF LIFE.*
③ EMILY VALENTINE FROM *BEVERLY HILLS, 90210.* I WAS SMITTEN FOR A HOT SECOND.
④ HELEN SLATER AS BILLIE JEAN DAVY IN *THE LEGEND OF BILLIE JEAN.*
THEN THERE WAS TERRY GRIFFITH IN *JUST ONE OF THE GUYS.*
"WHAT A FOX! DRESSES LIKE ELVIS COSTELLO. LOOKS LIKE THE KARATE KID. I'M GONNA GET HIM."
I DON'T THINK I HAD A CRUSH ON TERRY. I JUST WANTED TO DRESS LIKE HER AND BE ONE OF THE GUYS.
IN OTHER WORDS, I ALWAYS HAD AN AFFINITY FOR TOMBOYS.
WELL, I SURE AS HELL SCARED HIM, DIDN'T I?
IDGIE THREADGOODE

GINGER PROTECTION

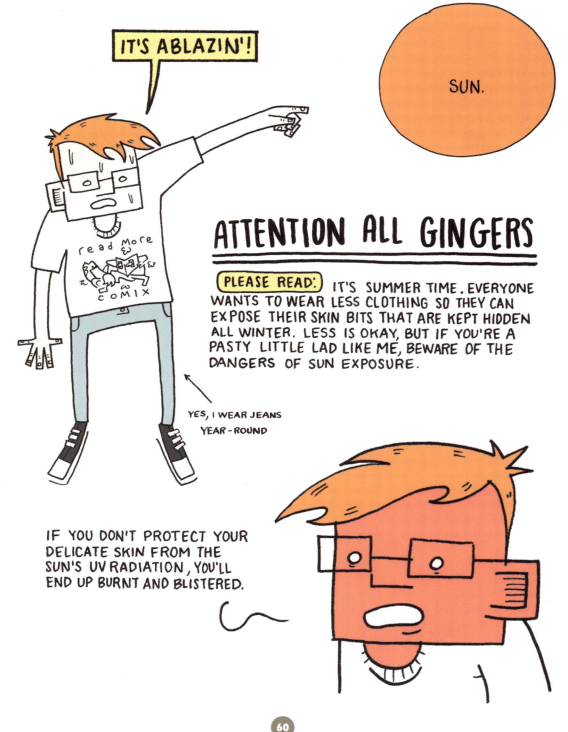

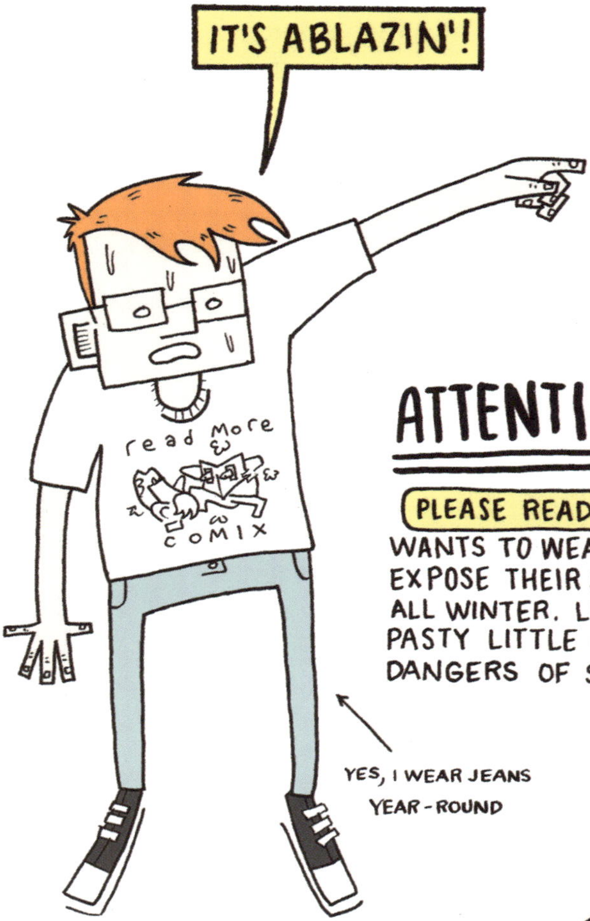
IT'S ABLAZIN'!
read More & COMIX
YES, I WEAR JEANS YEAR-ROUND

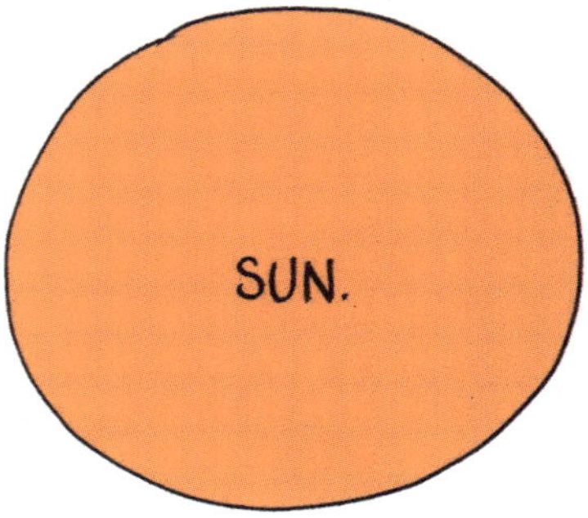
SUN.

ATTENTION ALL GINGERS

PLEASE READ: IT'S SUMMER TIME. EVERYONE WANTS TO WEAR LESS CLOTHING SO THEY CAN EXPOSE THEIR SKIN BITS THAT ARE KEPT HIDDEN ALL WINTER. LESS IS OKAY, BUT IF YOU'RE A PASTY LITTLE LAD LIKE ME, BEWARE OF THE DANGERS OF SUN EXPOSURE.

IF YOU DON'T PROTECT YOUR DELICATE SKIN FROM THE SUN'S UV RADIATION, YOU'LL END UP BURNT AND BLISTERED.

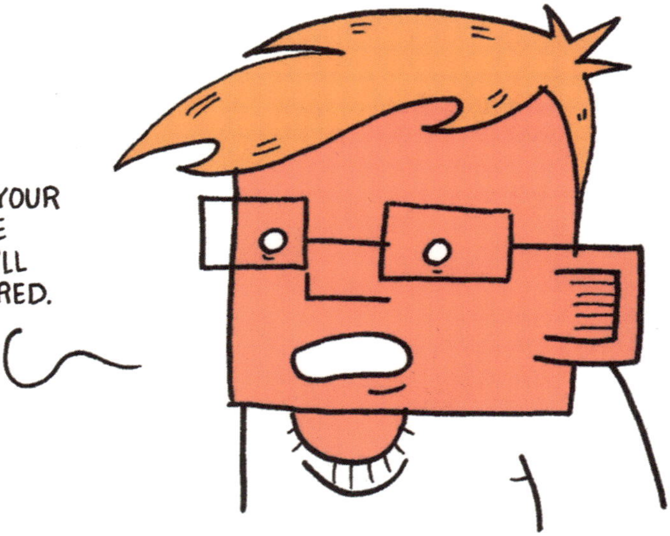

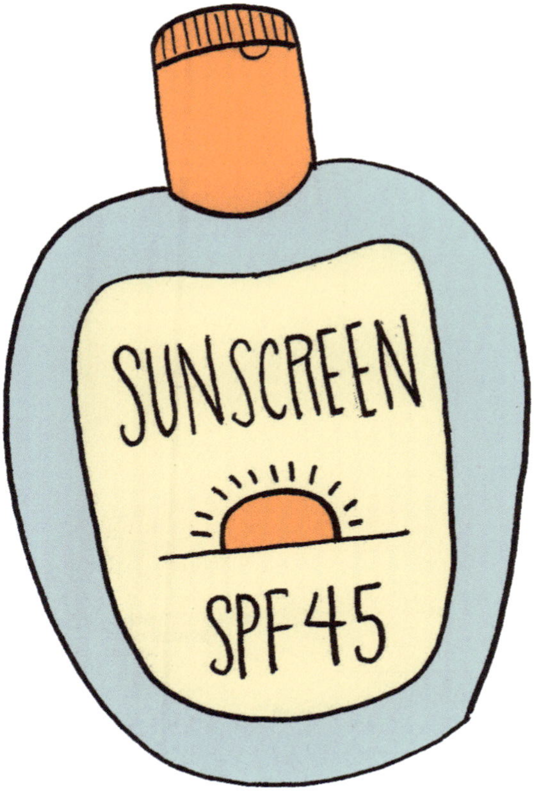
SUNSCREEN
SPF 45

DUE TO A MUTATED GENE, WE'RE ALREADY AT A HIGH RISK OF MELANOMA (THE DEADLIEST TYPE OF SKIN CANCER), SO DO YOURSELF A FAVOR AND BUY A BOTTLE OF SPF 45.

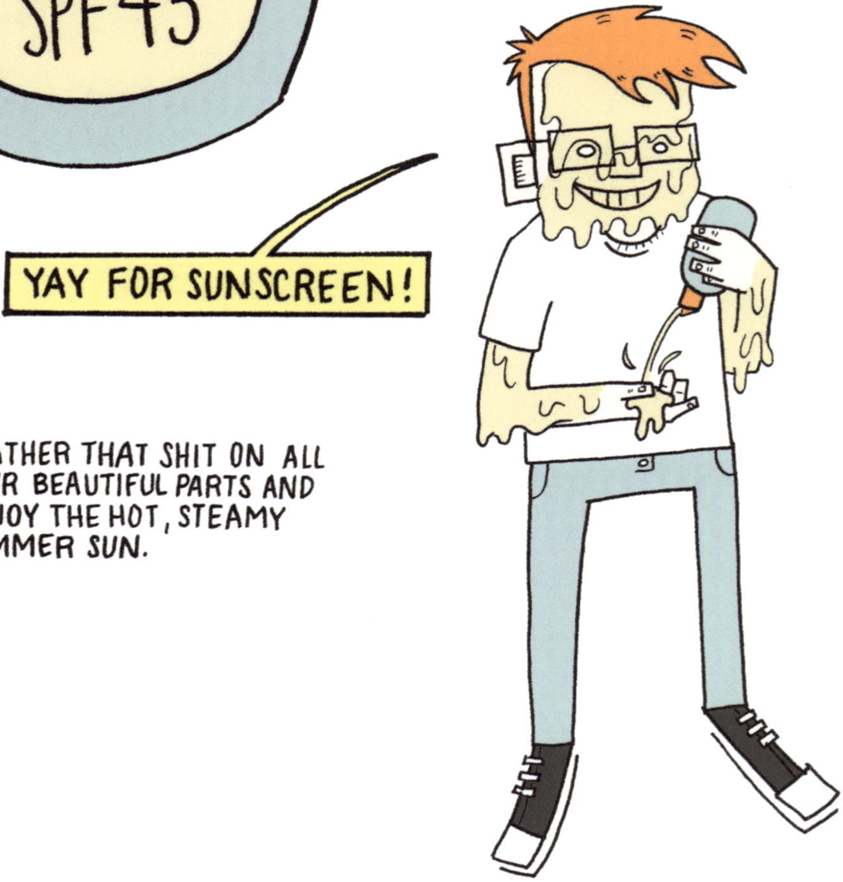
YAY FOR SUNSCREEN!

SLATHER THAT SHIT ON ALL YOUR BEAUTIFUL PARTS AND ENJOY THE HOT, STEAMY SUMMER SUN.

NOT A GUY

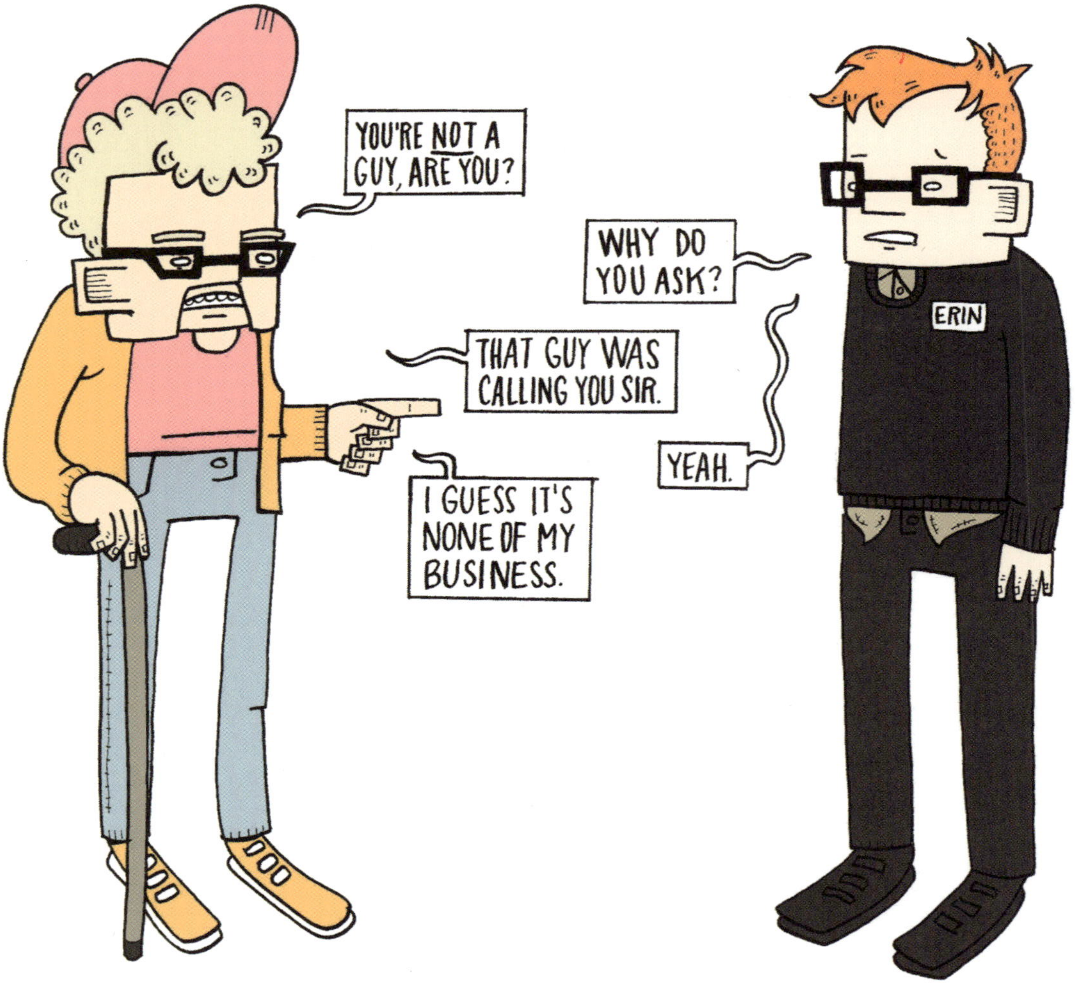
YOU'RE NOT A GUY, ARE YOU?
WHY DO YOU ASK?
THAT GUY WAS CALLING YOU SIR.
YEAH.
I GUESS IT'S NONE OF MY BUSINESS.
ERIN

GAMBLING FOR KIDS

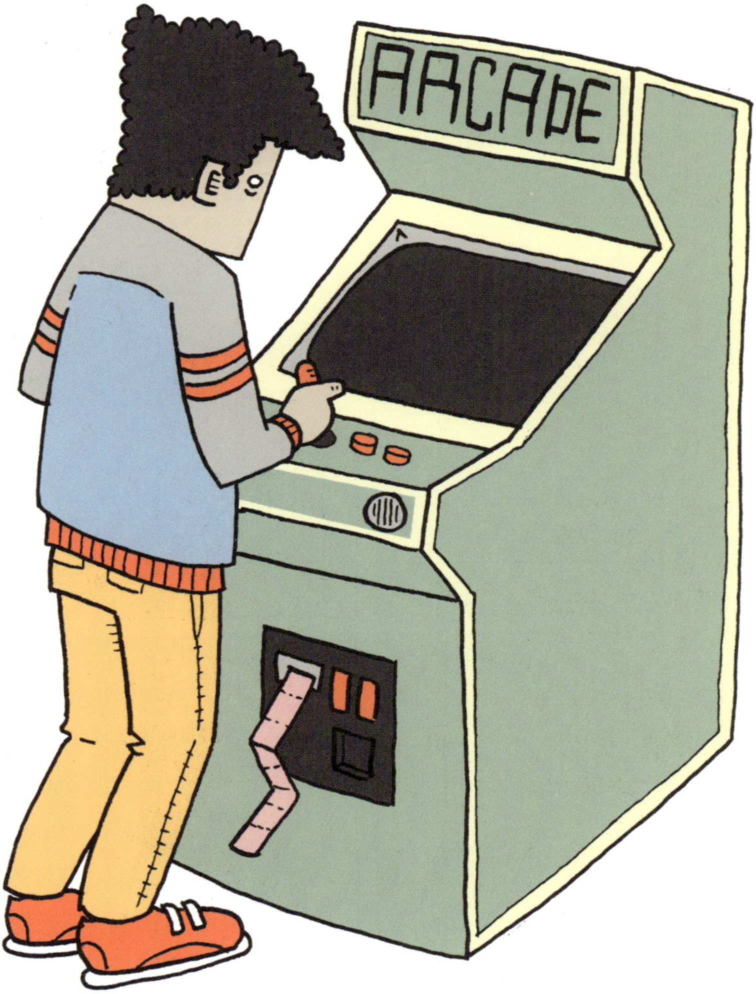

ARCADE

JERK

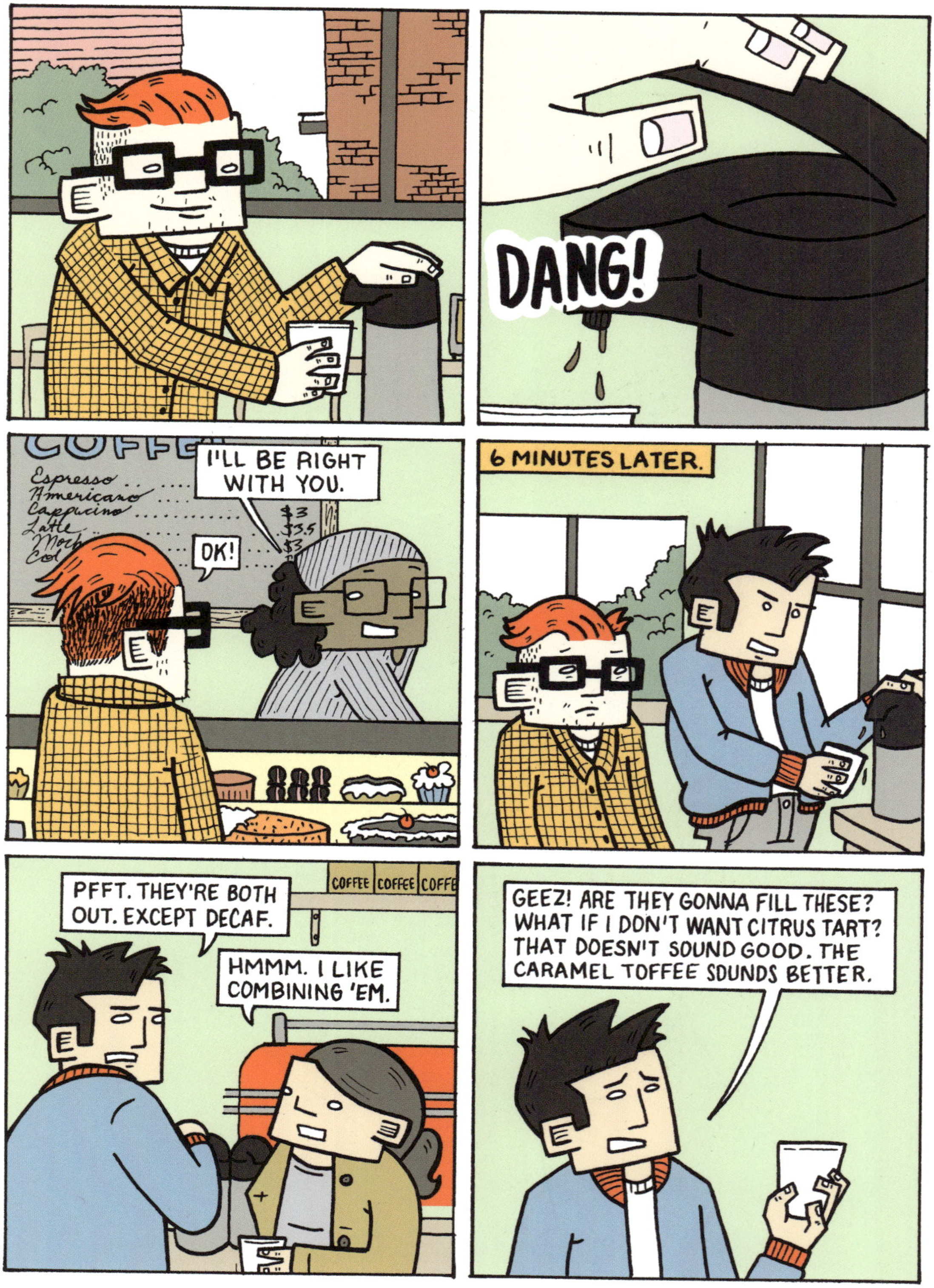
DANG!
Espresso
Americano
Cappucino
Latte
$3
$3.5
$3
I'LL BE RIGHT WITH YOU.
OK!
6 MINUTES LATER.
COFFEE
COFFEE
PFFT. THEY'RE BOTH OUT. EXCEPT DECAF.
HMMM. I LIKE COMBINING 'EM.
GEEZ! ARE THEY GONNA FILL THESE? WHAT IF I DON'T WANT CITRUS TART? THAT DOESN'T SOUND GOOD. THE CARAMEL TOFFEE SOUNDS BETTER.

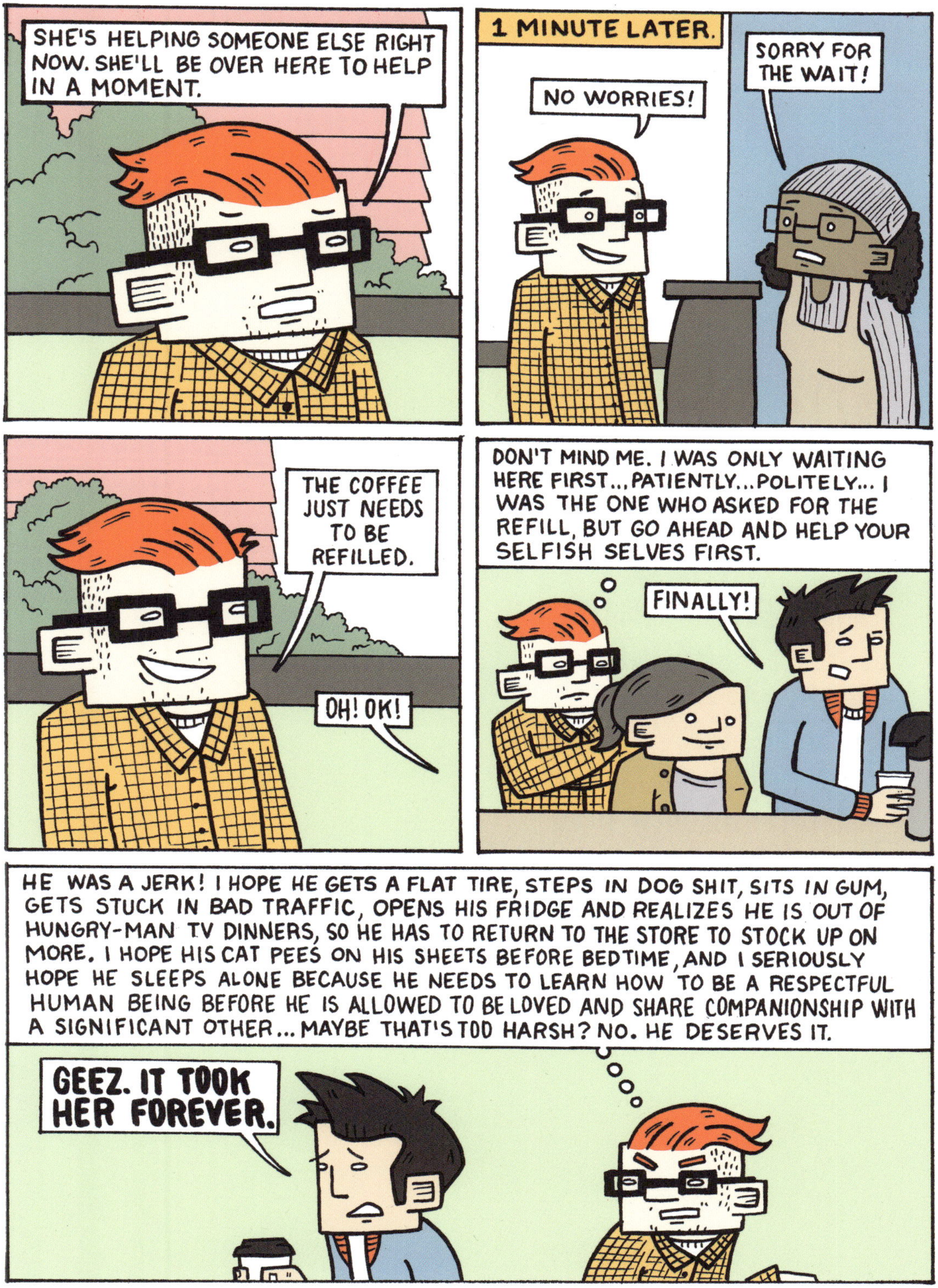
SHE'S HELPING SOMEONE ELSE RIGHT NOW. SHE'LL BE OVER HERE TO HELP IN A MOMENT.
1 MINUTE LATER.
SORRY FOR THE WAIT!
NO WORRIES!
THE COFFEE JUST NEEDS TO BE REFILLED.
OH! OK!
DON'T MIND ME. I WAS ONLY WAITING HERE FIRST... PATIENTLY... POLITELY... I WAS THE ONE WHO ASKED FOR THE REFILL, BUT GO AHEAD AND HELP YOUR SELFISH SELVES FIRST.
FINALLY!
HE WAS A JERK! I HOPE HE GETS A FLAT TIRE, STEPS IN DOG SHIT, SITS IN GUM, GETS STUCK IN BAD TRAFFIC, OPENS HIS FRIDGE AND REALIZES HE IS OUT OF HUNGRY-MAN TV DINNERS, SO HE HAS TO RETURN TO THE STORE TO STOCK UP ON MORE. I HOPE HIS CAT PEES ON HIS SHEETS BEFORE BEDTIME, AND I SERIOUSLY HOPE HE SLEEPS ALONE BECAUSE HE NEEDS TO LEARN HOW TO BE A RESPECTFUL HUMAN BEING BEFORE HE IS ALLOWED TO BE LOVED AND SHARE COMPANIONSHIP WITH A SIGNIFICANT OTHER... MAYBE THAT'S TOO HARSH? NO. HE DESERVES IT.
GEEZ. IT TOOK HER FOREVER.

OBSERVATION
SUNDAY, MAY 24, 2015

I NOTICED A CHILD ON MY STREET TOOK HOPSCOTCH TO A NEW LEVEL. WITH DIFFERENT COLORS OF CHALK, THEY DREW RECTANGLES ON THE SIDEWALK OF AN ENTIRE BLOCK. PERHAPS IT WASN'T HOPSCOTCH, BUT INSTEAD, A GEOMETRIC ABSTRACTION PIECE. EITHER WAY, I COULD TELL THIS KID GREW TIRED OF IT BECAUSE THE RECTANGLES GOT SLOPPIER, SMALLER, AND EVENTUALLY TURNED INTO PILL CAPSULES AND AIRPLANES.

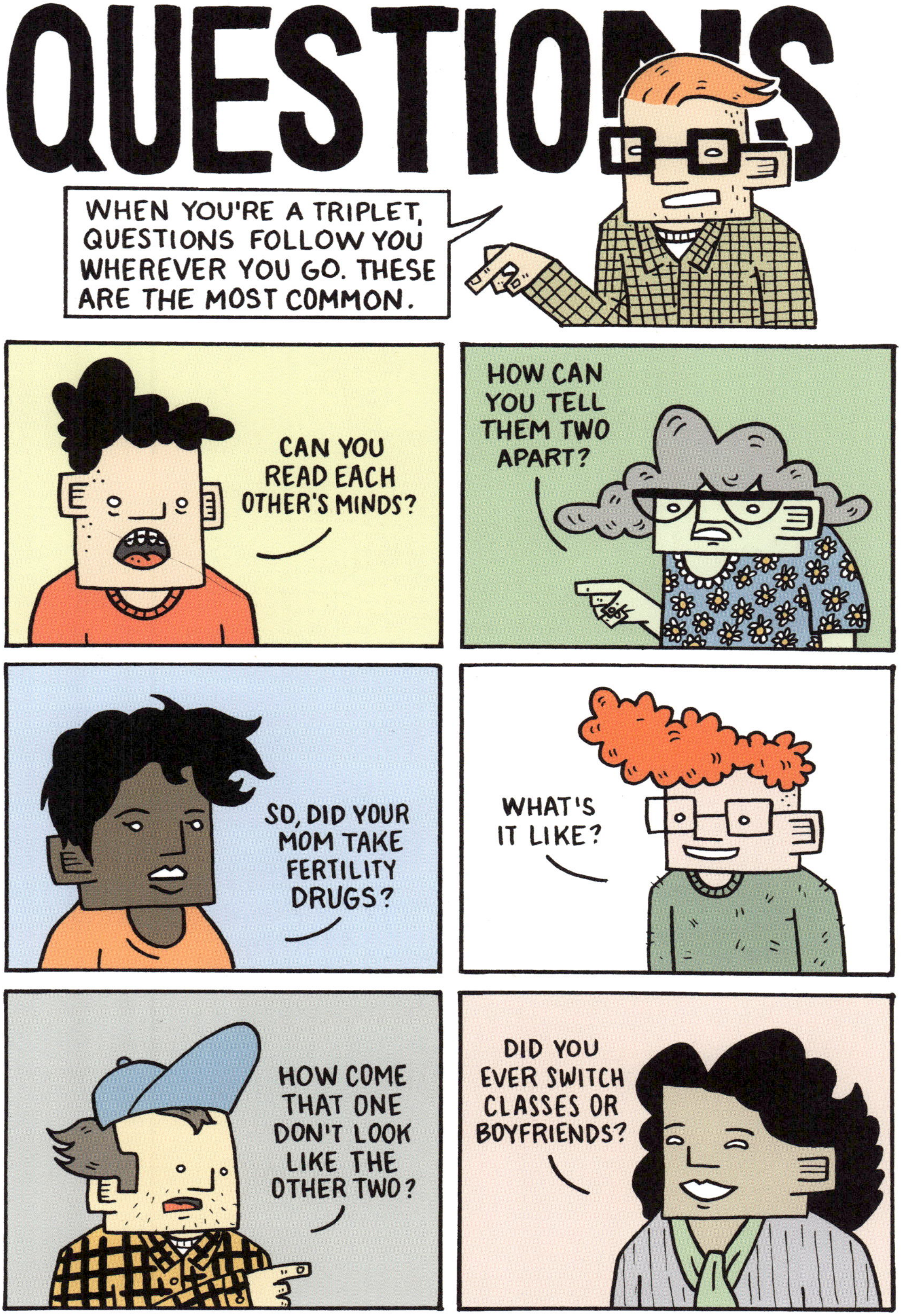
QUESTIONS
WHEN YOU'RE A TRIPLET, QUESTIONS FOLLOW YOU WHEREVER YOU GO. THESE ARE THE MOST COMMON.
CAN YOU READ EACH OTHER'S MINDS?
HOW CAN YOU TELL THEM TWO APART?
SO, DID YOUR MOM TAKE FERTILITY DRUGS?
WHAT'S IT LIKE?
HOW COME THAT ONE DON'T LOOK LIKE THE OTHER TWO?
DID YOU EVER SWITCH CLASSES OR BOYFRIENDS?

VOODOO DOLL ONE

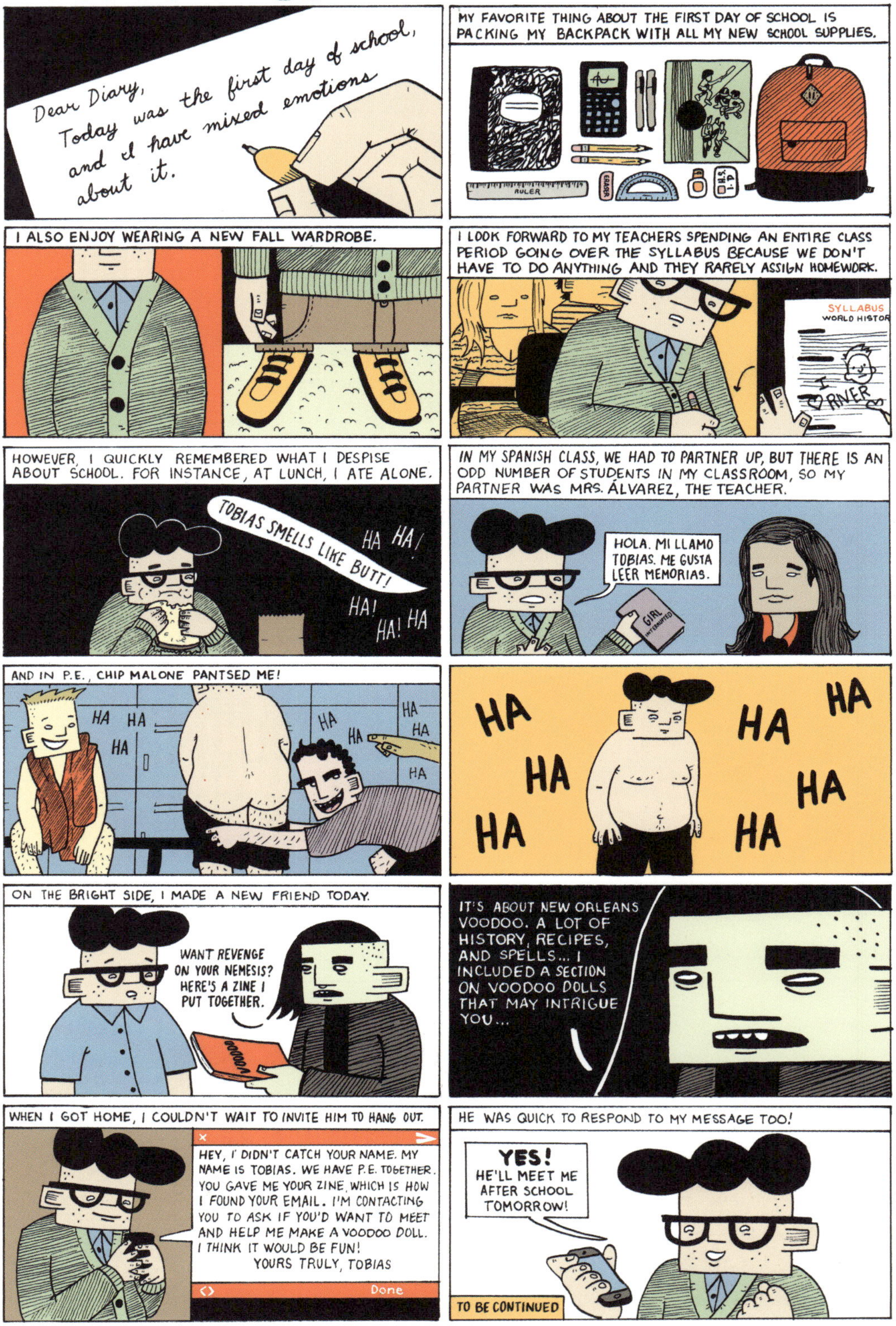

Dear Diary,
Today was the first day of school, and I have mixed emotions about it.
MY FAVORITE THING ABOUT THE FIRST DAY OF SCHOOL IS PACKING MY BACKPACK WITH ALL MY NEW SCHOOL SUPPLIES.
RULER
ERASER
I ALSO ENJOY WEARING A NEW FALL WARDROBE.
I LOOK FORWARD TO MY TEACHERS SPENDING AN ENTIRE CLASS PERIOD GOING OVER THE SYLLABUS BECAUSE WE DON'T HAVE TO DO ANYTHING AND THEY RARELY ASSIGN HOMEWORK.
SYLLABUS
HOWEVER, I QUICKLY REMEMBERED WHAT I DESPISE ABOUT SCHOOL. FOR INSTANCE, AT LUNCH, I ATE ALONE.
TOBIAS SMELLS LIKE BUTT!
HA HA! HA! HA! HA
IN MY SPANISH CLASS, WE HAD TO PARTNER UP, BUT THERE IS AN ODD NUMBER OF STUDENTS IN MY CLASSROOM, SO MY PARTNER WAS MRS. ÁLVAREZ, THE TEACHER.
HOLA. MI LLAMO TOBIAS. ME GUSTA LEER MEMORIAS.
GIRL INTERRUPTED
AND IN P.E., CHIP MALONE PANTSED ME!
HA HA HA HA HA HA HA HA
HA HA HA HA HA HA HA
ON THE BRIGHT SIDE, I MADE A NEW FRIEND TODAY.
WANT REVENGE ON YOUR NEMESIS? HERE'S A ZINE I PUT TOGETHER.
VOODOO
IT'S ABOUT NEW ORLEANS VOODOO. A LOT OF HISTORY, RECIPES, AND SPELLS... I INCLUDED A SECTION ON VOODOO DOLLS THAT MAY INTRIGUE YOU...
WHEN I GOT HOME, I COULDN'T WAIT TO INVITE HIM TO HANG OUT.
HEY, I DIDN'T CATCH YOUR NAME. MY NAME IS TOBIAS. WE HAVE P.E. TOGETHER. YOU GAVE ME YOUR ZINE, WHICH IS HOW I FOUND YOUR EMAIL. I'M CONTACTING YOU TO ASK IF YOU'D WANT TO MEET AND HELP ME MAKE A VOODOO DOLL. I THINK IT WOULD BE FUN!
YOURS TRULY, TOBIAS
Done
HE WAS QUICK TO RESPOND TO MY MESSAGE TOO!
YES! HE'LL MEET ME AFTER SCHOOL TOMORROW!
TO BE CONTINUED

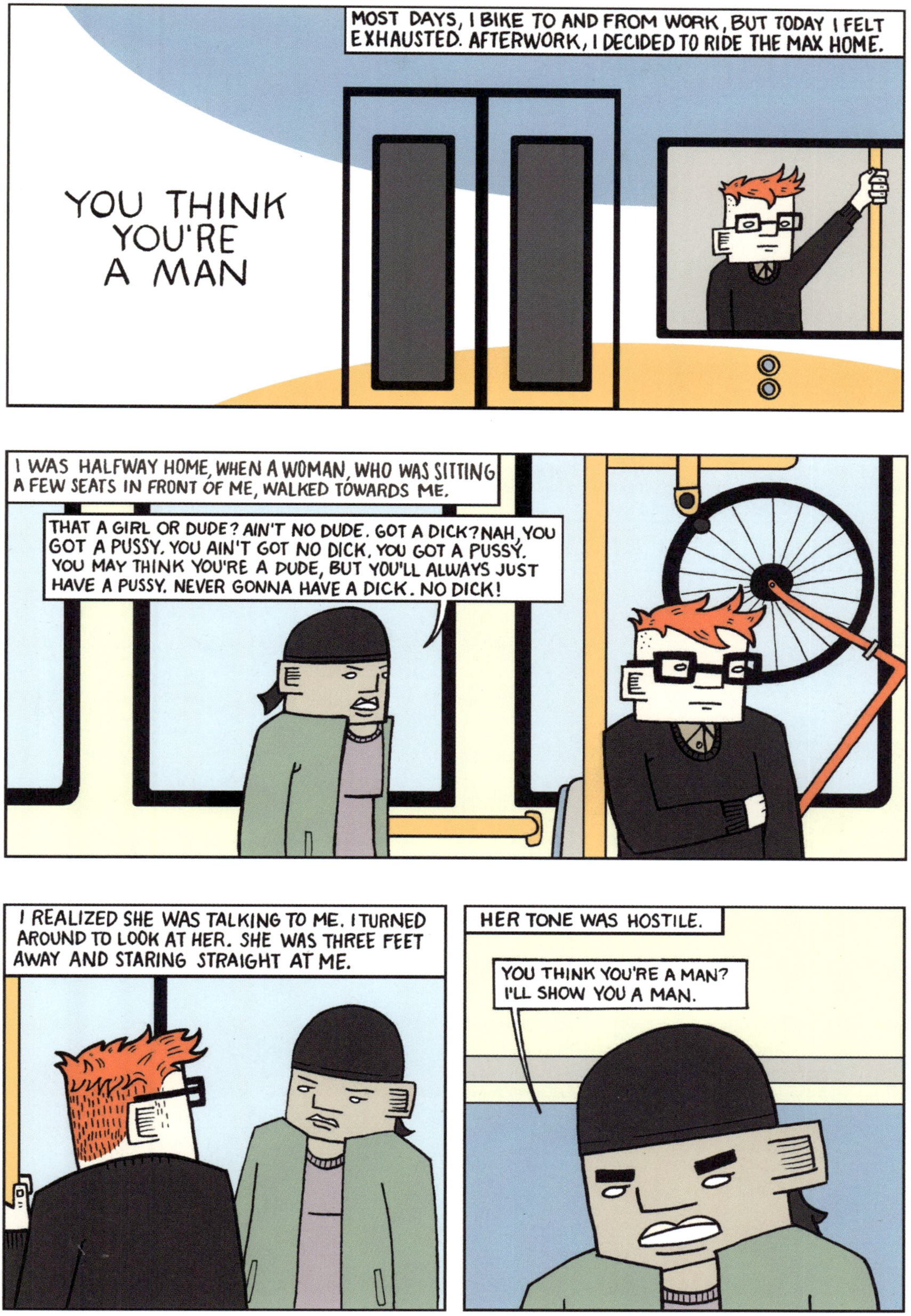
MOST DAYS, I BIKE TO AND FROM WORK, BUT TODAY I FELT EXHAUSTED. AFTERWORK, I DECIDED TO RIDE THE MAX HOME.
YOU THINK YOU'RE A MAN
I WAS HALFWAY HOME, WHEN A WOMAN, WHO WAS SITTING A FEW SEATS IN FRONT OF ME, WALKED TOWARDS ME.
THAT A GIRL OR DUDE? AIN'T NO DUDE. GOT A DICK? NAH, YOU GOT A PUSSY. YOU AIN'T GOT NO DICK. YOU GOT A PUSSY. YOU MAY THINK YOU'RE A DUDE, BUT YOU'LL ALWAYS JUST HAVE A PUSSY. NEVER GONNA HAVE A DICK. NO DICK!
I REALIZED SHE WAS TALKING TO ME. I TURNED AROUND TO LOOK AT HER. SHE WAS THREE FEET AWAY AND STARING STRAIGHT AT ME.
HER TONE WAS HOSTILE.
YOU THINK YOU'RE A MAN? I'LL SHOW YOU A MAN.

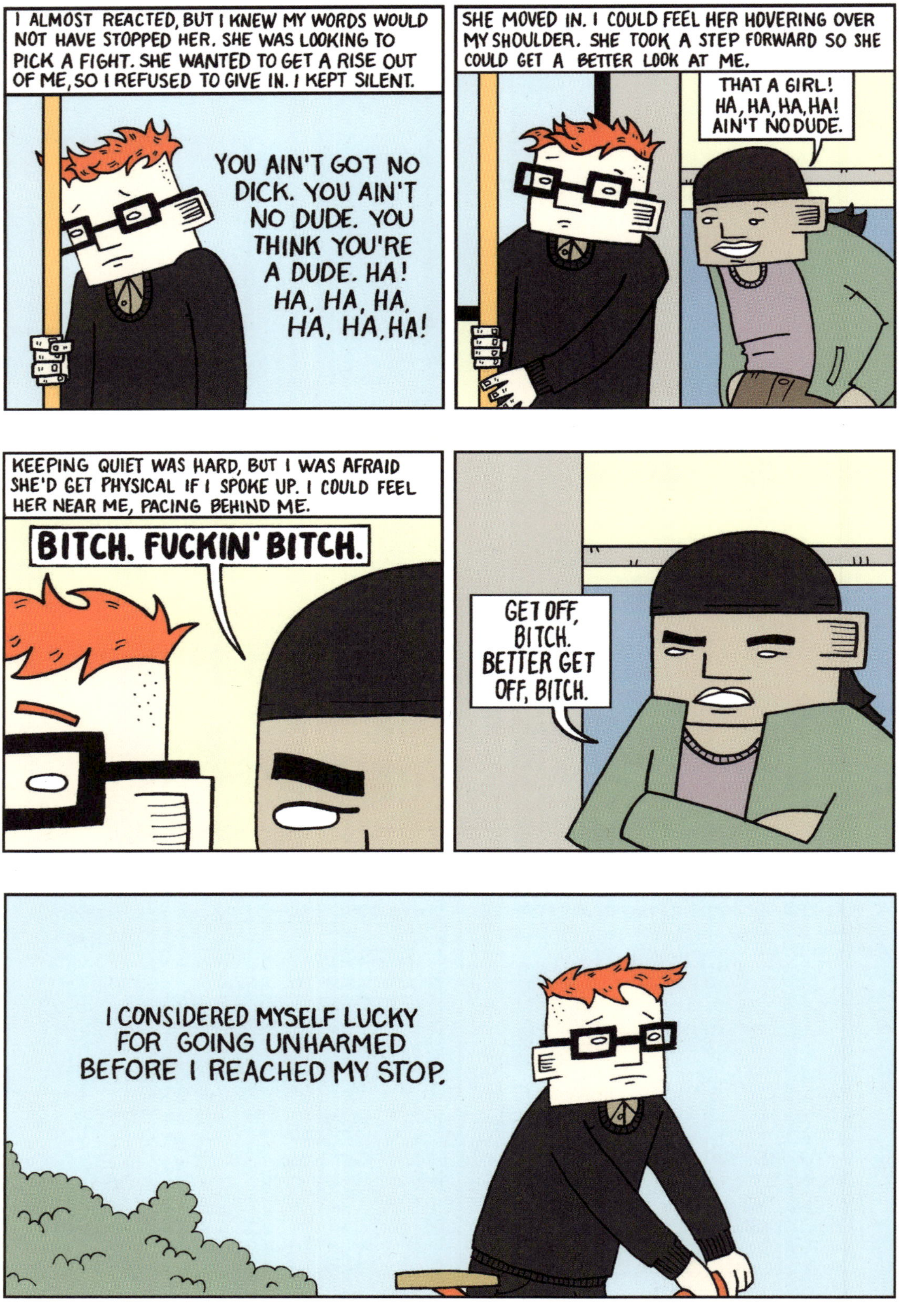
I ALMOST REACTED, BUT I KNEW MY WORDS WOULD NOT HAVE STOPPED HER. SHE WAS LOOKING TO PICK A FIGHT. SHE WANTED TO GET A RISE OUT OF ME, SO I REFUSED TO GIVE IN. I KEPT SILENT.
YOU AIN'T GOT NO DICK. YOU AIN'T NO DUDE. YOU THINK YOU'RE A DUDE. HA! HA, HA, HA, HA, HA, HA!
SHE MOVED IN. I COULD FEEL HER HOVERING OVER MY SHOULDER. SHE TOOK A STEP FORWARD SO SHE COULD GET A BETTER LOOK AT ME.
THAT A GIRL! HA, HA, HA, HA! AIN'T NO DUDE.
KEEPING QUIET WAS HARD, BUT I WAS AFRAID SHE'D GET PHYSICAL IF I SPOKE UP. I COULD FEEL HER NEAR ME, PACING BEHIND ME.
BITCH. FUCKIN' BITCH.
GET OFF, BITCH. BETTER GET OFF, BITCH.
I CONSIDERED MYSELF LUCKY FOR GOING UNHARMED BEFORE I REACHED MY STOP.

DALE

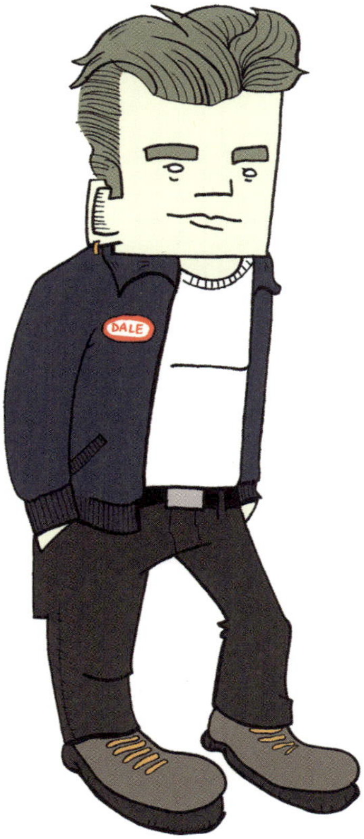
DALE

SOMETIMES, THE PEOPLE READIN' THESE THINGS DON'T CARE ABOUT THE PERSON'S INSIDES. THEY JUDGE A BOOK BY ITS COVER. I KNOW I'M KINDA SMALL, AND MY VOICE ISN'T AS DEEP AS THE GUYS IN THE SHOP, BUT I'M A GOOD PERSON. I'M KIND AND CARING. I TREAT WOMEN WITH RESPECT. I'M A GOOD LISTENER. I'M LOYAL... I'VE BEEN TOLD I'M NOT ALLOWED TO FIGHT IN A WAR BECAUSE THEY TELL ME I SHOULD WEAR A DRESS AND RAISE YOUNG ONES INSTEAD. I KNOW MY FACE IS NOT ROUGH, BUT THAT DOESN'T MEAN I'M NOT TOUGH. I KEEP A 'BLADE IN MY BACK POCKET, BUT I DON'T USE IT TO START ANY TROUBLE... I ENJOY READING, MOSTLY STEINBECK. AFTER THE SUN SETS, I LIKE TO SIT IN MY ARMCHAIR AND WATCH TV, OR I SIP OLD CROW WHILE I LISTEN TO RECORDS. I'M A PRETTY GOOD COOK. I LIKE DRIVIN' MY BIKE ON BACK ROADS. I LONG FOR A PRETTY GIRL, IN A PRETTY DRESS, TO SIT BEHIND ME AND WRAP HER ARMS, TIGHTLY, AROUND MY WAIST. I'M JUST LOOKING FOR A WOMAN WHO WILL LOVE ME FOR WHO I AM. IN RETURN, I WILL DO THE SAME. IMAGINE, ME AND YOU ON MY BIKE, GLIDING FOREVER, WITH THE WIND RACIN' THROUGH OUR HAIR. WE'LL STOP AT EVERY DIVE BAR ALONG THE WAY. WE'LL PLAY POOL AND YOU'LL BEAT ME. ON THE JUKEBOX, YOU'LL PICK THAT SONG BY JIMMY REED, "HONEST I DO," AND WE'LL BE THE ONLY TWO ON THE DANCE FLOOR. WE'LL FEEL SAFE IN EACH OTHER'S ARMS. SOME OF THE GUYS WILL FEEL INSECURE WHEN THEY SEE US DANCIN' THAT CLOSE TOGETHER. WHEN THEY SEE YOUR CHERRY RED LIPSTICK STAINED ON MY CHEEK, THEY'LL SAY "OUR KIND" AIN'T WELCOME THERE. WE'LL LAUGH AT THEIR FOOLISHNESS AND RUN AWAY. WE'LL START A LIFE SOMEWHERE FAR AWAY...

SHOWING OUT

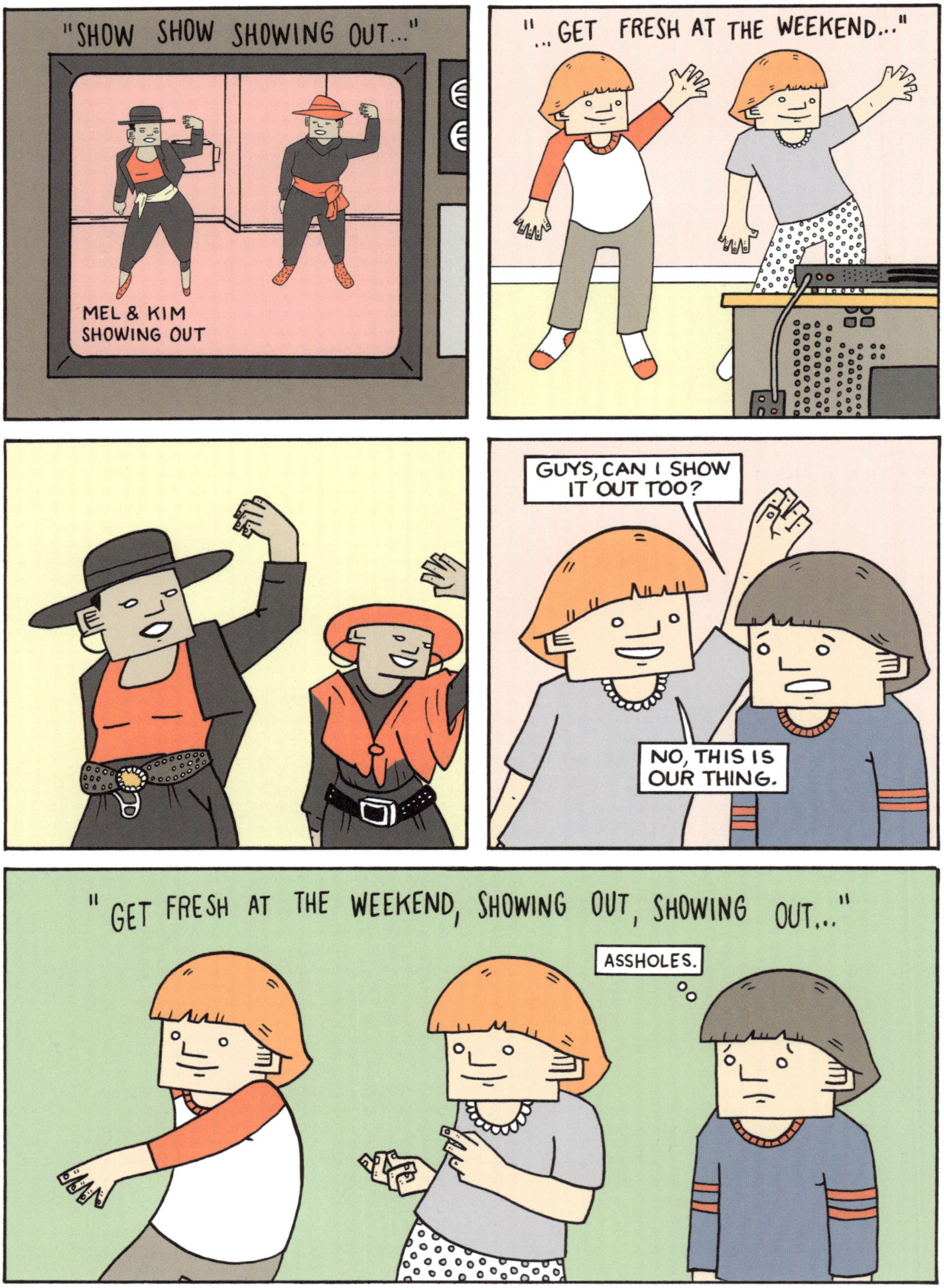
"SHOW SHOW SHOWING OUT..."
MEL & KIM
SHOWING OUT
"... GET FRESH AT THE WEEKEND..."
GUYS, CAN I SHOW IT OUT TOO?
NO, THIS IS OUR THING.
"GET FRESH AT THE WEEKEND, SHOWING OUT, SHOWING OUT..."
ASSHOLES.

I'LL SUE YOU

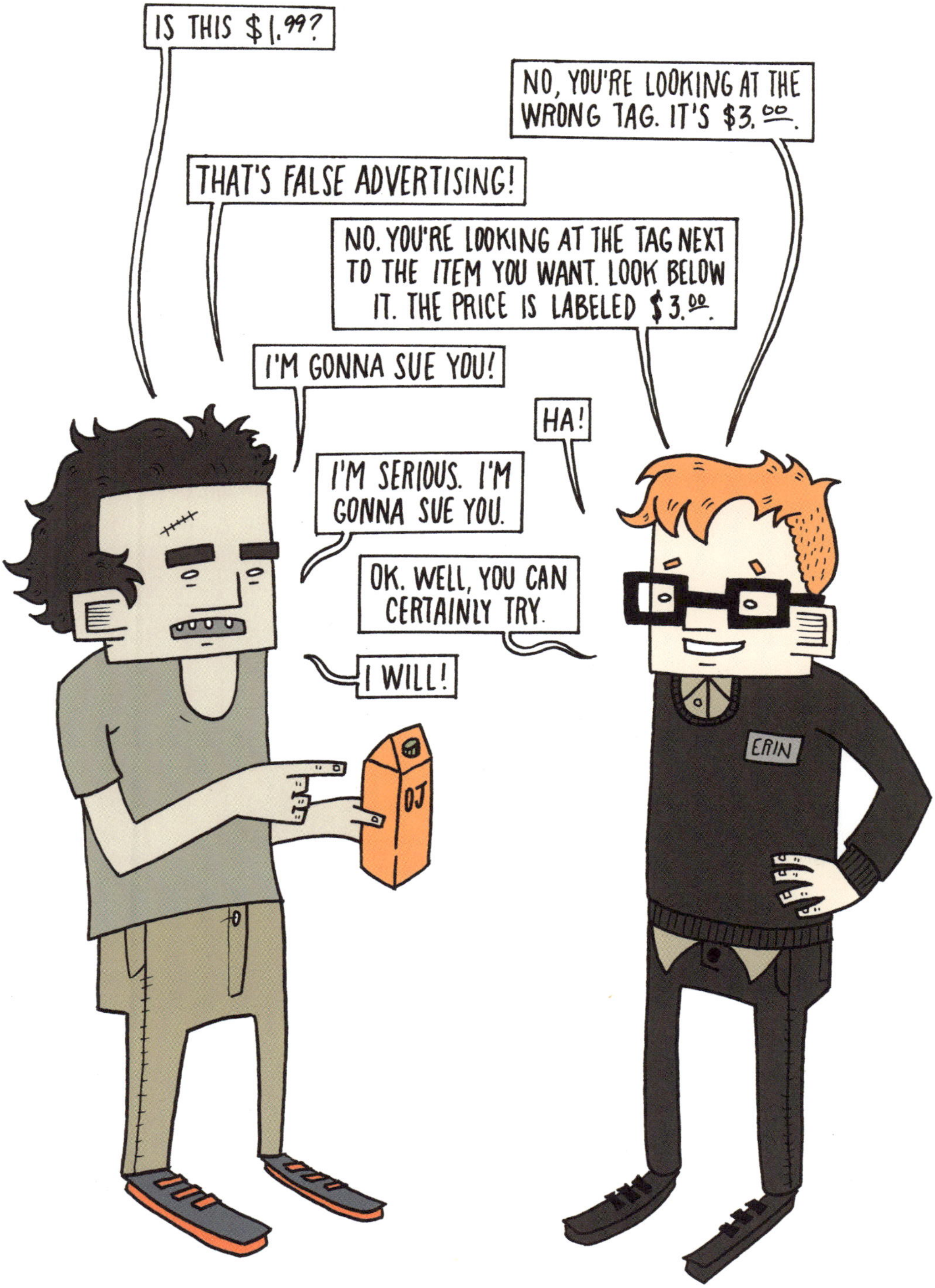
IS THIS $1.99?
NO, YOU'RE LOOKING AT THE WRONG TAG. IT'S $3.00.
THAT'S FALSE ADVERTISING!
NO. YOU'RE LOOKING AT THE TAG NEXT TO THE ITEM YOU WANT. LOOK BELOW IT. THE PRICE IS LABELED $3.00.
I'M GONNA SUE YOU!
HA!
I'M SERIOUS. I'M GONNA SUE YOU.
OK. WELL, YOU CAN CERTAINLY TRY.
I WILL!
OJ
ERIN

7 MONTHS ON TESTOSTERONE

IN ISSUE 2, I MADE A COMIC ILLUSTRATING THE EFFECTS TESTOSTERONE HAD ON MY BODY AT SEVEN WEEKS. THESE ARE THE EFFECTS TESTOSTERONE HAD ON MY BODY AT SEVEN MONTHS. AFTER TWO MONTHS, MY DOSE WAS INCREASED FROM .3 TO .5ML. THE CHANGES CONTINUED, AND THEY BECAME MORE NOTICEABLE.

CHECK OUT THE LIST OF CHANGES BELOW.

Ⓐ 7 WEEKS VS Ⓑ 7 MONTHS ON T

①. VOICE CONTINUES TO CHANGE

THE BIGGEST CHANGE HAS BEEN MY VOICE. AT 2.5 MONTHS IT BEGAN TO CRACK, BUT NO ONE NOTICED ANY CHANGES UNTIL AFTER 3 MONTHS.

YOU SOUND DIFFERENT.

IS MY VOICE DEEPER?

PERHAPS.

②. LOST MY ABILITY TO SING

I WAS NEVER MARIAH CAREY. I WAS JUST AVERAGE, BUT NOW I CAN'T SING A SINGLE SONG WITHOUT BUTCHERING IT BECAUSE I SQUEAK AND CRACK.

YOU GOT ME FEELING EMOTIONS.

DUDE, SING SOME BARRY WHITE OR STEPHIN MERRITT. YOUR HIGH NOTES SOUND SHITTY.

③. SORE THROAT/CLEARING THROAT

SINCE MY FIRST INJECTION, I ALWAYS FEEL LIKE I HAVE TO CLEAR MY THROAT. SOMETIMES, MY THROAT FEELS SORE, AND I'VE NOTICED IT PRECEDES ANY VOCAL CHANGES.

AHEM

I NEED A COUGH DROP OR A THROAT LOZENGE.

AHEM

④. BODY HAIR

I'VE NEVER BEEN VERY HAIRY EXCEPT FOR MY ARMS AND LEGS. HOWEVER, THAT HAIR IS NOW THICKER AND FULLER. I'VE ALSO SPROUTED NEW HAIRS.

'CAUSE I'M A GINGER, IT'S HARD TO SEE MY FACIAL HAIR, BUT IT DOES EXIST.

FURRY LEGS

NEW HAIR UNDER ARM

HAPPY TRAIL

5. WEIGHT GAIN

PRE-T, I WAS 109 lbs. IN 4 MONTHS, I GAINED 17 lbs. AFTER CHANGING MY DIET AND BIKING MORE, I LOST 6 lbs.

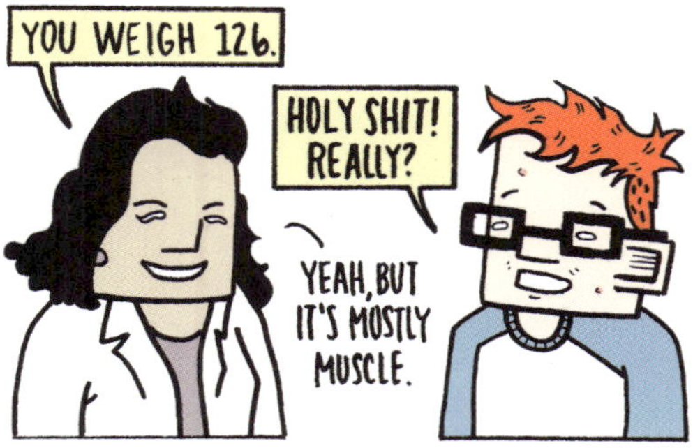
YOU WEIGH 126.
HOLY SHIT! REALLY?
YEAH, BUT IT'S MOSTLY MUSCLE.

6. OUTGROWING MY CLOTHES

BECAUSE I'M GAINING WEIGHT AND MUSCLE, I'VE HAD TO GET RID OF ALL MY JEANS AND A FEW SHIRTS. EVEN THE SPORTS BRAS AND BINDERS I USE TO COMPRESS MY CHEST FEEL TOO TIGHT AND PRESS INTO MY SKIN.

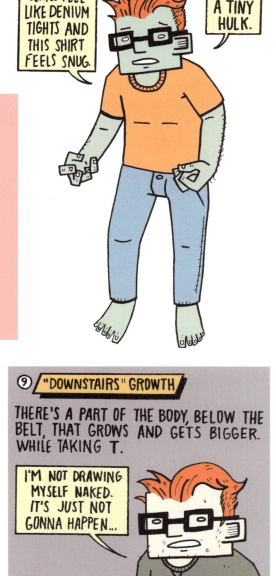

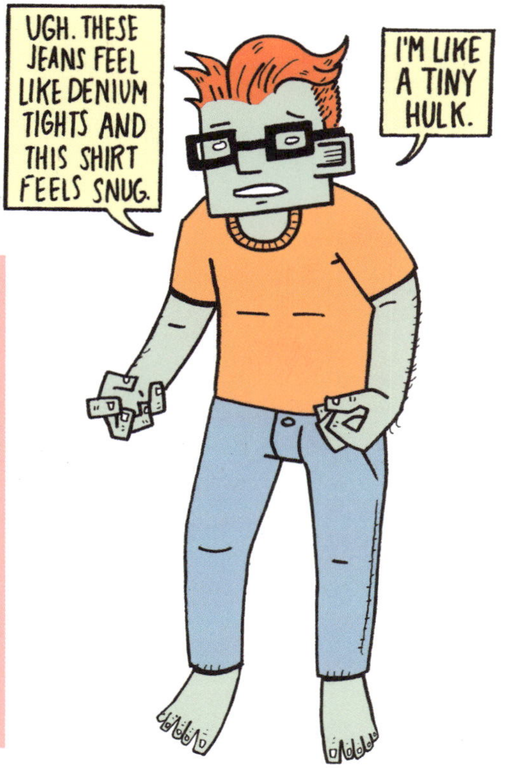
UGH. THESE JEANS FEEL LIKE DENIUM TIGHTS AND THIS SHIRT FEELS SNUG.
I'M LIKE A TINY HULK.

7. MUSCLE GAIN

TESTOSTERONE INCREASES MUSCLE MASS. FIRST, I NOTICED MY OBLIQUES GOT BIGGER, THEN MY SHOULDERS GOT BROADER, AND MY LEGS BLEW UP!

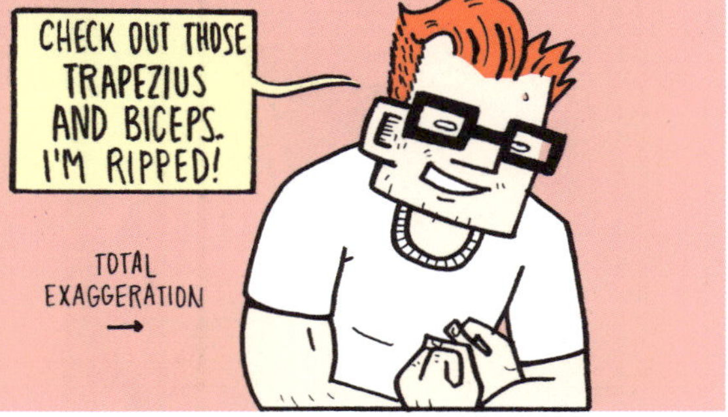
CHECK OUT THOSE TRAPEZIUS AND BICEPS. I'M RIPPED!
TOTAL EXAGGERATION →

8. INCREASE IN APPETITE

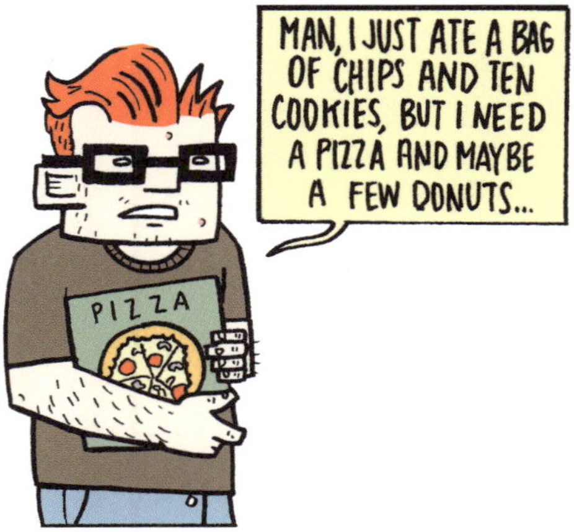
MAN, I JUST ATE A BAG OF CHIPS AND TEN COOKIES, BUT I NEED A PIZZA AND MAYBE A FEW DONUTS...
PIZZA

9. "DOWNSTAIRS" GROWTH

THERE'S A PART OF THE BODY, BELOW THE BELT, THAT GROWS AND GETS BIGGER WHILE TAKING T.

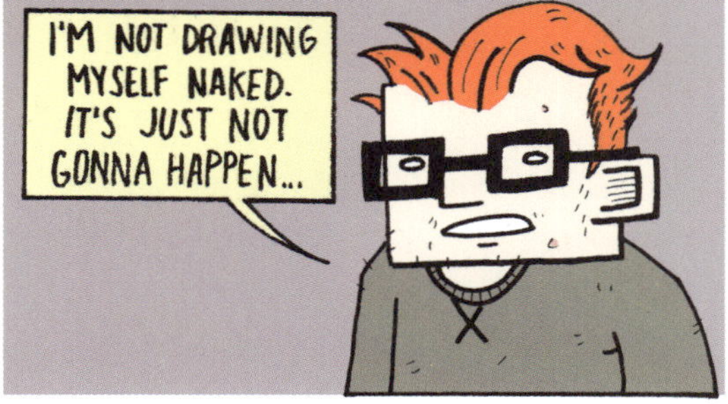
I'M NOT DRAWING MYSELF NAKED. IT'S JUST NOT GONNA HAPPEN...

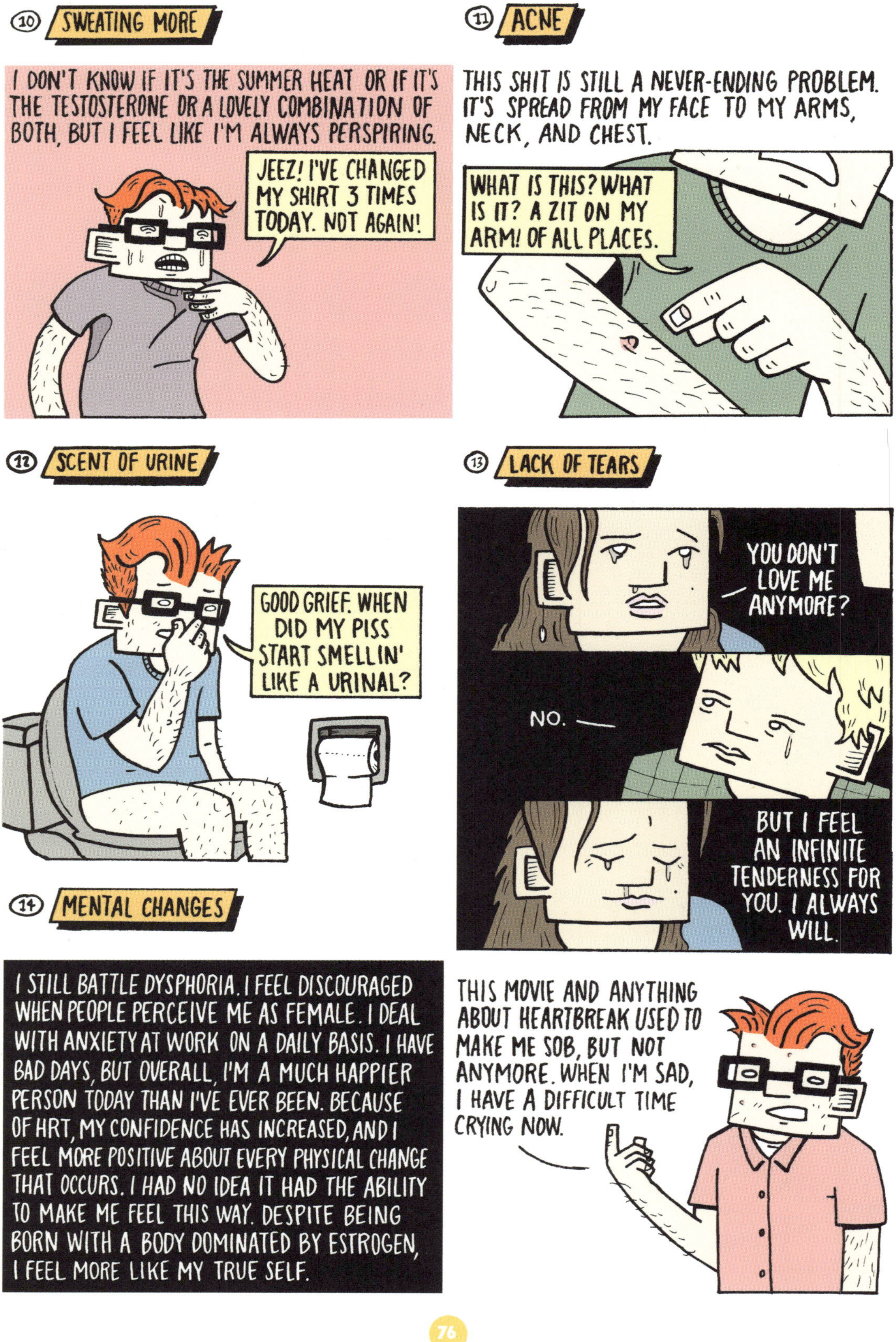

10 SWEATING MORE
I DON'T KNOW IF IT'S THE SUMMER HEAT OR IF IT'S THE TESTOSTERONE OR A LOVELY COMBINATION OF BOTH, BUT I FEEL LIKE I'M ALWAYS PERSPIRING.
JEEZ! I'VE CHANGED MY SHIRT 3 TIMES TODAY. NOT AGAIN!
11 ACNE
THIS SHIT IS STILL A NEVER-ENDING PROBLEM. IT'S SPREAD FROM MY FACE TO MY ARMS, NECK, AND CHEST.
WHAT IS THIS? WHAT IS IT? A ZIT ON MY ARM! OF ALL PLACES.
12 SCENT OF URINE
GOOD GRIEF. WHEN DID MY PISS START SMELLIN' LIKE A URINAL?
13 LACK OF TEARS
YOU DON'T LOVE ME ANYMORE?
NO.
BUT I FEEL AN INFINITE TENDERNESS FOR YOU. I ALWAYS WILL.
THIS MOVIE AND ANYTHING ABOUT HEARTBREAK USED TO MAKE ME SOB, BUT NOT ANYMORE. WHEN I'M SAD, I HAVE A DIFFICULT TIME CRYING NOW.
14 MENTAL CHANGES
I STILL BATTLE DYSPHORIA. I FEEL DISCOURAGED WHEN PEOPLE PERCEIVE ME AS FEMALE. I DEAL WITH ANXIETY AT WORK ON A DAILY BASIS. I HAVE BAD DAYS, BUT OVERALL, I'M A MUCH HAPPIER PERSON TODAY THAN I'VE EVER BEEN. BECAUSE OF HRT, MY CONFIDENCE HAS INCREASED, AND I FEEL MORE POSITIVE ABOUT EVERY PHYSICAL CHANGE THAT OCCURS. I HAD NO IDEA IT HAD THE ABILITY TO MAKE ME FEEL THIS WAY. DESPITE BEING BORN WITH A BODY DOMINATED BY ESTROGEN, I FEEL MORE LIKE MY TRUE SELF.

SAUVIE ISLAND

IN THE MORNING, I LEFT MY HOUSE IN ARBOR LODGE AND BIKED TO ST. JOHNS. WHILE RIDING OVER THE ST. JOHNS BRIDGE, I STOPPED TO LOOK AT SOME GRAFFITI AND SCRIBBLE ON THE BRIDGE.

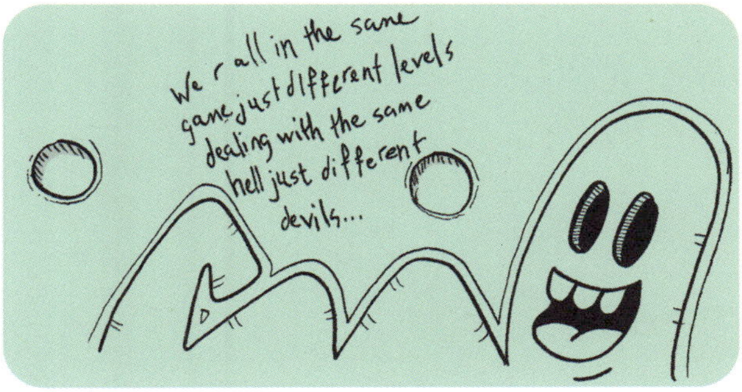
We r all in the same game just different levels dealing with the same hell just different devils...

I CONTINUED TO HEAD NORTH ON HWY 30, THROUGH LINNTON. EVENTUALLY, I MADE MY WAY TO SAUVIE ISLAND.

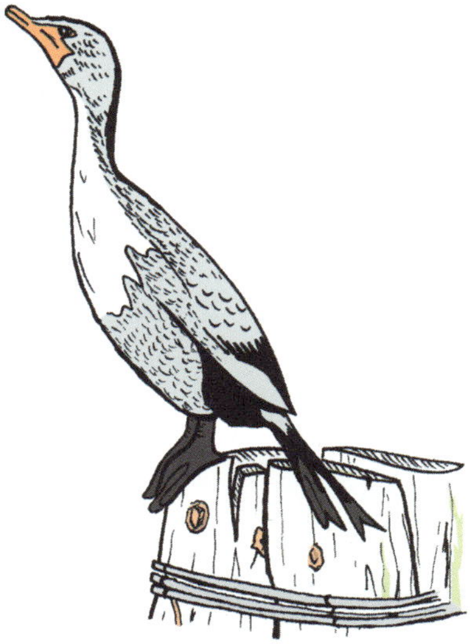

I PASSED MANY FARMS AND HEARD A VARIETY OF BIRDS CHIRPING.

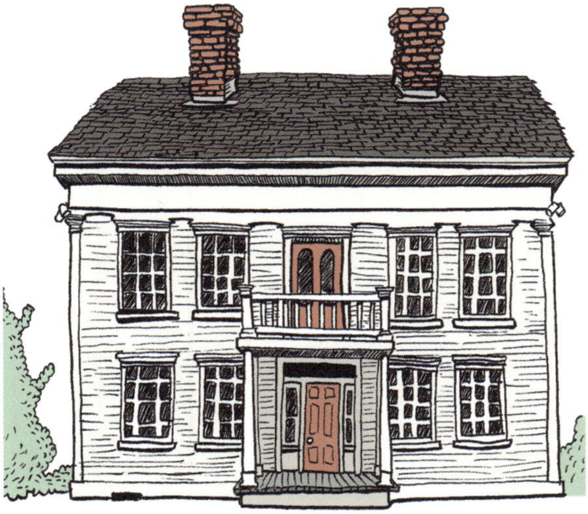

I STOPPED AT HOWELL TERRITORIAL PARK TO LOOK AT THE BYBEE-HOWELL HOUSE. I WANTED TO GO INSIDE, BUT IT WAS LOCKED. I PEEKED INSIDE THE WINDOW, HOPING AND FEARING TO SEE A GHOST, BUT I SAW NOTHING.

BEHIND THE HOUSE, THIRD GRADERS, ON A FIELD TRIP, PLAYED HIDE AND SEEK IN THE TREES.

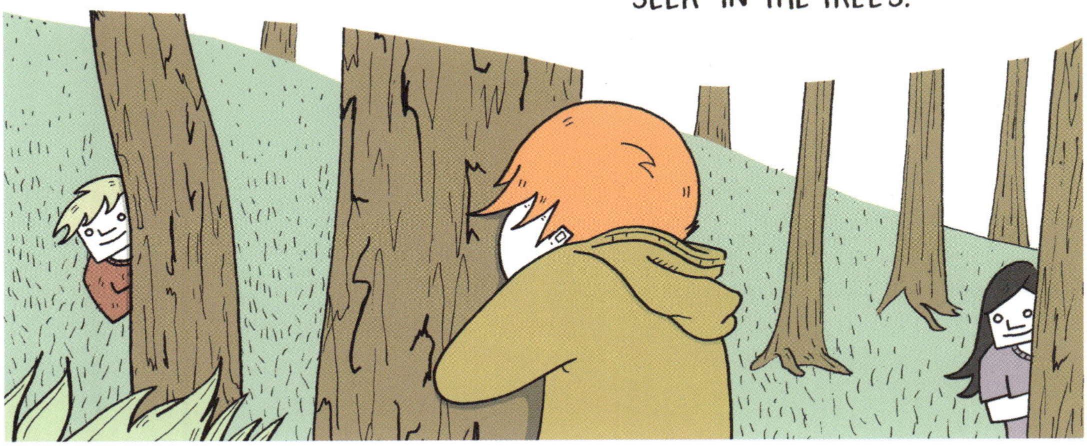

I LEFT THE PARK AND HEADED TO KRUGER'S MARKET WHERE I BOUGHT CHEAP VEGETABLES.

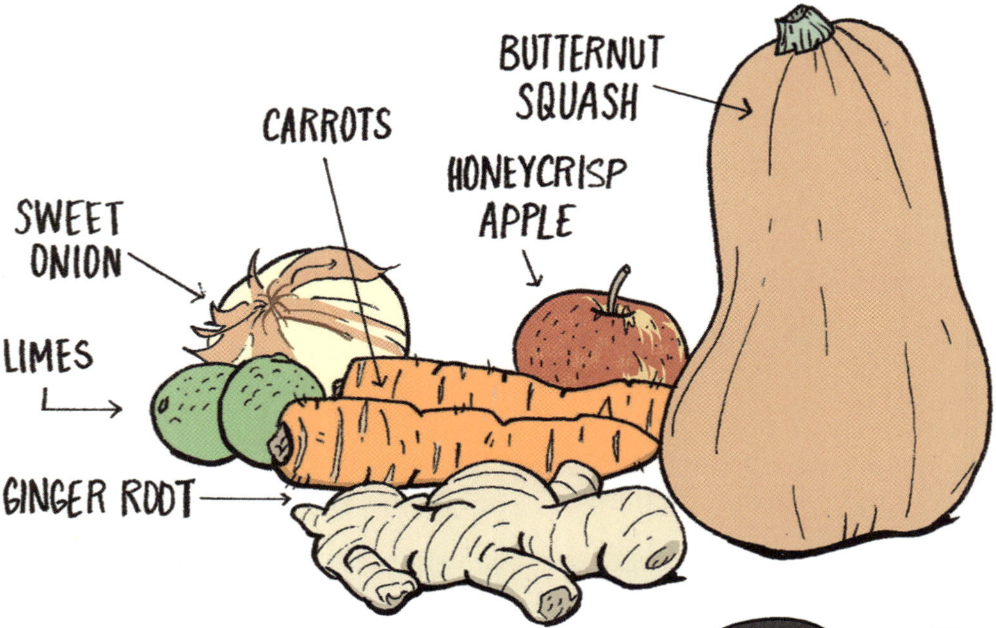
BUTTERNUT SQUASH
CARROTS
HONEYCRISP APPLE
SWEET ONION
LIMES
GINGER ROOT

WHILE STANDING IN THE PUMPKIN PATCH ALONE, I HEARD RUSTLING IN THE CORN FIELD. IF IT WERE DARK, I WOULD HAVE BEEN TERRIFIED, THINKING THE SOUND WAS FROM A CULT OF DEMONIC CHILDREN, WITH RUSTY SLING BLADES, OUT FOR BLOOD.

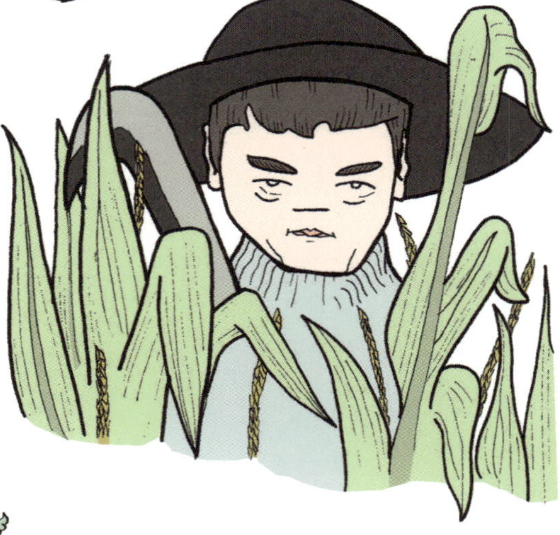

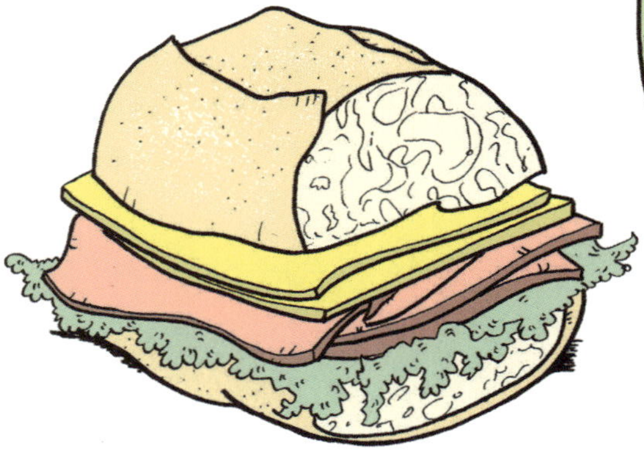

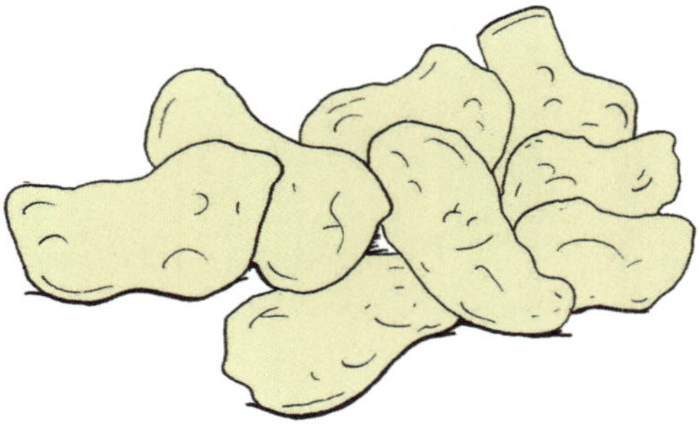

I BIKED AROUND THE ISLAND SOME MORE, BUT DECIDED TO HEAD BACK TO PORTLAND. I STOPPED IN ST. JOHNS AND SPENT $9.00 ON SOME BREAD, MEAT, AND CHEESE, AND EIGHT CHIPS.

AFTER LUNCH, I BIKED TO CATHEDRAL PARK. I READ A BOOK AND PASSED OUT UNDER THE BRIDGE.

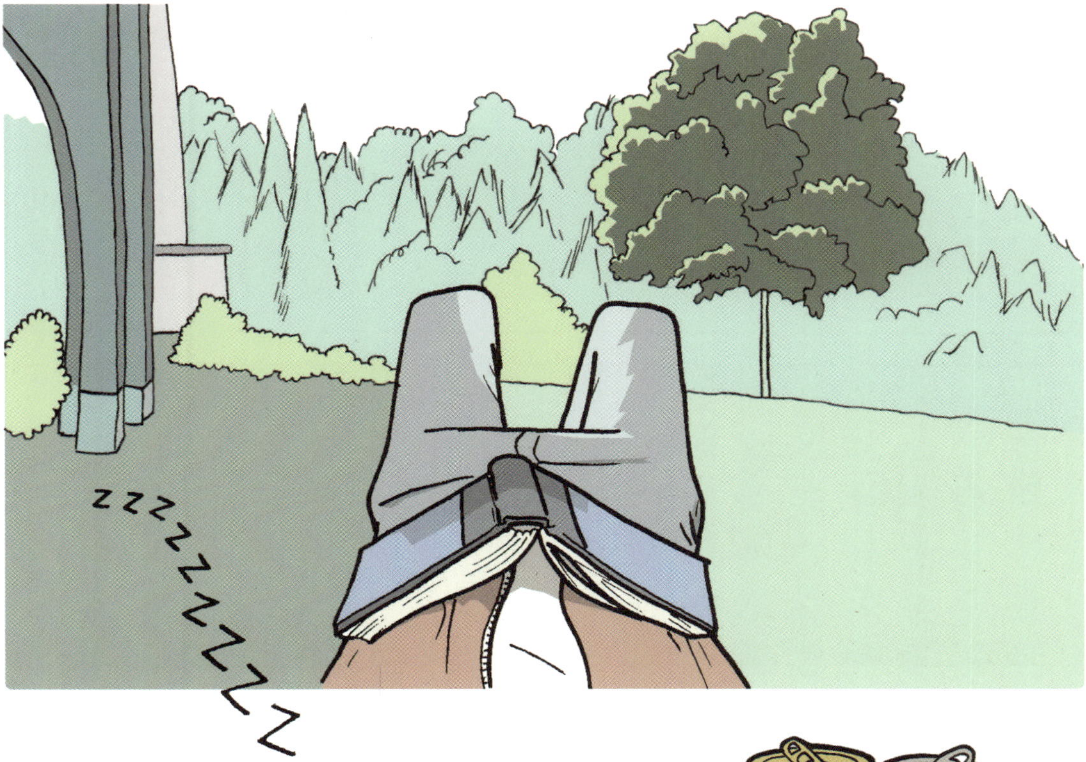
ZZZZZZZZZZZ

LATER IN THE EVENING, A FRIEND MET ME IN THE PARK. WE DECIDED TO WALK TO A BAR AND HAVE SOME ADULT BEVERAGES. AFTER THREE CHEAP BEERS AND GOOD CONVERSATION, I HEADED HOME IN THE DARK.

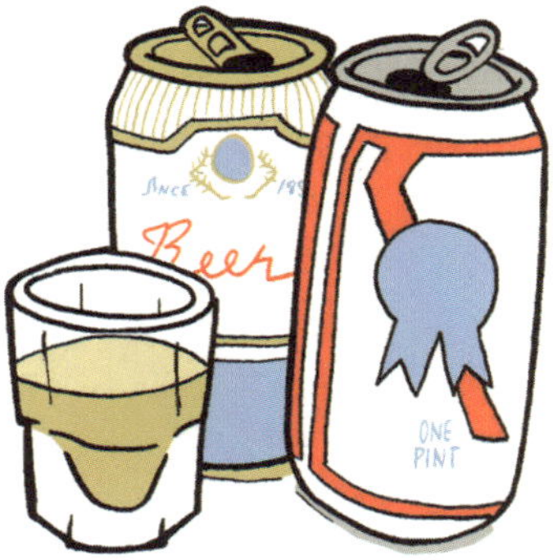
Beer
ONE PINT

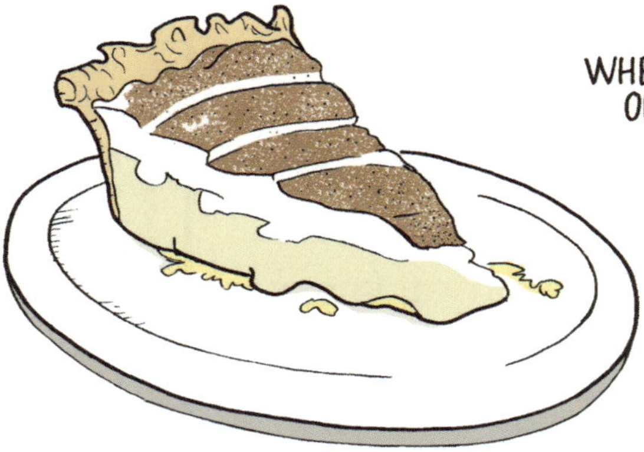

WHEN I ARRIVED HOME, MY ROOMATES WERE ON THEIR WAY TO RANDOM ORDER. THEY INVITED ME TO JOIN THEM. MY NIGHT ENDED WITH SITTING OUTSIDE THE COFFEE HOUSE AND EATING A SLICE OF BANANA CREAM PIE.

HASHTAG FOOD PICS

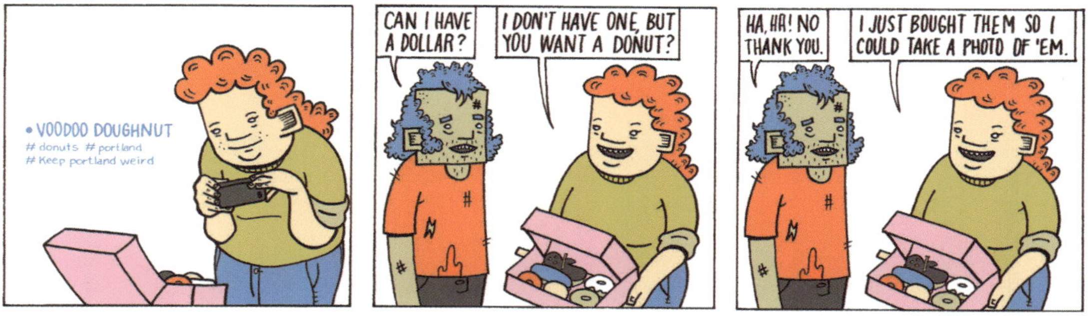
• VOODOO DOUGHNUT
donuts # portland
Keep portland weird
CAN I HAVE A DOLLAR?
I DON'T HAVE ONE, BUT YOU WANT A DONUT?
HA, HA! NO THANK YOU.
I JUST BOUGHT THEM SO I COULD TAKE A PHOTO OF 'EM.

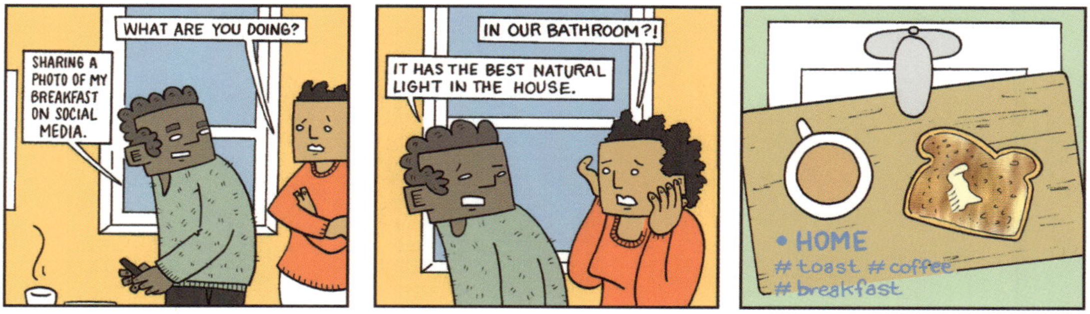
WHAT ARE YOU DOING?
SHARING A PHOTO OF MY BREAKFAST ON SOCIAL MEDIA.
IN OUR BATHROOM?!
IT HAS THE BEST NATURAL LIGHT IN THE HOUSE.
• HOME
toast # coffee
breakfast

I GOTTA SHARE THIS ON ALL OF MY SOCIAL MEDIA ACCOUNTS BECAUSE WHEN PEOPLE SEE THIS PAIN AU CHOCOLAT PHOTO I EDITED WITH SEVERAL FILTERS THEY'LL ENVY MY LIFESTYLE.

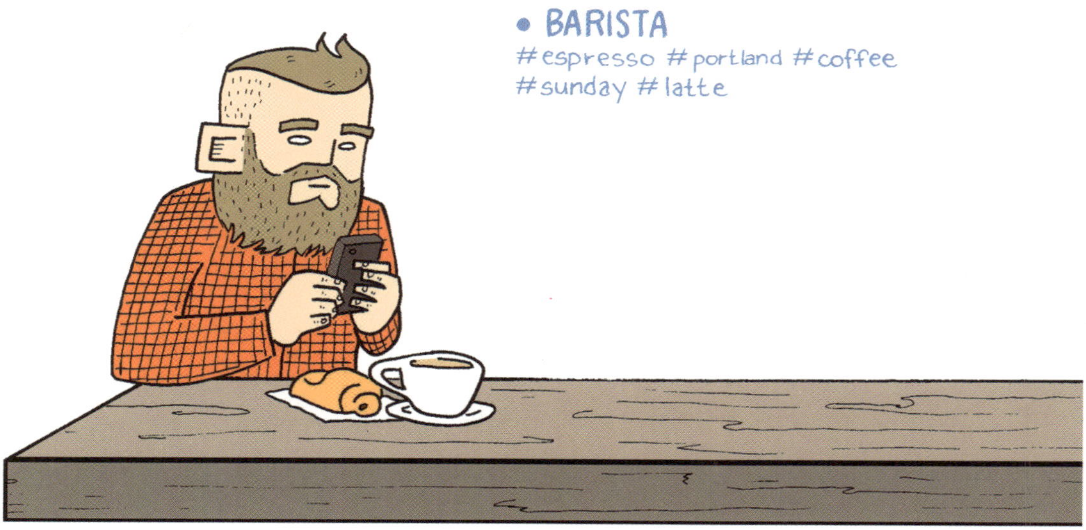
• BARISTA
#espresso #portland #coffee
#sunday #latte

SIBLING FIGHTING TECHNIQUES

A VISUAL GUIDE TO METHODS USED IN A SIBLING BRAWL, DEMONSTRATED BY TRIPLETS

HAIR PULLING

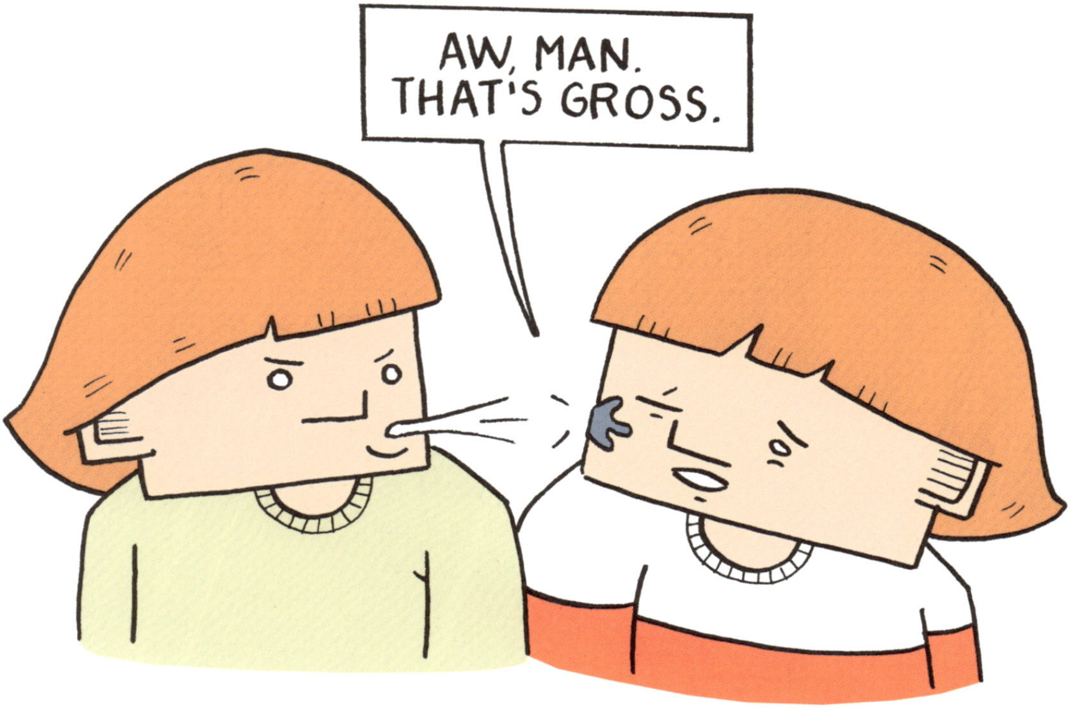
AW, MAN. THAT'S GROSS.

SPITTING

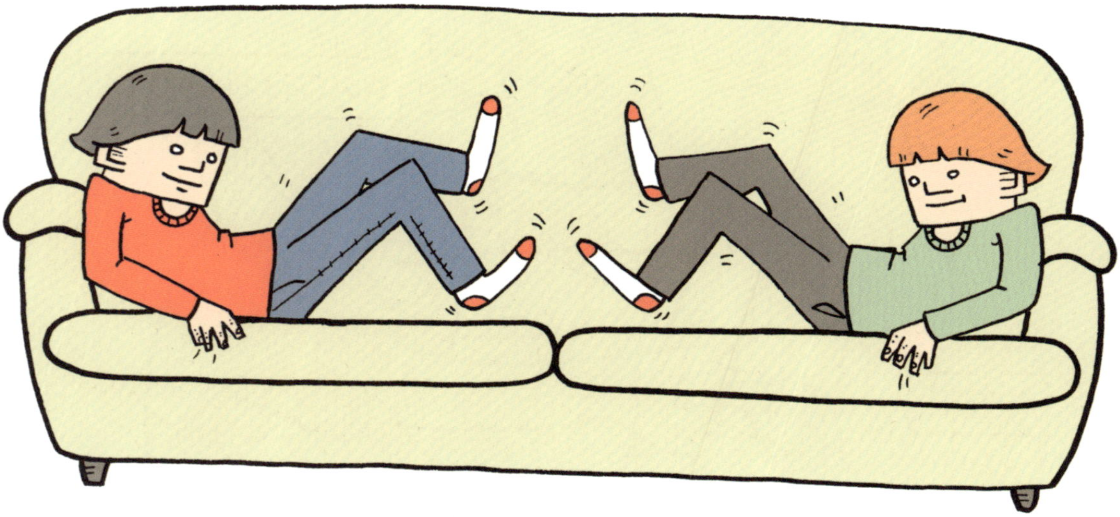

THE SHREDDER

TWO SIBLINGS WHO HAVE FORMED AN ALLIANCE SIT OPPOSITE OF EACH OTHER ON A COUCH WITH THEIR LEGS BENT, KICKING UP AND DOWN. WITH THE HEELS OF THEIR FEET, THEY PIERCE THE SOFA CUSHIONS BELOW THEM. WHEN THE THIRD SIBLING (THE OPPONENT) TRIES TO SIT ON THE COUCH, THE OTHER TWO SIBLINGS PERFORM THIS TECHNIQUE. THE ALLIES WIN EVERY TIME BECAUSE THE PAIN OF BEING PUNCHED BY FOUR HEELS IS UNBEARABLE FOR THE OUTNUMBERED SIBLING.

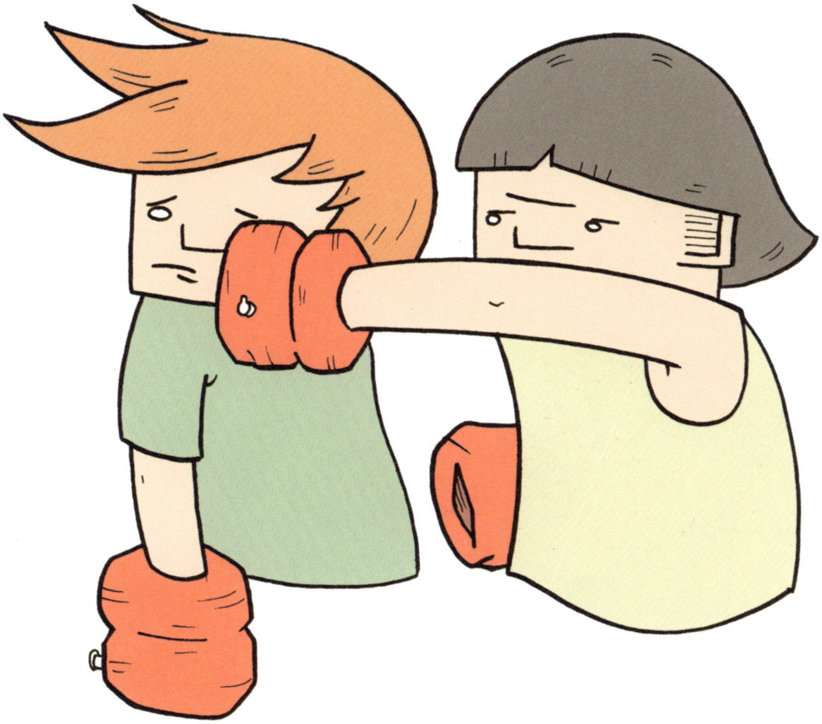

ARM-FLOATIE BOXING

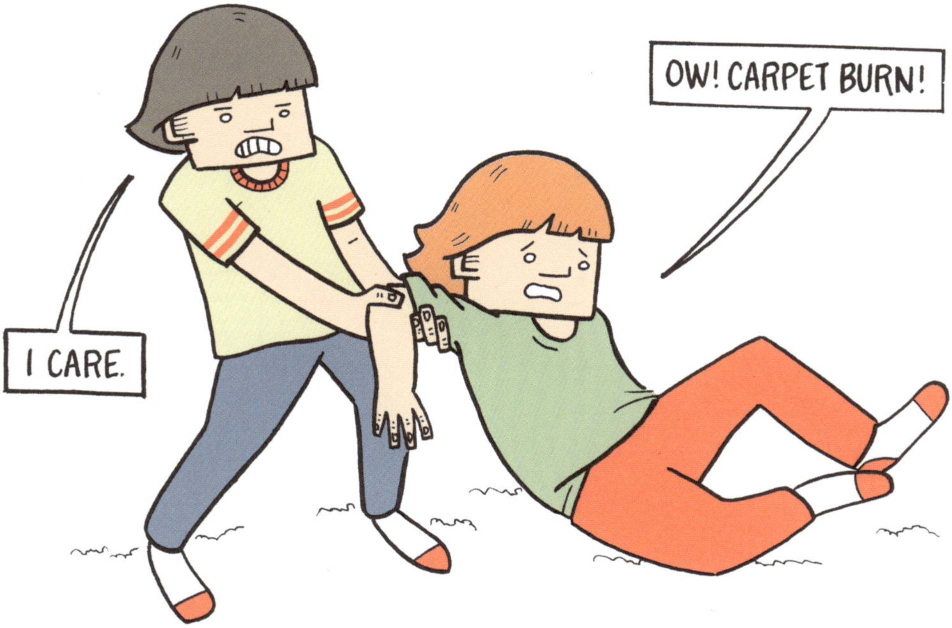
OW! CARPET BURN!
I CARE.

THE DROP & DRAG

SCRATCH 'N' BITE

FORK JAVELIN

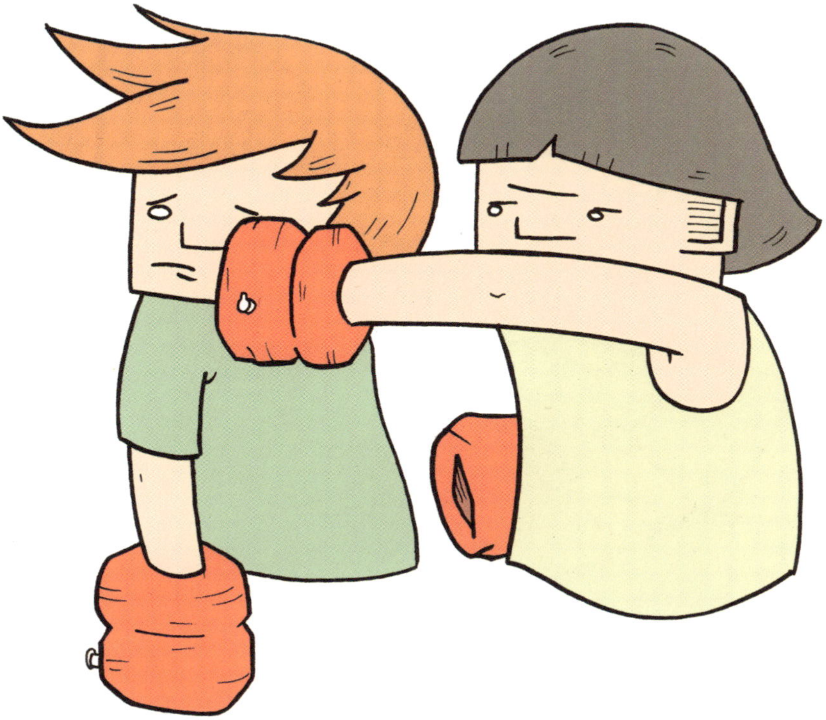

ARM-FLOATIE BOXING

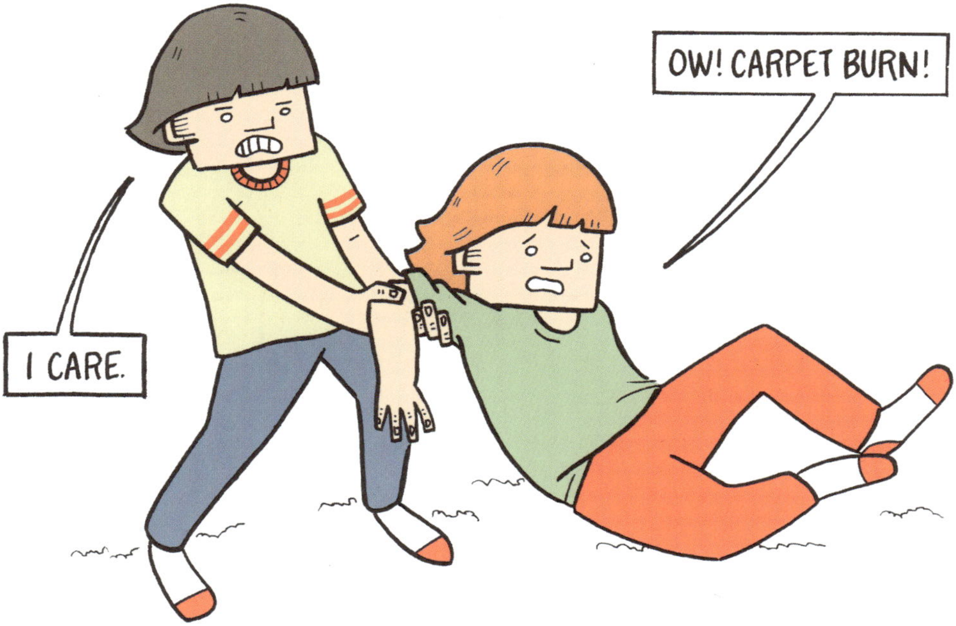
OW! CARPET BURN!
I CARE.

THE DROP & DRAG

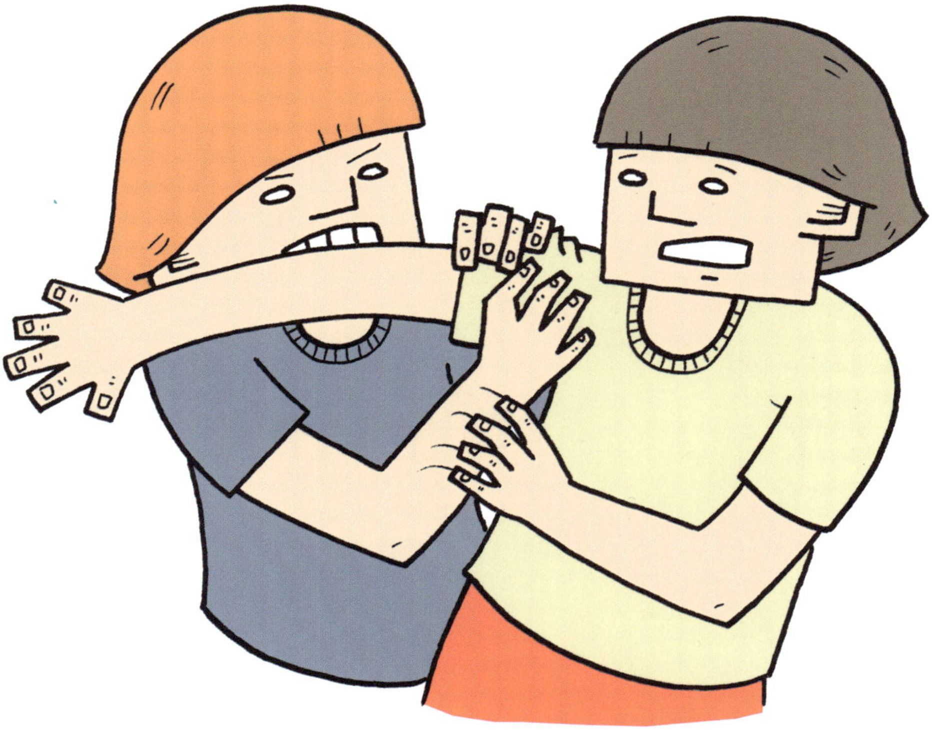

SCRATCH 'N' BITE

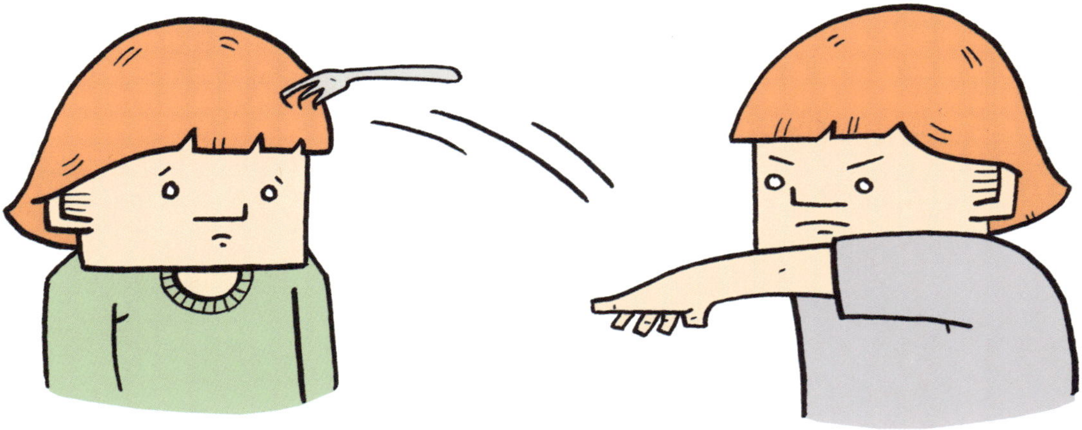

FORK JAVELIN

PACKING

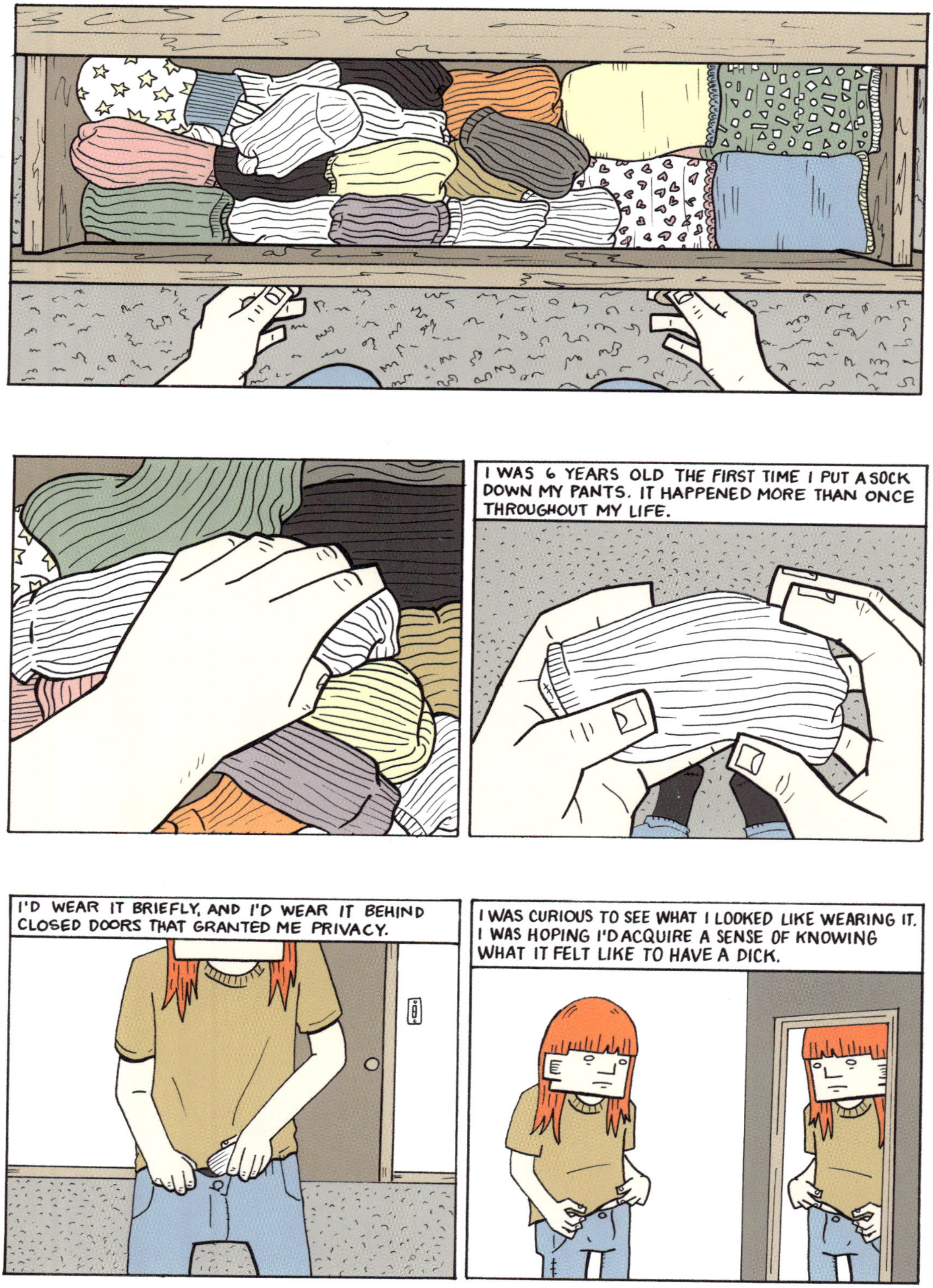
I WAS 6 YEARS OLD THE FIRST TIME I PUT A SOCK DOWN MY PANTS. IT HAPPENED MORE THAN ONCE THROUGHOUT MY LIFE.
I'D WEAR IT BRIEFLY, AND I'D WEAR IT BEHIND CLOSED DOORS THAT GRANTED ME PRIVACY.
I WAS CURIOUS TO SEE WHAT I LOOKED LIKE WEARING IT. I WAS HOPING I'D ACQUIRE A SENSE OF KNOWING WHAT IT FELT LIKE TO HAVE A DICK.

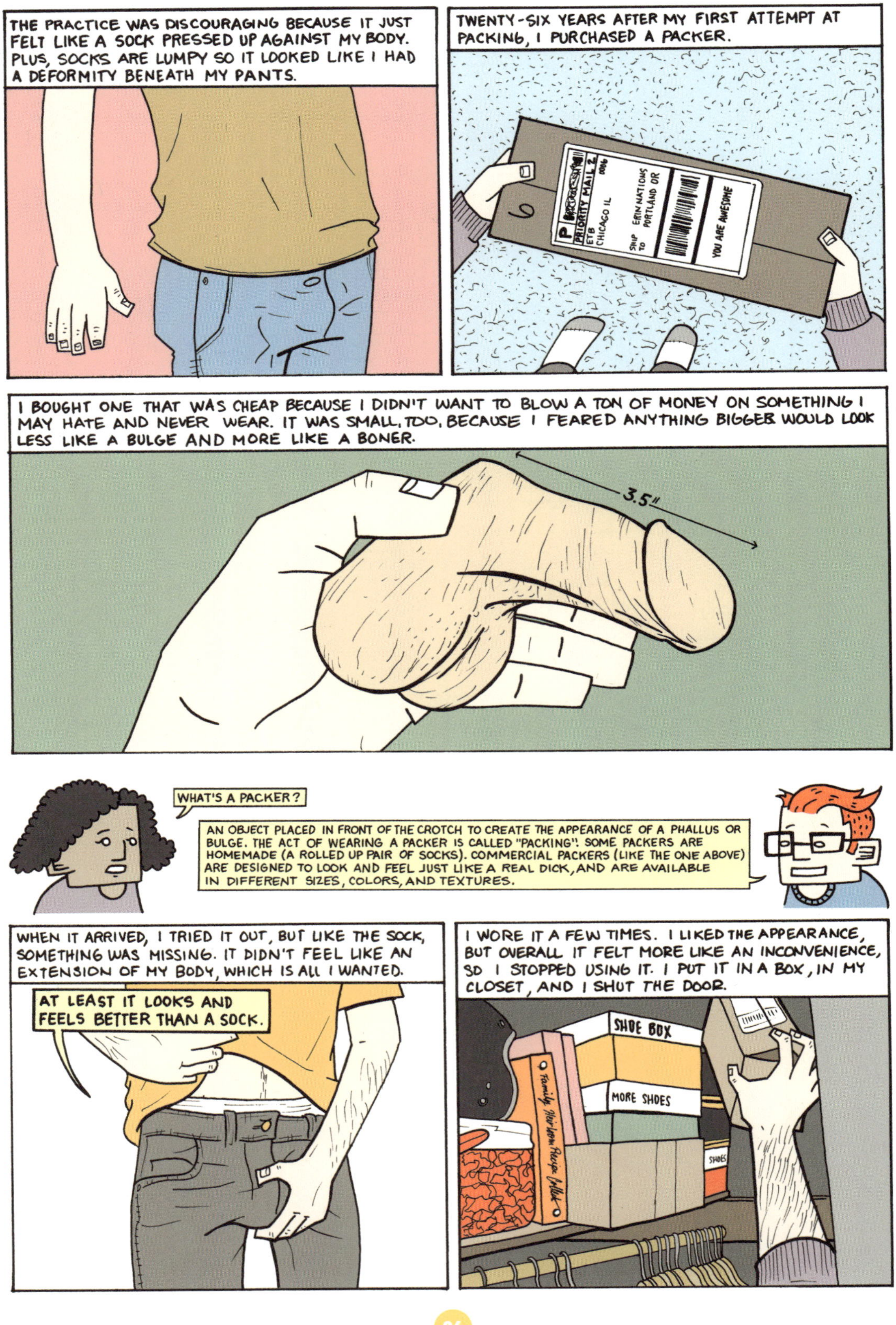

THE PRACTICE WAS DISCOURAGING BECAUSE IT JUST FELT LIKE A SOCK PRESSED UP AGAINST MY BODY. PLUS, SOCKS ARE LUMPY SO IT LOOKED LIKE I HAD A DEFORMITY BENEATH MY PANTS.
TWENTY-SIX YEARS AFTER MY FIRST ATTEMPT AT PACKING, I PURCHASED A PACKER.
PRIORITY MAIL 2
ETB
CHICAGO IL
SHIP TO
ERIN NATIONS
PORTLAND OR
YOU ARE AWESOME
I BOUGHT ONE THAT WAS CHEAP BECAUSE I DIDN'T WANT TO BLOW A TON OF MONEY ON SOMETHING I MAY HATE AND NEVER WEAR. IT WAS SMALL, TOO, BECAUSE I FEARED ANYTHING BIGGER WOULD LOOK LESS LIKE A BULGE AND MORE LIKE A BONER.
3.5"
WHAT'S A PACKER?
AN OBJECT PLACED IN FRONT OF THE CROTCH TO CREATE THE APPEARANCE OF A PHALLUS OR BULGE. THE ACT OF WEARING A PACKER IS CALLED "PACKING". SOME PACKERS ARE HOMEMADE (A ROLLED UP PAIR OF SOCKS). COMMERCIAL PACKERS (LIKE THE ONE ABOVE) ARE DESIGNED TO LOOK AND FEEL JUST LIKE A REAL DICK, AND ARE AVAILABLE IN DIFFERENT SIZES, COLORS, AND TEXTURES.
WHEN IT ARRIVED, I TRIED IT OUT, BUT LIKE THE SOCK, SOMETHING WAS MISSING. IT DIDN'T FEEL LIKE AN EXTENSION OF MY BODY, WHICH IS ALL I WANTED.
AT LEAST IT LOOKS AND FEELS BETTER THAN A SOCK.
I WORE IT A FEW TIMES. I LIKED THE APPEARANCE, BUT OVERALL IT FELT MORE LIKE AN INCONVENIENCE, SO I STOPPED USING IT. I PUT IT IN A BOX, IN MY CLOSET, AND I SHUT THE DOOR.
SHOE BOX
MORE SHOES
SHOES

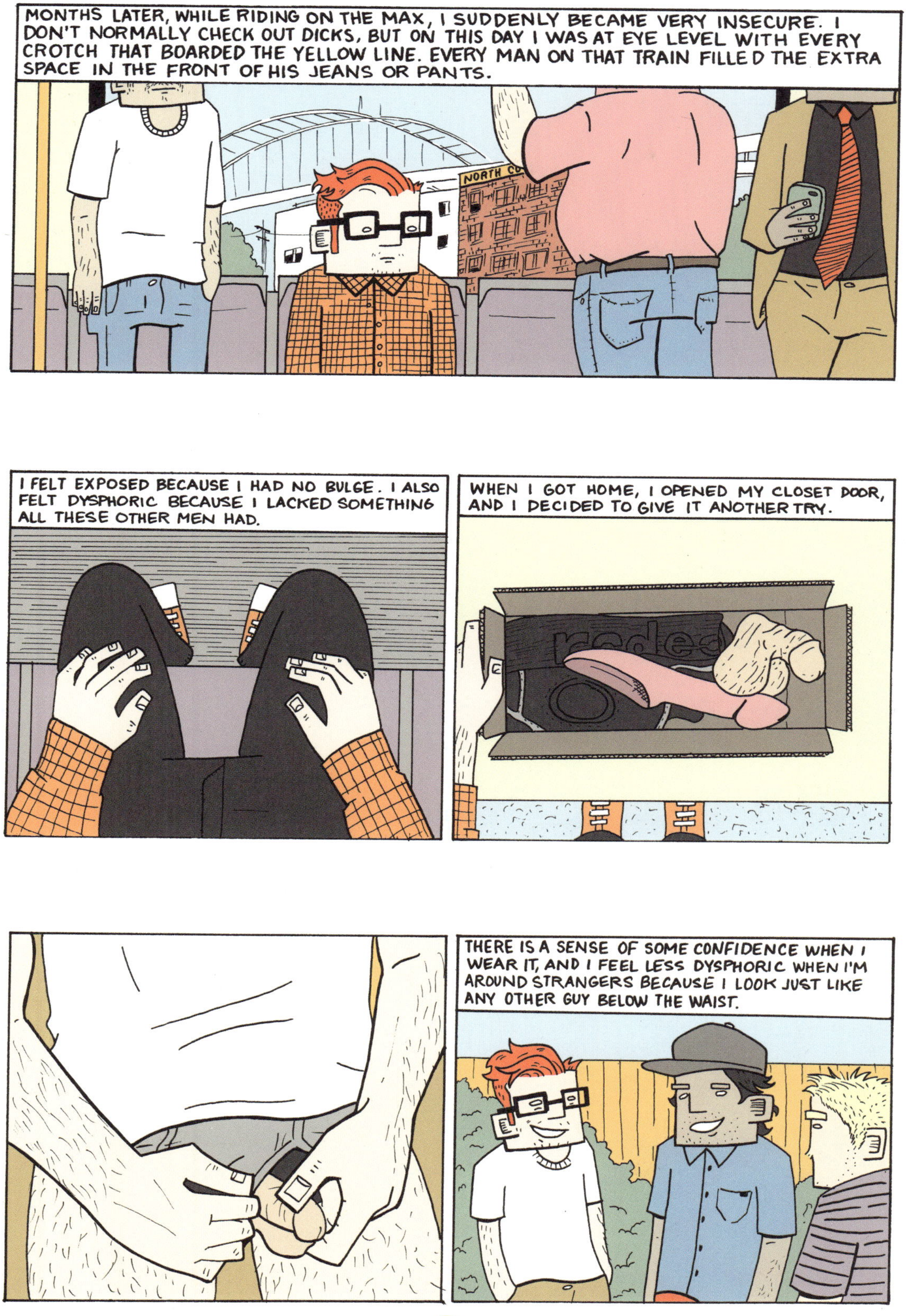
MONTHS LATER, WHILE RIDING ON THE MAX, I SUDDENLY BECAME VERY INSECURE. I DON'T NORMALLY CHECK OUT DICKS, BUT ON THIS DAY I WAS AT EYE LEVEL WITH EVERY CROTCH THAT BOARDED THE YELLOW LINE. EVERY MAN ON THAT TRAIN FILLED THE EXTRA SPACE IN THE FRONT OF HIS JEANS OR PANTS.
I FELT EXPOSED BECAUSE I HAD NO BULGE. I ALSO FELT DYSPHORIC BECAUSE I LACKED SOMETHING ALL THESE OTHER MEN HAD.
WHEN I GOT HOME, I OPENED MY CLOSET DOOR, AND I DECIDED TO GIVE IT ANOTHER TRY.
THERE IS A SENSE OF SOME CONFIDENCE WHEN I WEAR IT, AND I FEEL LESS DYSPHORIC WHEN I'M AROUND STRANGERS BECAUSE I LOOK JUST LIKE ANY OTHER GUY BELOW THE WAIST.

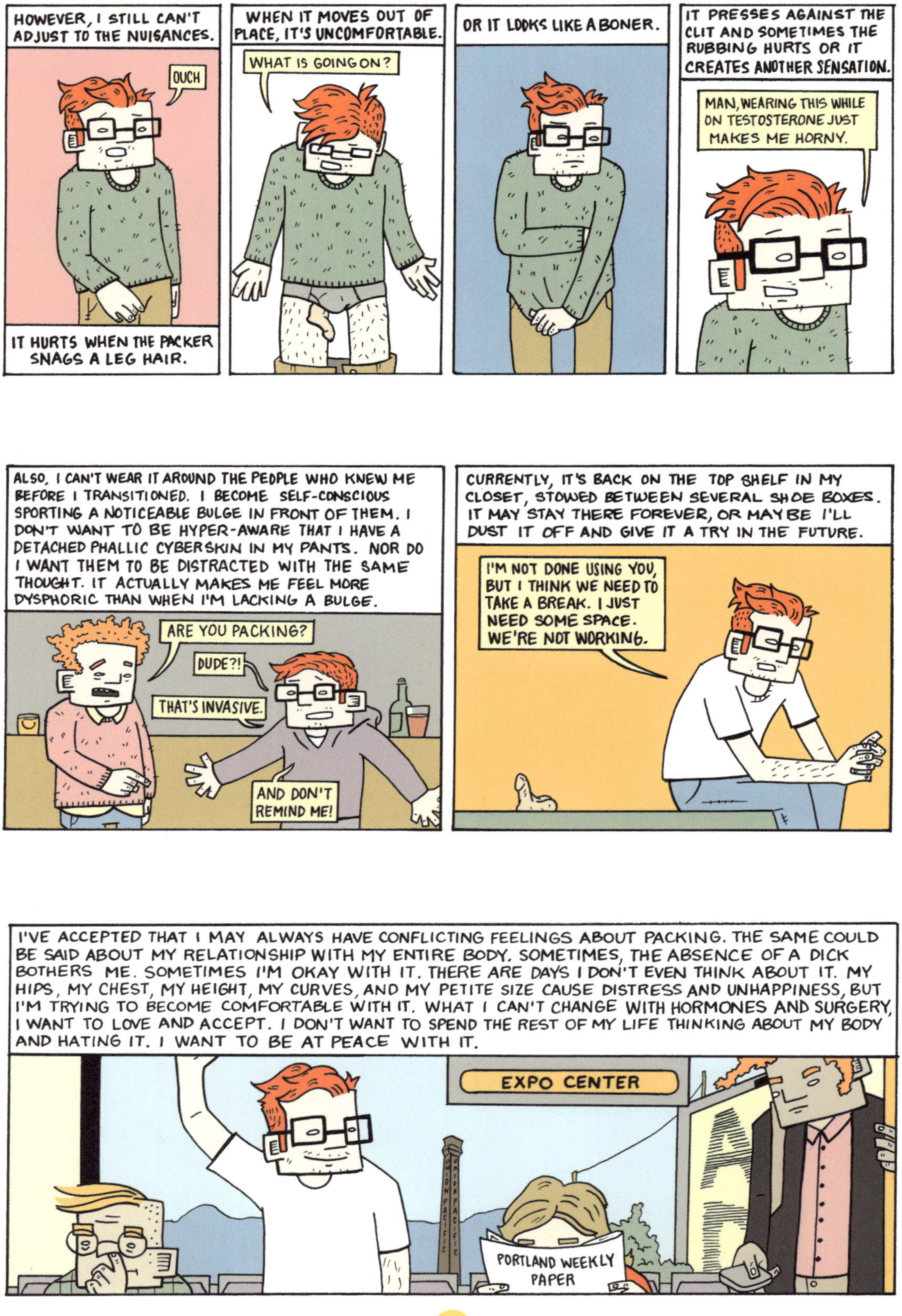

HOWEVER, I STILL CAN'T ADJUST TO THE NUISANCES.
OUCH
IT HURTS WHEN THE PACKER SNAGS A LEG HAIR.
WHEN IT MOVES OUT OF PLACE, IT'S UNCOMFORTABLE.
WHAT IS GOING ON?
OR IT LOOKS LIKE A BONER.
IT PRESSES AGAINST THE CLIT AND SOMETIMES THE RUBBING HURTS OR IT CREATES ANOTHER SENSATION.
MAN, WEARING THIS WHILE ON TESTOSTERONE JUST MAKES ME HORNY.
ALSO, I CAN'T WEAR IT AROUND THE PEOPLE WHO KNEW ME BEFORE I TRANSITIONED. I BECOME SELF-CONSCIOUS SPORTING A NOTICEABLE BULGE IN FRONT OF THEM. I DON'T WANT TO BE HYPER-AWARE THAT I HAVE A DETACHED PHALLIC CYBERSKIN IN MY PANTS. NOR DO I WANT THEM TO BE DISTRACTED WITH THE SAME THOUGHT. IT ACTUALLY MAKES ME FEEL MORE DYSPHORIC THAN WHEN I'M LACKING A BULGE.
ARE YOU PACKING?
DUDE?!
THAT'S INVASIVE.
AND DON'T REMIND ME!
CURRENTLY, IT'S BACK ON THE TOP SHELF IN MY CLOSET, STOWED BETWEEN SEVERAL SHOE BOXES. IT MAY STAY THERE FOREVER, OR MAYBE I'LL DUST IT OFF AND GIVE IT A TRY IN THE FUTURE.
I'M NOT DONE USING YOU, BUT I THINK WE NEED TO TAKE A BREAK. I JUST NEED SOME SPACE. WE'RE NOT WORKING.
I'VE ACCEPTED THAT I MAY ALWAYS HAVE CONFLICTING FEELINGS ABOUT PACKING. THE SAME COULD BE SAID ABOUT MY RELATIONSHIP WITH MY ENTIRE BODY. SOMETIMES, THE ABSENCE OF A DICK BOTHERS ME. SOMETIMES I'M OKAY WITH IT. THERE ARE DAYS I DON'T EVEN THINK ABOUT IT. MY HIPS, MY CHEST, MY HEIGHT, MY CURVES, AND MY PETITE SIZE CAUSE DISTRESS AND UNHAPPINESS, BUT I'M TRYING TO BECOME COMFORTABLE WITH IT. WHAT I CAN'T CHANGE WITH HORMONES AND SURGERY, I WANT TO LOVE AND ACCEPT. I DON'T WANT TO SPEND THE REST OF MY LIFE THINKING ABOUT MY BODY AND HATING IT. I WANT TO BE AT PEACE WITH IT.
EXPO CENTER
UNION PACIFIC
PORTLAND WEEKLY PAPER

THAT'S WHAT YOU GET

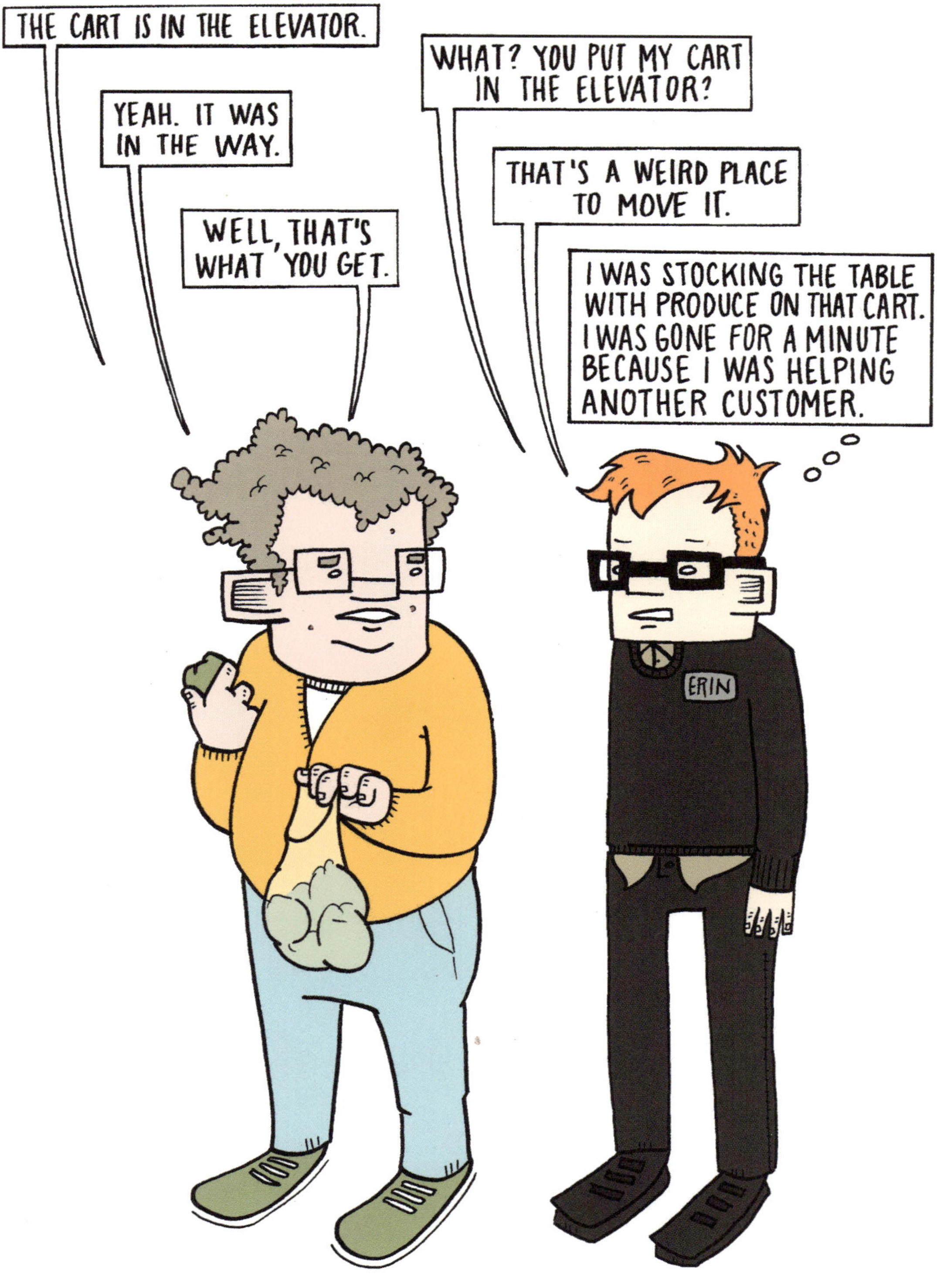

THE CART IS IN THE ELEVATOR.
WHAT? YOU PUT MY CART IN THE ELEVATOR?
YEAH. IT WAS IN THE WAY.
THAT'S A WEIRD PLACE TO MOVE IT.
I WAS STOCKING THE TABLE WITH PRODUCE ON THAT CART. I WAS GONE FOR A MINUTE BECAUSE I WAS HELPING ANOTHER CUSTOMER.
WELL, THAT'S WHAT YOU GET.
ERIN

I DON'T BELONG

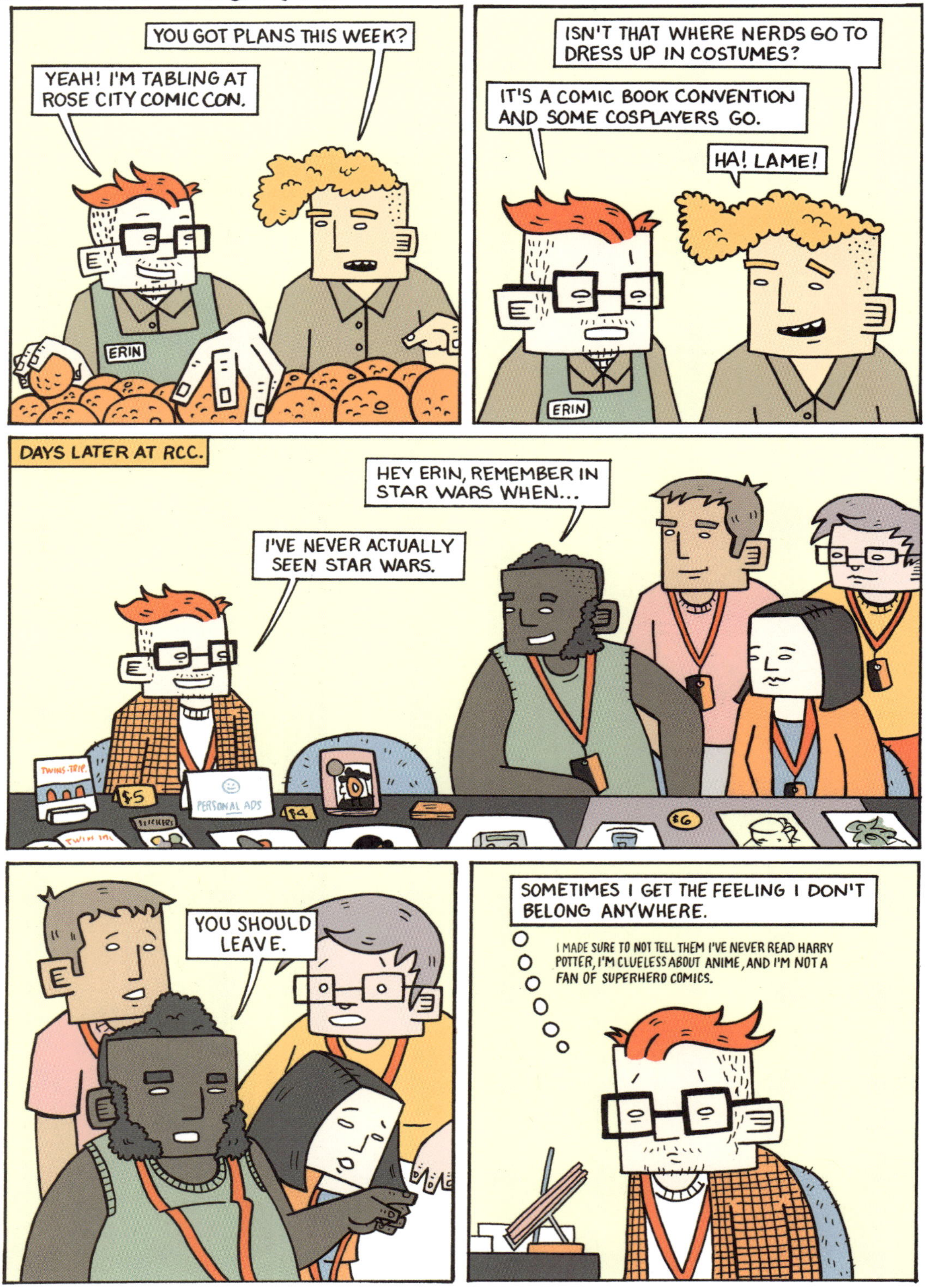
YOU GOT PLANS THIS WEEK?
YEAH! I'M TABLING AT ROSE CITY COMIC CON.
ERIN
ISN'T THAT WHERE NERDS GO TO DRESS UP IN COSTUMES?
IT'S A COMIC BOOK CONVENTION AND SOME COSPLAYERS GO.
HA! LAME!
ERIN
DAYS LATER AT RCC.
HEY ERIN, REMEMBER IN STAR WARS WHEN...
I'VE NEVER ACTUALLY SEEN STAR WARS.
TWINS TRIP
$5
PERSONAL ADS
$4
$6
YOU SHOULD LEAVE.
SOMETIMES I GET THE FEELING I DON'T BELONG ANYWHERE.
I MADE SURE TO NOT TELL THEM I'VE NEVER READ HARRY POTTER, I'M CLUELESS ABOUT ANIME, AND I'M NOT A FAN OF SUPERHERO COMICS.

WOMEN SHREDDING

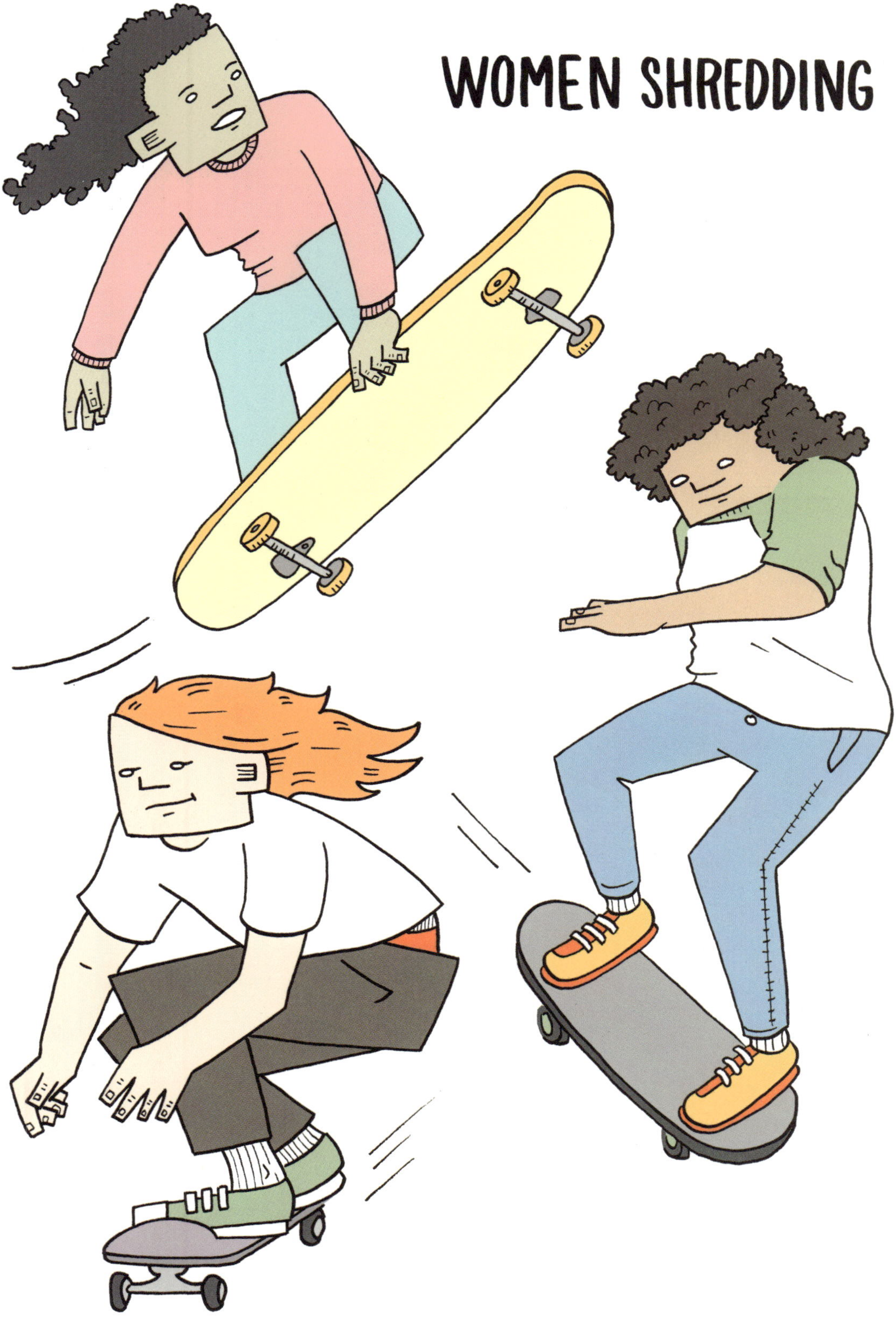

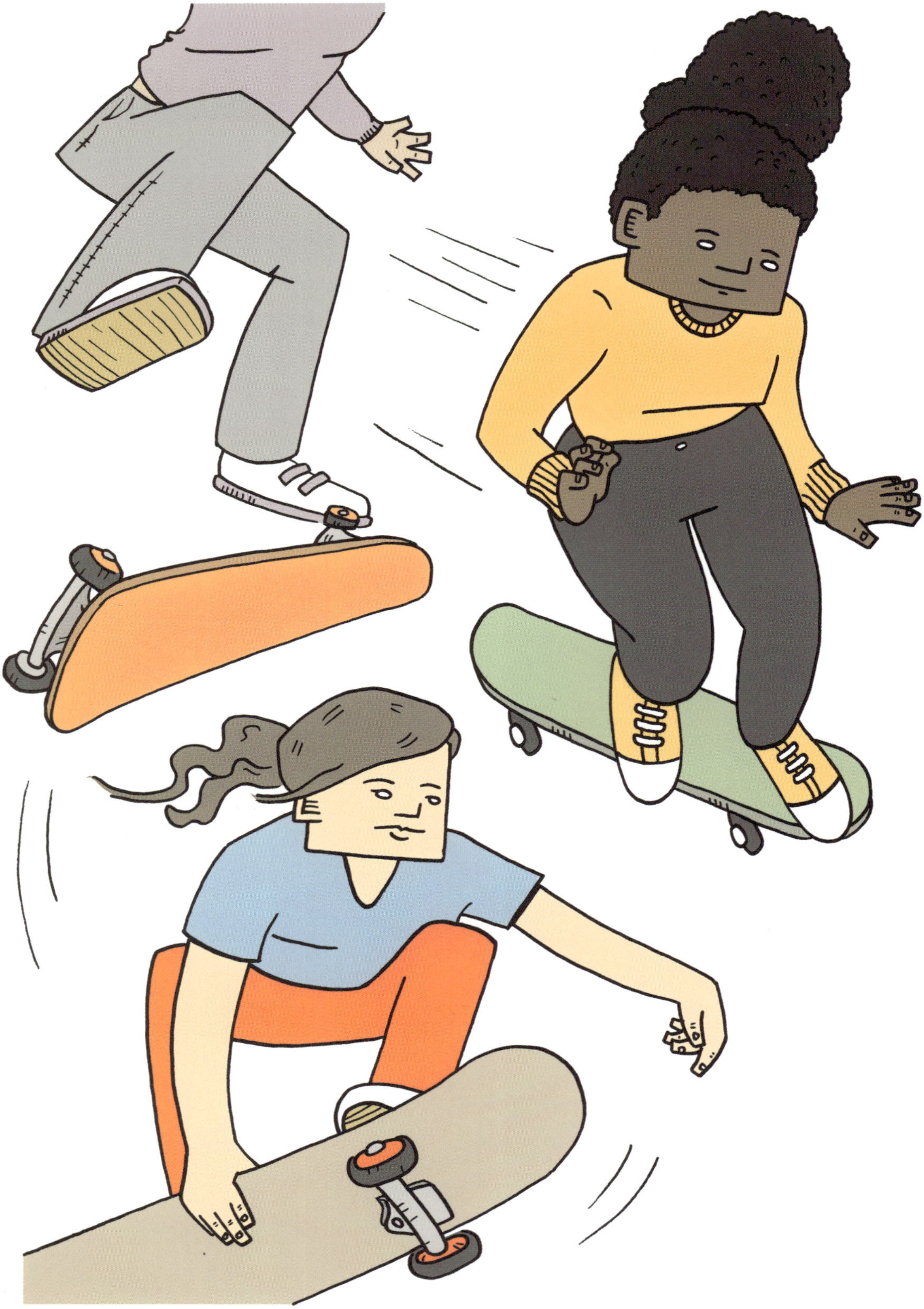

SKATE TRICKS FOR THE TIMID

AT A VERY YOUNG AGE, I YEARNED FOR A SKATEBOARD. SKATEBOARDING LOOKED FUN, AND I THOUGHT I WAS A BAD-ASS LITTLE DUDE THAT COULD SHRED.
I WAS DAYDREAMING. I COULDN'T MOVE 2 FEET ON A BOARD! DURING THE GIFT-GIVING HOLIDAYS, I NEVER ASKED MY FOLKS FOR A SKATEBOARD. WHEN I WAS A PIMPLED-FACE TEENAGER, I NEVER USED MY ALLOWANCE TO BUY ONE. DESPITE MY ENVY FOR SKATEBOARDERS AND MY DREAM OF BEING JUST LIKE ALL THE RAD FEMALE SKATERS I ADMIRED, I NEVER PURSUED IT.
I'M TOO TENSE AND AFRAID, AND I THINK DEEP DOWN I KNEW THAT. THERE ARE NO BRAKES OR HANDLES ON A SKATEBOARD. I NEED SECURITY TO FEEL SAFE.
I'M NOT SURE IF I'D BE ABLE TO GRIND, KICKFLIP, OR DO AN OLLIE, BUT I THINK I'D EXCEL AT SOME OF MY OWN TRICKS.

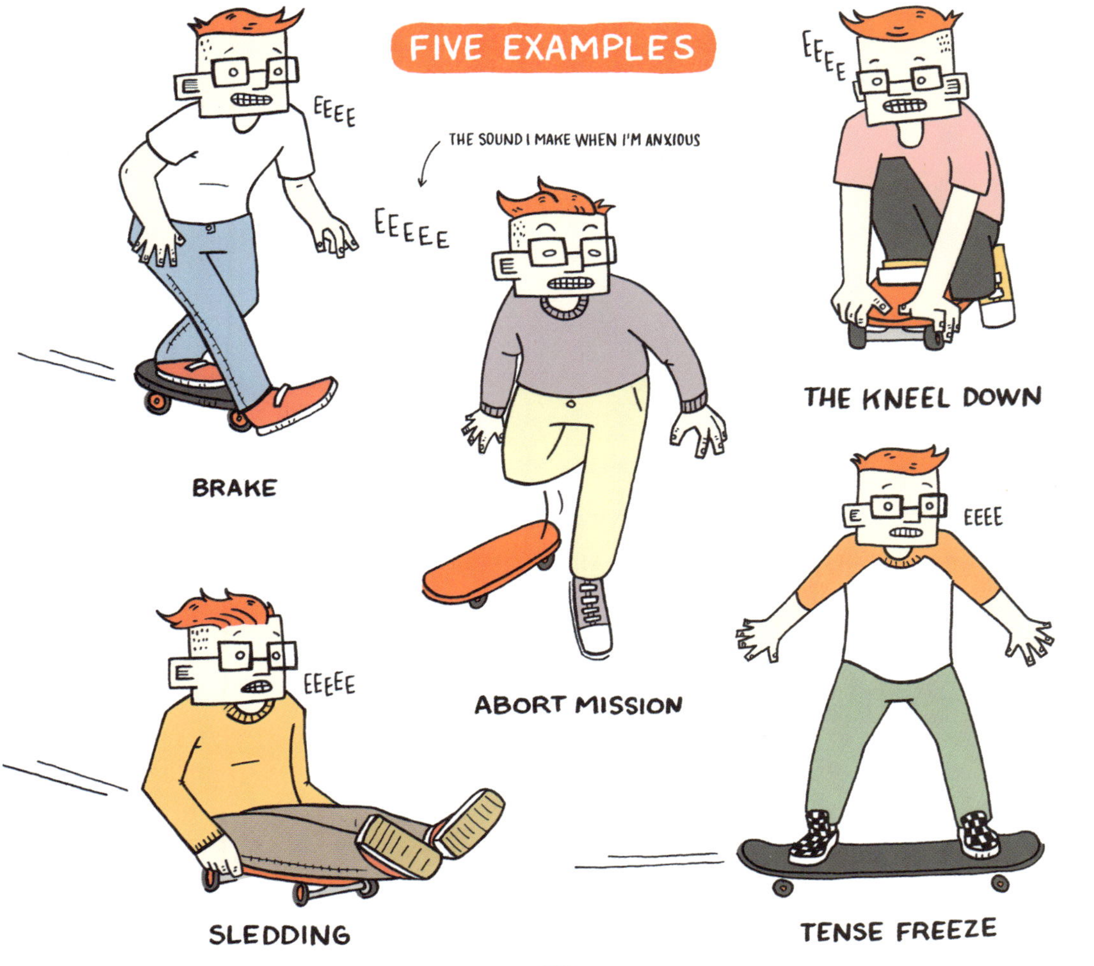
FIVE EXAMPLES
EEEE
BRAKE
THE SOUND I MAKE WHEN I'M ANXIOUS
EEEEE
ABORT MISSION
EEEE
THE KNEEL DOWN
EEEEE
SLEDDING
EEEE
TENSE FREEZE

RINGO

MY NAME IS RINGO. I'M 48 YEARS OLD. FOR 20 YEARS, I'VE WORKED
IN A CUBICLE, AT A DESK, IN FRONT OF A COMPUTER. I SPEND
HALF OF MY SHIFT CREATING NEW DESKTOP WALLPAPERS, TAKING
TRIPS TO THE BREAK ROOM TO REFILL MY COFFEE CUP, AND
FILLING OUT CROSSWORD PUZZLES IN THE MEN'S ROOM.
I LIKE COUPONING. IT'S SO EXCITING TO SAVE MONEY! IT'S ALSO
EXCITING TO FIND MONEY UNDER COUCH CUSHIONS! I LIKE
RETURNING MY ALUMINUM SODA CANS TO MY LOCAL RECYCLING
CENTER. I LIKE DECORATING MY HOUSE IN ADORABLE HANDMADE
ITEMS FROM THE CRAFT MALL. I HAVE AN EXTENSIVE VHS
COLLECTION OF LIFETIME ORIGINAL MOVIES. I LIKE POP MUSIC,
ESPECIALLY MILEY! SHE IS SO AUDACIOUS.
I BELIEVE HONESTY IS IMPORTANT, WHICH IS WHY I HAVE NO
PROBLEM ADMITTING SOME OF MY SHORTCOMINGS TO MY LOVE
SEEKERS. I HAVE PIMPLES ON MY BACK, AND MY BODY ODOR
SMELLS LIKE ROTTEN ONIONS. I HAVE BAD HALITOSIS, SO MY
KISSES TASTE METALLIC, AND SOMETIMES I COUGH UP TONSIL
STONES. THESE THINGS HAPPEN. NOBODY IS PERFECT.
AT MY AGE, I KNOW WHAT I WANT. I TRY NOT TO BE SUPERFICIAL,
BUT I WON'T LIE, I'M SEEKING SOMEONE WITH A BRONZE BOD',
AND LUSCIOUS LIPS, AND WHO SMELLS LIKE GARDENIAS. I'M
ONLY INTERESTED IN A LONG-TERM RELATIONSHIP BECAUSE I
WANT MY FIRST RELATIONSHIP TO BE MY LAST.
PLEASE RESPOND! I WANT TO GET TO KNOW YOU.

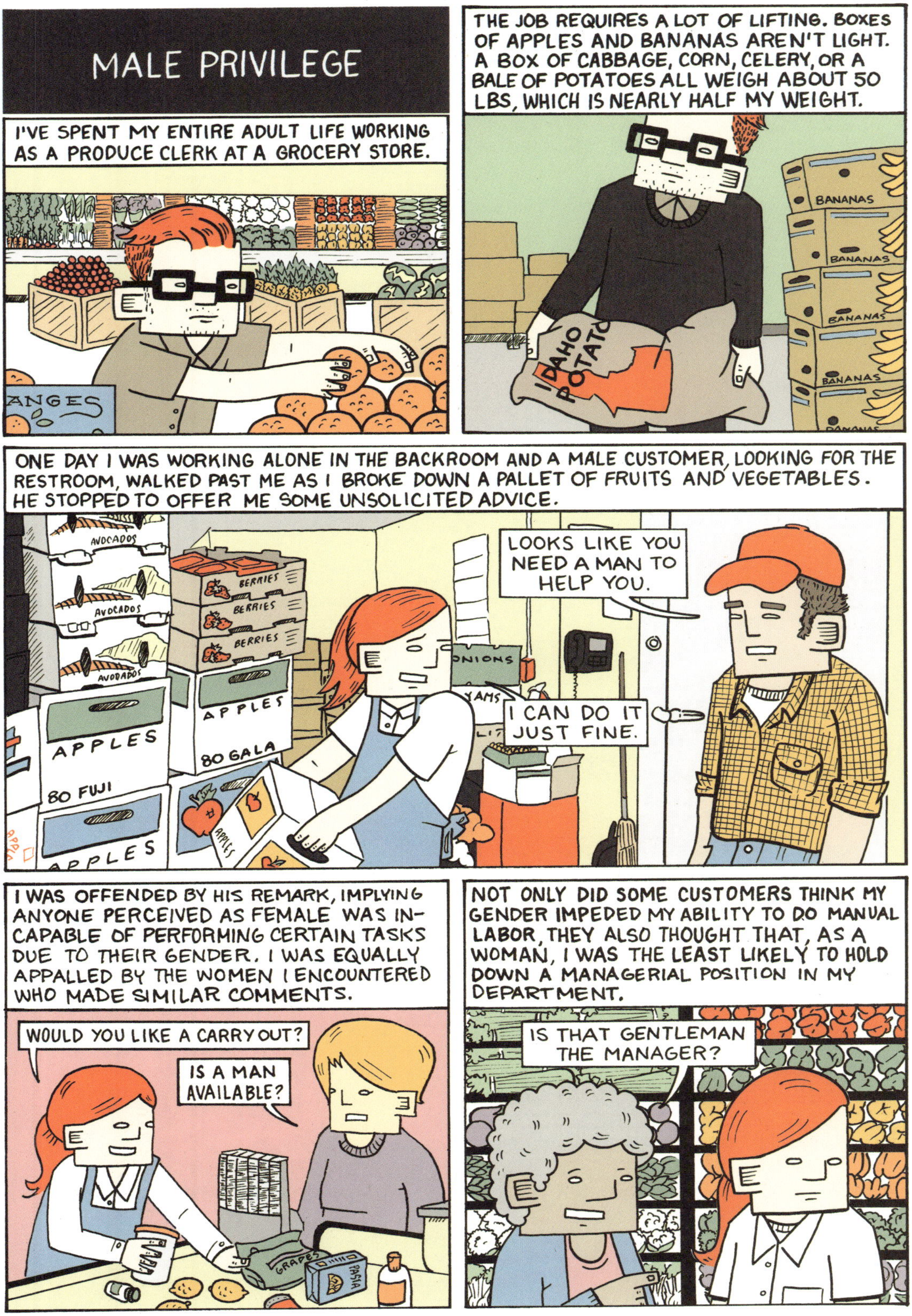
MALE PRIVILEGE
I'VE SPENT MY ENTIRE ADULT LIFE WORKING AS A PRODUCE CLERK AT A GROCERY STORE.
ANGES
THE JOB REQUIRES A LOT OF LIFTING. BOXES OF APPLES AND BANANAS AREN'T LIGHT. A BOX OF CABBAGE, CORN, CELERY, OR A BALE OF POTATOES ALL WEIGH ABOUT 50 LBS, WHICH IS NEARLY HALF MY WEIGHT.
BANANAS
BANANAS
BANANAS
BANANAS
ONE DAY I WAS WORKING ALONE IN THE BACKROOM AND A MALE CUSTOMER, LOOKING FOR THE RESTROOM, WALKED PAST ME AS I BROKE DOWN A PALLET OF FRUITS AND VEGETABLES. HE STOPPED TO OFFER ME SOME UNSOLICITED ADVICE.
AVOCADOS
AVOCADOS
AVOCADOS
BERRIES
BERRIES
BERRIES
APPLES
80 FUJI
APPLES
80 GALA
APPLES
ONIONS
YAMS
LOOKS LIKE YOU NEED A MAN TO HELP YOU.
I CAN DO IT JUST FINE.
I WAS OFFENDED BY HIS REMARK, IMPLYING ANYONE PERCEIVED AS FEMALE WAS INCAPABLE OF PERFORMING CERTAIN TASKS DUE TO THEIR GENDER. I WAS EQUALLY APPALLED BY THE WOMEN I ENCOUNTERED WHO MADE SIMILAR COMMENTS.
WOULD YOU LIKE A CARRYOUT?
IS A MAN AVAILABLE?
GRAPES
PASTA
NOT ONLY DID SOME CUSTOMERS THINK MY GENDER IMPEDED MY ABILITY TO DO MANUAL LABOR, THEY ALSO THOUGHT THAT, AS A WOMAN, I WAS THE LEAST LIKELY TO HOLD DOWN A MANAGERIAL POSITION IN MY DEPARTMENT.
IS THAT GENTLEMAN THE MANAGER?

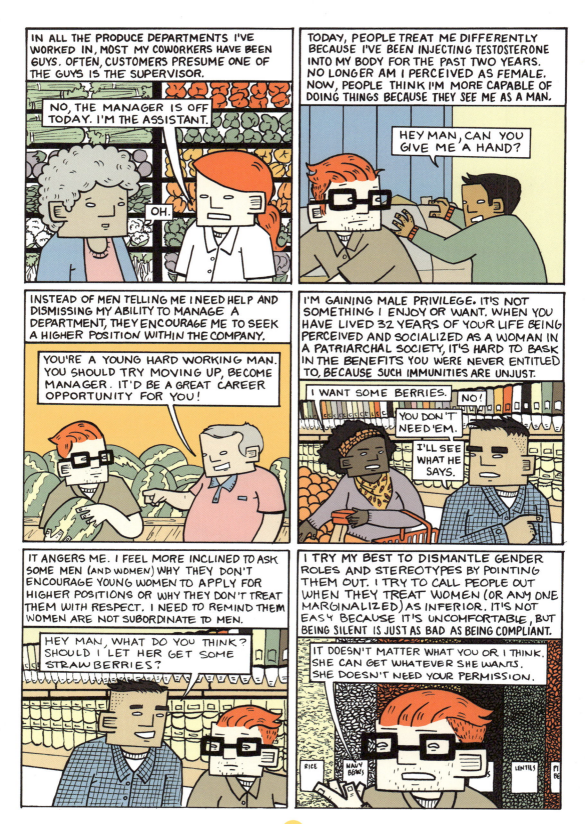

IN ALL THE PRODUCE DEPARTMENTS I'VE WORKED IN, MOST MY COWORKERS HAVE BEEN GUYS. OFTEN, CUSTOMERS PRESUME ONE OF THE GUYS IS THE SUPERVISOR.

NO, THE MANAGER IS OFF TODAY. I'M THE ASSISTANT.

OH.

TODAY, PEOPLE TREAT ME DIFFERENTLY BECAUSE I'VE BEEN INJECTING TESTOSTERONE INTO MY BODY FOR THE PAST TWO YEARS. NO LONGER AM I PERCEIVED AS FEMALE. NOW, PEOPLE THINK I'M MORE CAPABLE OF DOING THINGS BECAUSE THEY SEE ME AS A MAN.

HEY MAN, CAN YOU GIVE ME A HAND?

INSTEAD OF MEN TELLING ME I NEED HELP AND DISMISSING MY ABILITY TO MANAGE A DEPARTMENT, THEY ENCOURAGE ME TO SEEK A HIGHER POSITION WITHIN THE COMPANY.

YOU'RE A YOUNG HARD WORKING MAN. YOU SHOULD TRY MOVING UP, BECOME MANAGER. IT'D BE A GREAT CAREER OPPORTUNITY FOR YOU!

I'M GAINING MALE PRIVILEGE. IT'S NOT SOMETHING I ENJOY OR WANT. WHEN YOU HAVE LIVED 32 YEARS OF YOUR LIFE BEING PERCEIVED AND SOCIALIZED AS A WOMAN IN A PATRIARCHAL SOCIETY, IT'S HARD TO BASK IN THE BENEFITS YOU WERE NEVER ENTITLED TO, BECAUSE SUCH IMMUNITIES ARE UNJUST.

I WANT SOME BERRIES.

NO!

YOU DON'T NEED 'EM.

I'LL SEE WHAT HE SAYS.

IT ANGERS ME. I FEEL MORE INCLINED TO ASK SOME MEN (AND WOMEN) WHY THEY DON'T ENCOURAGE YOUNG WOMEN TO APPLY FOR HIGHER POSITIONS OR WHY THEY DON'T TREAT THEM WITH RESPECT. I NEED TO REMIND THEM WOMEN ARE NOT SUBORDINATE TO MEN.

HEY MAN, WHAT DO YOU THINK? SHOULD I LET HER GET SOME STRAWBERRIES?

I TRY MY BEST TO DISMANTLE GENDER ROLES AND STEREOTYPES BY POINTING THEM OUT. I TRY TO CALL PEOPLE OUT WHEN THEY TREAT WOMEN (OR ANY ONE MARGINALIZED) AS INFERIOR. IT'S NOT EASY BECAUSE IT'S UNCOMFORTABLE, BUT BEING SILENT IS JUST AS BAD AS BEING COMPLIANT.

IT DOESN'T MATTER WHAT YOU OR I THINK. SHE CAN GET WHATEVER SHE WANTS. SHE DOESN'T NEED YOUR PERMISSION.

RICE

NAVY BEANS

LENTILS

PI BE

VOODOO DOLL TWO

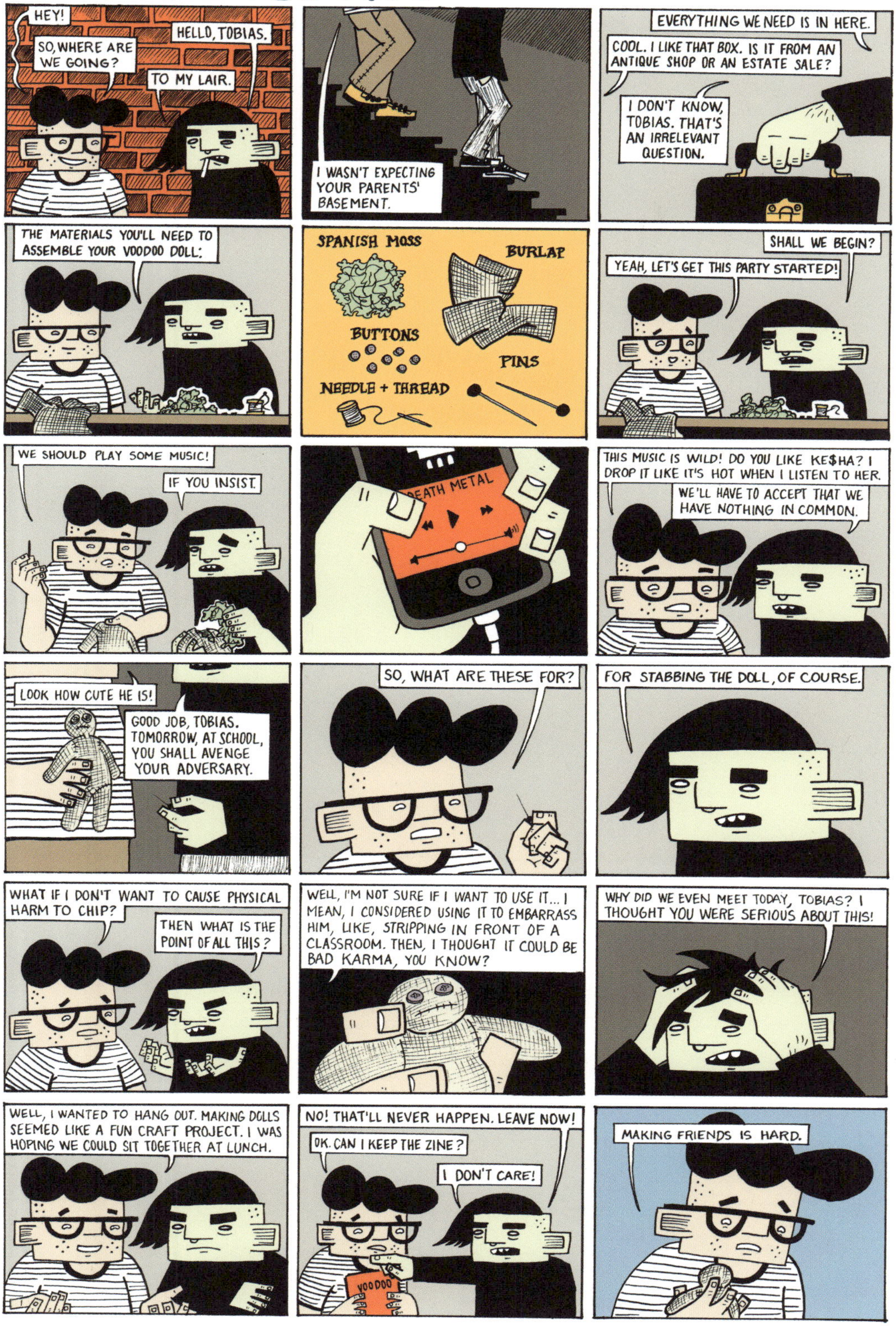

HEY!
SO, WHERE ARE WE GOING?
HELLO, TOBIAS.
TO MY LAIR.
I WASN'T EXPECTING YOUR PARENTS' BASEMENT.
EVERYTHING WE NEED IS IN HERE.
COOL. I LIKE THAT BOX. IS IT FROM AN ANTIQUE SHOP OR AN ESTATE SALE?
I DON'T KNOW, TOBIAS. THAT'S AN IRRELEVANT QUESTION.
THE MATERIALS YOU'LL NEED TO ASSEMBLE YOUR VOODOO DOLL:
SPANISH MOSS
BURLAP
BUTTONS
PINS
NEEDLE + THREAD
SHALL WE BEGIN?
YEAH, LET'S GET THIS PARTY STARTED!
WE SHOULD PLAY SOME MUSIC!
IF YOU INSIST.
DEATH METAL
THIS MUSIC IS WILD! DO YOU LIKE KE$HA? I DROP IT LIKE IT'S HOT WHEN I LISTEN TO HER.
WE'LL HAVE TO ACCEPT THAT WE HAVE NOTHING IN COMMON.
LOOK HOW CUTE HE IS!
GOOD JOB, TOBIAS. TOMORROW, AT SCHOOL, YOU SHALL AVENGE YOUR ADVERSARY.
SO, WHAT ARE THESE FOR?
FOR STABBING THE DOLL, OF COURSE.
WHAT IF I DON'T WANT TO CAUSE PHYSICAL HARM TO CHIP?
THEN WHAT IS THE POINT OF ALL THIS?
WELL, I'M NOT SURE IF I WANT TO USE IT... I MEAN, I CONSIDERED USING IT TO EMBARRASS HIM, LIKE, STRIPPING IN FRONT OF A CLASSROOM. THEN, I THOUGHT IT COULD BE BAD KARMA, YOU KNOW?
WHY DID WE EVEN MEET TODAY, TOBIAS? I THOUGHT YOU WERE SERIOUS ABOUT THIS!
WELL, I WANTED TO HANG OUT. MAKING DOLLS SEEMED LIKE A FUN CRAFT PROJECT. I WAS HOPING WE COULD SIT TOGETHER AT LUNCH.
NO! THAT'LL NEVER HAPPEN. LEAVE NOW!
OK. CAN I KEEP THE ZINE?
I DON'T CARE!
VOODOO
MAKING FRIENDS IS HARD.

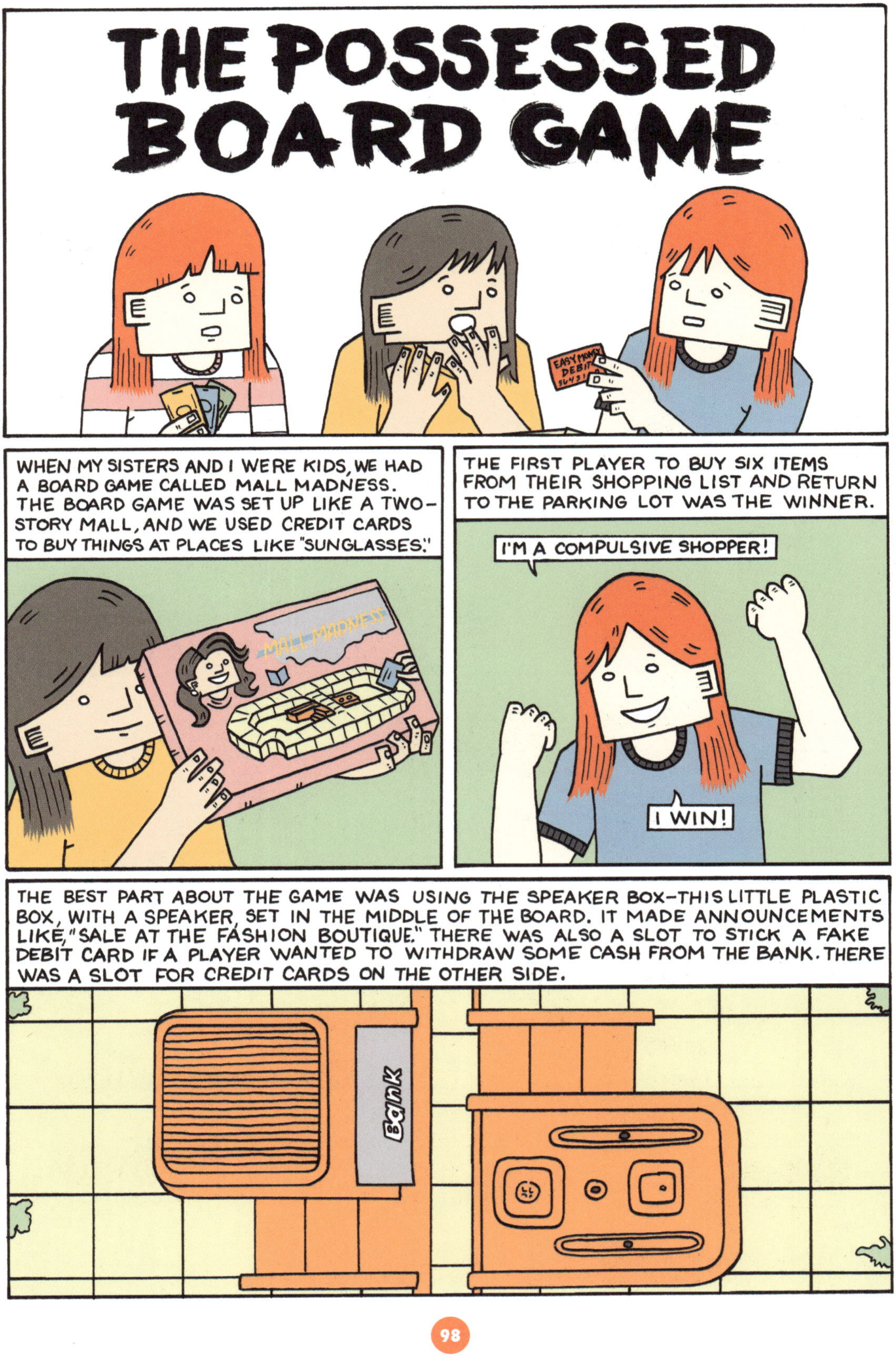
THE POSSESSED BOARD GAME
EASY MONEY DEBIT
WHEN MY SISTERS AND I WERE KIDS, WE HAD A BOARD GAME CALLED MALL MADNESS. THE BOARD GAME WAS SET UP LIKE A TWO-STORY MALL, AND WE USED CREDIT CARDS TO BUY THINGS AT PLACES LIKE "SUNGLASSES."
MALL MADNESS
THE FIRST PLAYER TO BUY SIX ITEMS FROM THEIR SHOPPING LIST AND RETURN TO THE PARKING LOT WAS THE WINNER.
I'M A COMPULSIVE SHOPPER!
I WIN!
THE BEST PART ABOUT THE GAME WAS USING THE SPEAKER BOX—THIS LITTLE PLASTIC BOX, WITH A SPEAKER, SET IN THE MIDDLE OF THE BOARD. IT MADE ANNOUNCEMENTS LIKE, "SALE AT THE FASHION BOUTIQUE." THERE WAS ALSO A SLOT TO STICK A FAKE DEBIT CARD IF A PLAYER WANTED TO WITHDRAW SOME CASH FROM THE BANK. THERE WAS A SLOT FOR CREDIT CARDS ON THE OTHER SIDE.
Bank

SOMETIMES, DURING A PLAYER'S TURN, AN EAGER VOICE FROM THE BOX PIPED UP. IT TOLD THE PLAYER TO MEET A FRIEND AT THE PIZZA SHOP BECAUSE THEY WERE HUNGRY. OTHER TIMES THE BOX WAS SASSY.

YOUR ITEM COST FIVE DOLLARS MORE!

IT WAS DEMANDING.

GO TO THE RESTROOM!

IT WAS TERRIBLY INCONVENIENT.

BANK CLOSED.

EVEN THOUGH WE LOVED THE SPEAKER BOX, WE WERE CONVINCED IT WAS POSSESSED BY A DEMONIC ENTITY! THE GAME WOULD GO UNTOUCHED FOR WEEKS. THE BOARD WOULD BE FOLDED UP IN A BOX. ALL THE LITTLE PIECES AND COMPONENTS WOULD BE STORED IN THEIR PROPER PLACE. THEN, IN THE MIDDLE OF THE NIGHT, WHILE WE WERE TUCKED AWAY IN OUR BEDS, THE LITTLE BOX SPOKE TO US.

OOH! LONG LINE. TRY AGAIN LATER!

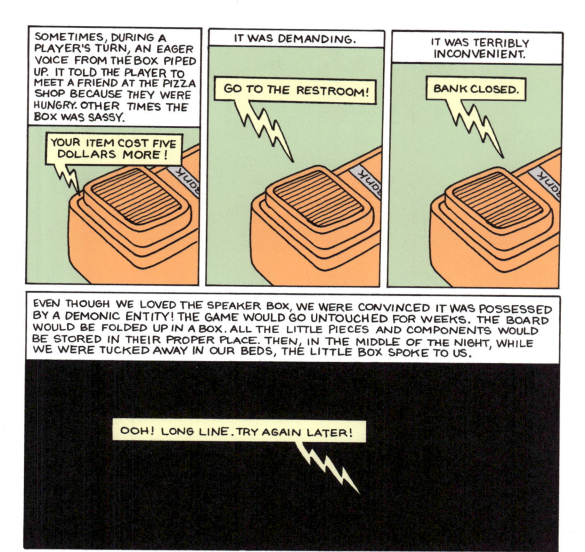

WHAT THE HELL WAS THAT?

YOU HEARD IT TOO?

YEAH! IT CAME FROM THE LIVING ROOM.

I THINK IT WAS MALL MADNESS!

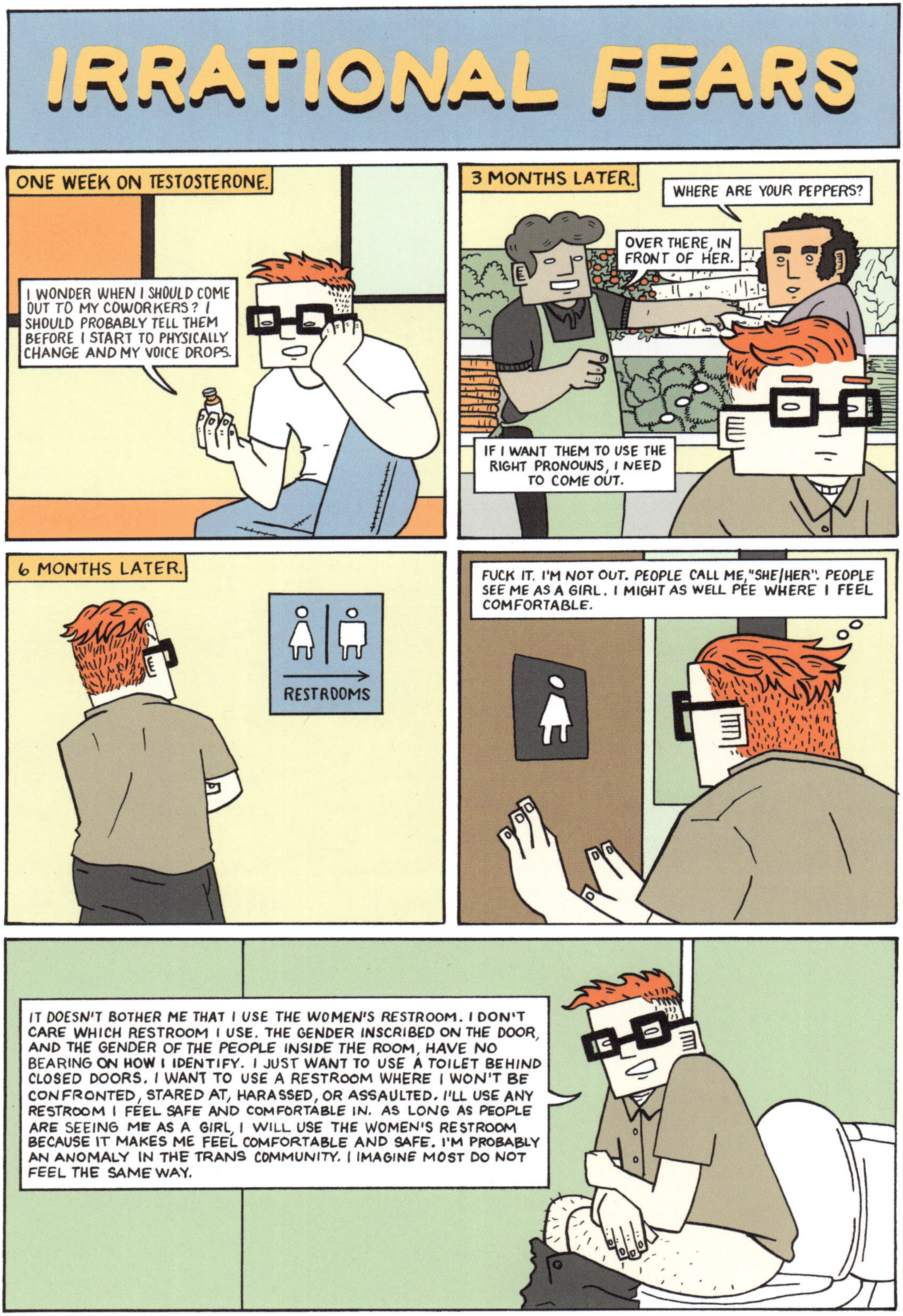
IRRATIONAL FEARS
ONE WEEK ON TESTOSTERONE.
I WONDER WHEN I SHOULD COME OUT TO MY COWORKERS? I SHOULD PROBABLY TELL THEM BEFORE I START TO PHYSICALLY CHANGE AND MY VOICE DROPS.
3 MONTHS LATER.
WHERE ARE YOUR PEPPERS?
OVER THERE, IN FRONT OF HER.
IF I WANT THEM TO USE THE RIGHT PRONOUNS, I NEED TO COME OUT.
6 MONTHS LATER.
RESTROOMS
FUCK IT. I'M NOT OUT. PEOPLE CALL ME, "SHE/HER". PEOPLE SEE ME AS A GIRL. I MIGHT AS WELL PEE WHERE I FEEL COMFORTABLE.
IT DOESN'T BOTHER ME THAT I USE THE WOMEN'S RESTROOM. I DON'T CARE WHICH RESTROOM I USE. THE GENDER INSCRIBED ON THE DOOR, AND THE GENDER OF THE PEOPLE INSIDE THE ROOM, HAVE NO BEARING ON HOW I IDENTIFY. I JUST WANT TO USE A TOILET BEHIND CLOSED DOORS. I WANT TO USE A RESTROOM WHERE I WON'T BE CONFRONTED, STARED AT, HARASSED, OR ASSAULTED. I'LL USE ANY RESTROOM I FEEL SAFE AND COMFORTABLE IN. AS LONG AS PEOPLE ARE SEEING ME AS A GIRL, I WILL USE THE WOMEN'S RESTROOM BECAUSE IT MAKES ME FEEL COMFORTABLE AND SAFE. I'M PROBABLY AN ANOMALY IN THE TRANS COMMUNITY. I IMAGINE MOST DO NOT FEEL THE SAME WAY.

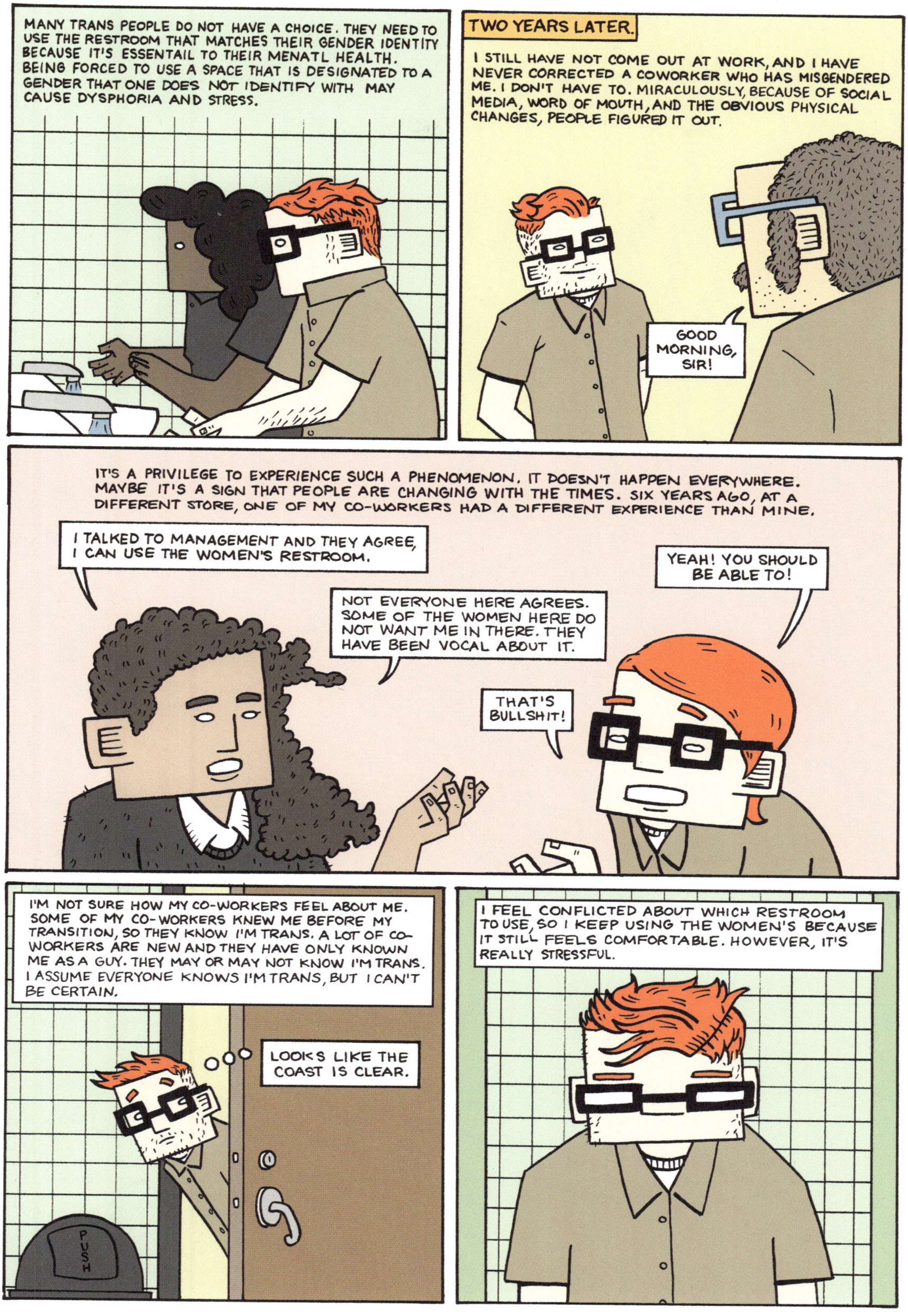
MANY TRANS PEOPLE DO NOT HAVE A CHOICE. THEY NEED TO USE THE RESTROOM THAT MATCHES THEIR GENDER IDENTITY BECAUSE IT'S ESSENTAIL TO THEIR MENATL HEALTH. BEING FORCED TO USE A SPACE THAT IS DESIGNATED TO A GENDER THAT ONE DOES NOT IDENTIFY WITH MAY CAUSE DYSPHORIA AND STRESS.
TWO YEARS LATER.
I STILL HAVE NOT COME OUT AT WORK, AND I HAVE NEVER CORRECTED A COWORKER WHO HAS MISGENDERED ME. I DON'T HAVE TO. MIRACULOUSLY, BECAUSE OF SOCIAL MEDIA, WORD OF MOUTH, AND THE OBVIOUS PHYSICAL CHANGES, PEOPLE FIGURED IT OUT.
GOOD MORNING, SIR!
IT'S A PRIVILEGE TO EXPERIENCE SUCH A PHENOMENON. IT DOESN'T HAPPEN EVERYWHERE. MAYBE IT'S A SIGN THAT PEOPLE ARE CHANGING WITH THE TIMES. SIX YEARS AGO, AT A DIFFERENT STORE, ONE OF MY CO-WORKERS HAD A DIFFERENT EXPERIENCE THAN MINE.
I TALKED TO MANAGEMENT AND THEY AGREE, I CAN USE THE WOMEN'S RESTROOM.
YEAH! YOU SHOULD BE ABLE TO!
NOT EVERYONE HERE AGREES. SOME OF THE WOMEN HERE DO NOT WANT ME IN THERE. THEY HAVE BEEN VOCAL ABOUT IT.
THAT'S BULLSHIT!
I'M NOT SURE HOW MY CO-WORKERS FEEL ABOUT ME. SOME OF MY CO-WORKERS KNEW ME BEFORE MY TRANSITION, SO THEY KNOW I'M TRANS. A LOT OF CO-WORKERS ARE NEW AND THEY HAVE ONLY KNOWN ME AS A GUY. THEY MAY OR MAY NOT KNOW I'M TRANS. I ASSUME EVERYONE KNOWS I'M TRANS, BUT I CAN'T BE CERTAIN.
LOOKS LIKE THE COAST IS CLEAR.
PUSH
I FEEL CONFLICTED ABOUT WHICH RESTROOM TO USE, SO I KEEP USING THE WOMEN'S BECAUSE IT STILL FEELS COMFORTABLE. HOWEVER, IT'S REALLY STRESSFUL.

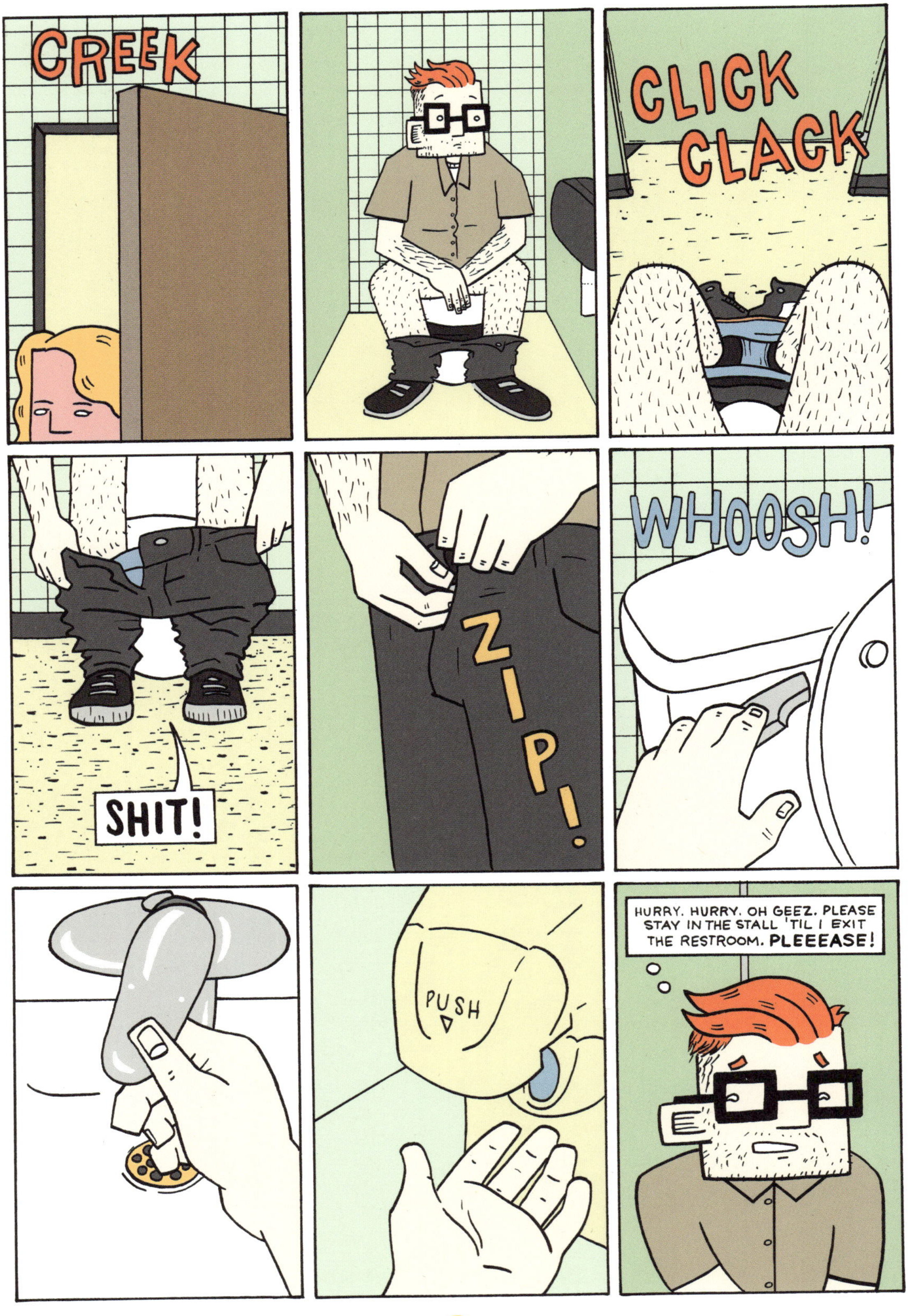
CREEK
CLICK CLACK
SHIT!
ZIP!
WHOOSH!
PUSH
HURRY. HURRY. OH GEEZ. PLEASE STAY IN THE STALL 'TIL I EXIT THE RESTROOM. PLEEEASE!

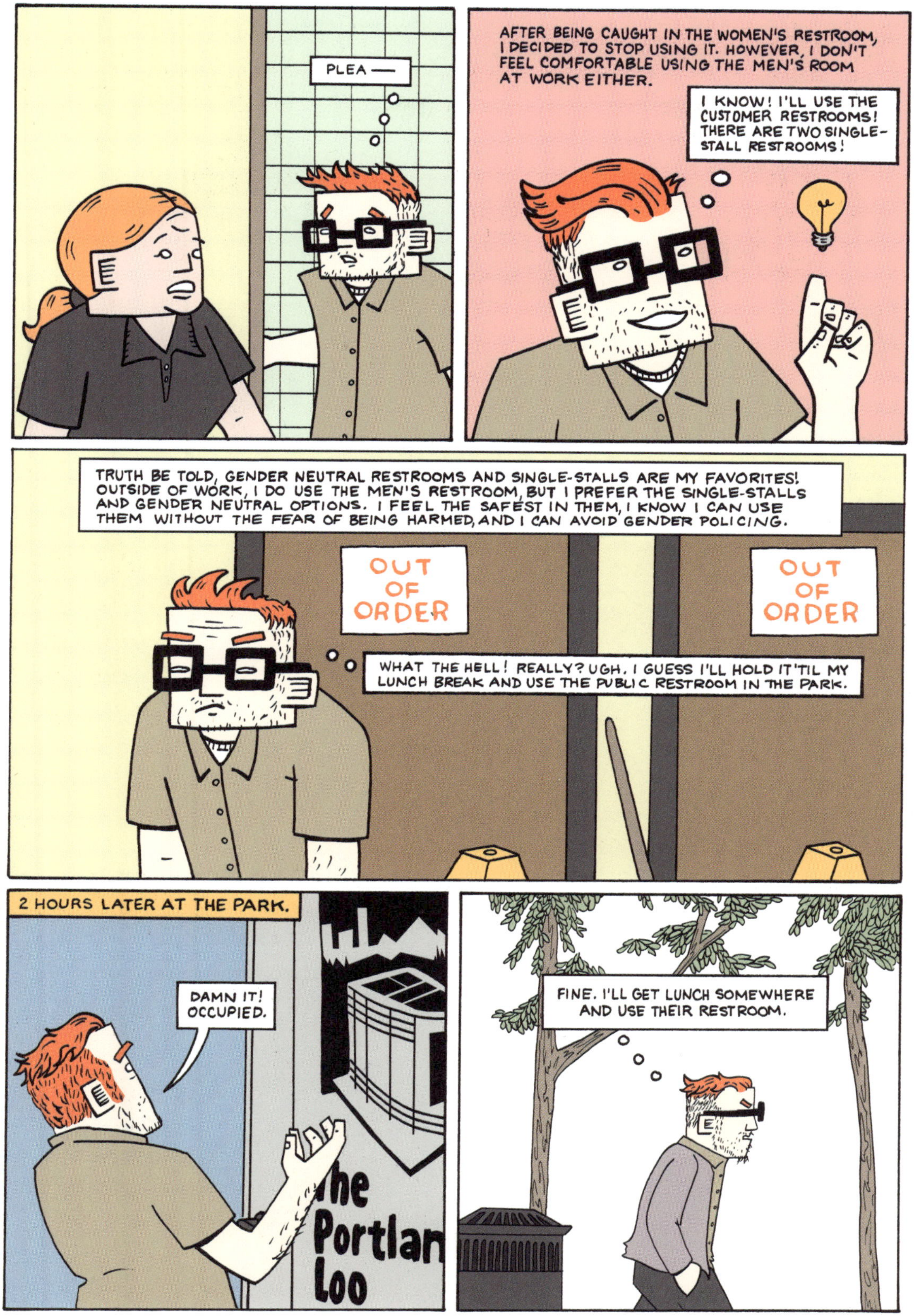
PLEA —
AFTER BEING CAUGHT IN THE WOMEN'S RESTROOM, I DECIDED TO STOP USING IT. HOWEVER, I DON'T FEEL COMFORTABLE USING THE MEN'S ROOM AT WORK EITHER.
I KNOW! I'LL USE THE CUSTOMER RESTROOMS! THERE ARE TWO SINGLE-STALL RESTROOMS!
TRUTH BE TOLD, GENDER NEUTRAL RESTROOMS AND SINGLE-STALLS ARE MY FAVORITES! OUTSIDE OF WORK, I DO USE THE MEN'S RESTROOM, BUT I PREFER THE SINGLE-STALLS AND GENDER NEUTRAL OPTIONS. I FEEL THE SAFEST IN THEM, I KNOW I CAN USE THEM WITHOUT THE FEAR OF BEING HARMED, AND I CAN AVOID GENDER POLICING.
OUT OF ORDER
OUT OF ORDER
WHAT THE HELL! REALLY? UGH. I GUESS I'LL HOLD IT 'TIL MY LUNCH BREAK AND USE THE PUBLIC RESTROOM IN THE PARK.
2 HOURS LATER AT THE PARK.
DAMN IT! OCCUPIED.
FINE. I'LL GET LUNCH SOMEWHERE AND USE THEIR RESTROOM.

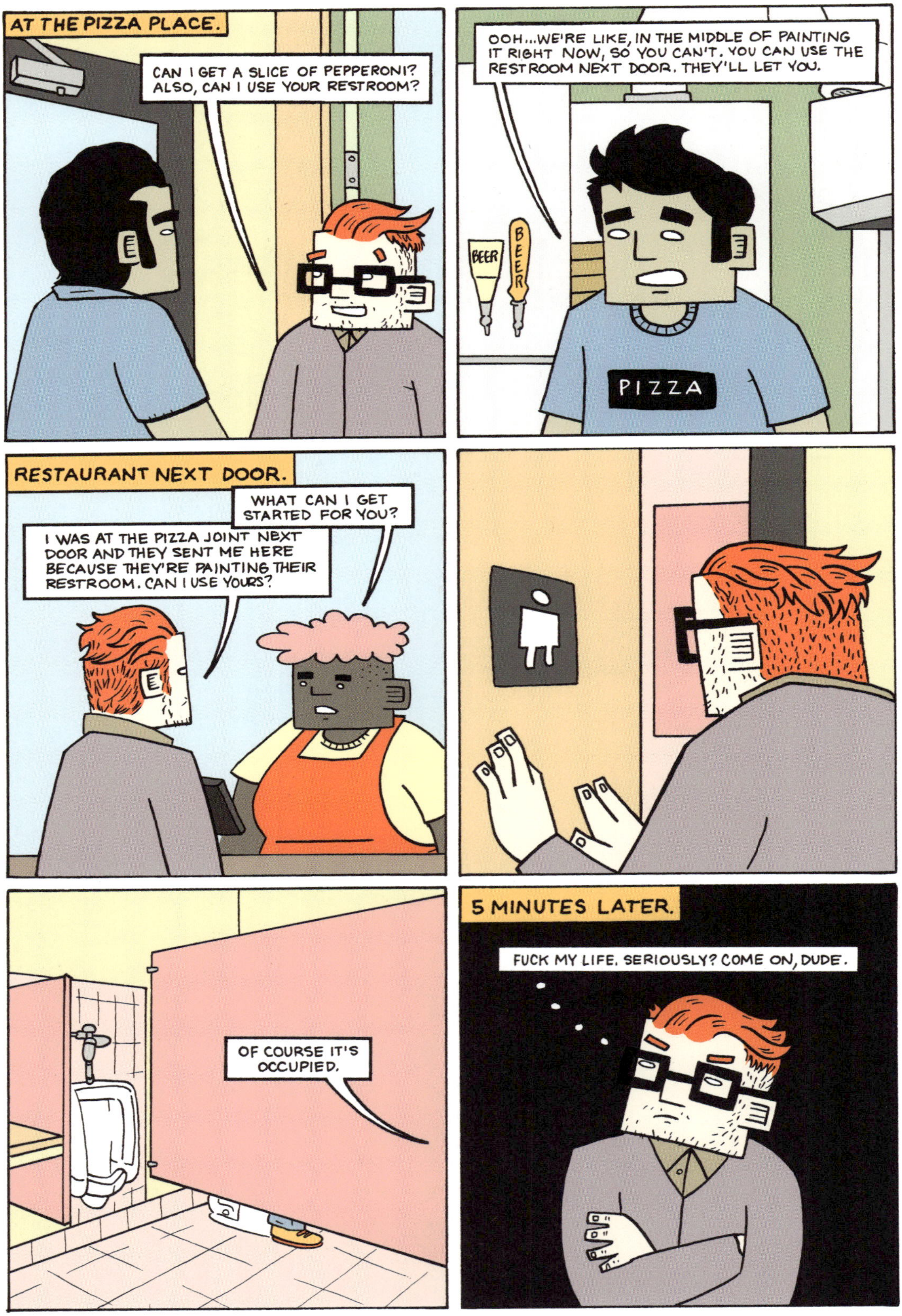
AT THE PIZZA PLACE.
CAN I GET A SLICE OF PEPPERONI? ALSO, CAN I USE YOUR RESTROOM?
OOH...WE'RE LIKE, IN THE MIDDLE OF PAINTING IT RIGHT NOW, SO YOU CAN'T. YOU CAN USE THE RESTROOM NEXT DOOR. THEY'LL LET YOU.
BEER
BEER
PIZZA
RESTAURANT NEXT DOOR.
WHAT CAN I GET STARTED FOR YOU?
I WAS AT THE PIZZA JOINT NEXT DOOR AND THEY SENT ME HERE BECAUSE THEY'RE PAINTING THEIR RESTROOM. CAN I USE YOURS?
OF COURSE IT'S OCCUPIED.
5 MINUTES LATER.
FUCK MY LIFE. SERIOUSLY? COME ON, DUDE.

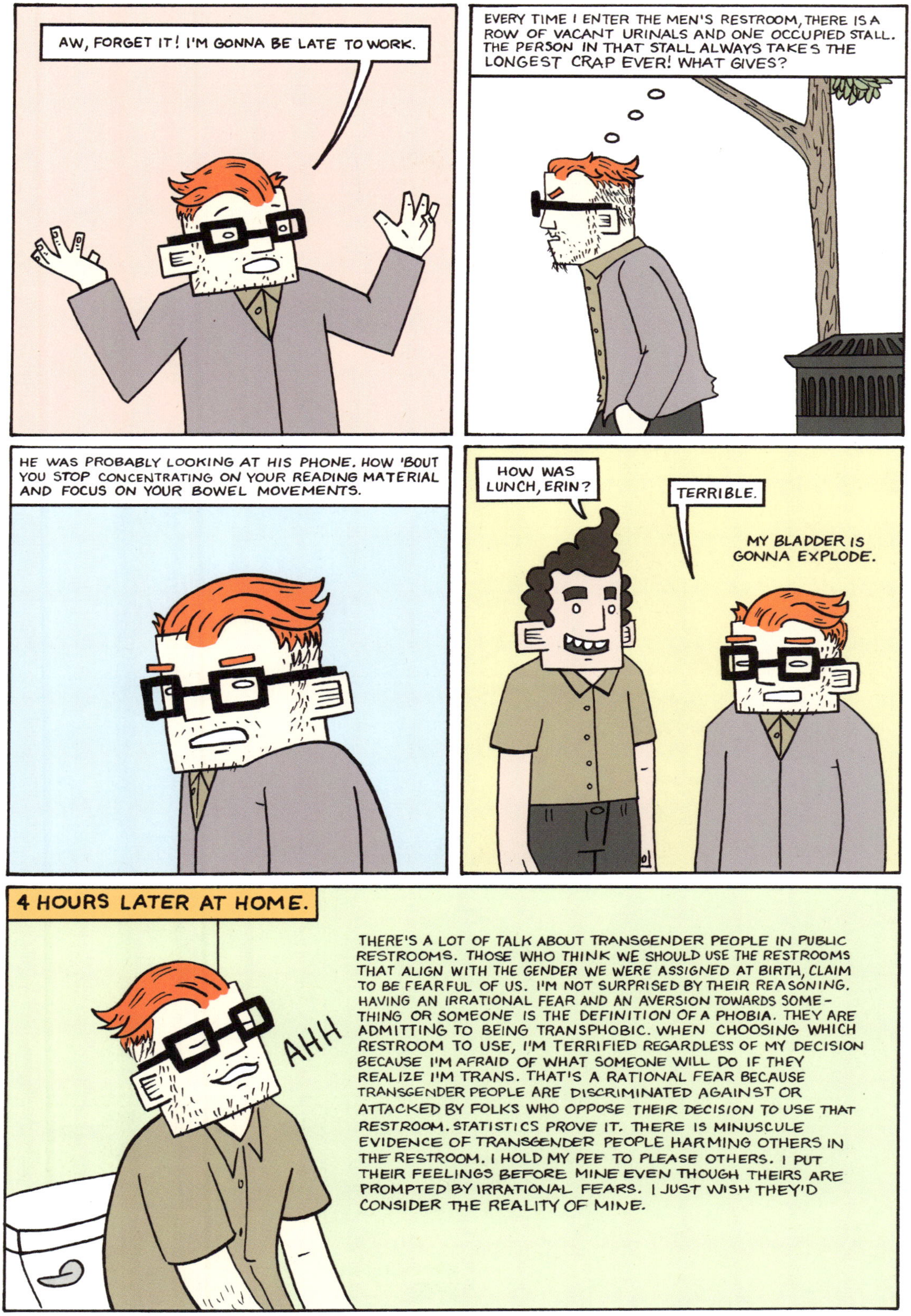

AW, FORGET IT! I'M GONNA BE LATE TO WORK.
EVERY TIME I ENTER THE MEN'S RESTROOM, THERE IS A ROW OF VACANT URINALS AND ONE OCCUPIED STALL. THE PERSON IN THAT STALL ALWAYS TAKES THE LONGEST CRAP EVER! WHAT GIVES?
HE WAS PROBABLY LOOKING AT HIS PHONE. HOW 'BOUT YOU STOP CONCENTRATING ON YOUR READING MATERIAL AND FOCUS ON YOUR BOWEL MOVEMENTS.
HOW WAS LUNCH, ERIN?
TERRIBLE.
MY BLADDER IS GONNA EXPLODE.
4 HOURS LATER AT HOME.
AHH
THERE'S A LOT OF TALK ABOUT TRANSGENDER PEOPLE IN PUBLIC RESTROOMS. THOSE WHO THINK WE SHOULD USE THE RESTROOMS THAT ALIGN WITH THE GENDER WE WERE ASSIGNED AT BIRTH, CLAIM TO BE FEARFUL OF US. I'M NOT SURPRISED BY THEIR REASONING. HAVING AN IRRATIONAL FEAR AND AN AVERSION TOWARDS SOME-THING OR SOMEONE IS THE DEFINITION OF A PHOBIA. THEY ARE ADMITTING TO BEING TRANSPHOBIC. WHEN CHOOSING WHICH RESTROOM TO USE, I'M TERRIFIED REGARDLESS OF MY DECISION BECAUSE I'M AFRAID OF WHAT SOMEONE WILL DO IF THEY REALIZE I'M TRANS. THAT'S A RATIONAL FEAR BECAUSE TRANSGENDER PEOPLE ARE DISCRIMINATED AGAINST OR ATTACKED BY FOLKS WHO OPPOSE THEIR DECISION TO USE THAT RESTROOM. STATISTICS PROVE IT. THERE IS MINUSCULE EVIDENCE OF TRANSGENDER PEOPLE HARMING OTHERS IN THE RESTROOM. I HOLD MY PEE TO PLEASE OTHERS. I PUT THEIR FEELINGS BEFORE MINE EVEN THOUGH THEIRS ARE PROMPTED BY IRRATIONAL FEARS. I JUST WISH THEY'D CONSIDER THE REALITY OF MINE.

HAND-HOLDING

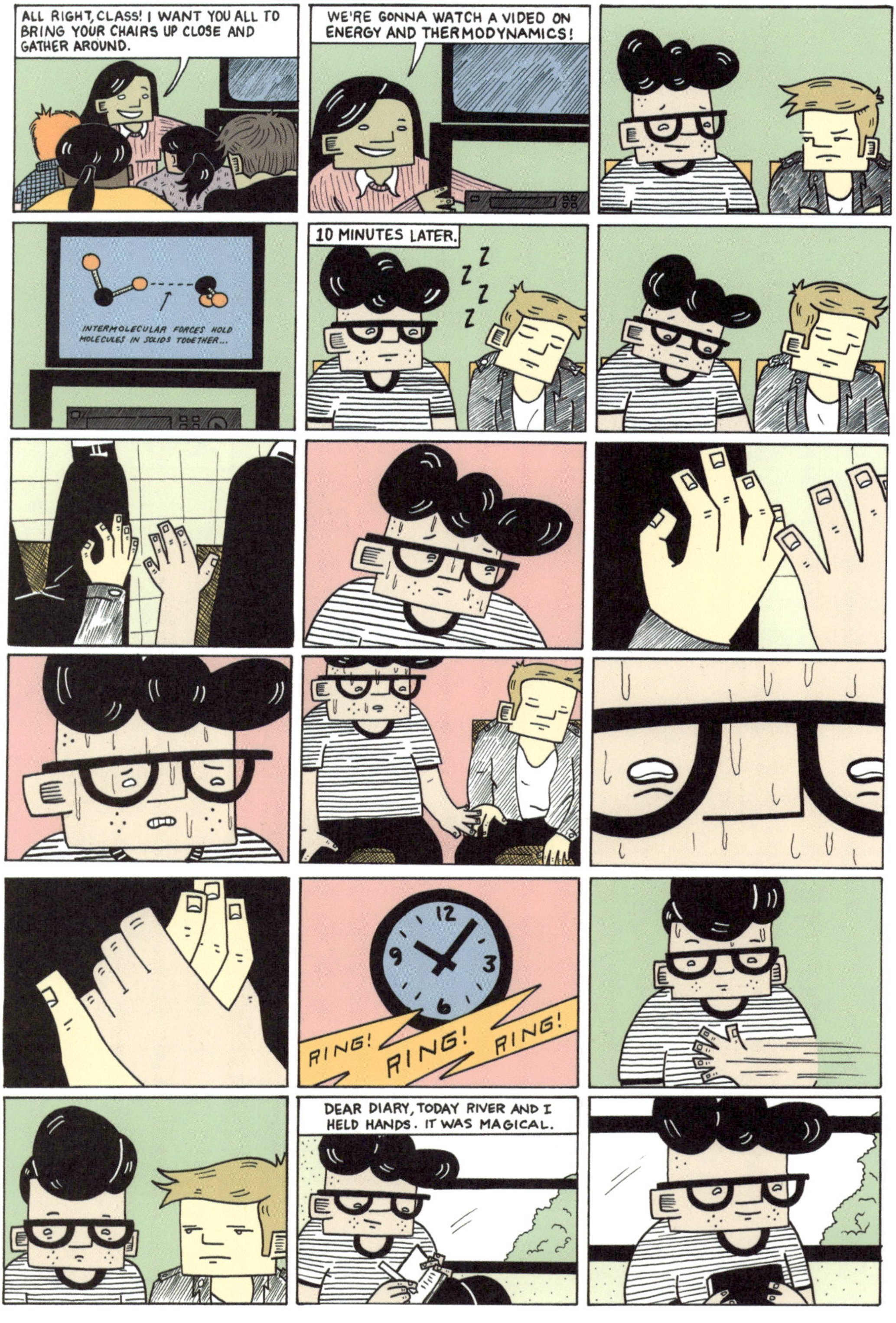

ALL RIGHT, CLASS! I WANT YOU ALL TO BRING YOUR CHAIRS UP CLOSE AND GATHER AROUND.
WE'RE GONNA WATCH A VIDEO ON ENERGY AND THERMODYNAMICS!
INTERMOLECULAR FORCES HOLD MOLECULES IN SOLIDS TOGETHER...
10 MINUTES LATER.
Z Z Z Z
12
3
6
9
RING!
RING!
RING!
DEAR DIARY, TODAY RIVER AND I HELD HANDS. IT WAS MAGICAL.

PRIMARY COLORS

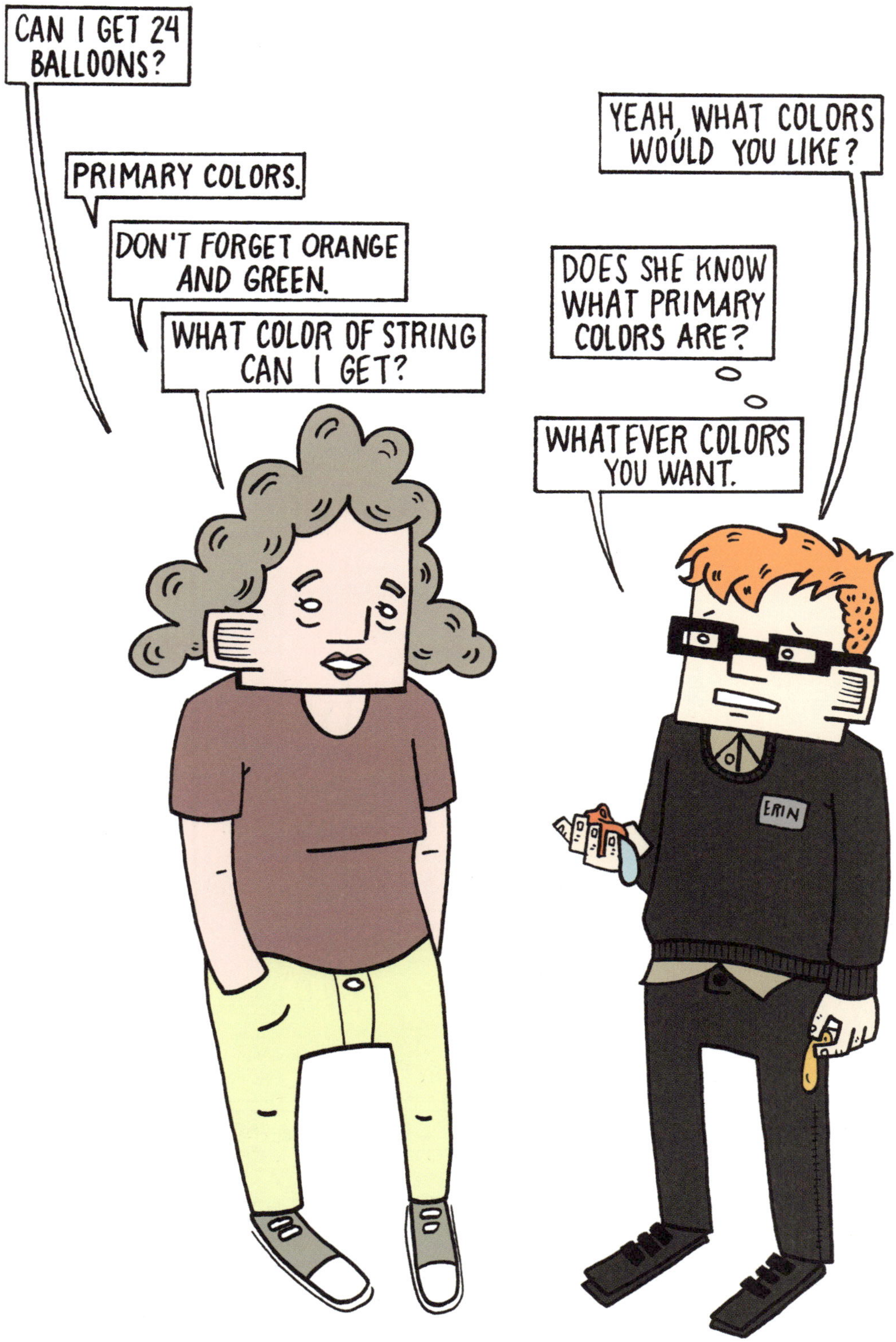
CAN I GET 24 BALLOONS?
YEAH, WHAT COLORS WOULD YOU LIKE?
PRIMARY COLORS.
DON'T FORGET ORANGE AND GREEN.
DOES SHE KNOW WHAT PRIMARY COLORS ARE?
WHAT COLOR OF STRING CAN I GET?
WHATEVER COLORS YOU WANT.
ERIN

TATUM

I'M REQUESTING A LOVER WHO SMELLS LIKE SANDALWOOD AND WHO WORKS WITH THEIR HANDS.

MY NAME IS TATUM. MY AGE IS IRRELEVANT.

I HAVE A YOUTHFUL SPIRIT AND UNPARALLELED WISDOM.

A TYPICAL DAY FOR ME BEGINS WITH TAKING A DEEP BREATH AND THEN EXHALING. AFTER RISING, I FIND A WARM SHAFT OF LIGHT TO SIT IN, DRINK MATCHA TEA OUT OF A MASON JAR, AND READ KEROUAC.

I'M AN ARTIST THAT WEARS PAINT ON MY PANTS TO PROVE IT. I REFUSE TO WORK FOR THE MAN AND BE OPPRESSED. WHEN I LEAVE MY GRANDMA'S NEST, I WILL GET BY WITH BARTER AND ART COMMISSIONS.

FOR A COMPANION, I'M SEEKING AN OLD SOUL LIKE MYSELF. I DESIRE SOMEONE WITH THE STRENGTH AND COURAGE OF AN EAGLE. I WANT SOMEONE WHO WILL EXPRESS HIS/HERSELF SENSUALLY AND EXUDE HARMONY. I WANT A MATE WHO ENJOYS CATCHING BUTTERFLIES WHILE BAREFOOT. WE'LL CLIMB AND DWELL IN TREES LIKE ORANGUTANS. WE'LL HIDE UNDER WATERFALLS AND SPEND ENDLESS HOURS FEELING EACH OTHER'S VALLEYS AND HILLS AS OUR TONGUES AND LIPS COPULATE.

IF YOU FEEL MY WORDS, FOLLOW YOUR HEART AND SEND ME A SIGNAL.

ONE WEEK AT THE SOU'WESTER

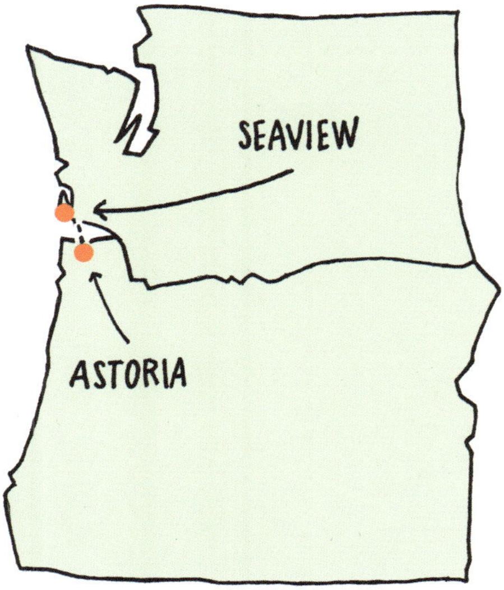
SEAVIEW
ASTORIA

FIFTEEN MILES NORTH OF ASTORIA, OREGON LIES THE SOU'WESTER LODGE. IT'S LOCATED IN SEAVIEW, WASHINGTON, ON THE LONG BEACH PENINSULA.

THE SOU'WESTER IS DESCRIBED AS A "BOHEMIAN RESORT." GUESTS HAVE THE OPTION OF STAYING AT THE LODGE, A COTTAGE, OR ONE OF THE MANY VINTAGE TRAILERS.

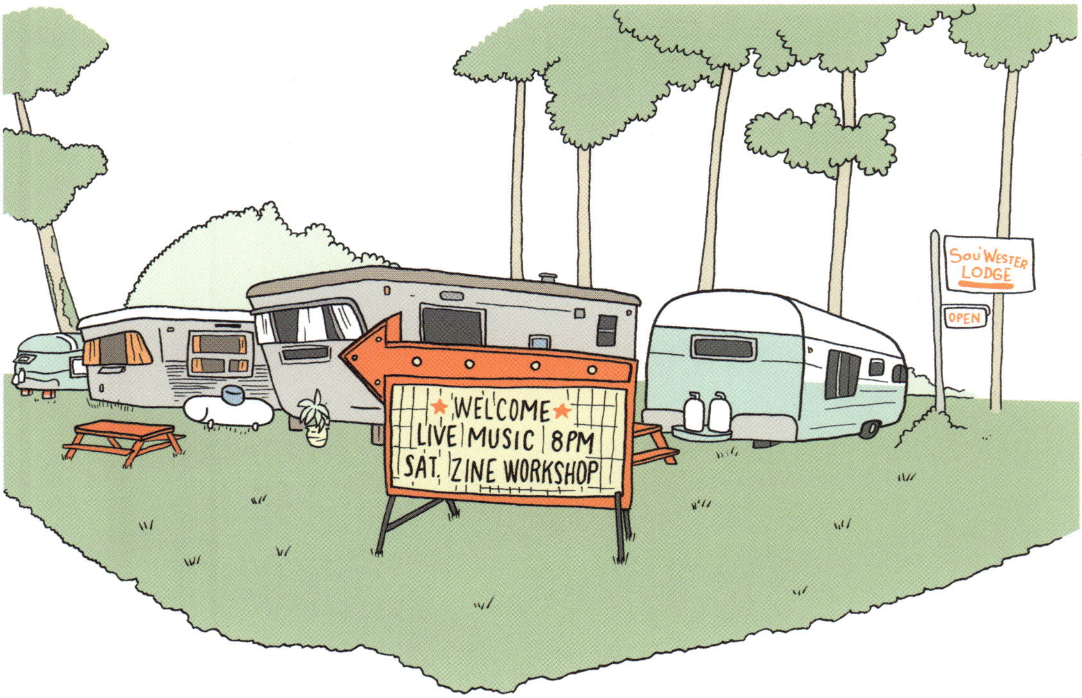
SOU'WESTER LODGE
OPEN
WELCOME
LIVE MUSIC 8PM
SAT. ZINE WORKSHOP

I SPENT A WEEK IN ONE OF THE TRAILERS DURING MY ARTIST RESIDENCY THERE.

THE ZELMAR CRUISER

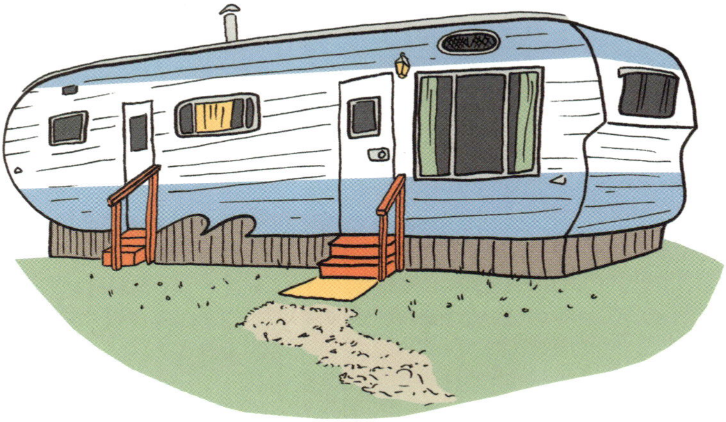

BEFORE ARRIVING, I STOPPED AT THE MERRY TIME RESTAURANT AND LOUNGE IN ASTORIA. A FRIEND, WHO WAS GIVING ME A LIFT, JOINED ME. WE HAD A SHOT OF WHISKEY AND A PABST.

A FACE MASK OF SLOTH WAS NAILED ABOVE THE DOOR. IT SEEMED APPROPRIATE CONSIDERING THE GOONIES WAS FILMED IN ASTORIA. ONCE UPON A TIME, PEOPLE COULD VISIT THE GOONIES' HOUSE. UNFORTUNATELY, THE OWNER OF THE HOUSE AND HER NEIGHBORS PUT AN END TO THAT LAST YEAR BECAUSE SOME TOURISTS WERE BEING DICKS.

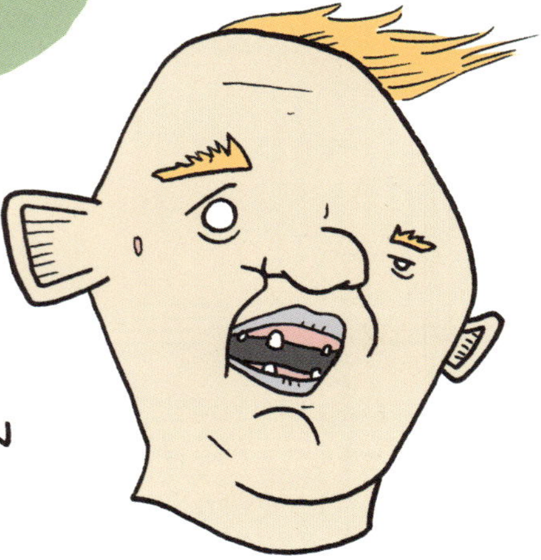

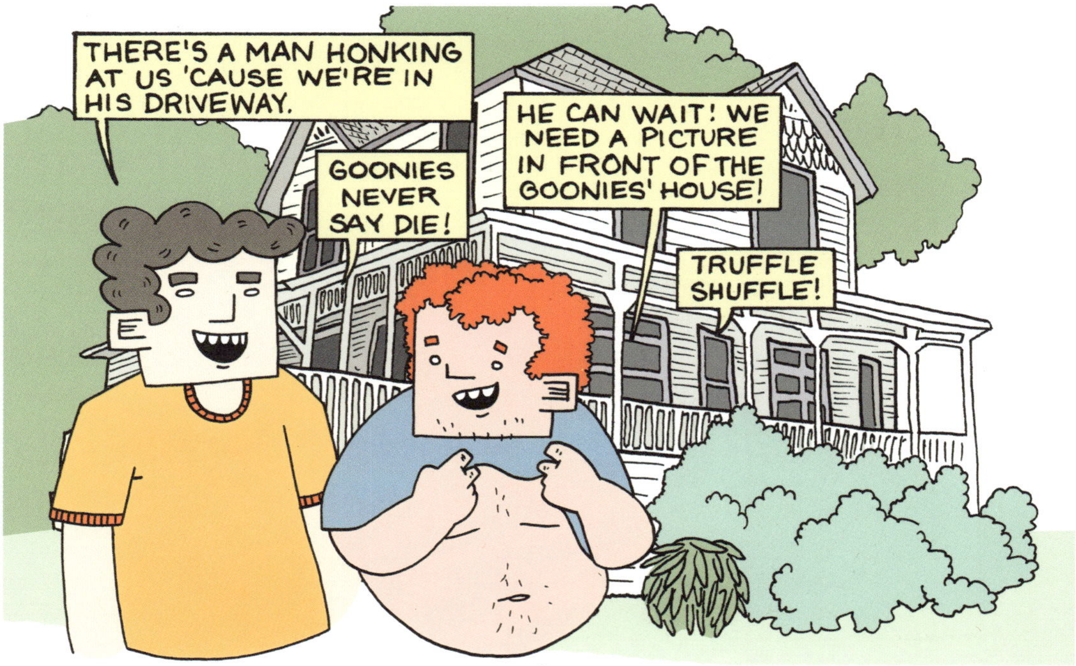
THERE'S A MAN HONKING AT US 'CAUSE WE'RE IN HIS DRIVEWAY.
GOONIES NEVER SAY DIE!
HE CAN WAIT! WE NEED A PICTURE IN FRONT OF THE GOONIES' HOUSE!
TRUFFLE SHUFFLE!

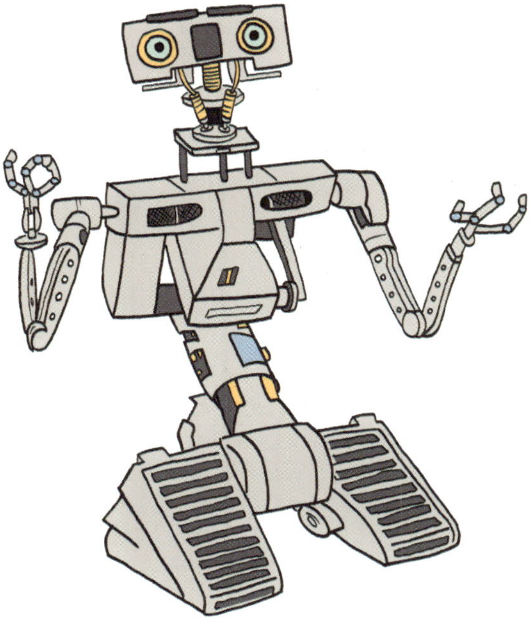

VISITORS SHOULD NOT FRET. A FEW BLOCKS AWAY IS JOHN JACOB ASTOR ELEMENTARY, WHICH IS THE SCHOOL THAT APPEARS IN KINDERGARTEN COP. ANYONE IS FREE TO VIEW THAT BUILDING. OTHER NOTABLE MOVIES THAT HAVE BEEN FILMED IN ASTORIA INCLUDE SHORT CIRCUIT AND FREE WILLY.

AROUND 4:00 PM, WE ARRIVED AT THE SOU'WESTER. WE SPLIT A BEER. THEN, MY FRIEND HEADED BACK TO PORTLAND. I SPENT THE REMAINDER OF THE DAY WRITING AND LISTENING TO HANK WILLIAMS ON A FISHER PRICE PORTABLE RECORD PLAYER THAT WAS SUPPLIED BY THE LODGE.

THE FOLLOWING DAY, I WOKE UP AT 5AM, PREPARED BREAKFAST, MADE COFFEE, LISTENED TO A PODCAST, AND BEGAN WORKING. I FELL INTO THE SAME ROUTINE EVERY DAY.

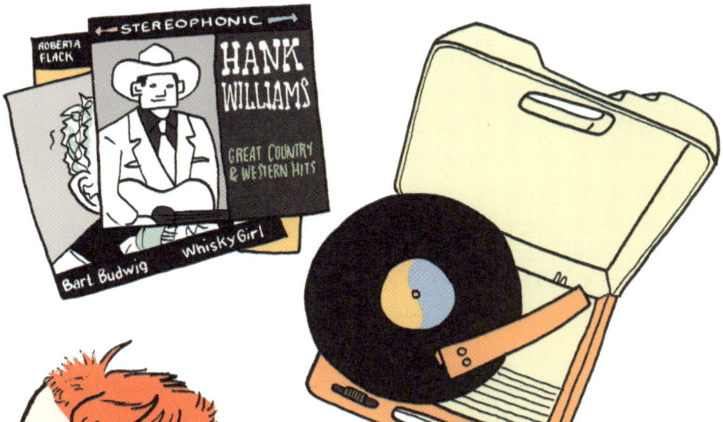
ROBERTA FLACK
STEREOPHONIC
HANK WILLIAMS
GREAT COUNTRY & WESTERN HITS
Bart Budwig
WhiskyGirl

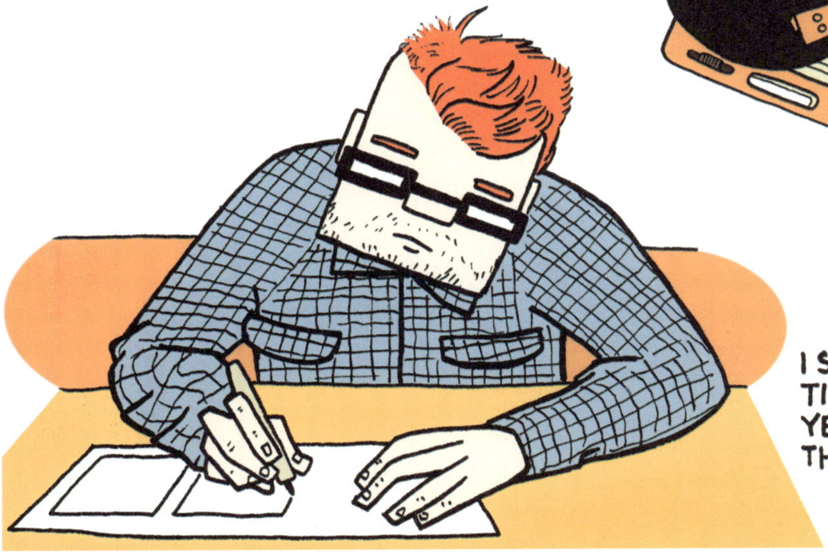

I SPENT MOST MY TIME AT THE LITTLE YELLOW TABLE IN THE KITCHEN.

WHILE WORKING, I LISTENED TO BIRDS CHIRPING OUTSIDE THE WINDOW, VINYL RECORDS SPINNING, AND PITTER-PATTER FROM THE RAIN HITTING THE TRAILER. IT RAINED FOR TWO DAYS STRAIGHT.

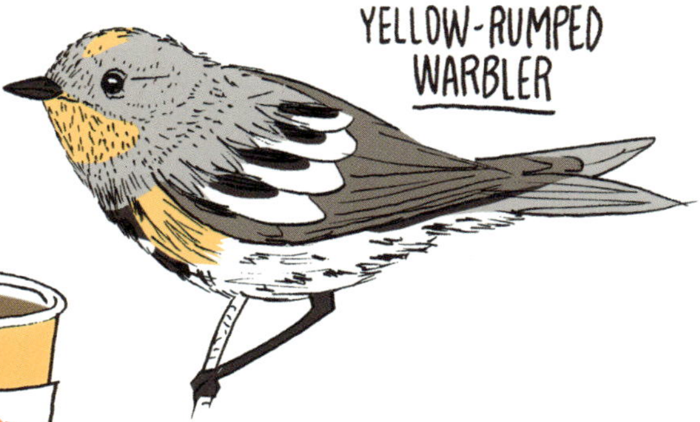

YELLOW-RUMPED WARBLER

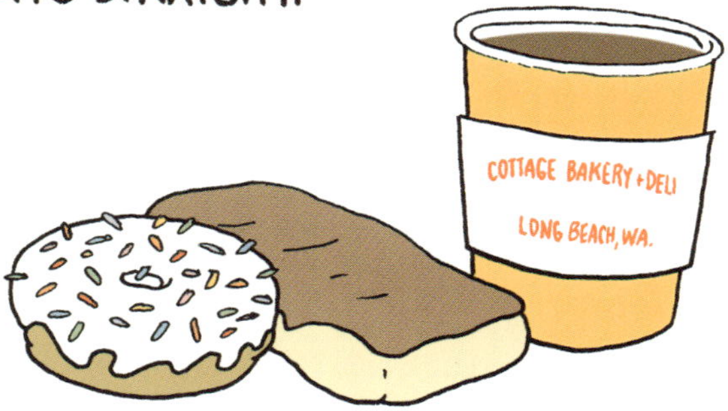
COTTAGE BAKERY + DELI
LONG BEACH, WA.

AFTER THREE DAYS, I BEGAN TO EXPERIENCE CABIN FEVER. I DECIDED TO WALK A MILE TO LONG BEACH. I GRABBED A COUPLE DONUTS AND COFFEE BECAUSE I NEEDED THEM FOR SURVIVAL.

WHEN I LEFT THE DONUT SHOP, I HIT UP MARSH'S FREE MUSEUM.

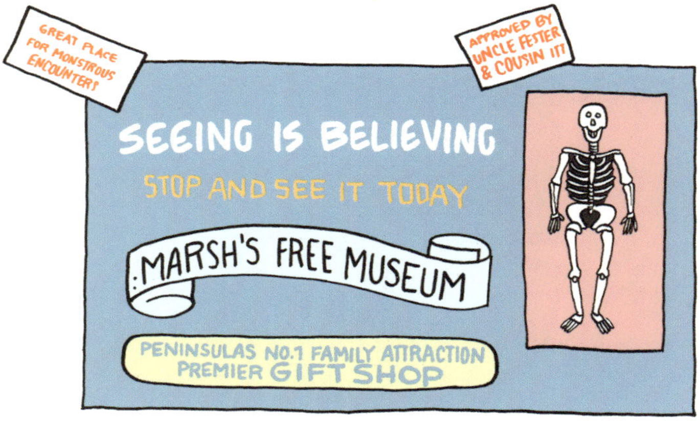
GREAT PLACE FOR MONSTROUS ENCOUNTERS
APPROVED BY UNCLE FESTER & COUSIN ITT
SEEING IS BELIEVING
STOP AND SEE IT TODAY
MARSH'S FREE MUSEUM
PENINSULAS NO.1 FAMILY ATTRACTION
PREMIER GIFT SHOP

THE MUSEUM WAS FILLED WITH BULLSHIT THAT'S SOLD EXCLUSIVELY AT COASTAL TOURIST TRAPS.

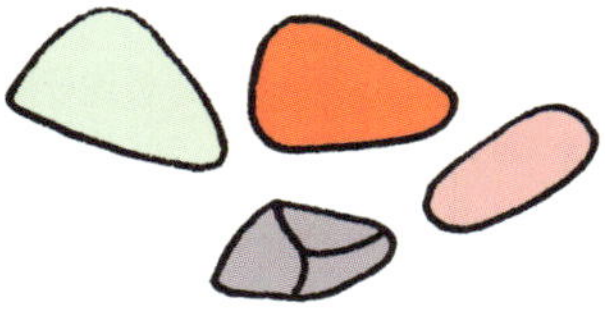

SHINY ROCKS

NOVELTY BIKE PLATES WITH NAMES

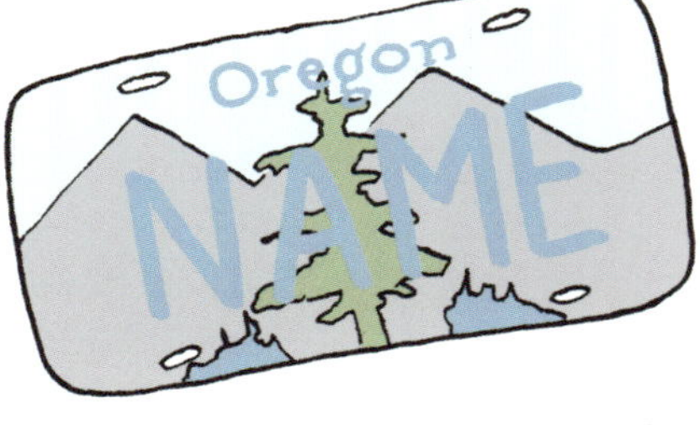
Oregon
NAME

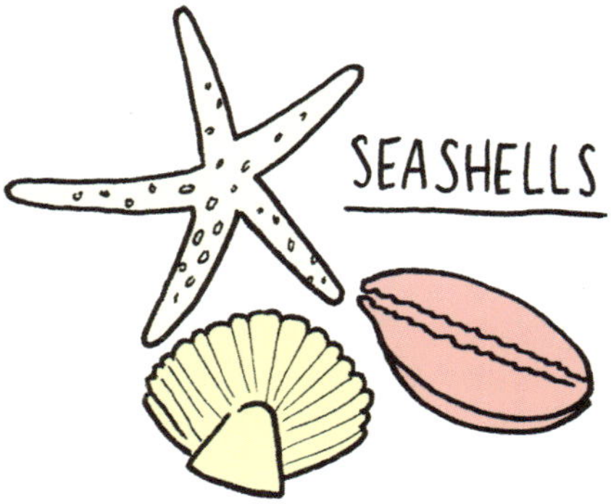

SEASHELLS

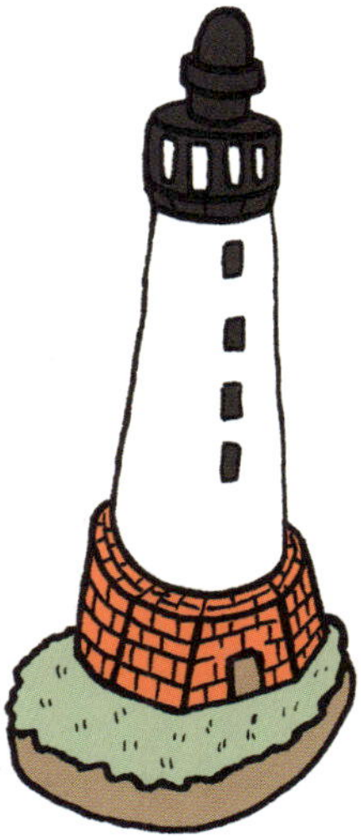

NAUTICAL PARAPHERNALIA

UNCONTROLLABLE
HOT STUFF
PASSIONATE
BURNING
WILD
NAUGHTY BUT NICE
MILD
HARMLESS
CLAMMY
TRY AGAIN
TEST YOUR LOVE!
25¢

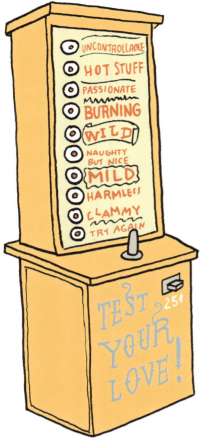

MARSH'S ALSO HOUSED SEVERAL OLD PENNY ARCADES SUCH AS PEEP SHOW MACHINES, LOVE TESTERS, AND FORTUNE-TELLERS. NONE OF THEM WORKED.

MARSH'S MAJOR CLAIM TO FAME IS JAKE THE ALLIGATOR MAN. JAKE IS PART ALLIGATOR AND PART MAN. HIS MUMMIFIED BODY RESIDES IN A GLASS BOX WITH SAND AND A PIECE OF DRIFTWOOD. JAKE COULD BE A HOAX. HOWEVER, IN '93 HE WAS ON THE COVER OF THE WEEKLY WORLD NEWS, SO CLEARLY HE'S LEGIT.

I DECIDED I COULDN'T LEAVE MARSH'S WITHOUT A SOUVENIR. I BOUGHT A BUTTON AND A PENCIL THAT I'LL NEVER USE. THESE TREASURES WILL BE PLACED IN A DRAWER AND FORGOTTEN ABOUT, BUT AT THE TIME I FELT LIKE I NEEDED THEM.

MY FRIEND JAKE
SHA'S FREE MUSEUM

WASH
"WORLD'S LARGEST FRYING PAN." NOT TO SCALE.

AS I WALKED HOME, I SPOTTED THE "WORLD'S LARGEST FRYING PAN." THIS CLAIM IS DEBATABLE. AFTER DOING AN INTERNET SEARCH, I LEARNED THE WORLD'S LARGEST FRYING PAN ALSO RESIDES IN IOWA AND NORTH CAROLINA.

THE NIGHT BEFORE I LEFT, MY FRIEND RETURNED TO PICK ME UP. WE DRANK WHISKEY AND LISTENED TO RECORDS.

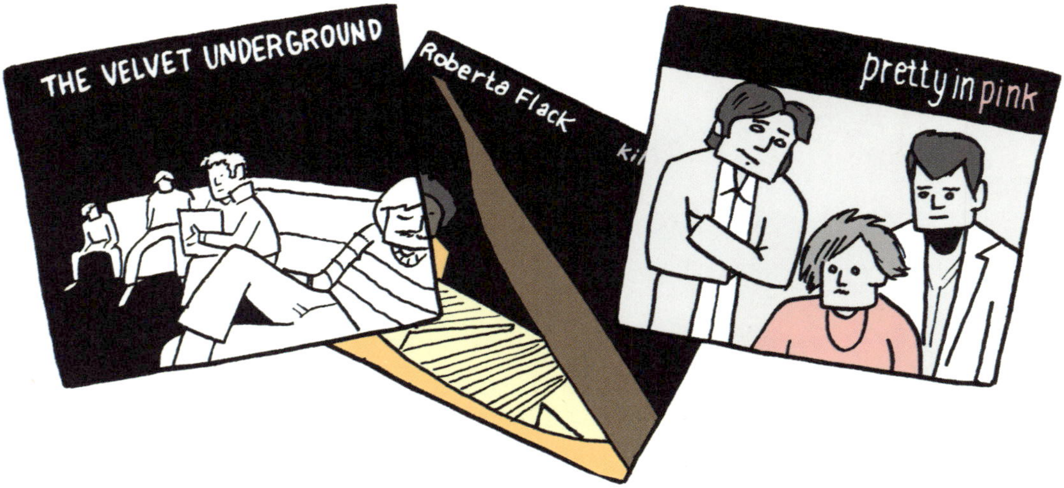
THE VELVET UNDERGROUND
Roberta Flack
pretty in pink

AS WE WATCHED THE SUNSET ON THE BEACH, WE ATE PIZZA AND DRANK BEER.

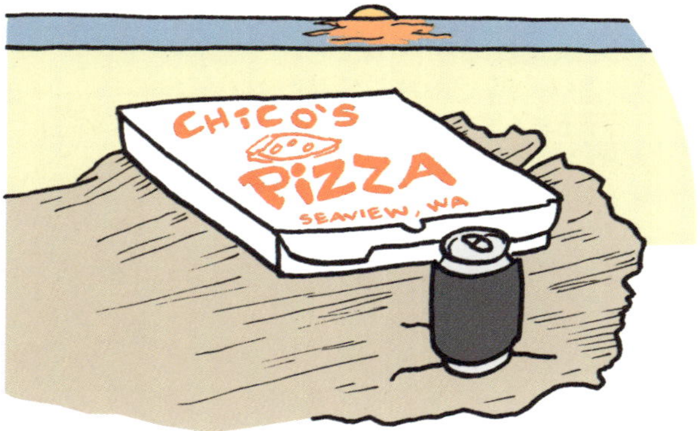
CHICO'S
PIZZA
SEAVIEW, WA

WE ENDED THE NIGHT AT ROD'S LAMPLIGHTER, A DIVE BAR NEXT DOOR. IT WAS BRIGHTLY LIT AND OFF-PUTTING. A DRUNK WOMAN AND A DRUNK MAN WERE THE ONLY OTHER PATRONS IN THE BAR. THEY PLEADED WITH US TO SING KARAOKE. WE DECLINED. THEY SANG "ROCK LOBSTER" AND "DON'T STOP BELIEVIN'."

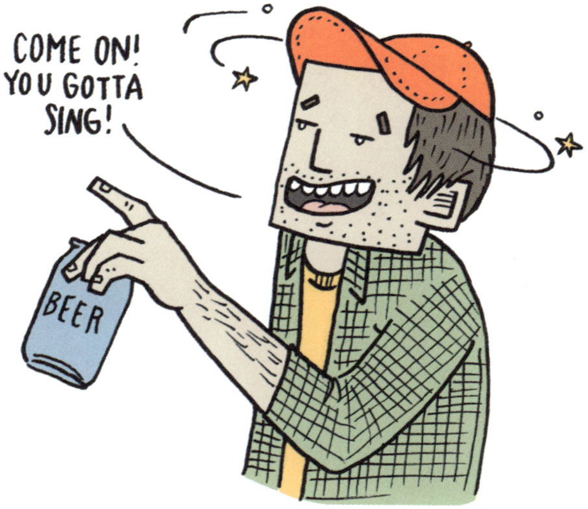
COME ON! YOU GOTTA SING!
BEER

THE NEXT MORNING, I RETURNED ALL THE RECORDS I BORROWED. I PACKED MY ART SUPPLIES AND PUT AWAY THE LOOSE PAGES OF COMICS I HAD COMPLETED.
I CHECKED OUT.
WE GOT ON THE 101 AND HEADED HOME.

UNREQUITED LOVE

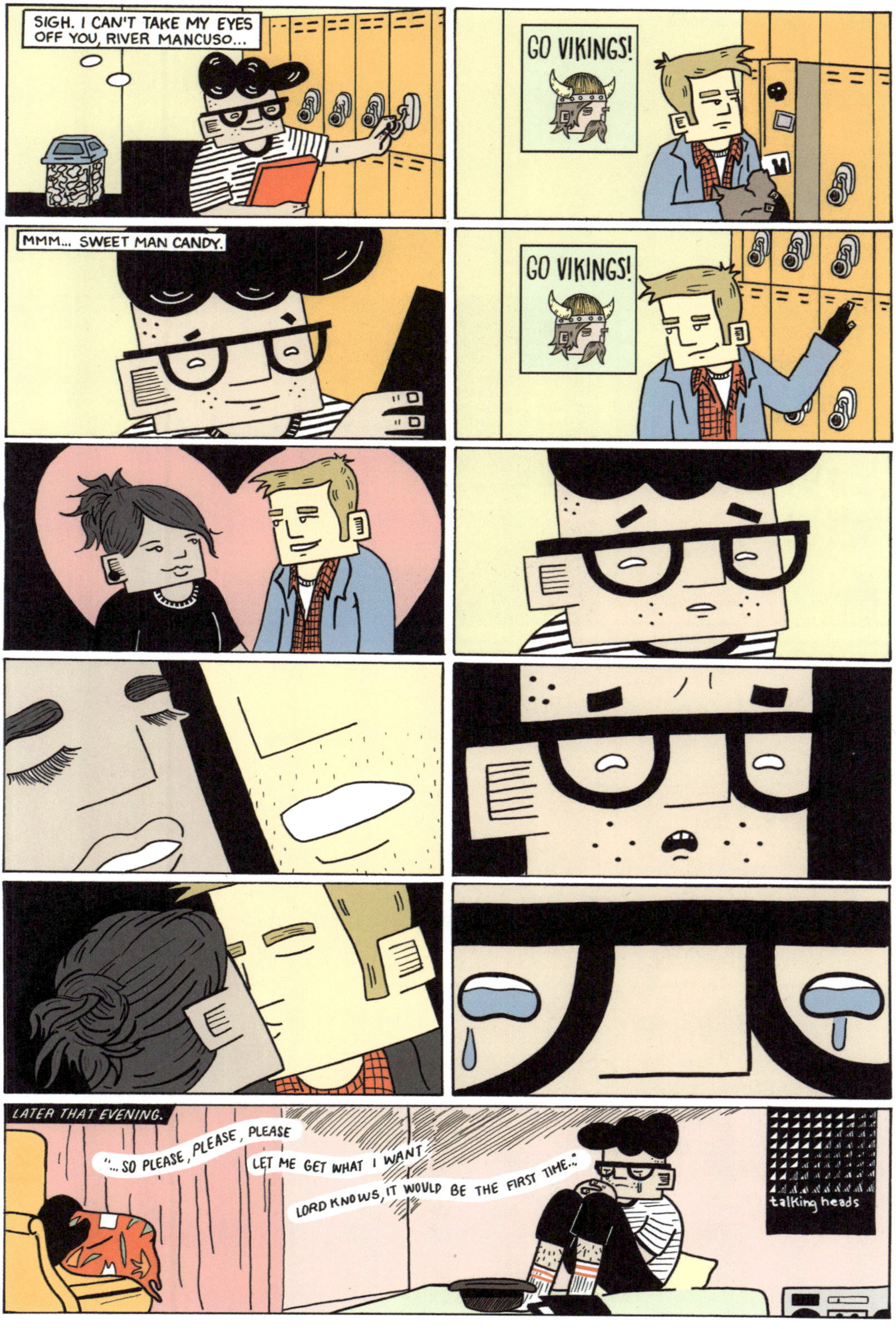

SIGH. I CAN'T TAKE MY EYES OFF YOU, RIVER MANCUSO...
GO VIKINGS!
MMM... SWEET MAN CANDY.
GO VIKINGS!
LATER THAT EVENING.
"... SO PLEASE, PLEASE, PLEASE
LET ME GET WHAT I WANT
LORD KNOWS, IT WOULD BE THE FIRST TIME..."
talking heads

VASECTOMY

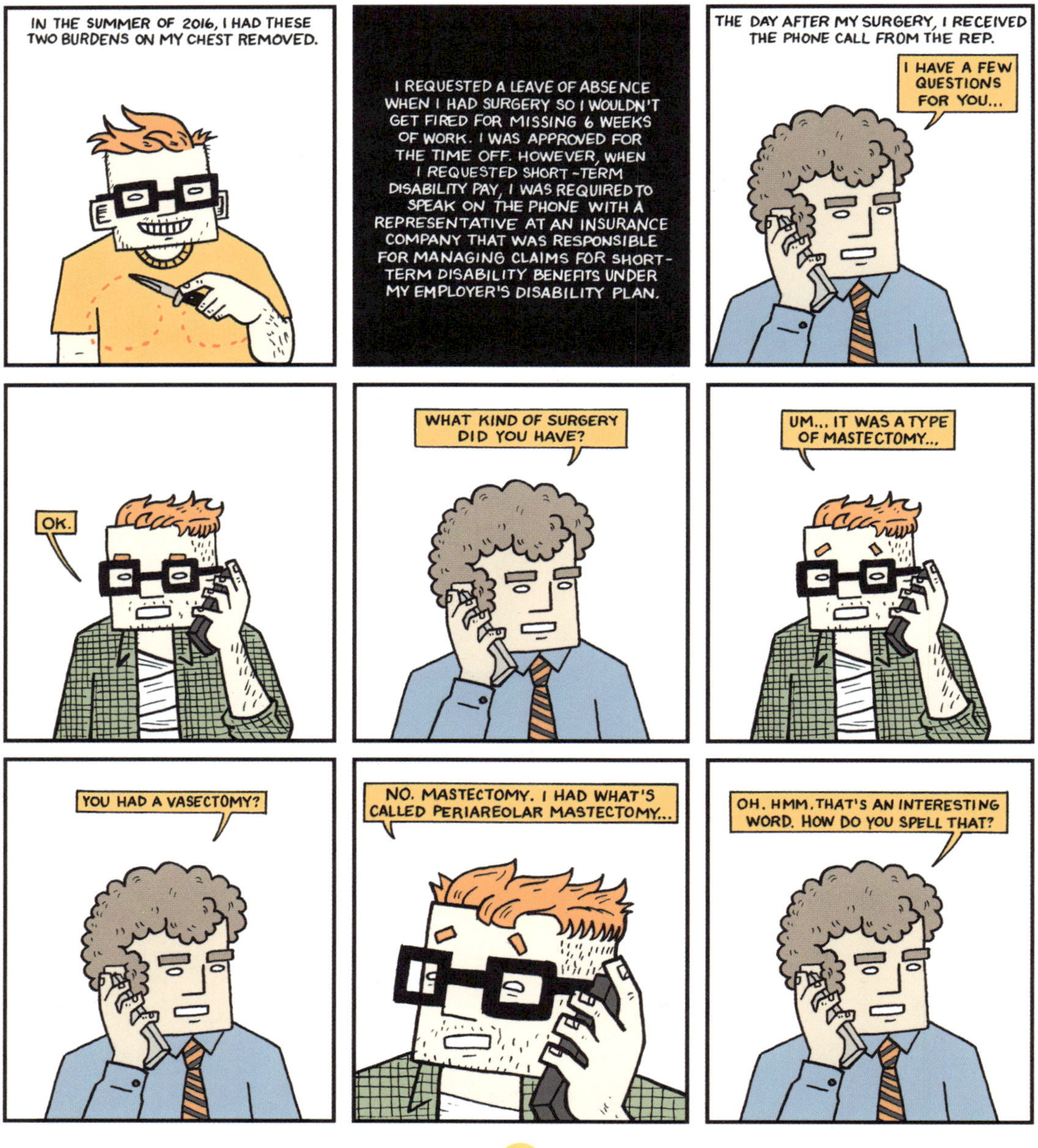
IN THE SUMMER OF 2016, I HAD THESE TWO BURDENS ON MY CHEST REMOVED.
I REQUESTED A LEAVE OF ABSENCE WHEN I HAD SURGERY SO I WOULDN'T GET FIRED FOR MISSING 6 WEEKS OF WORK. I WAS APPROVED FOR THE TIME OFF. HOWEVER, WHEN I REQUESTED SHORT-TERM DISABILITY PAY, I WAS REQUIRED TO SPEAK ON THE PHONE WITH A REPRESENTATIVE AT AN INSURANCE COMPANY THAT WAS RESPONSIBLE FOR MANAGING CLAIMS FOR SHORT-TERM DISABILITY BENEFITS UNDER MY EMPLOYER'S DISABILITY PLAN.
THE DAY AFTER MY SURGERY, I RECEIVED THE PHONE CALL FROM THE REP.
I HAVE A FEW QUESTIONS FOR YOU...
OK.
WHAT KIND OF SURGERY DID YOU HAVE?
UM... IT WAS A TYPE OF MASTECTOMY...
YOU HAD A VASECTOMY?
NO. MASTECTOMY. I HAD WHAT'S CALLED PERIAREOLAR MASTECTOMY...
OH. HMM. THAT'S AN INTERESTING WORD. HOW DO YOU SPELL THAT?

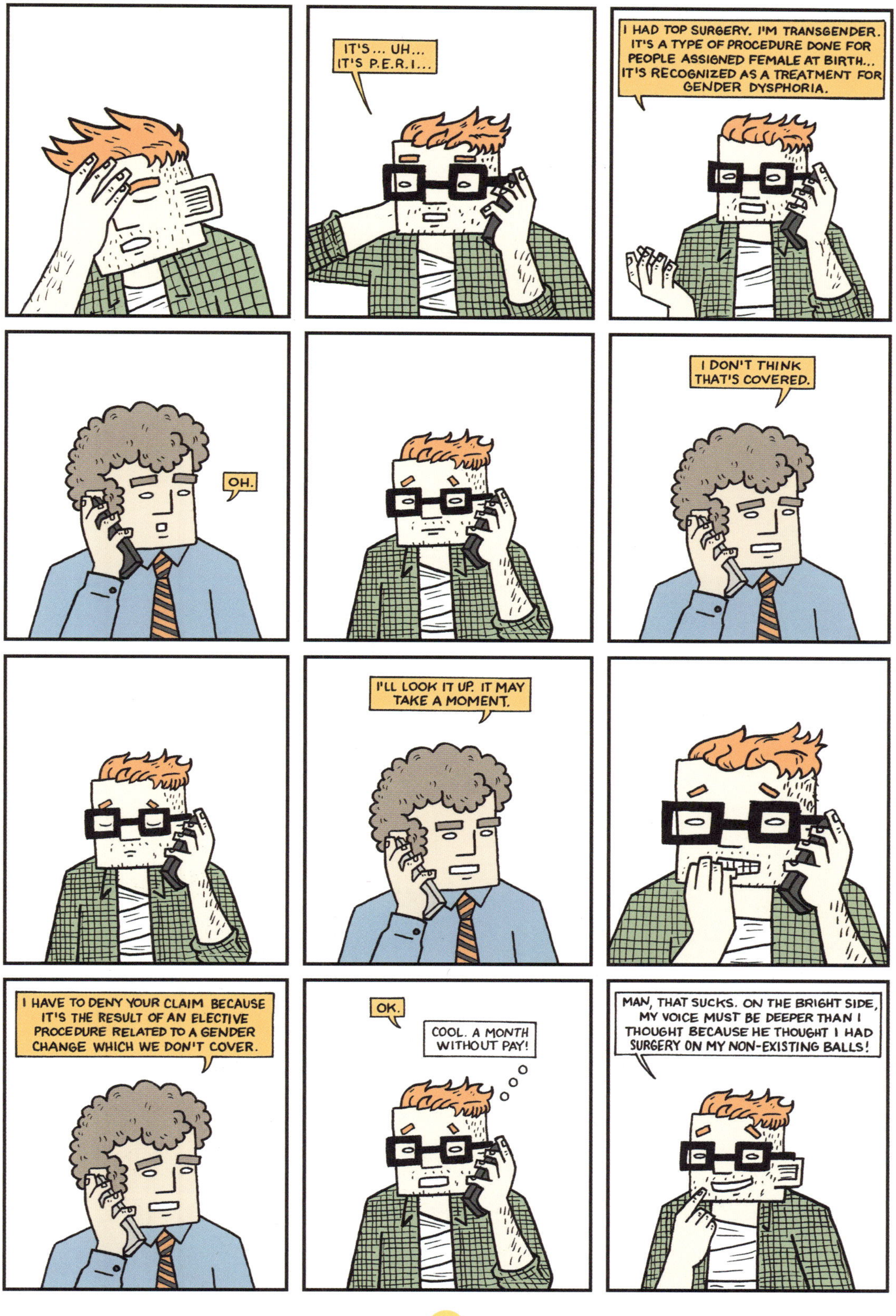
IT'S... UH... IT'S P.E.R.I...
I HAD TOP SURGERY. I'M TRANSGENDER. IT'S A TYPE OF PROCEDURE DONE FOR PEOPLE ASSIGNED FEMALE AT BIRTH... IT'S RECOGNIZED AS A TREATMENT FOR GENDER DYSPHORIA.
OH.
I DON'T THINK THAT'S COVERED.
I'LL LOOK IT UP. IT MAY TAKE A MOMENT.
I HAVE TO DENY YOUR CLAIM BECAUSE IT'S THE RESULT OF AN ELECTIVE PROCEDURE RELATED TO A GENDER CHANGE WHICH WE DON'T COVER.
OK.
COOL. A MONTH WITHOUT PAY!
MAN, THAT SUCKS. ON THE BRIGHT SIDE, MY VOICE MUST BE DEEPER THAN I THOUGHT BECAUSE HE THOUGHT I HAD SURGERY ON MY NON-EXISTING BALLS!

ORGANIC CUCUMBERS

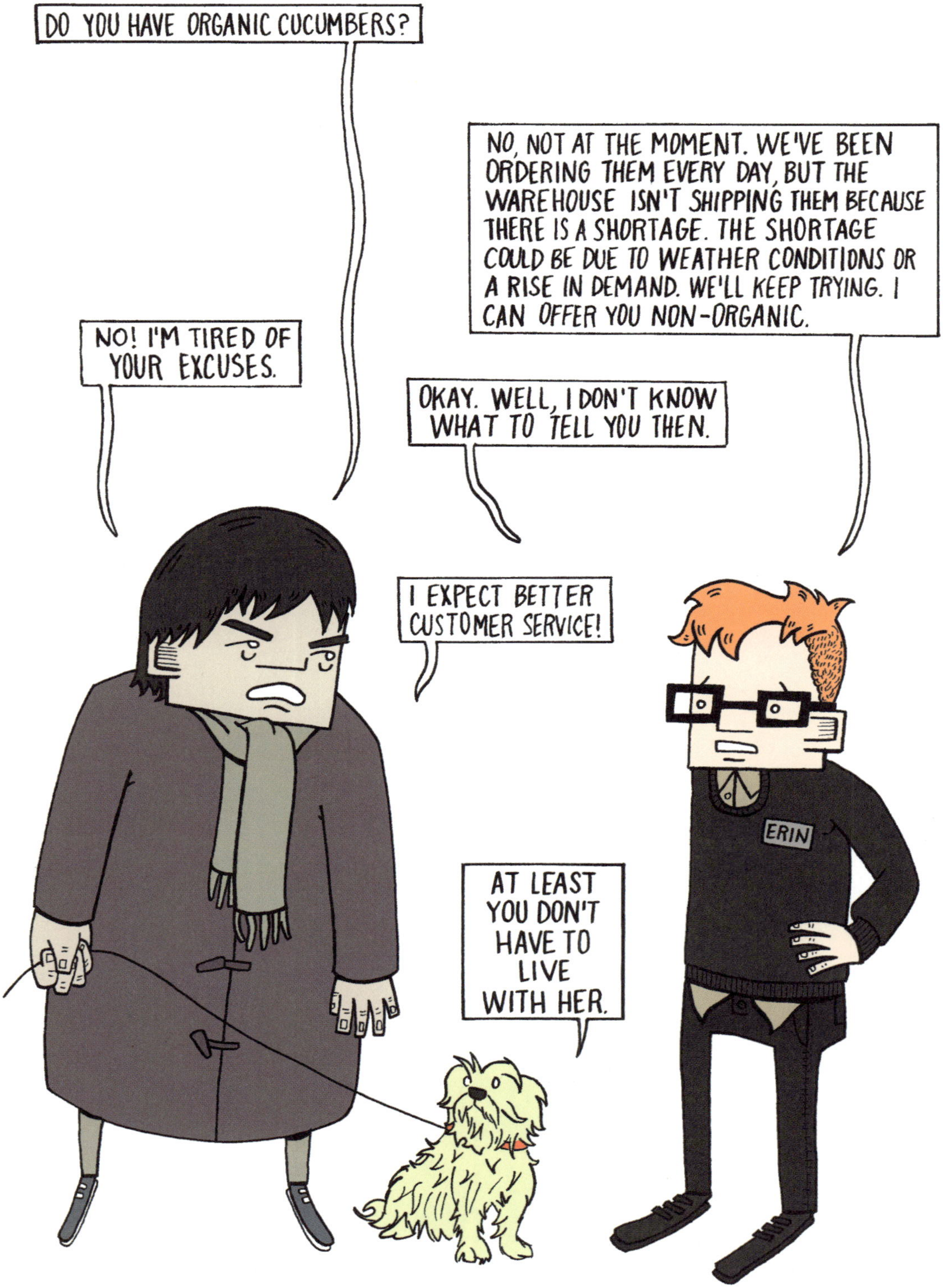

DO YOU HAVE ORGANIC CUCUMBERS?
NO, NOT AT THE MOMENT. WE'VE BEEN ORDERING THEM EVERY DAY, BUT THE WAREHOUSE ISN'T SHIPPING THEM BECAUSE THERE IS A SHORTAGE. THE SHORTAGE COULD BE DUE TO WEATHER CONDITIONS OR A RISE IN DEMAND. WE'LL KEEP TRYING. I CAN OFFER YOU NON-ORGANIC.
NO! I'M TIRED OF YOUR EXCUSES.
OKAY. WELL, I DON'T KNOW WHAT TO TELL YOU THEN.
I EXPECT BETTER CUSTOMER SERVICE!
ERIN
AT LEAST YOU DON'T HAVE TO LIVE WITH HER.

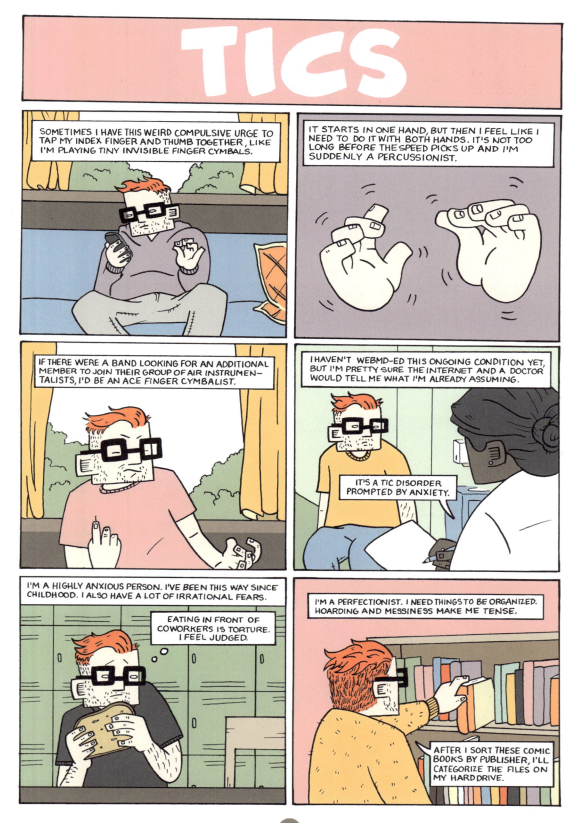

TICS

SOMETIMES I HAVE THIS WEIRD COMPULSIVE URGE TO TAP MY INDEX FINGER AND THUMB TOGETHER, LIKE I'M PLAYING TINY INVISIBLE FINGER CYMBALS.

IT STARTS IN ONE HAND, BUT THEN I FEEL LIKE I NEED TO DO IT WITH BOTH HANDS. IT'S NOT TOO LONG BEFORE THE SPEED PICKS UP AND I'M SUDDENLY A PERCUSSIONIST.

IF THERE WERE A BAND LOOKING FOR AN ADDITIONAL MEMBER TO JOIN THEIR GROUP OF AIR INSTRUMENTALISTS, I'D BE AN ACE FINGER CYMBALIST.

I HAVEN'T WEBMD-ED THIS ONGOING CONDITION YET, BUT I'M PRETTY SURE THE INTERNET AND A DOCTOR WOULD TELL ME WHAT I'M ALREADY ASSUMING.

IT'S A TIC DISORDER PROMPTED BY ANXIETY.

I'M A HIGHLY ANXIOUS PERSON. I'VE BEEN THIS WAY SINCE CHILDHOOD. I ALSO HAVE A LOT OF IRRATIONAL FEARS.

EATING IN FRONT OF COWORKERS IS TORTURE. I FEEL JUDGED.

I'M A PERFECTIONIST. I NEED THINGS TO BE ORGANIZED. HOARDING AND MESSINESS MAKE ME TENSE.

AFTER I SORT THESE COMIC BOOKS BY PUBLISHER, I'LL CATEGORIZE THE FILES ON MY HARD DRIVE.

I HAVE A TENDENCY TO DOUBT MYSELF, I'M SELF-CONSCIOUS, AND SOCIAL SITUATIONS ARE HELLA STRESSFUL.

MY WORST FEAR!

ERIN, COME ON! DANCE!

NO THANKS. JUST GONNA DROWN MYSELF IN BOOZE UNTIL I'M RELAXED ENOUGH TO RESIDE IN THIS HELL.

DANCE! DANCE! DANCE! DANCE! DANCE! DANCE! DANCE! DANCE! DANCE! NCE! DANCE! DANCE!

DANCE! DANCE! DANCE! DANCE! DANCE! DANCE! DANCE! DANCE! DANCE! DANCE! DAN DANCE! DAN DANCE

SOMEONE PLEASE RESCUE ME FROM THIS NIGHTMARE.

DID I MENTION, I ALSO SUFFER FROM SLEEP DEPRIVATION REGULARLY? ON AVERAGE, I SLEEP 4-6 HOURS A NIGHT BECAUSE I HAVE BODY ACHES THAT A PERSON OF MY AGE SHOULD NOT HAVE. PLUS, THE FELINE I ADOPTED WAKES ME UP SEVERAL TIMES DURING MY SLUMBER.

ALERT! THE FOOD IS STALE I REPEAT, THE FOOD IS BAD! REFILL STAT! BEFORE I DIE FROM STARVATION!

USUALLY, THE TICS OCCUR WHEN I'M STRESSED AND HAVEN'T HAD ENOUGH SLEEP. INSTEAD OF VISITING A THERAPIST, DOING SOME RELAXATION EXERCISES, MEDITATING, OR TAKING PILLS, I'M JUST GOING TO EMBRACE MY EMBARRASSING RANDOM FITS OF REPETITIVE MOVEMENT. I'M GOING TO DO SOMETHING ONLY AN ANAL-RETENTIVE PERSON WOULD DO. I'M GOING TO MAKE A VISUAL LIST OF SOME OF THE MOTOR AND VOCAL TICS I'VE HAD SINCE CHILDHOOD. SOME HAVE EXPIRED. SOME GO INTO REMISSION. SOME LIKE TO STICK AROUND. BEAR IN MIND, I'M NOT THE LEAST BIT ASHAMED NOR DO I FEEL DISPIRITED BY THESE QUIRKS. I'M HUMBLE.

BENDING MY NECK BACKWARDS

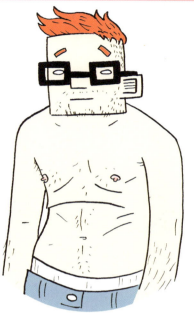

SUCKING IN MY GUT OR CONTRACTING MY ABDOMINAL MUSCLES.

MAKING FUNNY FACES WHILE DRAWING OR DOING HOMEWORK
(ONLY PREVALENT AS A CHILD)

ROCKING BACK AND FORTH

GO AHEAD AND LAUGH. I KNOW THE SIGHT OF AN ADULT ROCKING BACK AND FORTH LOOKS PECULIAR, BUT I SPENT A LOT OF TIME IN A WIND-UP BABY SWING WHEN I WAS AN INFANT. IT WAS SOOTHING. I DON'T CARE HOW SILLY I LOOK. THIS SHIT WORKS! INSTEAD OF POPPING PAXIL, I BODY ROCK AND LET THE ENDORPHINS FLY UNTIL I'M AT EASE.

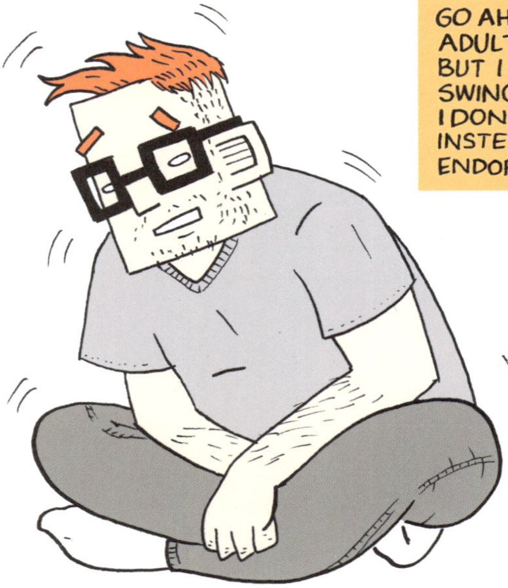

BLINKING REALLY HARD

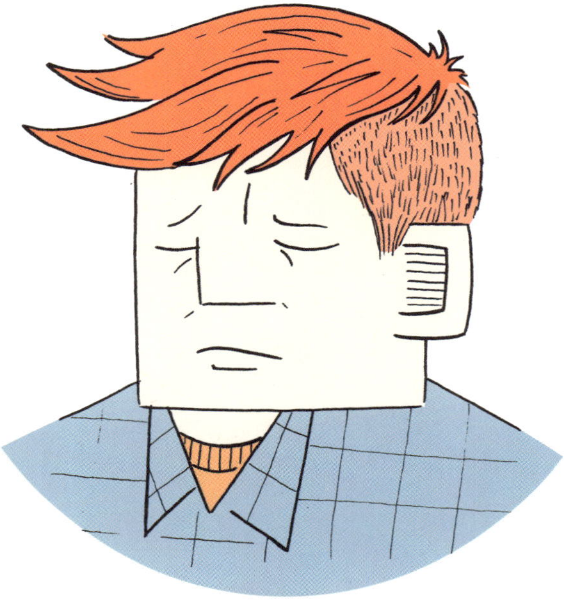

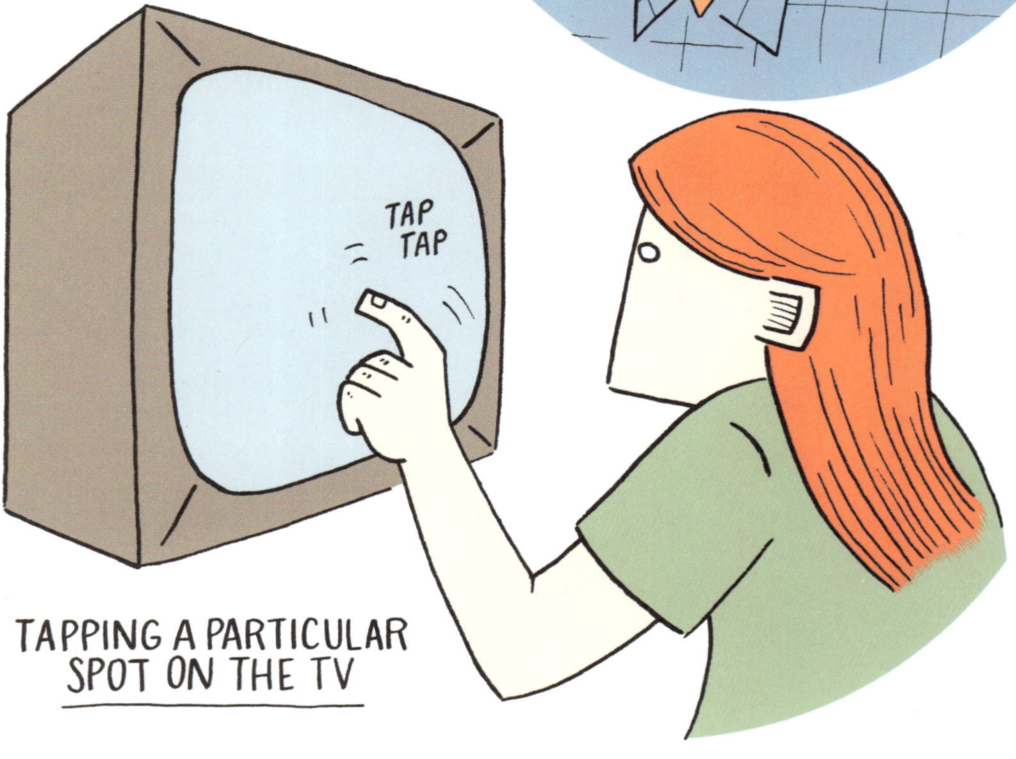
TAP
TAP

TAPPING A PARTICULAR SPOT ON THE TV

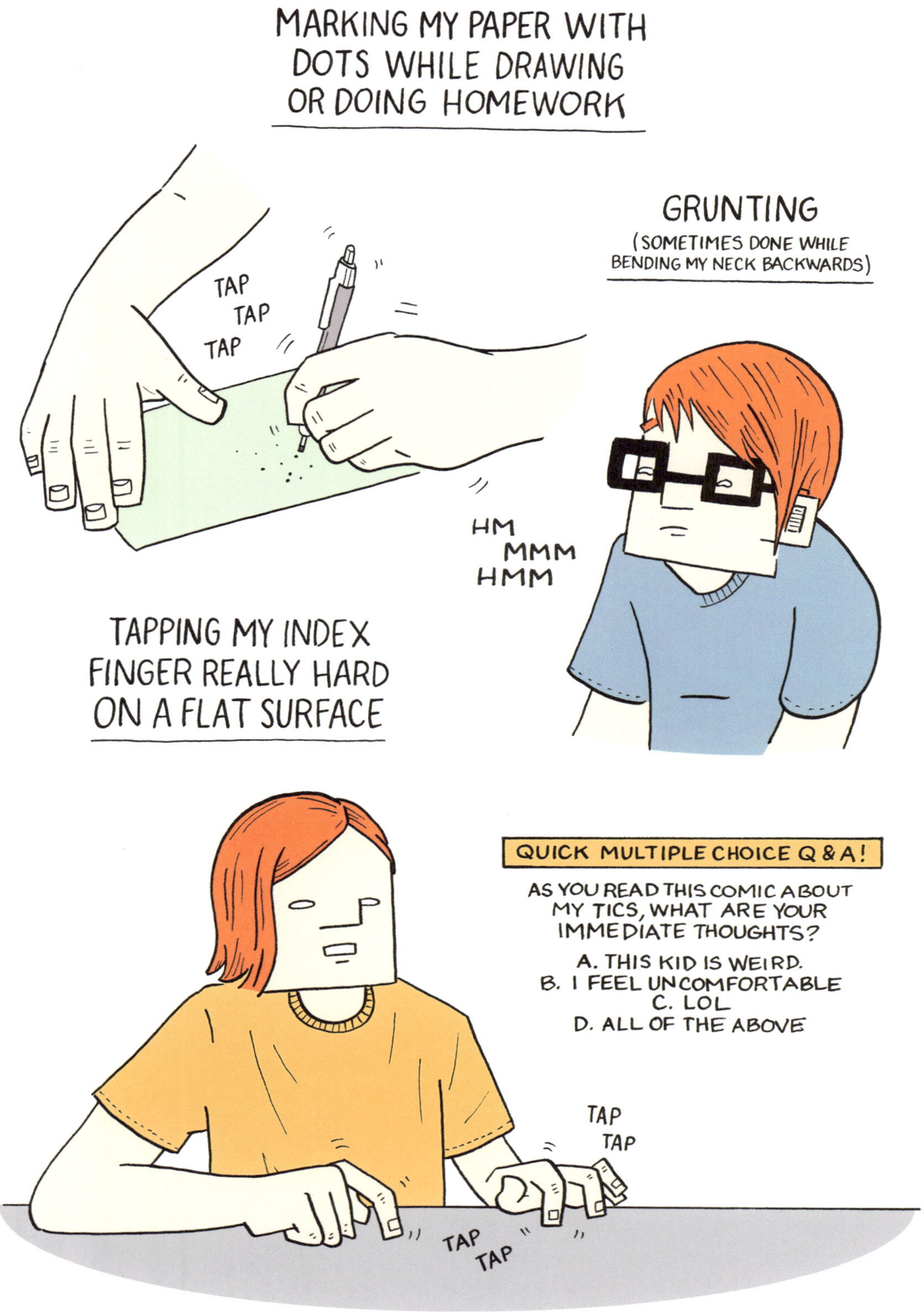
MARKING MY PAPER WITH DOTS WHILE DRAWING OR DOING HOMEWORK
TAP TAP TAP
GRUNTING
(SOMETIMES DONE WHILE BENDING MY NECK BACKWARDS)
HM MMM HMM
TAPPING MY INDEX FINGER REALLY HARD ON A FLAT SURFACE
QUICK MULTIPLE CHOICE Q & A!
AS YOU READ THIS COMIC ABOUT MY TICS, WHAT ARE YOUR IMMEDIATE THOUGHTS?
A. THIS KID IS WEIRD.
B. I FEEL UNCOMFORTABLE
C. LOL
D. ALL OF THE ABOVE
TAP TAP
TAP TAP

MILO

FRIENDS CALL ME MILO. I'M 26. I HAVE TWO PART TIME JOBS. I'M A PRODUCE CLERK AT A LOCAL GROCERY STORE, AND I ALSO REPAIR/BUILD BIKES.

MY BEST FRIEND IS CHESTER. HE'S MY TWO-YEAR-OLD PIT BULL MIX. HE'S A REAL CHARMER AND LOVES TO CUDDLE.

IN MY SPARE TIME, I LIKE TO DOODLE, MAKE ZINES, PLAY CARDS, EXPLORE THE CITY AT NIGHT, READ SMALL PRESS BOOKS BY QUEER AUTHORS, AND DRINK CHEAP BEER AT DIVE BARS WITH MY FRIENDS.

I HAVE NO PIERCINGS, BUT I HAVE A TATTOO OF ALF.

I'M OK WITH A COMMITTED RELATIONSHIP OR SOMETHING CASUAL. I'M DOWN FOR A GOOD TIME.

IF PLAYING SKEE-BALL AT THE NICKEL ARCADE, GRABBING A RAD SLICE OF PIZZA, AND CATCHING A LATE SHOWING OF A JOHN HUGHES FILM AT THE LAURELHURST SOUNDS LIKE A GOOD PLAN, SEND ME A MESSAGE.

SUPER SOAKERS

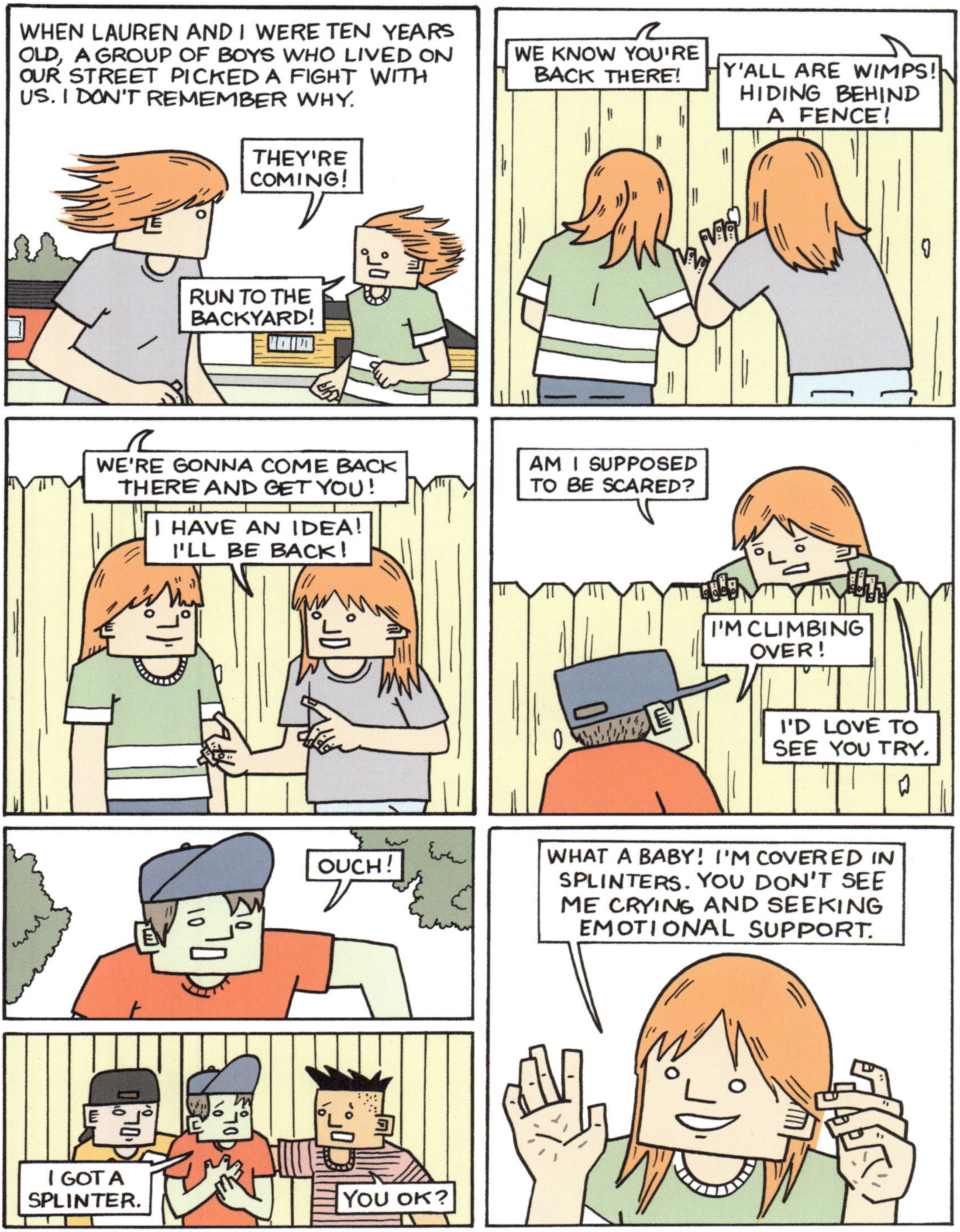
WHEN LAUREN AND I WERE TEN YEARS OLD, A GROUP OF BOYS WHO LIVED ON OUR STREET PICKED A FIGHT WITH US. I DON'T REMEMBER WHY.
THEY'RE COMING!
RUN TO THE BACKYARD!
WE KNOW YOU'RE BACK THERE!
Y'ALL ARE WIMPS! HIDING BEHIND A FENCE!
WE'RE GONNA COME BACK THERE AND GET YOU!
I HAVE AN IDEA! I'LL BE BACK!
AM I SUPPOSED TO BE SCARED?
I'M CLIMBING OVER!
I'D LOVE TO SEE YOU TRY.
OUCH!
I GOT A SPLINTER.
YOU OK?
WHAT A BABY! I'M COVERED IN SPLINTERS. YOU DON'T SEE ME CRYING AND SEEKING EMOTIONAL SUPPORT.

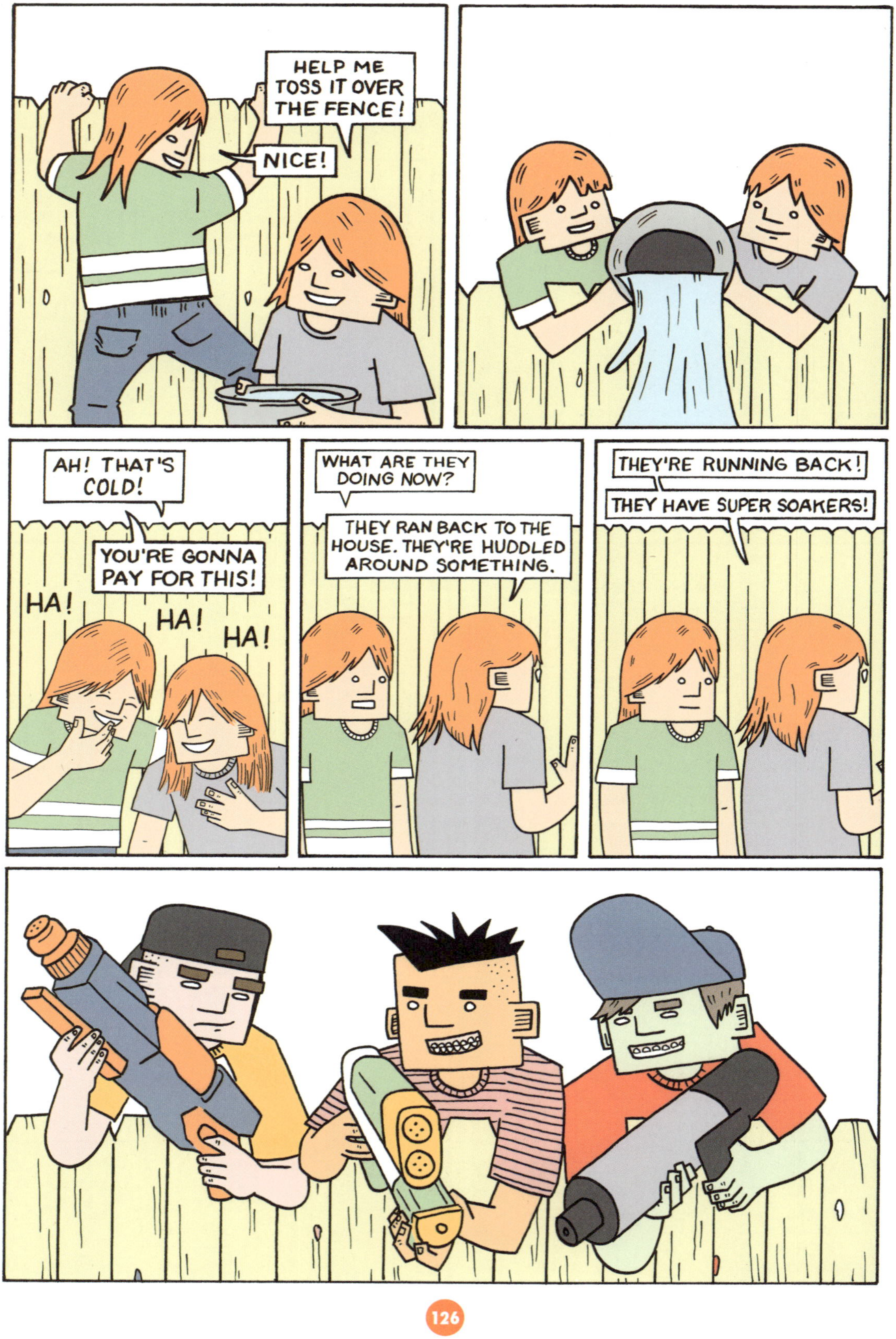
HELP ME TOSS IT OVER THE FENCE!
NICE!
AH! THAT'S COLD!
YOU'RE GONNA PAY FOR THIS!
HA!
HA!
HA!
WHAT ARE THEY DOING NOW?
THEY RAN BACK TO THE HOUSE. THEY'RE HUDDLED AROUND SOMETHING.
THEY'RE RUNNING BACK!
THEY HAVE SUPER SOAKERS!

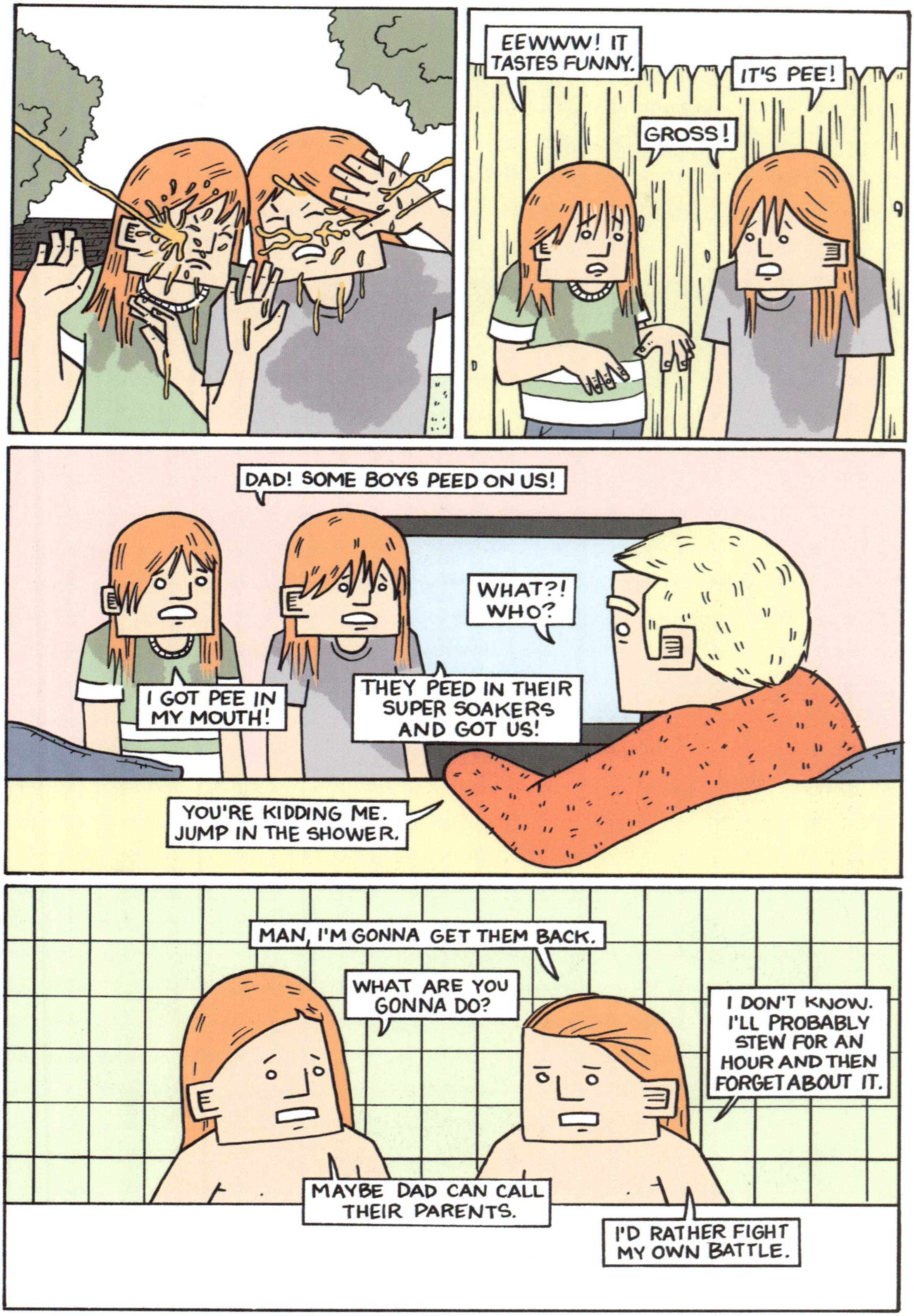
EEWWW! IT TASTES FUNNY.
IT'S PEE!
GROSS!
DAD! SOME BOYS PEED ON US!
WHAT?! WHO?
I GOT PEE IN MY MOUTH!
THEY PEED IN THEIR SUPER SOAKERS AND GOT US!
YOU'RE KIDDING ME. JUMP IN THE SHOWER.
MAN, I'M GONNA GET THEM BACK.
WHAT ARE YOU GONNA DO?
I DON'T KNOW. I'LL PROBABLY STEW FOR AN HOUR AND THEN FORGET ABOUT IT.
MAYBE DAD CAN CALL THEIR PARENTS.
I'D RATHER FIGHT MY OWN BATTLE.

MOVING ON

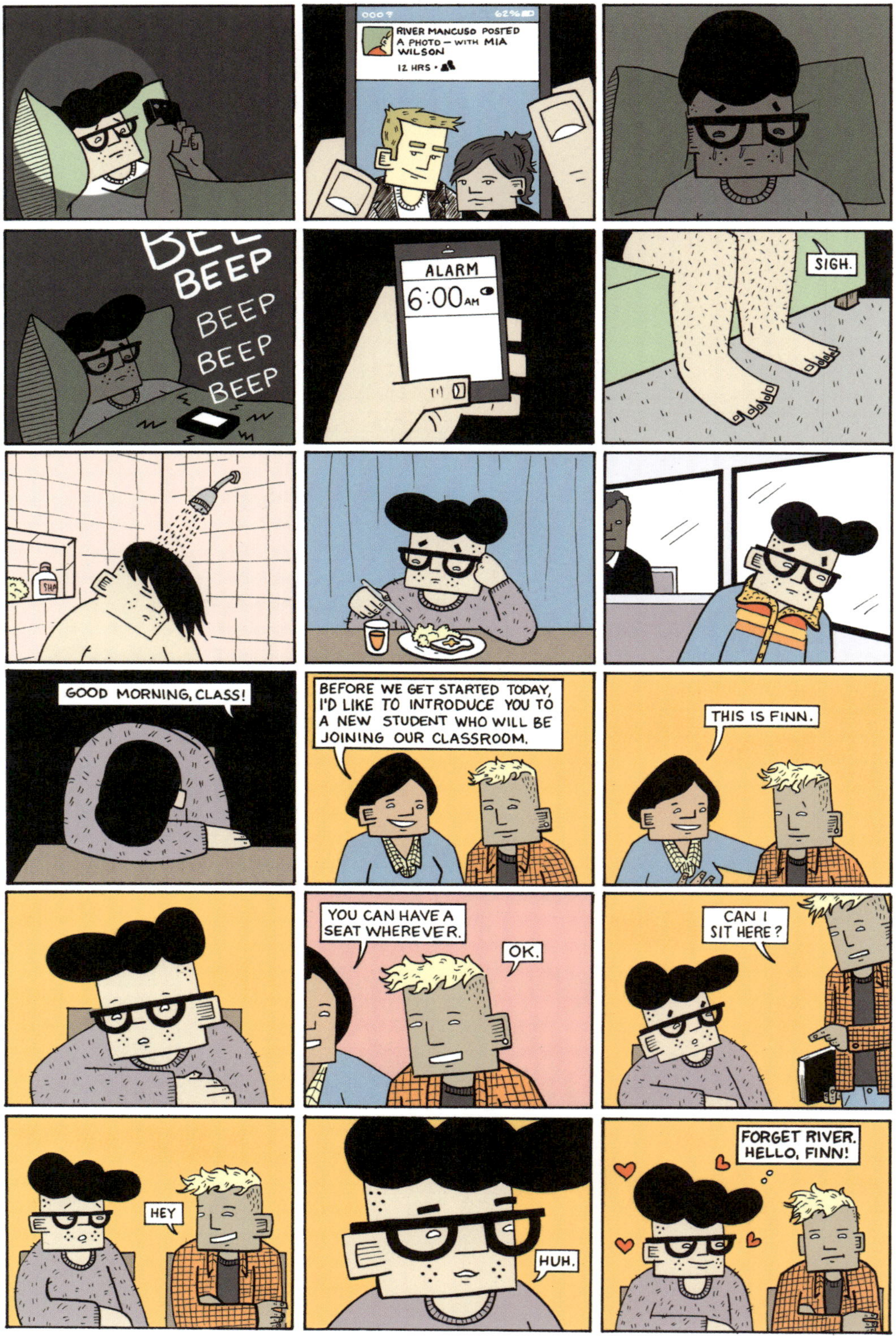

RIVER MANCUSO POSTED A PHOTO — WITH MIA WILSON
12 HRS •
BEEP
BEEP
BEEP
BEEP
ALARM
6:00 AM
SIGH.
GOOD MORNING, CLASS!
BEFORE WE GET STARTED TODAY, I'D LIKE TO INTRODUCE YOU TO A NEW STUDENT WHO WILL BE JOINING OUR CLASSROOM.
THIS IS FINN.
YOU CAN HAVE A SEAT WHEREVER.
OK.
CAN I SIT HERE?
HEY
HUH.
FORGET RIVER. HELLO, FINN!

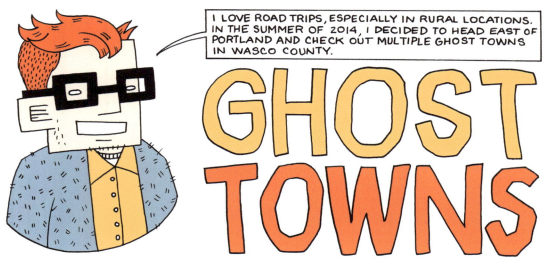

I LOVE ROAD TRIPS, ESPECIALLY IN RURAL LOCATIONS. IN THE SUMMER OF 2014, I DECIDED TO HEAD EAST OF PORTLAND AND CHECK OUT MULTIPLE GHOST TOWNS IN WASCO COUNTY.

GHOST TOWNS

I'M NOT SURE WHAT LURES ME TO DESOLATED LOCATIONS. MAYBE IT'S THE ABSENCE OF PEOPLE. IT'S NOT THAT I HATE PEOPLE. I JUST ENJOY TAKING IN MY ENVIRONMENT IN SOLITUDE.

ACCORDING TO THE INTERNET, OREGON HAS THE MOST GHOST TOWNS IN THE UNITED STATES. I CHOSE TO CHECK OUT A FEW IN NORTH-CENTRAL OREGON BECAUSE THERE'S A GOOD NUMBER IN THE REGION. ALSO, THE DRIVE WASN'T TOO FAR FROM HOME.

WA-14
THE DALLES
PORTLAND
BOYD
DUFUR
US-197
SHANIKO
OR-218
ANTELOPE

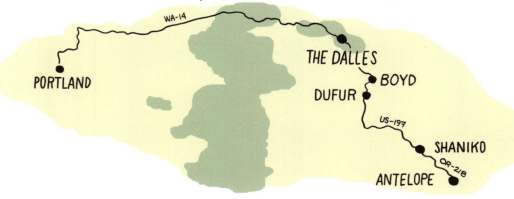

WHEN I PASSED THE DALLES AND HEADED SOUTH ON ROUTE 197, I FELT A LITTLE NERVOUS ABOUT BEING ALONE IN A LAND WITHOUT PEOPLE AND ROAD TRIP AMENITIES. AT TIMES, MY CELL PHONE RECEPTION WAS TERRIBLE. I WONDERED WHAT WOULD HAPPEN IF I RAN OUT OF GAS, EVEN THOUGH MY TANK WAS FULL. I WAS AFRAID THE CAR WOULD BREAK DOWN, OR I'D GET A FLAT TIRE. WHAT IF I CAME IN CONTACT WITH A SERIAL KILLER? I WAS ILL PREPARED, BUT I TRIED TO IGNORE MY FEARS AND PRESS FORWARD.

HI! COULD YOU HELP ME GET SOMETHING OUT OF THE TRUNK OF MY CAR?
UH...
FUCK NO!
RUN!

I LANDED 16 MILES SOUTH OF THE DALLES, IN DUFUR. IT'S A SMALL TOWN WITH A POPULATION OF A LITTLE OVER 600. I PLANNED TO STAY OVERNIGHT, SO I MADE RESERVATIONS AT THE HISTORIC BALCH HOTEL.

WHEN I ENTERED THE THREE-STORY BRICK BUILDING, THE OWNER GREETED ME AT THE FRONT DESK. SHE WAS SWEET AND PLEASANT. AS SHE WALKED ME TO MY ROOM, SHE TOLD ME ABOUT THE SERVICES THEY PROVIDED, THE BREAKFAST IN THE MORNING, AND WHERE I COULD FIND THE BATHROOM. SHE INFORMED ME THAT HER ROOM WAS JUST DOWN THE HALL FROM MINE. FOR SOME REASON, I FELT SAFER KNOWING THIS. WE WERE THE ONLY TWO IN THE HOTEL. I FELT SOMEWHAT RELIEVED BECAUSE IT MEANT I'D HAVE THE SHARED BATHROOM ALL TO MYSELF. HOWEVER, I WAS UNNERVED TO STAY AT AN EMPTY ESTABLISHMENT THAT WAS INTENDED TO ACCOMMODATE MANY OCCUPANTS.

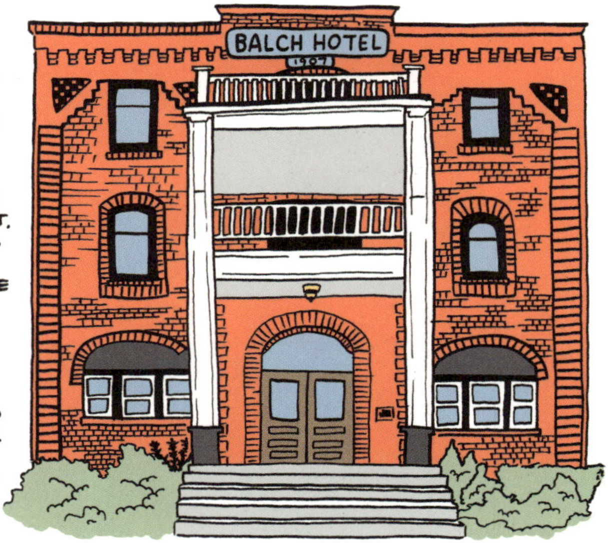
BALCH HOTEL

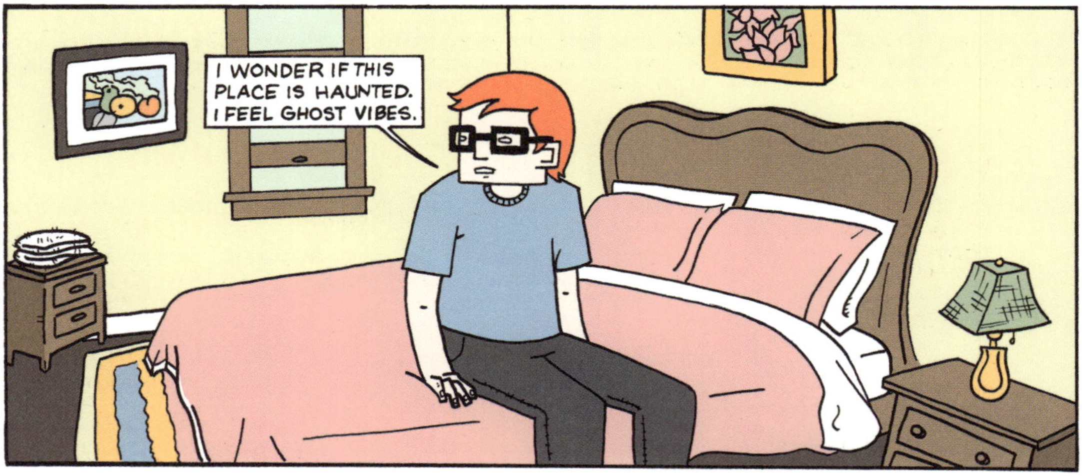
I WONDER IF THIS PLACE IS HAUNTED. I FEEL GHOST VIBES.

I INVESTIGATED MY ROOM AFTER SHE STEPPED AWAY. IT WAS OLD, AND THE FLOORS CREAKED. THERE WAS NO A.C., NO TV, AND NO TELEPHONE, BUT THERE WAS WI-FI. ANTIQUES FURNISHED THE ROOM. A LITTLE PORCELAIN SINK STOOD NEXT TO THE BED. I THOUGHT IT WAS UNUSUAL, BUT AT LEAST I DIDN'T HAVE TO LEAVE MY ROOM TO BRUSH MY TEETH.

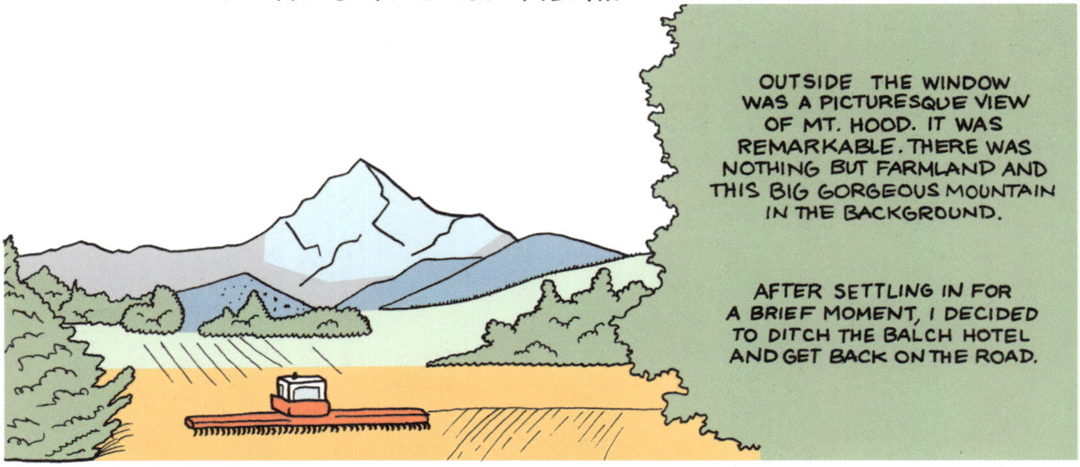
OUTSIDE THE WINDOW WAS A PICTURESQUE VIEW OF MT. HOOD. IT WAS REMARKABLE. THERE WAS NOTHING BUT FARMLAND AND THIS BIG GORGEOUS MOUNTAIN IN THE BACKGROUND.
AFTER SETTLING IN FOR A BRIEF MOMENT, I DECIDED TO DITCH THE BALCH HOTEL AND GET BACK ON THE ROAD.

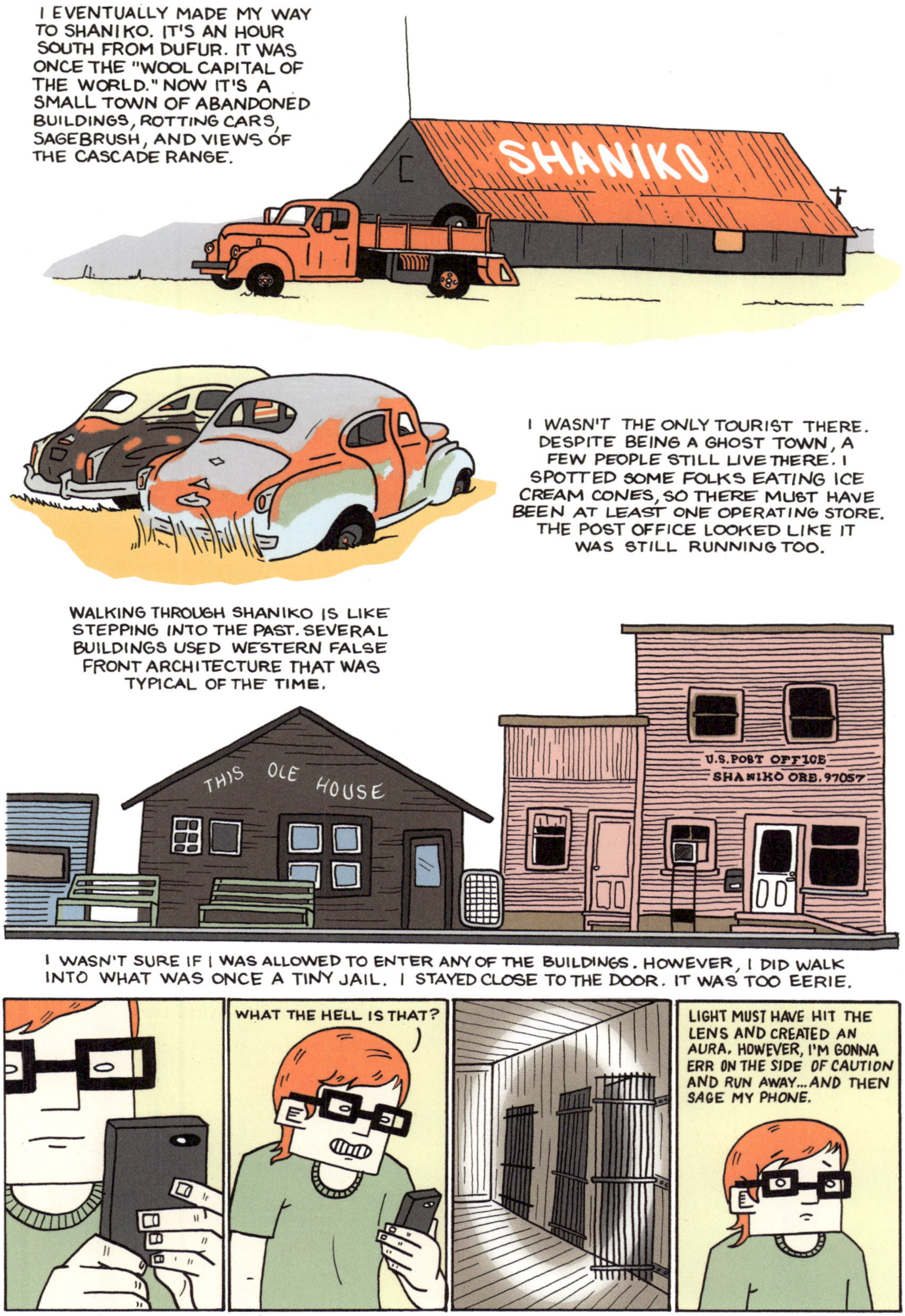
I EVENTUALLY MADE MY WAY TO SHANIKO. IT'S AN HOUR SOUTH FROM DUFUR. IT WAS ONCE THE "WOOL CAPITAL OF THE WORLD." NOW IT'S A SMALL TOWN OF ABANDONED BUILDINGS, ROTTING CARS, SAGEBRUSH, AND VIEWS OF THE CASCADE RANGE.
SHANIKO
I WASN'T THE ONLY TOURIST THERE. DESPITE BEING A GHOST TOWN, A FEW PEOPLE STILL LIVE THERE. I SPOTTED SOME FOLKS EATING ICE CREAM CONES, SO THERE MUST HAVE BEEN AT LEAST ONE OPERATING STORE. THE POST OFFICE LOOKED LIKE IT WAS STILL RUNNING TOO.
WALKING THROUGH SHANIKO IS LIKE STEPPING INTO THE PAST. SEVERAL BUILDINGS USED WESTERN FALSE FRONT ARCHITECTURE THAT WAS TYPICAL OF THE TIME.
THIS OLE HOUSE
U.S. POST OFFICE
SHANIKO ORE. 97057
I WASN'T SURE IF I WAS ALLOWED TO ENTER ANY OF THE BUILDINGS. HOWEVER, I DID WALK INTO WHAT WAS ONCE A TINY JAIL. I STAYED CLOSE TO THE DOOR. IT WAS TOO EERIE.
WHAT THE HELL IS THAT?
LIGHT MUST HAVE HIT THE LENS AND CREATED AN AURA. HOWEVER, I'M GONNA ERR ON THE SIDE OF CAUTION AND RUN AWAY... AND THEN SAGE MY PHONE.

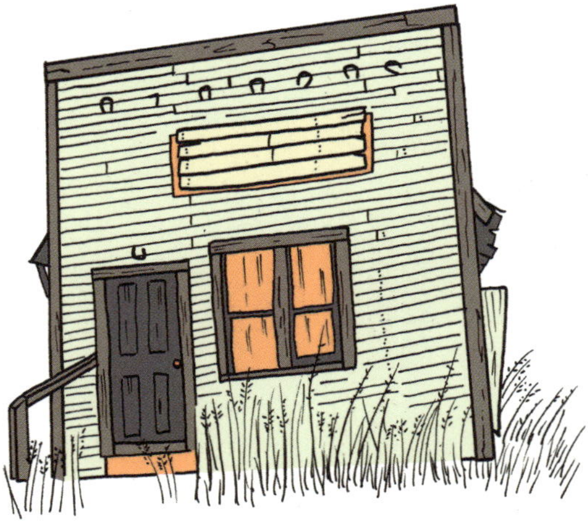

I WANTED TO MAKE ONE MORE STOP AND BE BACK IN DUFUR BEFORE DUSK, SO I LEFT SHANIKO AND JUMPED ON ROUTE 218 TOWARDS ANTELOPE.

ONLY A HANDFUL OF PEOPLE LIVE IN ANTELOPE. WHEN I DROVE THROUGH, I GOT THE SENSE I WASN'T WELCOMED THERE. THE TWO OR THREE PEOPLE I MADE EYE CONTACT WITH, AS I SLOWLY CRUISED PAST THEIR HOMES, GAVE ME LONG, HARD STARES. MAYBE I WAS PROJECTING MY FEARS ONTO THEM. I HAD A CAMERA, WHICH SCREAMED "TOURIST!" I GET IT. I'M OVERCOME WITH THE SAME IRRITABILITY WHEN I SEE TOURISTS WASTING HOURS IN A LINE OUTSIDE OF VOODOO DOUGHNUTS IN PORTLAND. ALSO, I HAD SHORT HAIR, A FEMININE BUILD, I DRESSED MASCULINE, AND I WAS ANDROGYNOUS. I DIDN'T EXACTLY FIT THE DEMOGRAPHIC OF THIS PODUNK TOWN. I'M NOT SURE WHAT ASSUMPTIONS THEY HAD OF ME BASED ON MY APPEARANCE. I WAS WELL AWARE THAT I FIT A STEREOTYPE. I ONLY HOPED THEY DIDN'T HAVE A PHOBIA OF THAT TYPE.

MY VISIT WAS SHORT. I WANDERED AROUND THE PARAMETERS OF THE OLD SCHOOLHOUSE AND TOOK PHOTOS OF 3 VACANT BUILDINGS. THE PREMISE WAS VERY HAUNTING. A SINGLE METAL SLIDE, A RUSTED MERRY-GO-ROUND, SWING SET, AND BASKETBALL COURT ENCLOSED BY A CHAIN LINK FENCE, WERE LOCATED IN FRONT OF THE SCHOOL. I WANTED TO GO INSIDE, BUT IT WAS LOCKED. EVEN IF I WAS ABLE TO TRESPASS, I WAS TOO CHICKENSHIT TO EXPLORE THE BUILDING. I PEERED THROUGH A WINDOW. TO MY SURPRISE, THE INTERIOR LOOKED LIKE A FUNCTIONING SCHOOL.

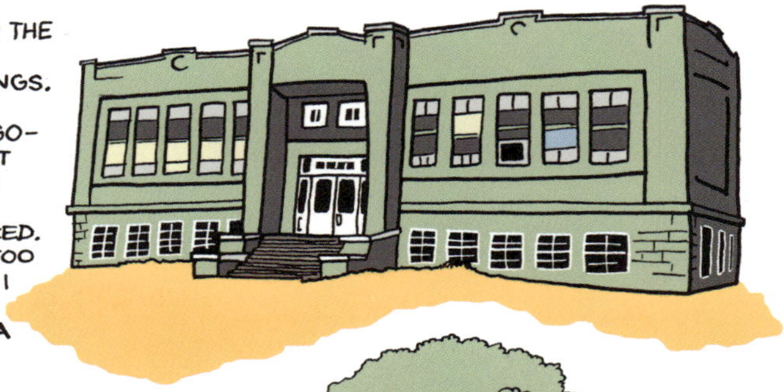

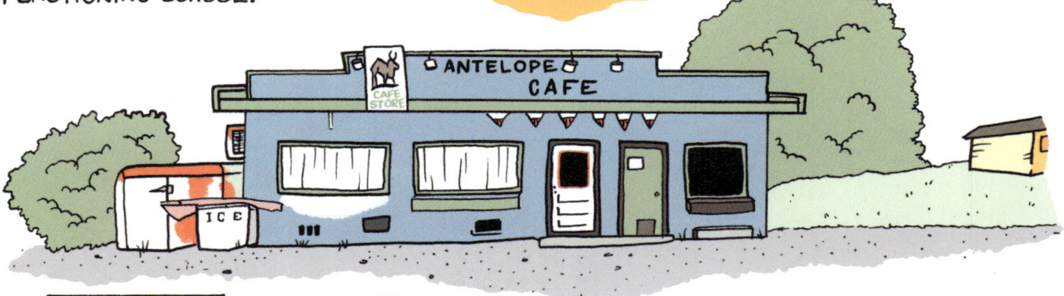
ANTELOPE CAFE
CAFE STORE
ICE

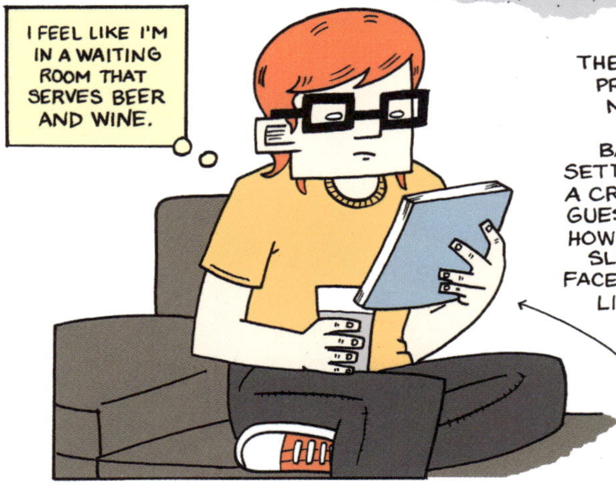
I FEEL LIKE I'M IN A WAITING ROOM THAT SERVES BEER AND WINE.

THE SCHOOL AND THE TOWN WERE PRETTY UPSETTING, SO I MADE NO POINT OF STAYING LONG.

BACK AT THE BALCH HOTEL, I SETTLED IN THE LOBBY AND DRANK A CRAFT BEER. BY THAT TIME, MORE GUESTS HAD ARRIVED. CONSIDERING HOW MUCH I ENJOY SOLITUDE, I WAS SLIGHTLY THRILLED TO SEE MORE FACES. I NO LONGER FELT LIKE I WAS LIVING IN THE TWILIGHT ZONE.

A PHOTOGRAPHY BOOK OF WASHINGTON LANDSCAPES I FOUND ON THE COFFEE TABLE. I WAS TOO LAZY TO WALK TO MY ROOM AND GET MY BOOK.

I GRABBED DINNER AT A GROCERY STORE DOWN THE STREET. THE PULLED PORK SANDWICH SERVED WITH FRIES WAS THE KINDA GARBAGE FOOD I WANTED TO DEVOUR, SO I ORDERED IT TO GO. I FELT UNDER-WHELMED WHEN THE SERVER HANDED ME MY MEAL. I DIDN'T VOICE A COMPLAINT. I DIDN'T REFUSE IT OR RETURN IT. I SMILED AND THANKED HER GRACIOUSLY. I WALKED A FEW BLOCKS, SAT DOWN AT A PICNIC TABLE, AND ATE MY DISAPPOINTING MEAL AS THE SUN SET.

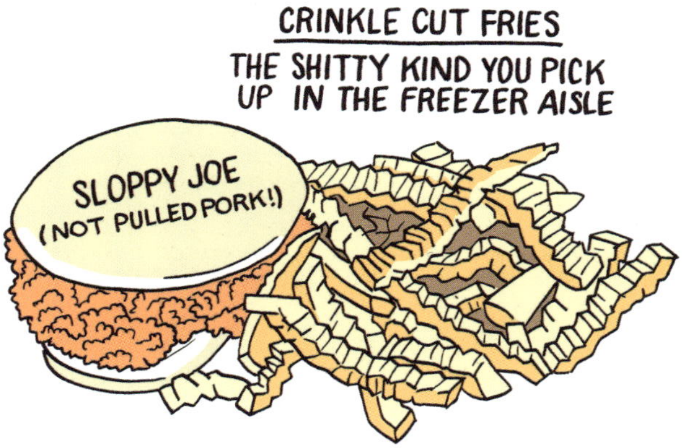
CRINKLE CUT FRIES
THE SHITTY KIND YOU PICK UP IN THE FREEZER AISLE
SLOPPY JOE (NOT PULLED PORK!)

THAT NIGHT, AS I LAID IN BED, IN THE DARK, WITH THE BLANKETS PULLED OVER MY HEAD, I HAD TROUBLE FALLING ASLEEP. MULTIPLE SCENARIOS RAN IN MY MIND.

I WAS AFRAID I WOULD OPEN MY EYES AND SEE A LITTLE BOY STANDING THREE FEET FROM MY FACE...

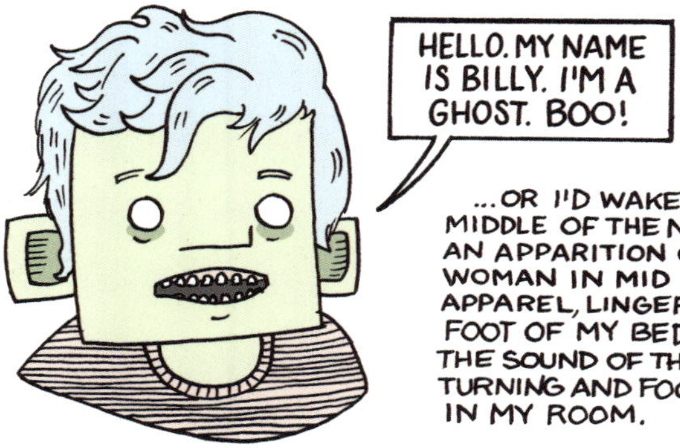
HELLO. MY NAME IS BILLY. I'M A GHOST. BOO!

...OR I'D WAKE UP IN THE MIDDLE OF THE NIGHT AND SEE AN APPARITION OF AN OLDER WOMAN IN MID 19TH CENTURY APPAREL, LINGERING AT THE FOOT OF MY BED. I ANTICIPATED THE SOUND OF THE DOORKNOB TURNING AND FOOT STEPS IN MY ROOM.

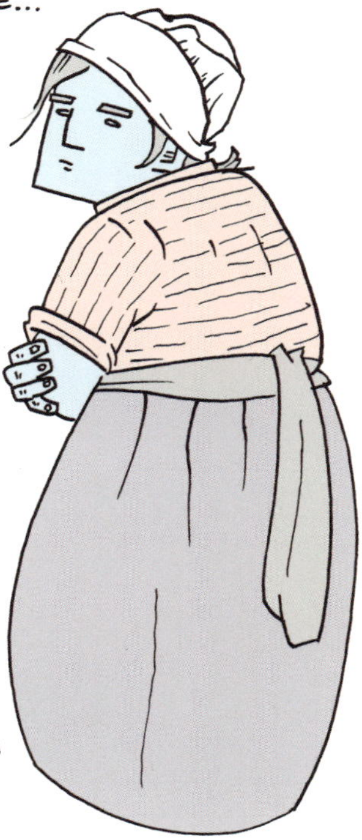

LUCKILY, I WOKE UP THE NEXT MORNING FREE FROM NIGHT TERRORS AND GHOSTLY VISIONS.

WHEN I SAT DOWN FOR BREAKFAST, THE OWNER CAME TO VISIT ME. WE CHATTED FOR A LITTLE BIT. I TOLD HER I WAS IN TOWN TO CHECK OUT GHOST TOWNS. SHE PERKED UP WITH EXCITEMENT AND HANDED ME A MAP OF TOWNS TO CHECK OUT. WHEN I TOLD HER I VISITED SHANIKO AND ANTELOPE, SHE ASKED IF I HAD EVER HEARD ABOUT BHAGWAN SHREE RAJNEESH.

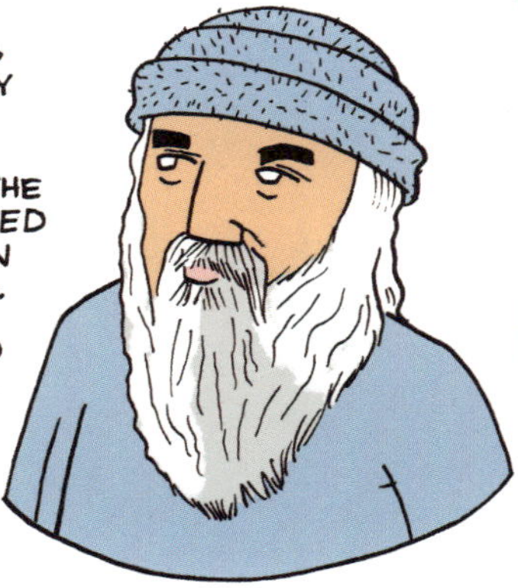

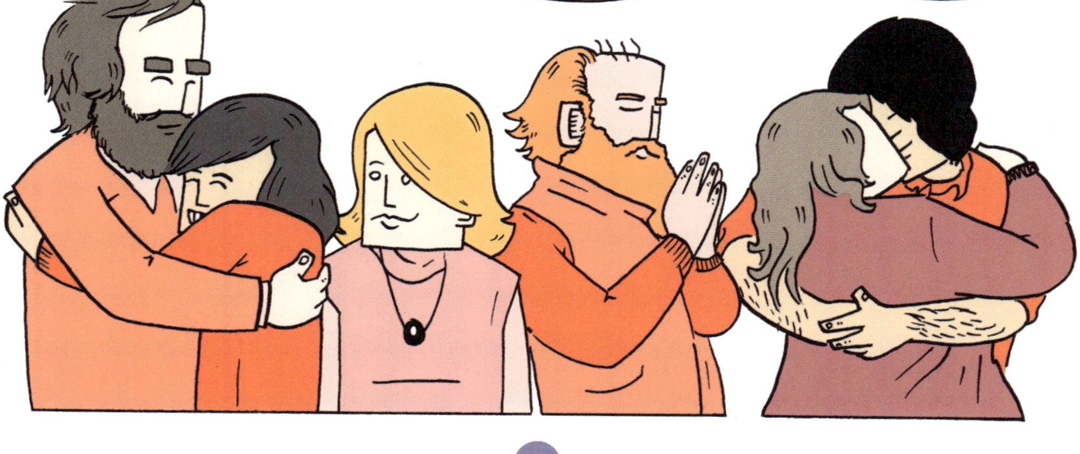

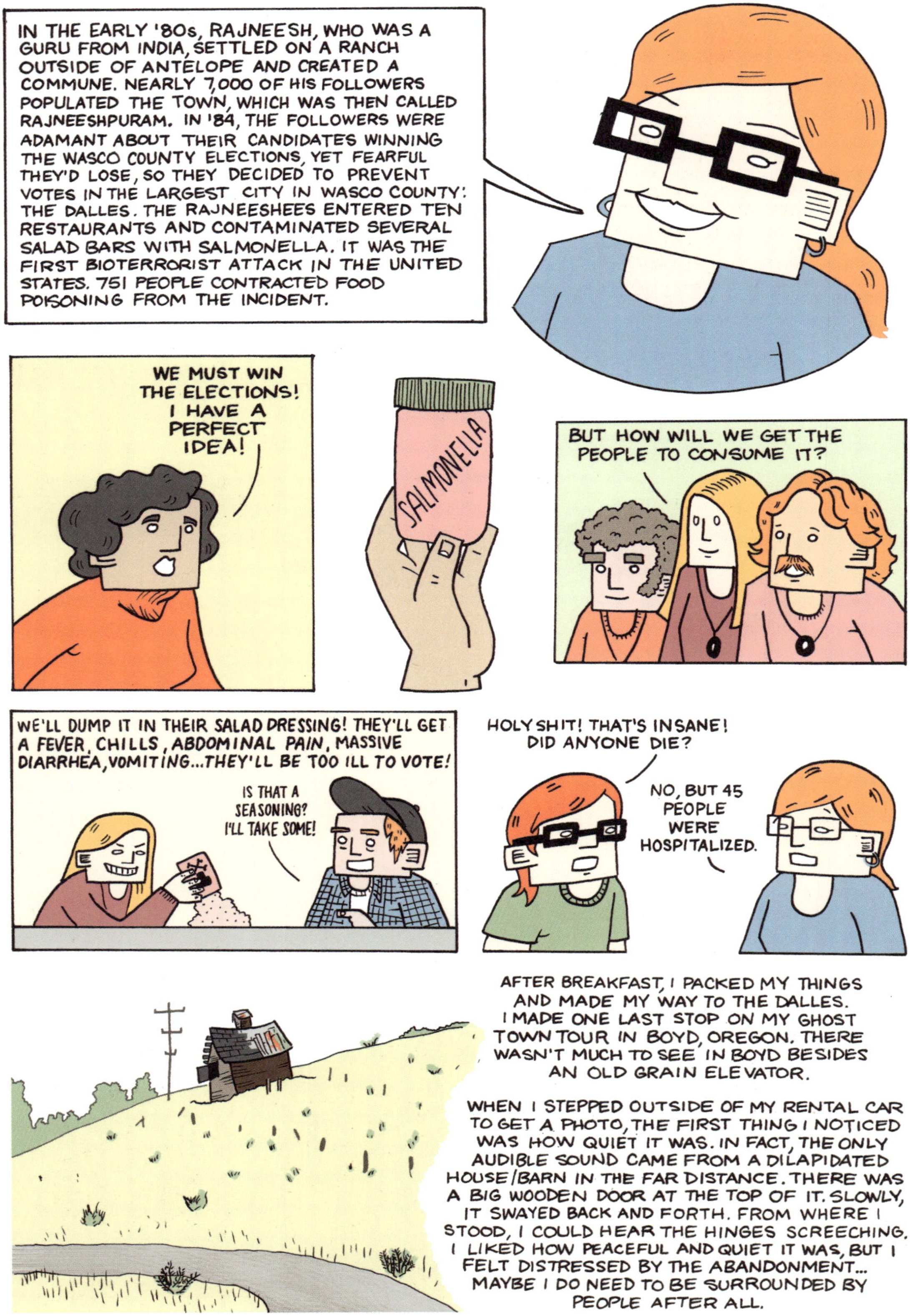
IN THE EARLY '80s, RAJNEESH, WHO WAS A GURU FROM INDIA, SETTLED ON A RANCH OUTSIDE OF ANTELOPE AND CREATED A COMMUNE. NEARLY 7,000 OF HIS FOLLOWERS POPULATED THE TOWN, WHICH WAS THEN CALLED RAJNEESHPURAM. IN '84, THE FOLLOWERS WERE ADAMANT ABOUT THEIR CANDIDATES WINNING THE WASCO COUNTY ELECTIONS, YET FEARFUL THEY'D LOSE, SO THEY DECIDED TO PREVENT VOTES IN THE LARGEST CITY IN WASCO COUNTY: THE DALLES. THE RAJNEESHEES ENTERED TEN RESTAURANTS AND CONTAMINATED SEVERAL SALAD BARS WITH SALMONELLA. IT WAS THE FIRST BIOTERRORIST ATTACK IN THE UNITED STATES. 751 PEOPLE CONTRACTED FOOD POISONING FROM THE INCIDENT.
WE MUST WIN THE ELECTIONS! I HAVE A PERFECT IDEA!
SALMONELLA
BUT HOW WILL WE GET THE PEOPLE TO CONSUME IT?
WE'LL DUMP IT IN THEIR SALAD DRESSING! THEY'LL GET A FEVER, CHILLS, ABDOMINAL PAIN, MASSIVE DIARRHEA, VOMITING...THEY'LL BE TOO ILL TO VOTE!
IS THAT A SEASONING? I'LL TAKE SOME!
HOLY SHIT! THAT'S INSANE! DID ANYONE DIE?
NO, BUT 45 PEOPLE WERE HOSPITALIZED.
AFTER BREAKFAST, I PACKED MY THINGS AND MADE MY WAY TO THE DALLES. I MADE ONE LAST STOP ON MY GHOST TOWN TOUR IN BOYD, OREGON. THERE WASN'T MUCH TO SEE IN BOYD BESIDES AN OLD GRAIN ELEVATOR.
WHEN I STEPPED OUTSIDE OF MY RENTAL CAR TO GET A PHOTO, THE FIRST THING I NOTICED WAS HOW QUIET IT WAS. IN FACT, THE ONLY AUDIBLE SOUND CAME FROM A DILAPIDATED HOUSE/BARN IN THE FAR DISTANCE. THERE WAS A BIG WOODEN DOOR AT THE TOP OF IT. SLOWLY, IT SWAYED BACK AND FORTH. FROM WHERE I STOOD, I COULD HEAR THE HINGES SCREECHING. I LIKED HOW PEACEFUL AND QUIET IT WAS, BUT I FELT DISTRESSED BY THE ABANDONMENT... MAYBE I DO NEED TO BE SURROUNDED BY PEOPLE AFTER ALL.

TEENAGE BOY

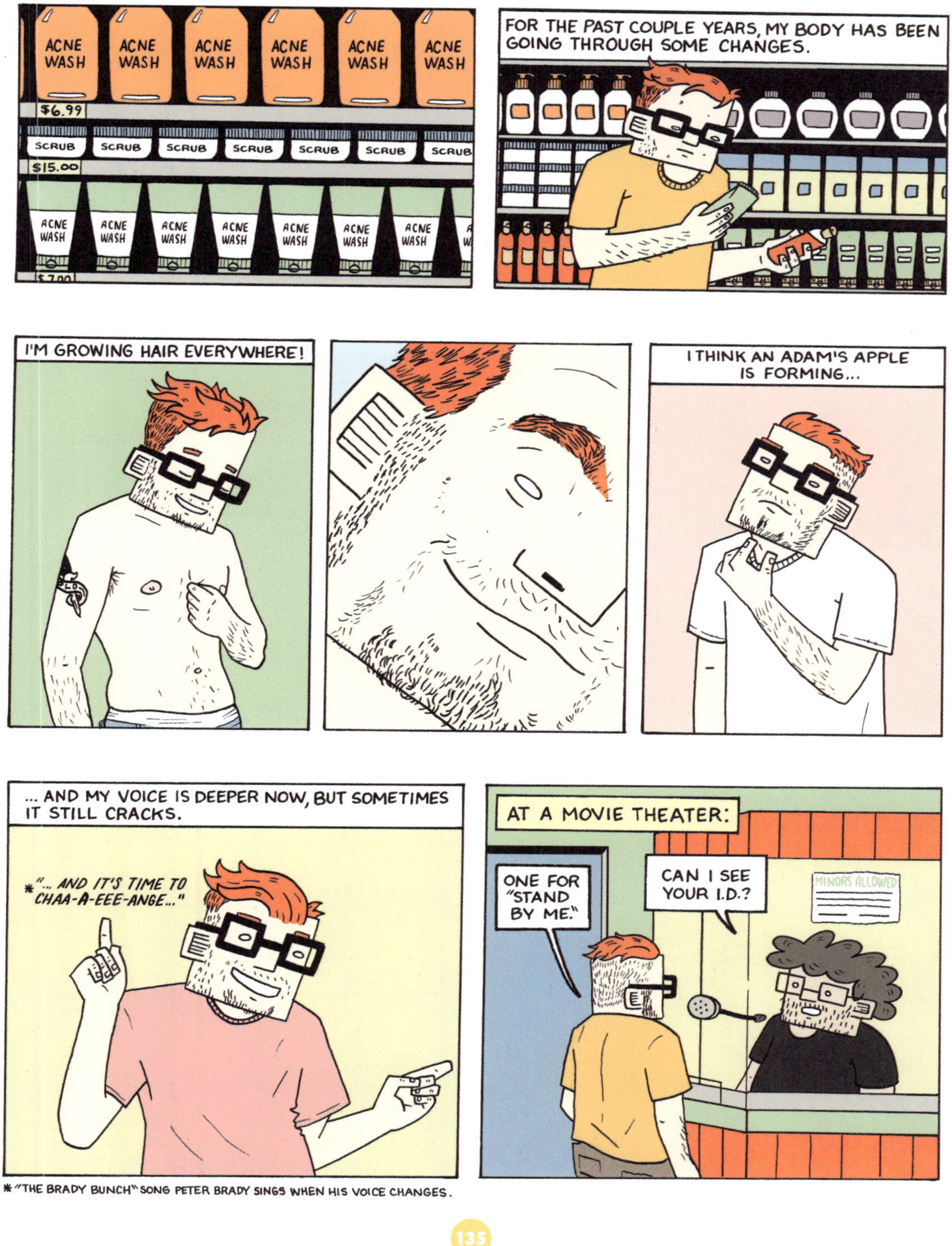

ACNE WASH
$6.99
SCRUB
$15.00
ACNE WASH
FOR THE PAST COUPLE YEARS, MY BODY HAS BEEN GOING THROUGH SOME CHANGES.
I'M GROWING HAIR EVERYWHERE!
I THINK AN ADAM'S APPLE IS FORMING...
... AND MY VOICE IS DEEPER NOW, BUT SOMETIMES IT STILL CRACKS.
*"... AND IT'S TIME TO CHAA-A-EEE-ANGE..."
AT A MOVIE THEATER:
ONE FOR "STAND BY ME."
CAN I SEE YOUR I.D.?
MINORS ALLOWED

* "THE BRADY BUNCH" SONG PETER BRADY SINGS WHEN HIS VOICE CHANGES.

OH! DAMN. YOU DO NOT LOOK 34.
YEAH, I KNOW.
IT'S NOT UNCOMMON FOR PEOPLE TO MISTAKE ME FOR A TEENAGER. I'M 5'4", PRETTY SCRAWNY, AND I'M GOING THROUGH PUBERTY.
CRAP TO FEED MY RAVENOUS APPETITE
SODA
I'M NOT EXPERIENCING A DELAYED PUBERTY. I'M EXPERIENCING MY SECOND PUBERTY. I'M TRANS-GENDER, AND WHEN A TRANS PERSON TRANSITIONS WITH HORMONE REPLACEMENT THERAPY, THEY DEVELOP SECONDARY SEX CHARACTERISTICS ASSOCIATED WITH THE GENDER THEY IDENTIFY WITH. AS A TRANS MAN, I INJECT TESTOSTERONE. THIS HORMONE IS THE REASON WHY FOLKS GROW FACIAL HAIR, HAVE DEEP VOICES, AND HAVE A HIGH LIBIDO.
AS A KID, I ENVIED MALE BODIES. I YEARNED FOR A PHYSICAL APPEARANCE I KNEW I'D NEVER ACQUIRE. YOU CAN ONLY IMAGINE HOW HAPPY I AM TODAY, TO SEE MY BODY SLOWLY RESEMBLE WHAT I ALWAYS DESIRED.
H.R.T. IS WONDERFUL! PRAISE CHEMISTRY.
PUBERTY HAS BEEN EXCITING! I MISSED OUT ON THIS EXCITEMENT THE FIRST TIME, 20 YEARS AGO.
YOUR BODY IS GOING THROUGH MANY CHANGES. THIS STAGE IN YOUR LIFE IS CALLED PUBERTY. YOU'LL DEVELOP BREASTS AND START YOUR MENSTRUAL PERIOD. YOU ARE **BECOMING WOMEN**.

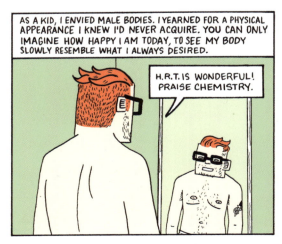

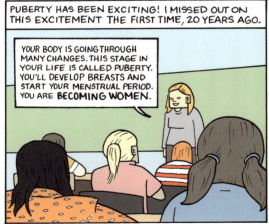

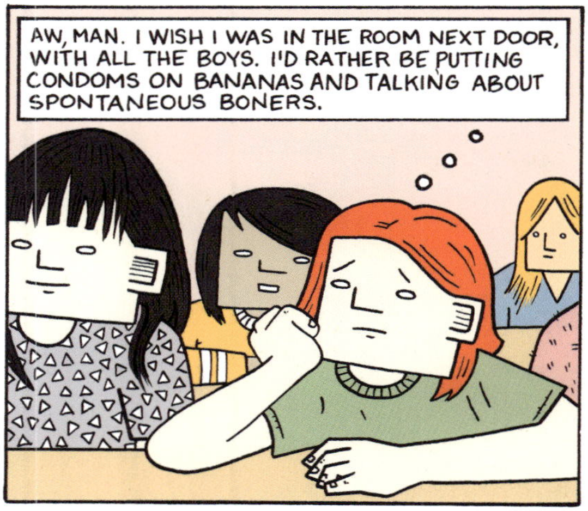
AW, MAN. I WISH I WAS IN THE ROOM NEXT DOOR, WITH ALL THE BOYS. I'D RATHER BE PUTTING CONDOMS ON BANANAS AND TALKING ABOUT SPONTANEOUS BONERS.

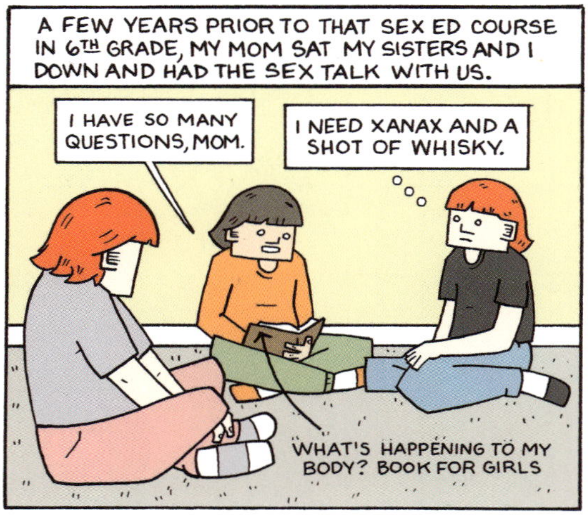
A FEW YEARS PRIOR TO THAT SEX ED COURSE IN 6TH GRADE, MY MOM SAT MY SISTERS AND I DOWN AND HAD THE SEX TALK WITH US.
I HAVE SO MANY QUESTIONS, MOM.
I NEED XANAX AND A SHOT OF WHISKY.
WHAT'S HAPPENING TO MY BODY? BOOK FOR GIRLS

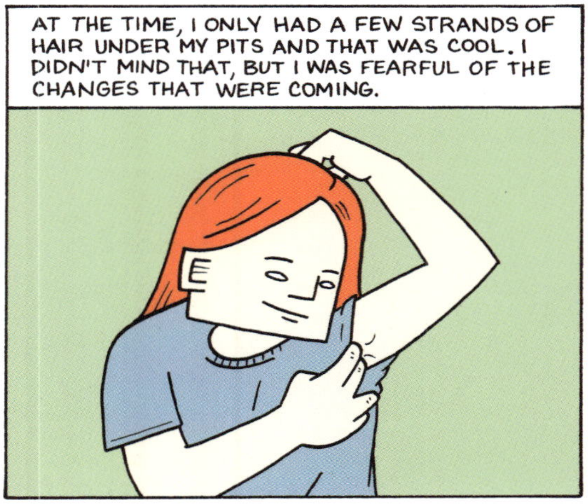
AT THE TIME, I ONLY HAD A FEW STRANDS OF HAIR UNDER MY PITS AND THAT WAS COOL. I DIDN'T MIND THAT, BUT I WAS FEARFUL OF THE CHANGES THAT WERE COMING.

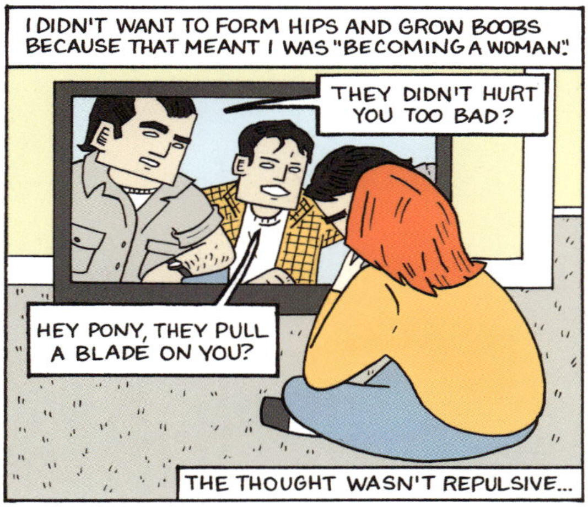
I DIDN'T WANT TO FORM HIPS AND GROW BOOBS BECAUSE THAT MEANT I WAS "BECOMING A WOMAN."
THEY DIDN'T HURT YOU TOO BAD?
HEY PONY, THEY PULL A BLADE ON YOU?
THE THOUGHT WASN'T REPULSIVE...

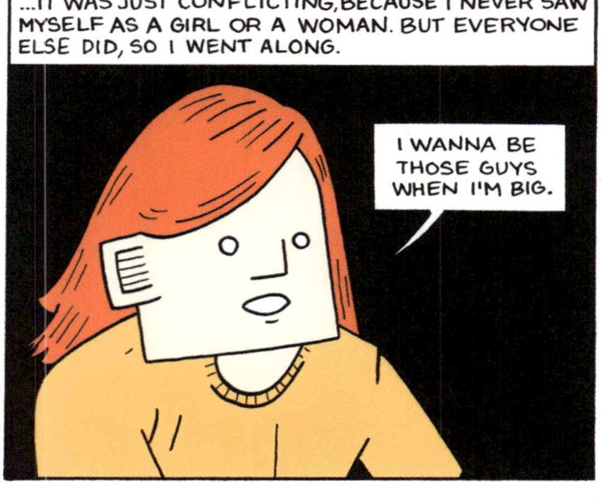
...IT WAS JUST CONFLICTING, BECAUSE I NEVER SAW MYSELF AS A GIRL OR A WOMAN. BUT EVERYONE ELSE DID, SO I WENT ALONG.
I WANNA BE THOSE GUYS WHEN I'M BIG.

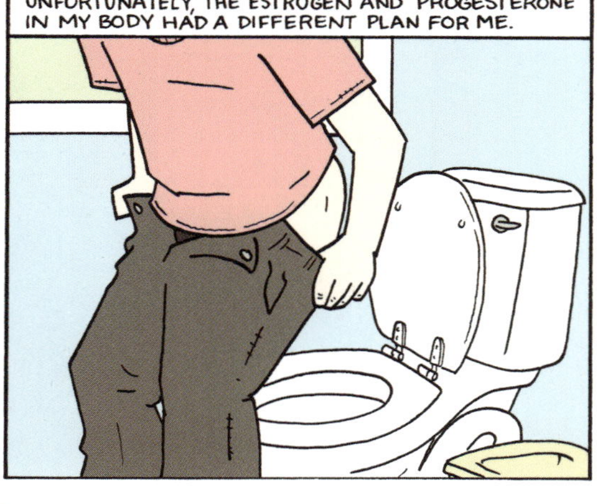
UNFORTUNATELY, THE ESTROGEN AND PROGESTERONE IN MY BODY HAD A DIFFERENT PLAN FOR ME.

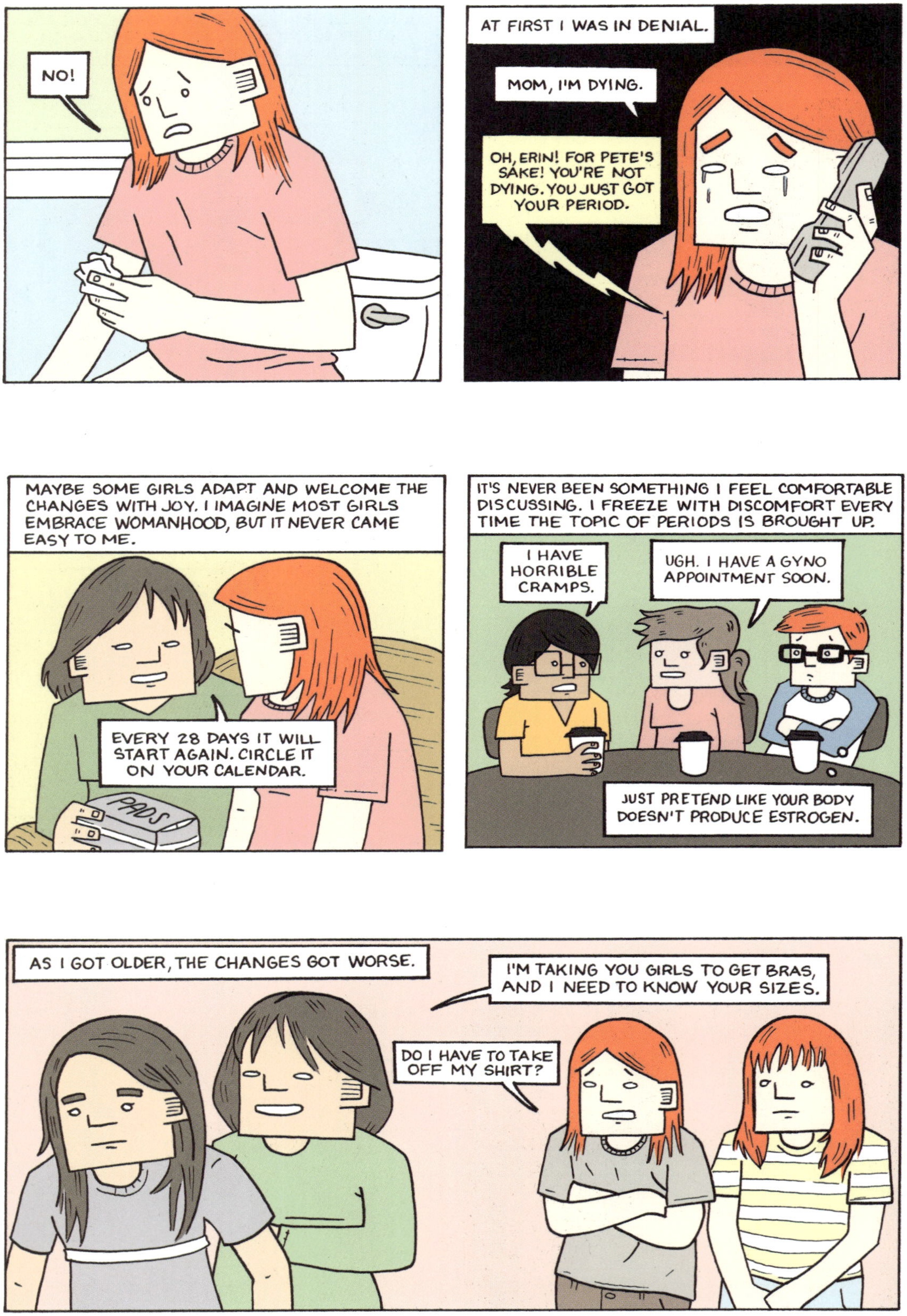
NO!
AT FIRST I WAS IN DENIAL.
MOM, I'M DYING.
OH, ERIN! FOR PETE'S SAKE! YOU'RE NOT DYING. YOU JUST GOT YOUR PERIOD.
MAYBE SOME GIRLS ADAPT AND WELCOME THE CHANGES WITH JOY. I IMAGINE MOST GIRLS EMBRACE WOMANHOOD, BUT IT NEVER CAME EASY TO ME.
EVERY 28 DAYS IT WILL START AGAIN. CIRCLE IT ON YOUR CALENDAR.
PADS
IT'S NEVER BEEN SOMETHING I FEEL COMFORTABLE DISCUSSING. I FREEZE WITH DISCOMFORT EVERY TIME THE TOPIC OF PERIODS IS BROUGHT UP.
I HAVE HORRIBLE CRAMPS.
UGH. I HAVE A GYNO APPOINTMENT SOON.
JUST PRETEND LIKE YOUR BODY DOESN'T PRODUCE ESTROGEN.
AS I GOT OLDER, THE CHANGES GOT WORSE.
I'M TAKING YOU GIRLS TO GET BRAS, AND I NEED TO KNOW YOUR SIZES.
DO I HAVE TO TAKE OFF MY SHIRT?

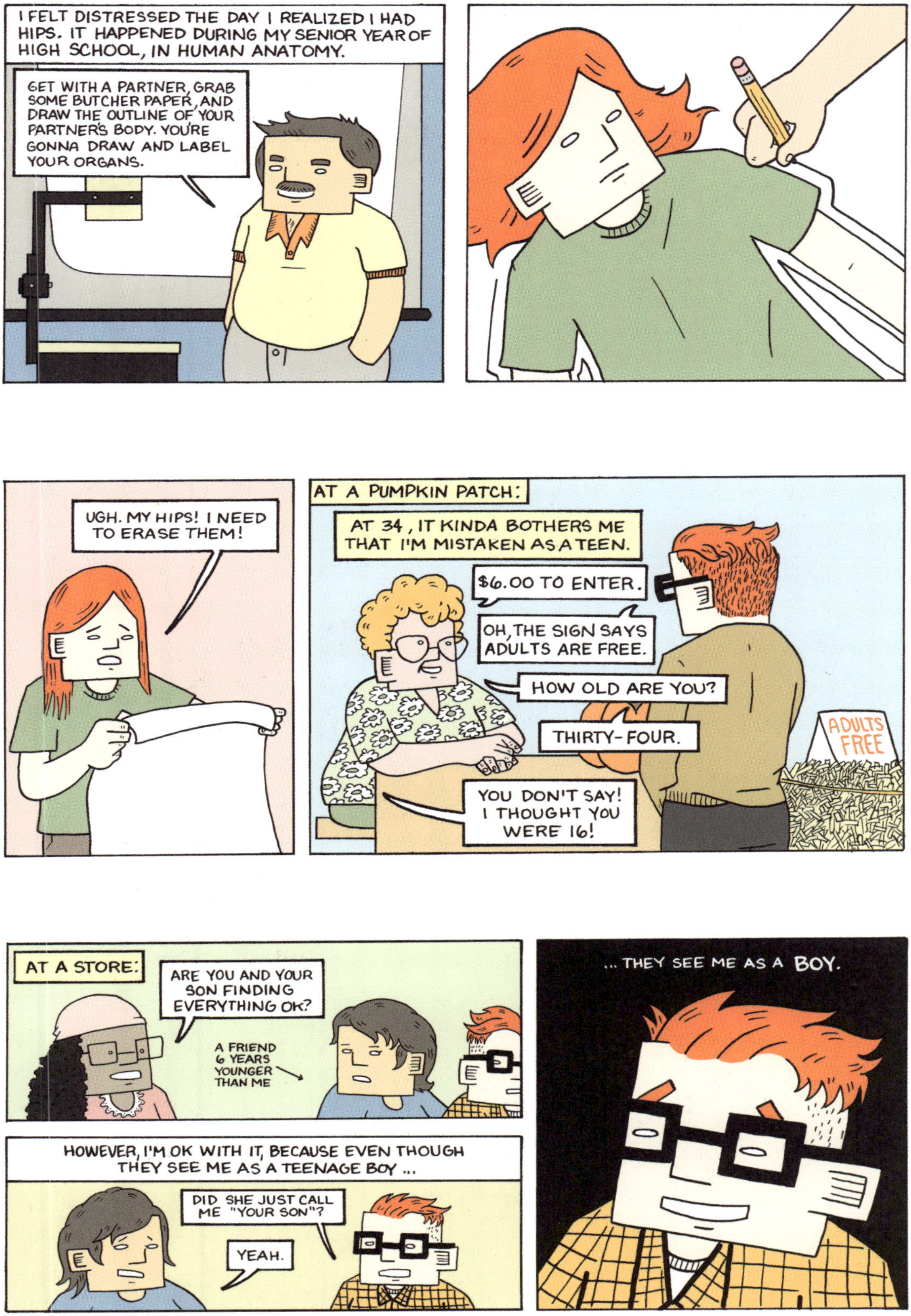

I FELT DISTRESSED THE DAY I REALIZED I HAD HIPS. IT HAPPENED DURING MY SENIOR YEAR OF HIGH SCHOOL, IN HUMAN ANATOMY.
GET WITH A PARTNER, GRAB SOME BUTCHER PAPER, AND DRAW THE OUTLINE OF YOUR PARTNER'S BODY. YOU'RE GONNA DRAW AND LABEL YOUR ORGANS.
UGH. MY HIPS! I NEED TO ERASE THEM!
AT A PUMPKIN PATCH:
AT 34, IT KINDA BOTHERS ME THAT I'M MISTAKEN AS A TEEN.
$6.00 TO ENTER.
OH, THE SIGN SAYS ADULTS ARE FREE.
HOW OLD ARE YOU?
THIRTY-FOUR.
ADULTS FREE
YOU DON'T SAY! I THOUGHT YOU WERE 16!
AT A STORE:
ARE YOU AND YOUR SON FINDING EVERYTHING OK?
A FRIEND 6 YEARS YOUNGER THAN ME
HOWEVER, I'M OK WITH IT, BECAUSE EVEN THOUGH THEY SEE ME AS A TEENAGE BOY ...
DID SHE JUST CALL ME "YOUR SON"?
YEAH.
... THEY SEE ME AS A BOY.

FIXATING ON FINN

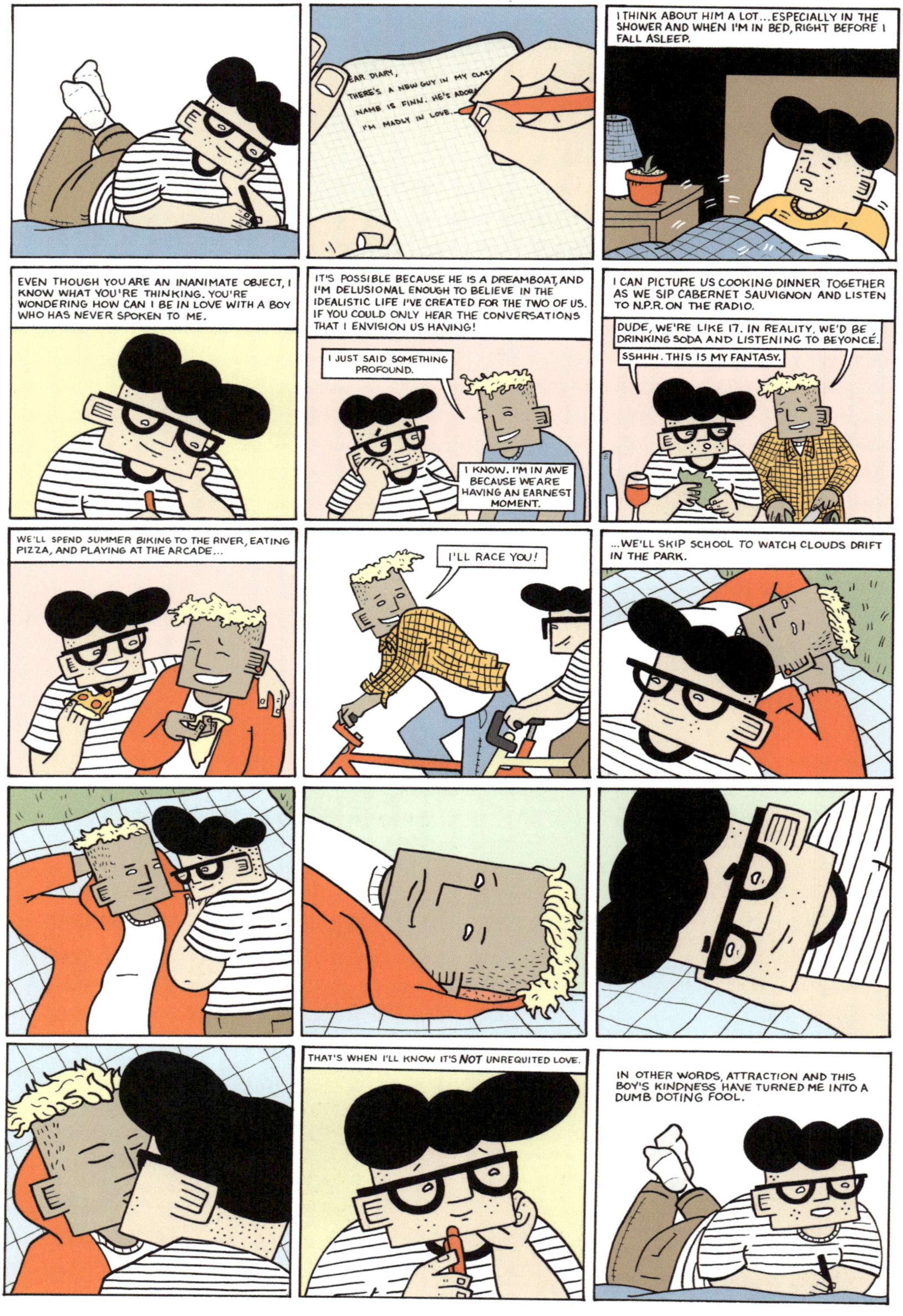
EAR DIARY,
THERE'S A NEW GUY IN MY CLASS
NAME IS FINN. HE'S ADORA
I'M MADLY IN LOVE.
I THINK ABOUT HIM A LOT... ESPECIALLY IN THE SHOWER AND WHEN I'M IN BED, RIGHT BEFORE I FALL ASLEEP.
EVEN THOUGH YOU ARE AN INANIMATE OBJECT, I KNOW WHAT YOU'RE THINKING. YOU'RE WONDERING HOW CAN I BE IN LOVE WITH A BOY WHO HAS NEVER SPOKEN TO ME.
IT'S POSSIBLE BECAUSE HE IS A DREAMBOAT, AND I'M DELUSIONAL ENOUGH TO BELIEVE IN THE IDEALISTIC LIFE I'VE CREATED FOR THE TWO OF US. IF YOU COULD ONLY HEAR THE CONVERSATIONS THAT I ENVISION US HAVING!
I JUST SAID SOMETHING PROFOUND.
I KNOW. I'M IN AWE BECAUSE WE'ARE HAVING AN EARNEST MOMENT.
I CAN PICTURE US COOKING DINNER TOGETHER AS WE SIP CABERNET SAUVIGNON AND LISTEN TO N.P.R. ON THE RADIO.
DUDE, WE'RE LIKE 17. IN REALITY, WE'D BE DRINKING SODA AND LISTENING TO BEYONCÉ.
SSHHH. THIS IS MY FANTASY.
WE'LL SPEND SUMMER BIKING TO THE RIVER, EATING PIZZA, AND PLAYING AT THE ARCADE...
I'LL RACE YOU!
...WE'LL SKIP SCHOOL TO WATCH CLOUDS DRIFT IN THE PARK.
THAT'S WHEN I'LL KNOW IT'S NOT UNREQUITED LOVE.
IN OTHER WORDS, ATTRACTION AND THIS BOY'S KINDNESS HAVE TURNED ME INTO A DUMB DOTING FOOL.

HUBERT

MY NAME IS HUBERT. I'M 27. I'M LOOKING FOR A DATE.
I CAN'T COOK, BUT I KNOW WHERE TO FIND THE BEST PIZZA
AND THE BEST KOREAN FOOD CART.
I SHOWER THREE TIMES A WEEK, I NEVER COMB MY HAIR, I GO
COMMANDO, AND I WEAR THE SAME JEANS EVERY DAY.
HOWEVER, I BRUSH AFTER EVERY MEAL AND FLOSS DAILY.
I WANNA DATE SOMEONE WHO WANTS TO SHOP FOR RECORDS
AT AN UNDERGROUND HOLE IN THE WALL. IT'S THE KIND OF
SHOP THAT'S PLASTERED WITH GIG POSTERS AND STOCKED WITH
OBSCURE RECORDS. THE FOLKS WHO WORK THERE ARE KIND OF
PRETENTIOUS, BUT IT MAKES US FEEL COOL BECAUSE WE
DISCOVERED A SECRET PLACE THAT CATERS TO A NICHE CROWD.
I'M LOOKING FOR SOMEONE WHO WANTS TO BUY ZINES AT AN
ANARCHIST BOOKSTORE. WE'LL DRINK COFFEE AND READ
LITERATURE AT A LOCALLY-OWNED COFFEEHOUSE. WE'LL SMOKE
CIGARETTES, DRINK BEER, AND TALK ABOUT POETRY, ART AND
HISTORY AT A DIVE BAR. WE'LL SLEEP IN 'TIL 10, AND THEN GET
BREAKFAST AT A QUAINT SPOT THAT WAS ONCE SOMEONE'S
TWO-STORY HOUSE. NOW IT'S A JOINT THAT MAKES GOOD
OMELETTES AND HOME FRIES. IT'S THE KIND OF PLACE THAT
SERVES BEVERAGES IN MUGS FROM DIFFERENT THRIFT STORES.
I'M ATTRACTED TO MODS, BUT I'M OPEN TO ANYONE.
IF YOU ALSO LIKE TO PROCESS YOUR EMOTIONS IN A JOURNAL,
YOU SHOULD HIT ME UP.

NAVEL ORANGES

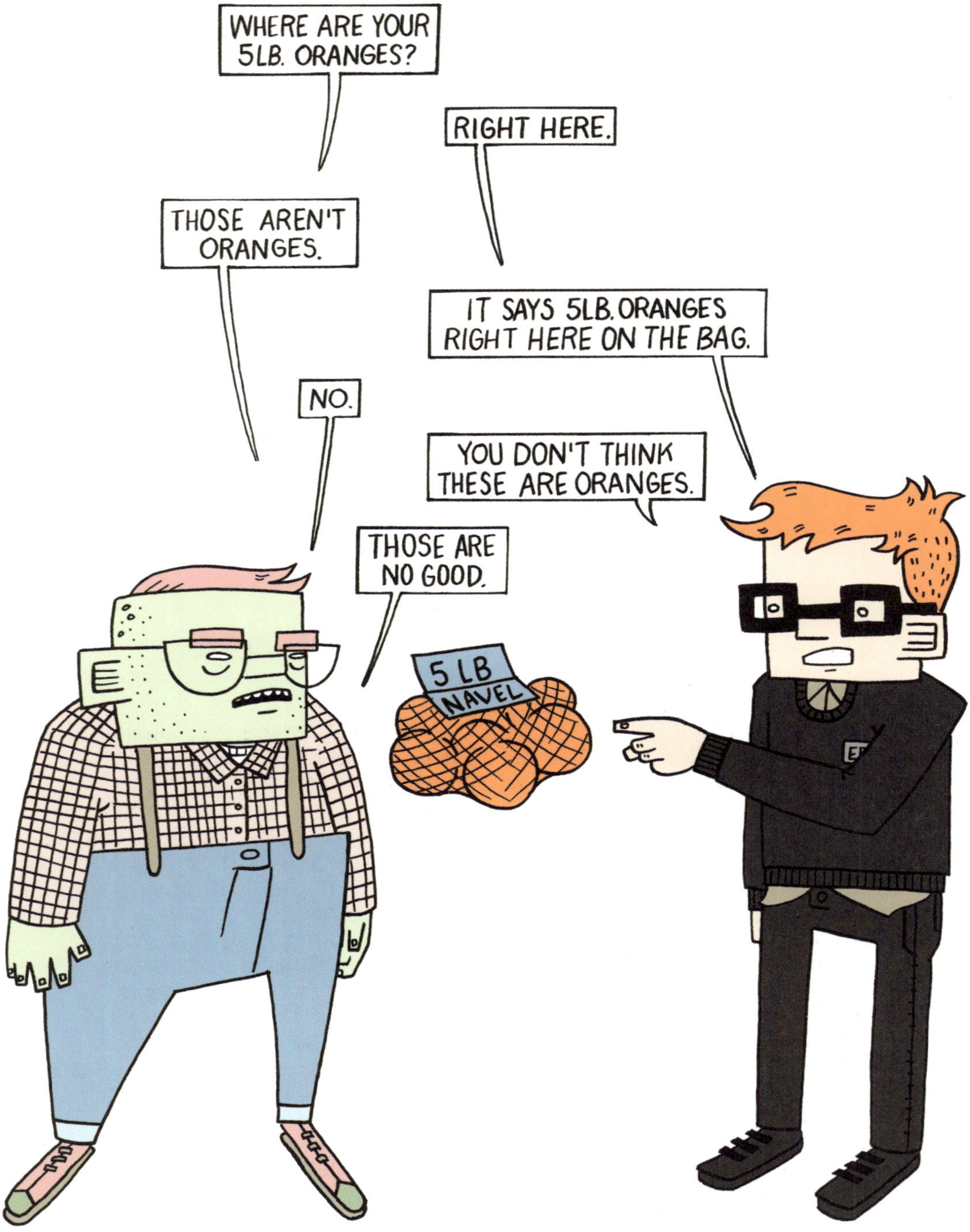
WHERE ARE YOUR 5LB. ORANGES?
RIGHT HERE.
THOSE AREN'T ORANGES.
IT SAYS 5LB. ORANGES RIGHT HERE ON THE BAG.
NO.
YOU DON'T THINK THESE ARE ORANGES.
THOSE ARE NO GOOD.
5 LB
NAVEL

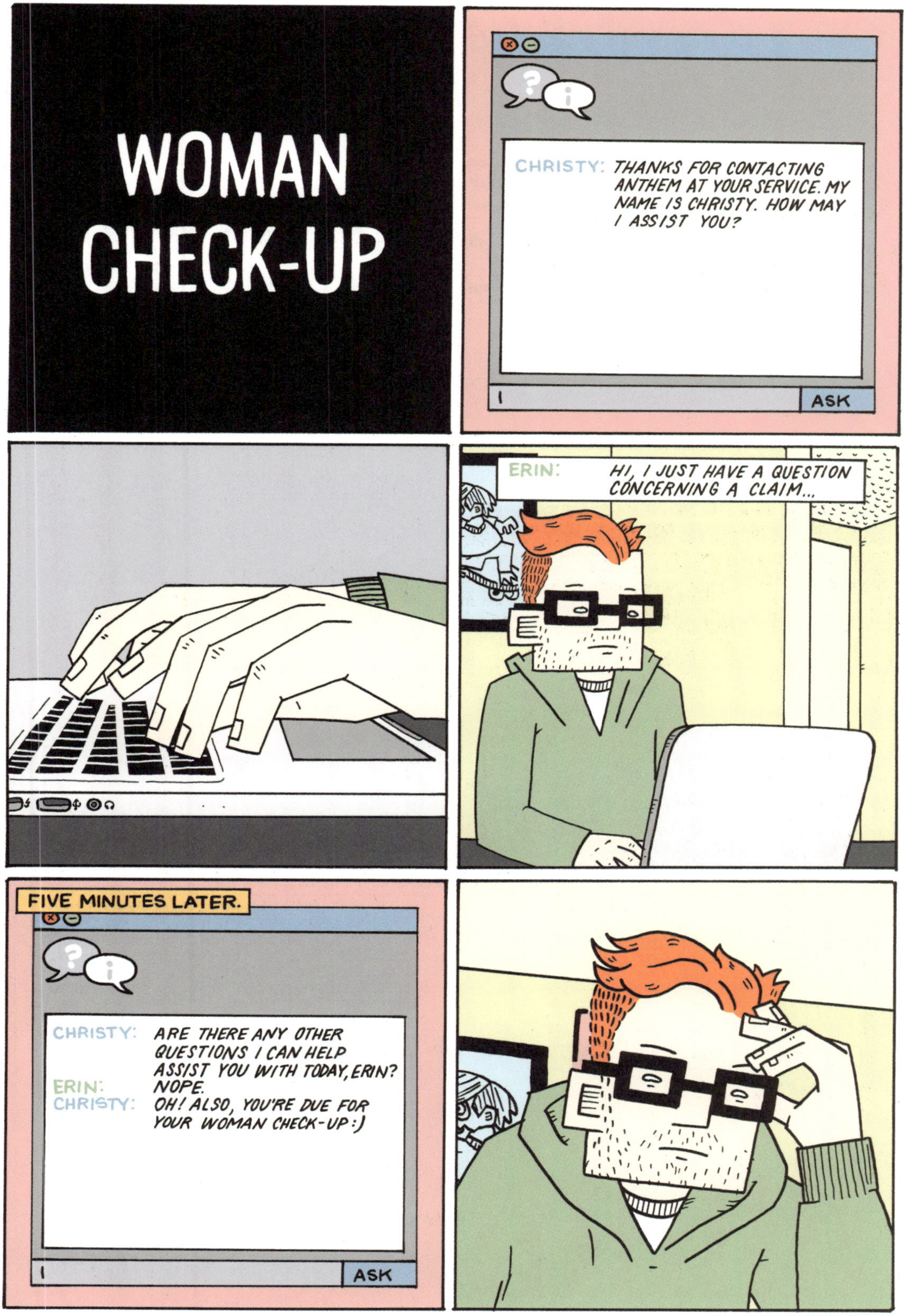
WOMAN CHECK-UP
CHRISTY: THANKS FOR CONTACTING ANTHEM AT YOUR SERVICE. MY NAME IS CHRISTY. HOW MAY I ASSIST YOU?
ASK
ERIN: HI, I JUST HAVE A QUESTION CONCERNING A CLAIM...
FIVE MINUTES LATER.
CHRISTY: ARE THERE ANY OTHER QUESTIONS I CAN HELP ASSIST YOU WITH TODAY, ERIN?
ERIN: NOPE.
CHRISTY: OH! ALSO, YOU'RE DUE FOR YOUR WOMAN CHECK-UP :)
ASK

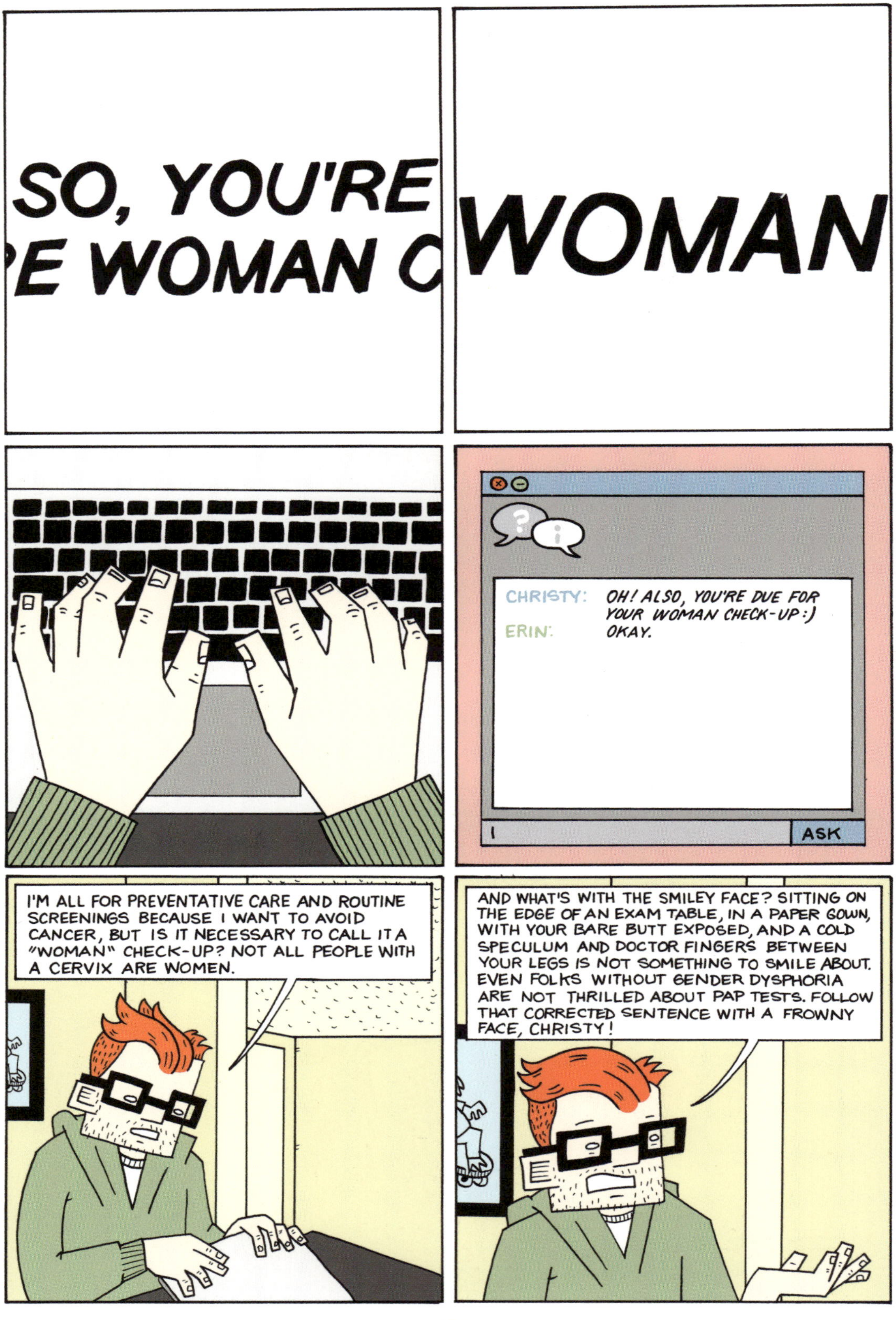
SO, YOU'RE
E WOMAN C
WOMAN
CHRISTY: OH! ALSO, YOU'RE DUE FOR YOUR WOMAN CHECK-UP :)
ERIN: OKAY.
ASK
I'M ALL FOR PREVENTATIVE CARE AND ROUTINE SCREENINGS BECAUSE I WANT TO AVOID CANCER, BUT IS IT NECESSARY TO CALL IT A "WOMAN" CHECK-UP? NOT ALL PEOPLE WITH A CERVIX ARE WOMEN.
AND WHAT'S WITH THE SMILEY FACE? SITTING ON THE EDGE OF AN EXAM TABLE, IN A PAPER GOWN, WITH YOUR BARE BUTT EXPOSED, AND A COLD SPECULUM AND DOCTOR FINGERS BETWEEN YOUR LEGS IS NOT SOMETHING TO SMILE ABOUT. EVEN FOLKS WITHOUT GENDER DYSPHORIA ARE NOT THRILLED ABOUT PAP TESTS. FOLLOW THAT CORRECTED SENTENCE WITH A FROWNY FACE, CHRISTY!

AUDIENCE

IT WASN'T UNCOMMON FOR MY FAMILY TO PULL PRANKS ON EACH OTHER.

ONE TIME, AFTER WE SAW THE MOVIE "IT," I SNUCK INTO THE BATHROOM WHEN LAUREN WAS TAKING A SHOWER.

THERE'S A SCENE IN THE FILM WHEN PENNY-WISE THE CLOWN APPEARS WHILE A BOY IS TAKING A SHOWER. I THOUGHT IT WOULD BE FUNNY TO HOLD A RED TOWEL (THE COLOR OF PENNYWISE'S HAIR) ABOVE THE SHOWER DOOR.

WHEN LAUREN TURNED AROUND AND SAW THE RED, SHE SCREAMED. I LAUGHED.

"...WELL, RHONDA YOU LOOK SO FINE..."

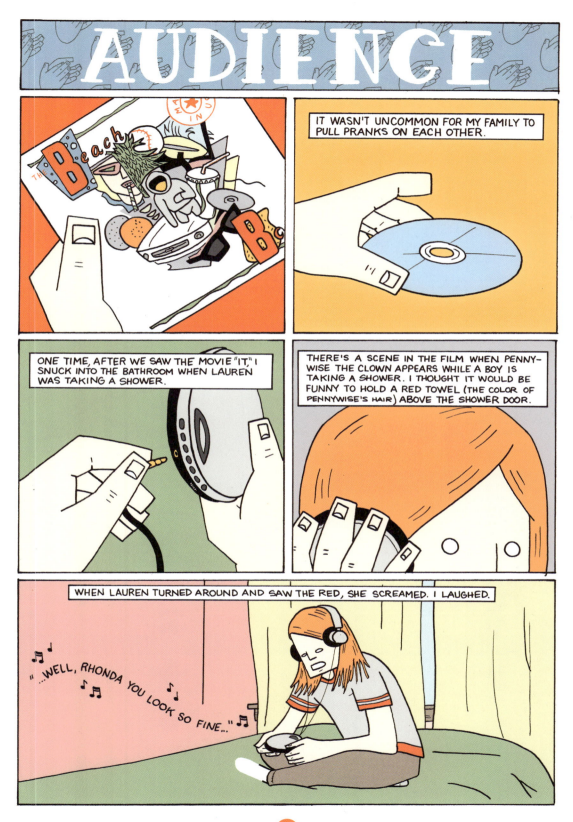

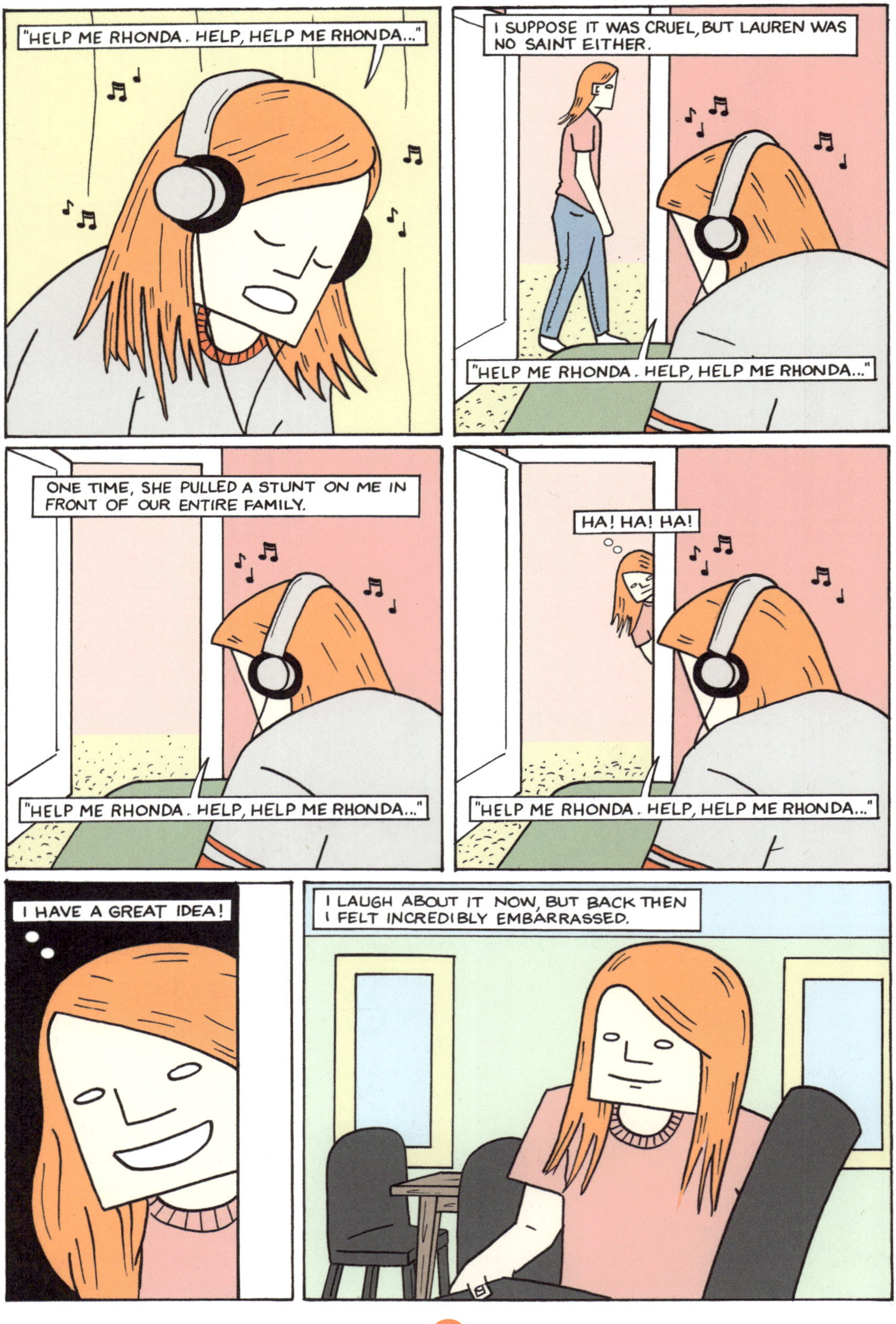
"HELP ME RHONDA. HELP, HELP ME RHONDA..."
I SUPPOSE IT WAS CRUEL, BUT LAUREN WAS NO SAINT EITHER.
"HELP ME RHONDA. HELP, HELP ME RHONDA..."
ONE TIME, SHE PULLED A STUNT ON ME IN FRONT OF OUR ENTIRE FAMILY.
"HELP ME RHONDA. HELP, HELP ME RHONDA..."
HA! HA! HA!
"HELP ME RHONDA. HELP, HELP ME RHONDA..."
I HAVE A GREAT IDEA!
I LAUGH ABOUT IT NOW, BUT BACK THEN I FELT INCREDIBLY EMBARRASSED.

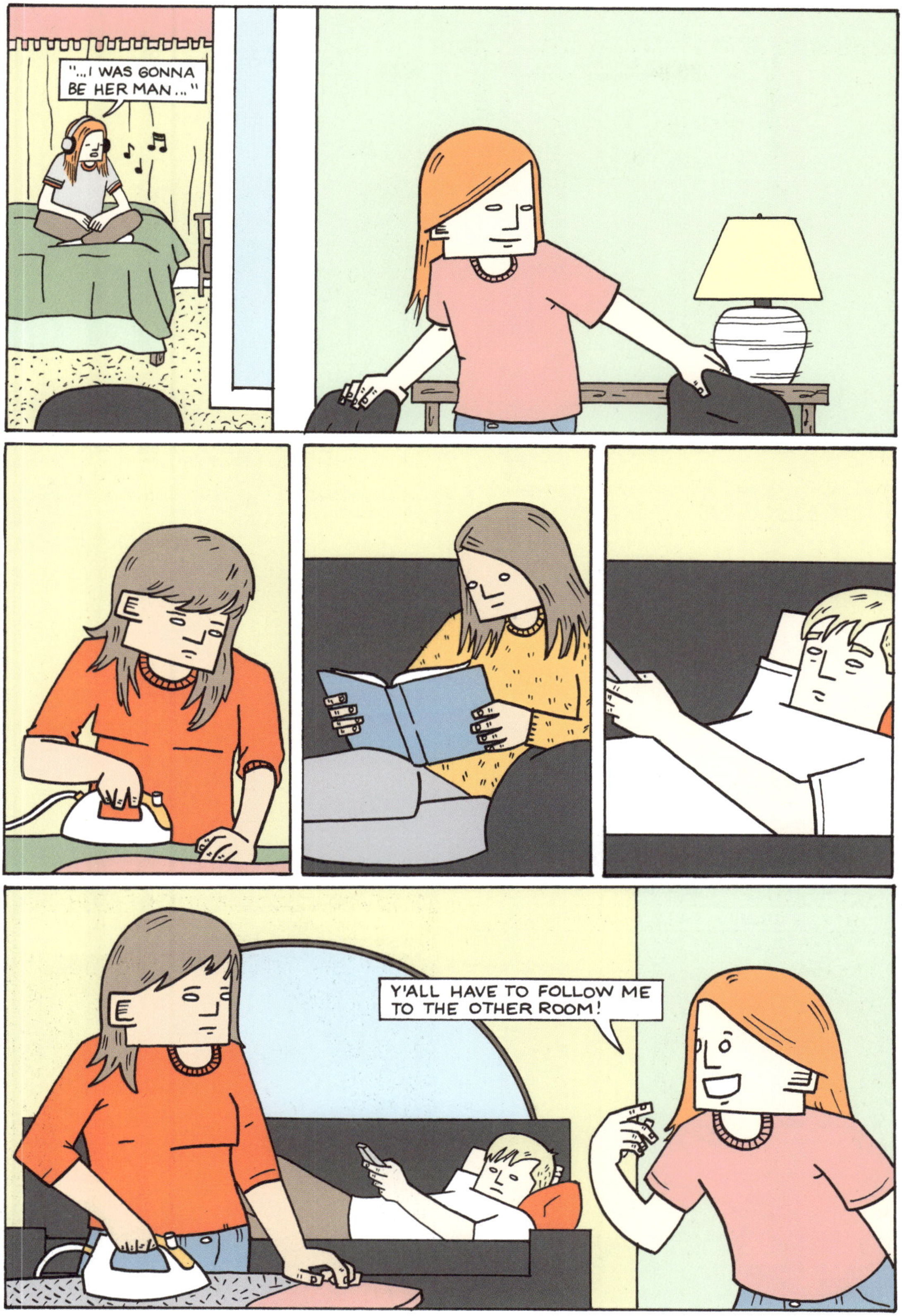
"...I WAS GONNA BE HER MAN..."
Y'ALL HAVE TO FOLLOW ME TO THE OTHER ROOM!

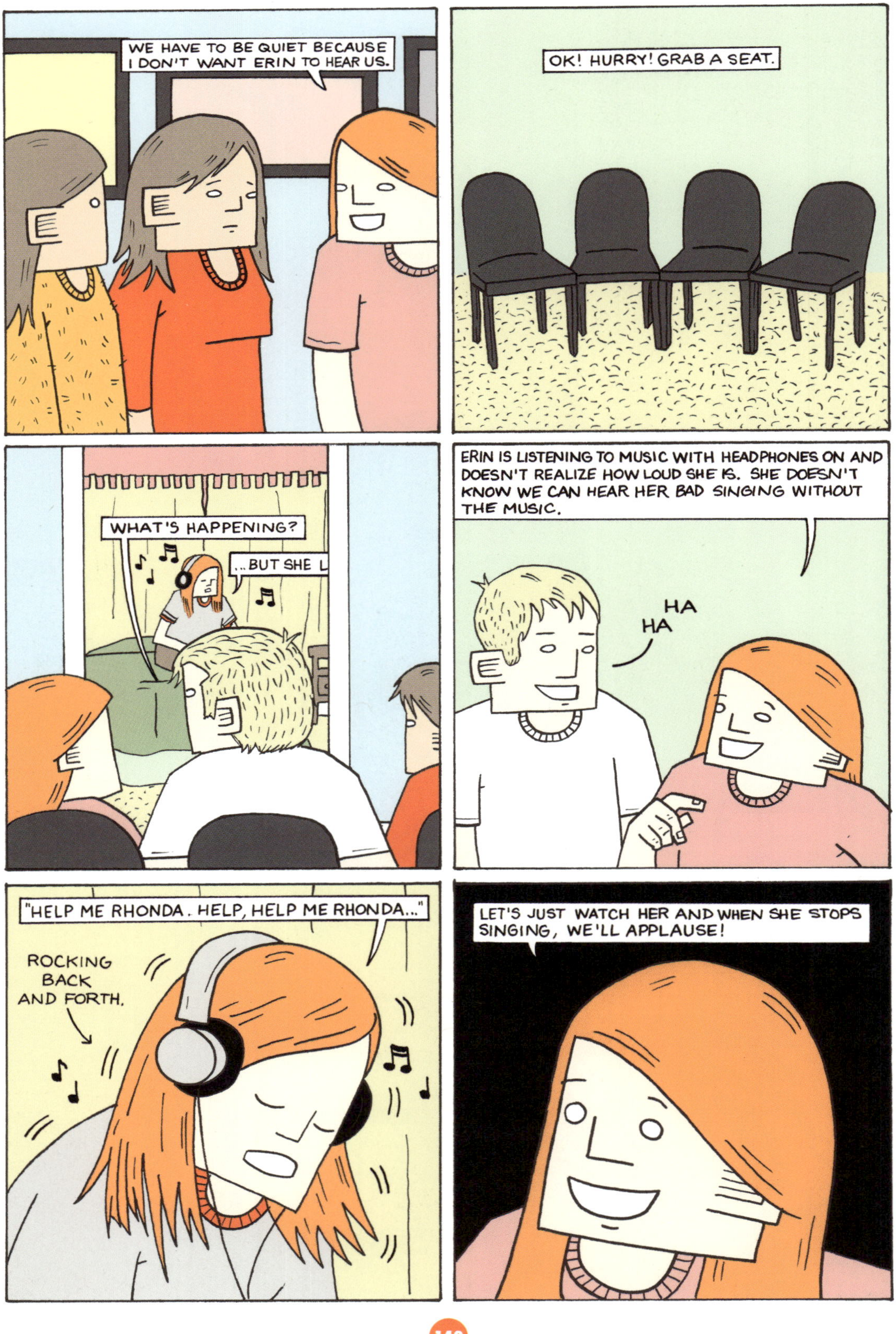
WE HAVE TO BE QUIET BECAUSE I DON'T WANT ERIN TO HEAR US.
OK! HURRY! GRAB A SEAT.
WHAT'S HAPPENING?
...BUT SHE L
ERIN IS LISTENING TO MUSIC WITH HEADPHONES ON AND DOESN'T REALIZE HOW LOUD SHE IS. SHE DOESN'T KNOW WE CAN HEAR HER BAD SINGING WITHOUT THE MUSIC.
HA HA
"HELP ME RHONDA. HELP, HELP ME RHONDA..."
ROCKING BACK AND FORTH.
LET'S JUST WATCH HER AND WHEN SHE STOPS SINGING, WE'LL APPLAUSE!

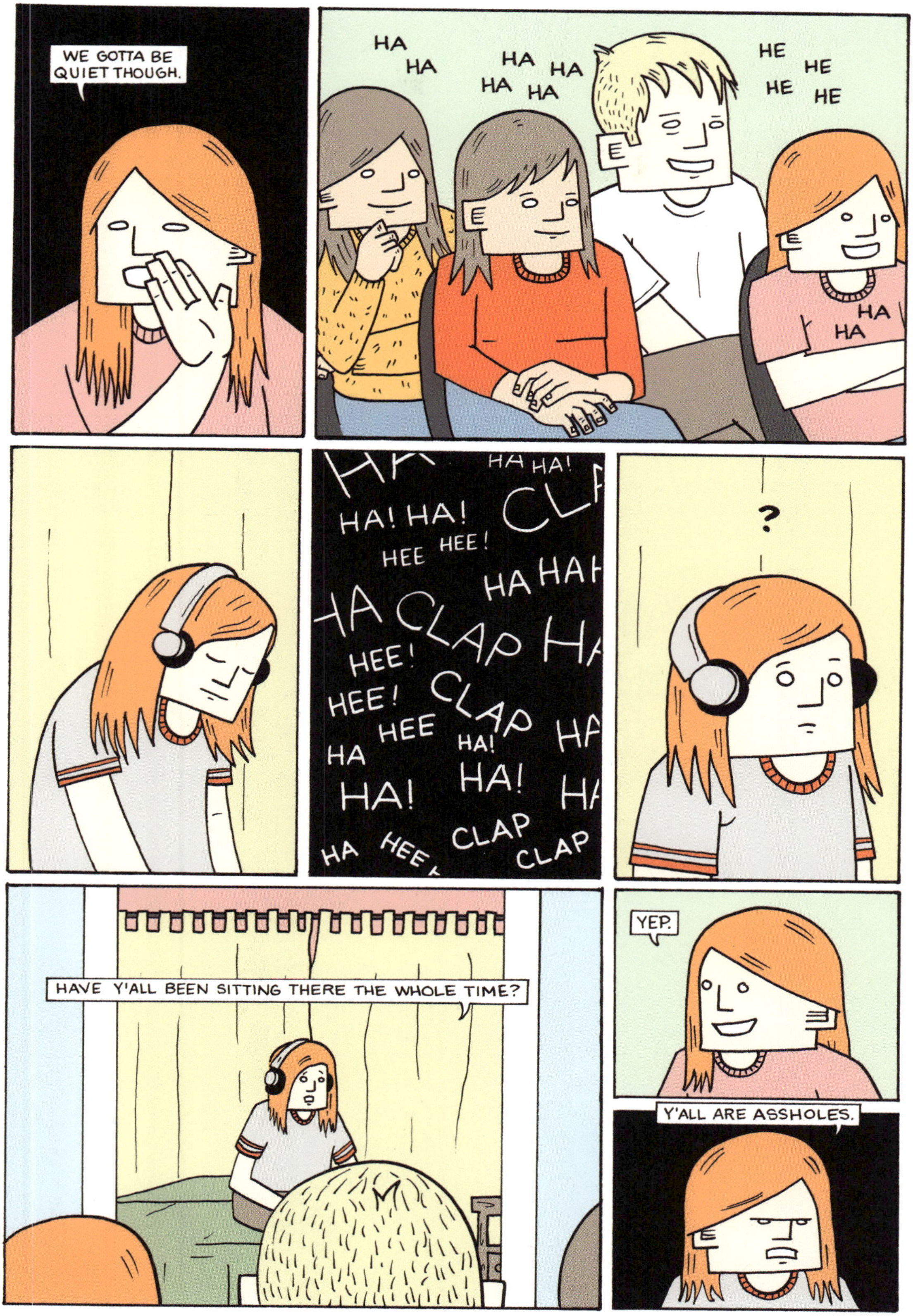
WE GOTTA BE QUIET THOUGH.
HA HA HA HA HA HA
HE HE HE HE
HA HA
HA! HA! HEE HEE! HA HA HA CLAP HEE! HEE! CLAP HEE HA! HA HA! HA! CLAP CLAP
?
HAVE Y'ALL BEEN SITTING THERE THE WHOLE TIME?
YEP.
Y'ALL ARE ASSHOLES.

WHAT DO I KNOW?

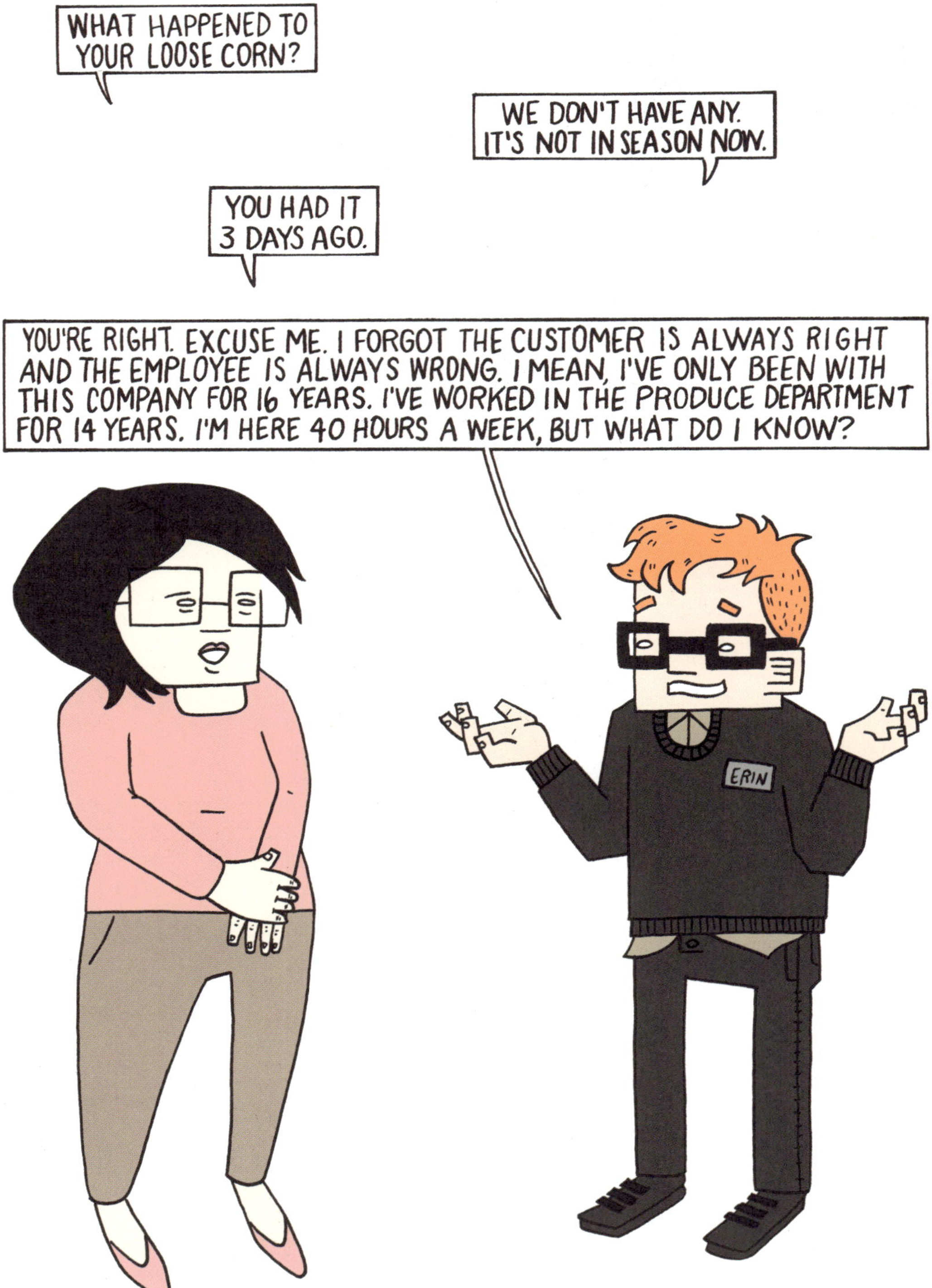
WHAT HAPPENED TO YOUR LOOSE CORN?
WE DON'T HAVE ANY. IT'S NOT IN SEASON NOW.
YOU HAD IT 3 DAYS AGO.
YOU'RE RIGHT. EXCUSE ME. I FORGOT THE CUSTOMER IS ALWAYS RIGHT AND THE EMPLOYEE IS ALWAYS WRONG. I MEAN, I'VE ONLY BEEN WITH THIS COMPANY FOR 16 YEARS. I'VE WORKED IN THE PRODUCE DEPARTMENT FOR 14 YEARS. I'M HERE 40 HOURS A WEEK, BUT WHAT DO I KNOW?
ERIN

ROGER

I DON'T LIKE CHILDREN. IF YOU HAVE KIDS, IT'S A DEAL BREAKER.
IF YOU WANT KIDS, IT'S A DEAL BREAKER. I'M 52. I'M NOT IN
THE MOOD TO WASTE MY RETIREMENT ON KID CRAFTS, DIAPERS,
AND PLAYDATES.

I DON'T LIKE PETS. IF YOU HAVE PETS, IT'S A DEAL BREAKER. CATS
ARE SPITEFUL DEMONS WHO WILL PEE ON YOUR BELONGINGS IF
YOU UPSET THEIR DAILY ROUTINES. DOGS WANT TO BE YOUR BEST
FRIEND. I DON'T NEED ANY MORE FRIENDS. FISH ARE POINTLESS.
BIRDS ONLY CHIRP AND POOP.

I HATE PICKY FOOD EATERS. IF YOU HAVE DIETARY RESTRICTIONS,
IT'S A DEAL BREAKER. I HAVE REFINED TASTE. FOOD IS AN
EXPERIENCE. I LIKE TO SHARE IT WITH OTHERS. I ENJOY
TALKING ABOUT IT. HOW AM I SUPPOSED TO MAKE DRAGON FRUIT
COCKTAILS IF YOU ONLY EAT FOOD GROWN WITHIN 100 MILES OF
YOUR HOUSE, BECAUSE YOU'RE TRYING TO REDUCE GREEN-
HOUSE GASES? AND I DON'T WANT TO HEAR ABOUT HOW
GLUTEN GIVES YOU SOFT STOOLS WHILE WE'RE EATING DINNER.
OTHER DEAL BREAKERS INCLUDE COUCH POTATOES, HOADERS,
OPEN-MOUTH EATERS, SLOW WALKERS, SOCIAL MEDIA ADDICTS,
PHONE TEXTERS, NAIL-BITERS, AND BAD PENMANSHIP.

MY NAME IS ROGER. I DON'T HAVE ANY VENEREAL DISEASES
THAT I KNOW OF. I'M MEDIOCRE. I'D CALL MY STYLE "OUTLET
MALL." I SMELL LIKE DRUG STORE AFTERSHAVE AND
LISTERINE MOUTHWASH.

WAYS TO ASK OUT A BOY

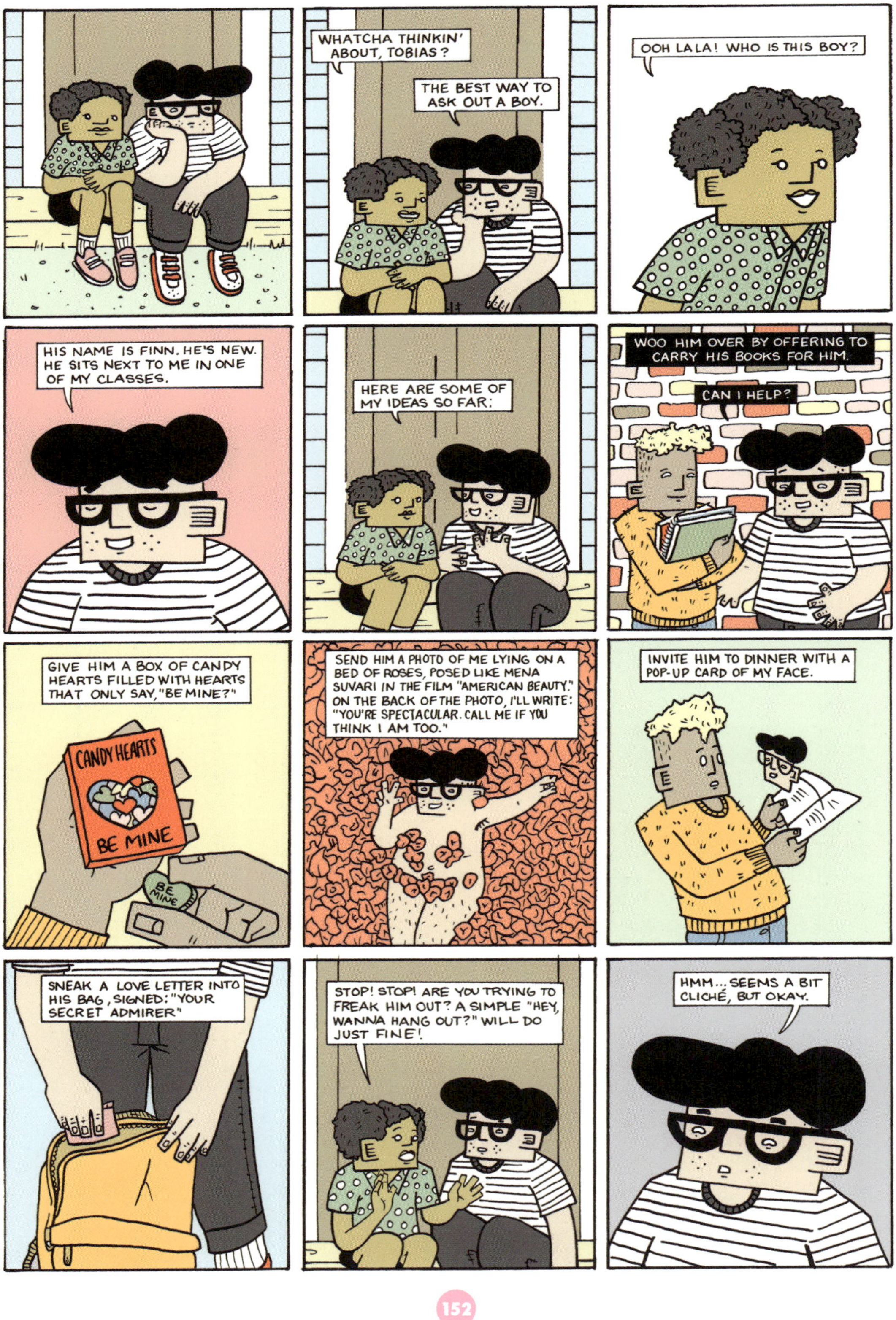

WHATCHA THINKIN' ABOUT, TOBIAS?
THE BEST WAY TO ASK OUT A BOY.
OOH LA LA! WHO IS THIS BOY?
HIS NAME IS FINN. HE'S NEW. HE SITS NEXT TO ME IN ONE OF MY CLASSES.
HERE ARE SOME OF MY IDEAS SO FAR:
WOO HIM OVER BY OFFERING TO CARRY HIS BOOKS FOR HIM.
CAN I HELP?
GIVE HIM A BOX OF CANDY HEARTS FILLED WITH HEARTS THAT ONLY SAY, "BE MINE?"
CANDY HEARTS
BE MINE
BE MINE
SEND HIM A PHOTO OF ME LYING ON A BED OF ROSES, POSED LIKE MENA SUVARI IN THE FILM "AMERICAN BEAUTY." ON THE BACK OF THE PHOTO, I'LL WRITE: "YOU'RE SPECTACULAR. CALL ME IF YOU THINK I AM TOO."
INVITE HIM TO DINNER WITH A POP-UP CARD OF MY FACE.
SNEAK A LOVE LETTER INTO HIS BAG, SIGNED: "YOUR SECRET ADMIRER"
STOP! STOP! ARE YOU TRYING TO FREAK HIM OUT? A SIMPLE "HEY, WANNA HANG OUT?" WILL DO JUST FINE!
HMM... SEEMS A BIT CLICHÉ, BUT OKAY.

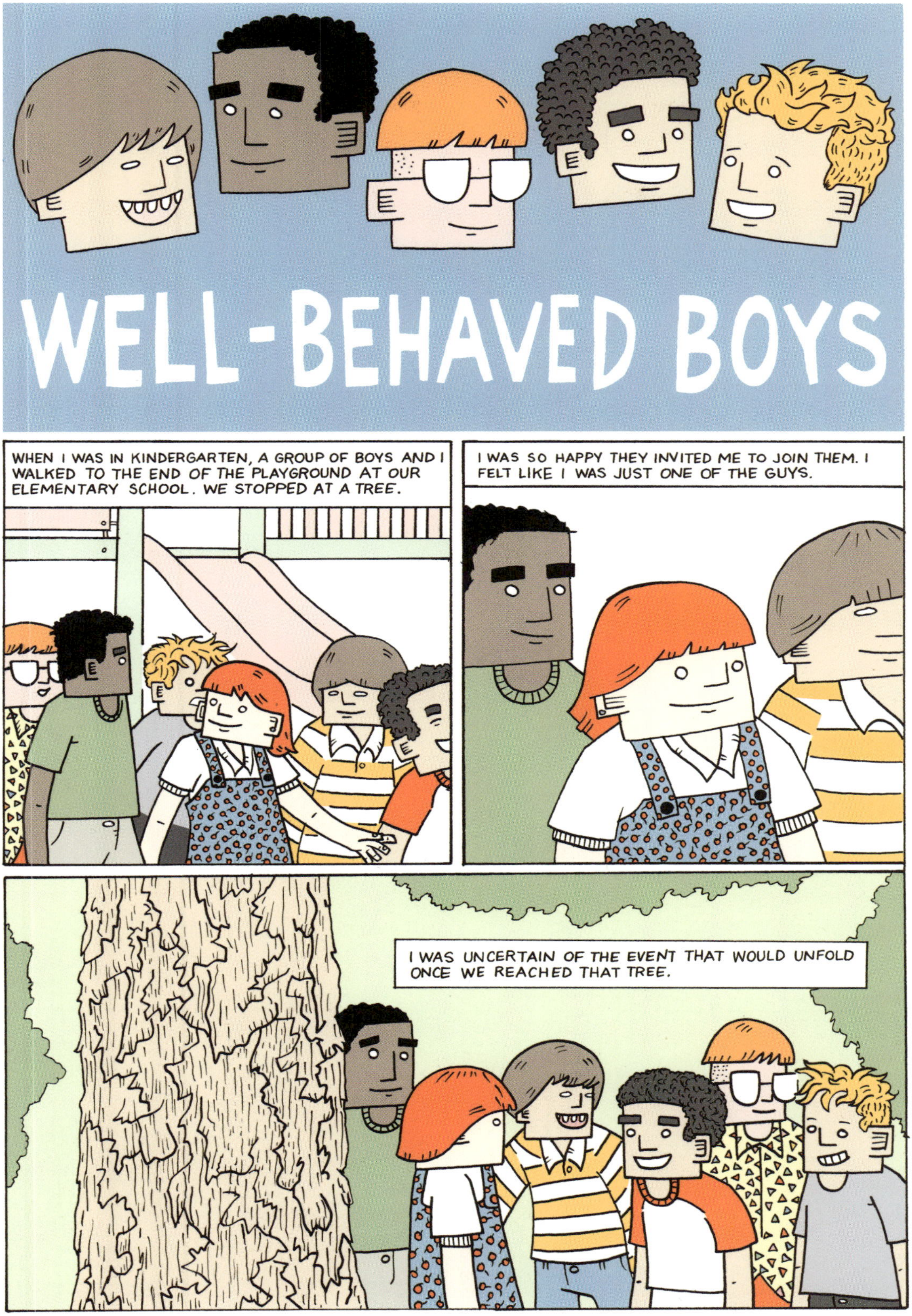
WELL-BEHAVED BOYS
WHEN I WAS IN KINDERGARTEN, A GROUP OF BOYS AND I WALKED TO THE END OF THE PLAYGROUND AT OUR ELEMENTARY SCHOOL. WE STOPPED AT A TREE.
I WAS SO HAPPY THEY INVITED ME TO JOIN THEM. I FELT LIKE I WAS JUST ONE OF THE GUYS.
I WAS UNCERTAIN OF THE EVENT THAT WOULD UNFOLD ONCE WE REACHED THAT TREE.

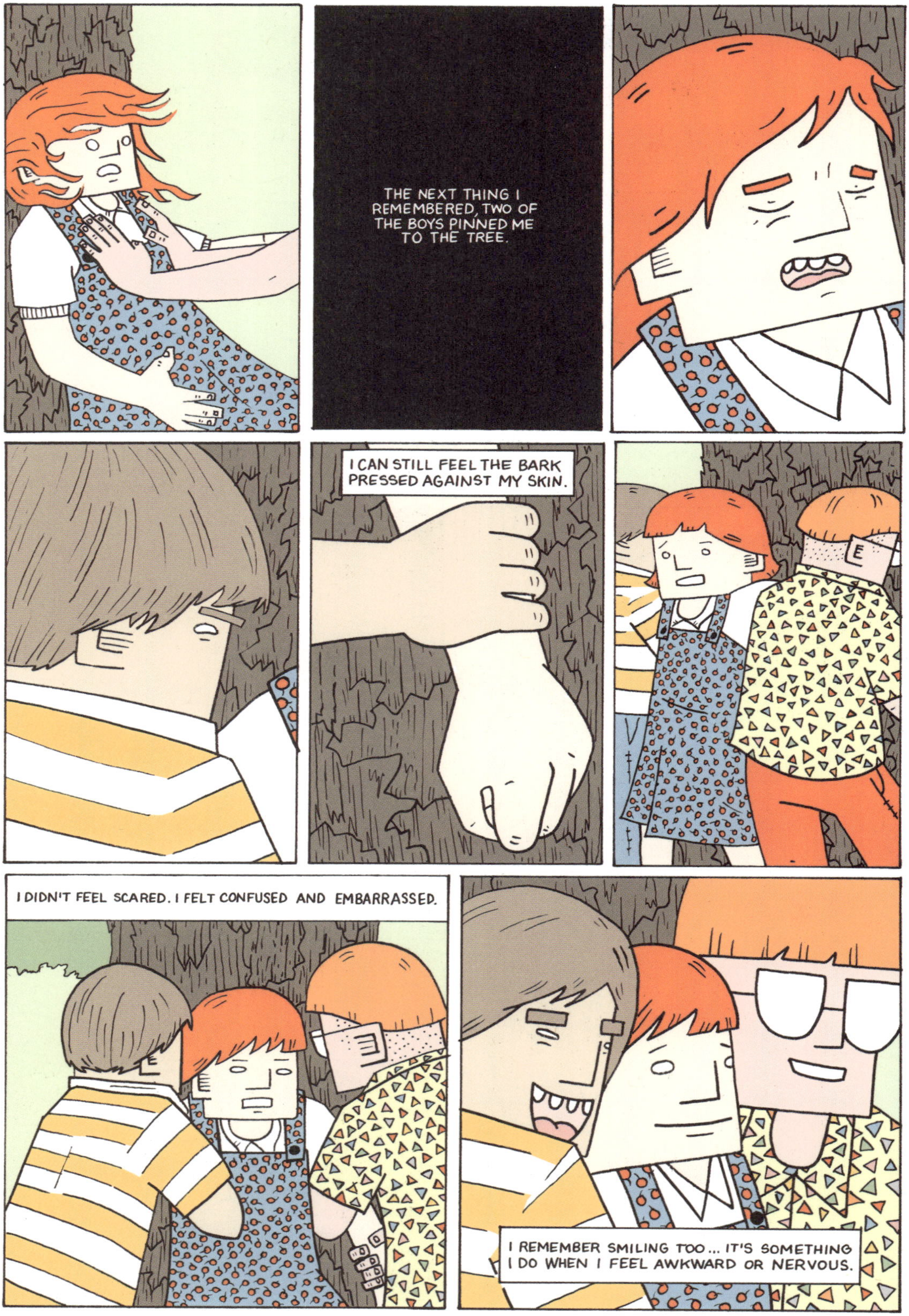

THE NEXT THING I REMEMBERED, TWO OF THE BOYS PINNED ME TO THE TREE.
I CAN STILL FEEL THE BARK PRESSED AGAINST MY SKIN.
I DIDN'T FEEL SCARED. I FELT CONFUSED AND EMBARRASSED.
I REMEMBER SMILING TOO... IT'S SOMETHING I DO WHEN I FEEL AWKWARD OR NERVOUS.

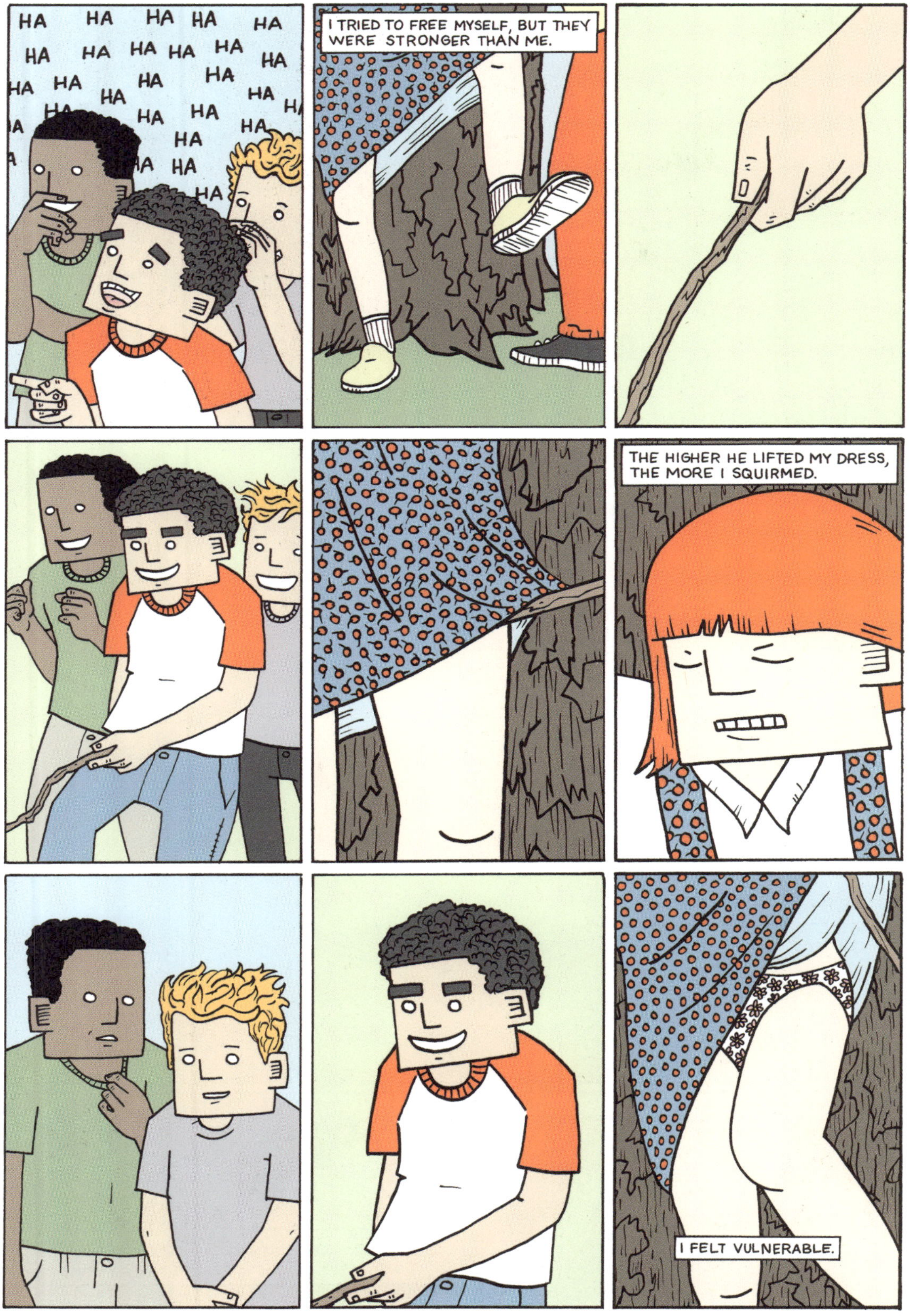
HA HA HA HA HA HA HA HA HA HA HA HA HA HA HA HA HA HA HA HA HA HA HA
I TRIED TO FREE MYSELF, BUT THEY WERE STRONGER THAN ME.
THE HIGHER HE LIFTED MY DRESS, THE MORE I SQUIRMED.
I FELT VULNERABLE.

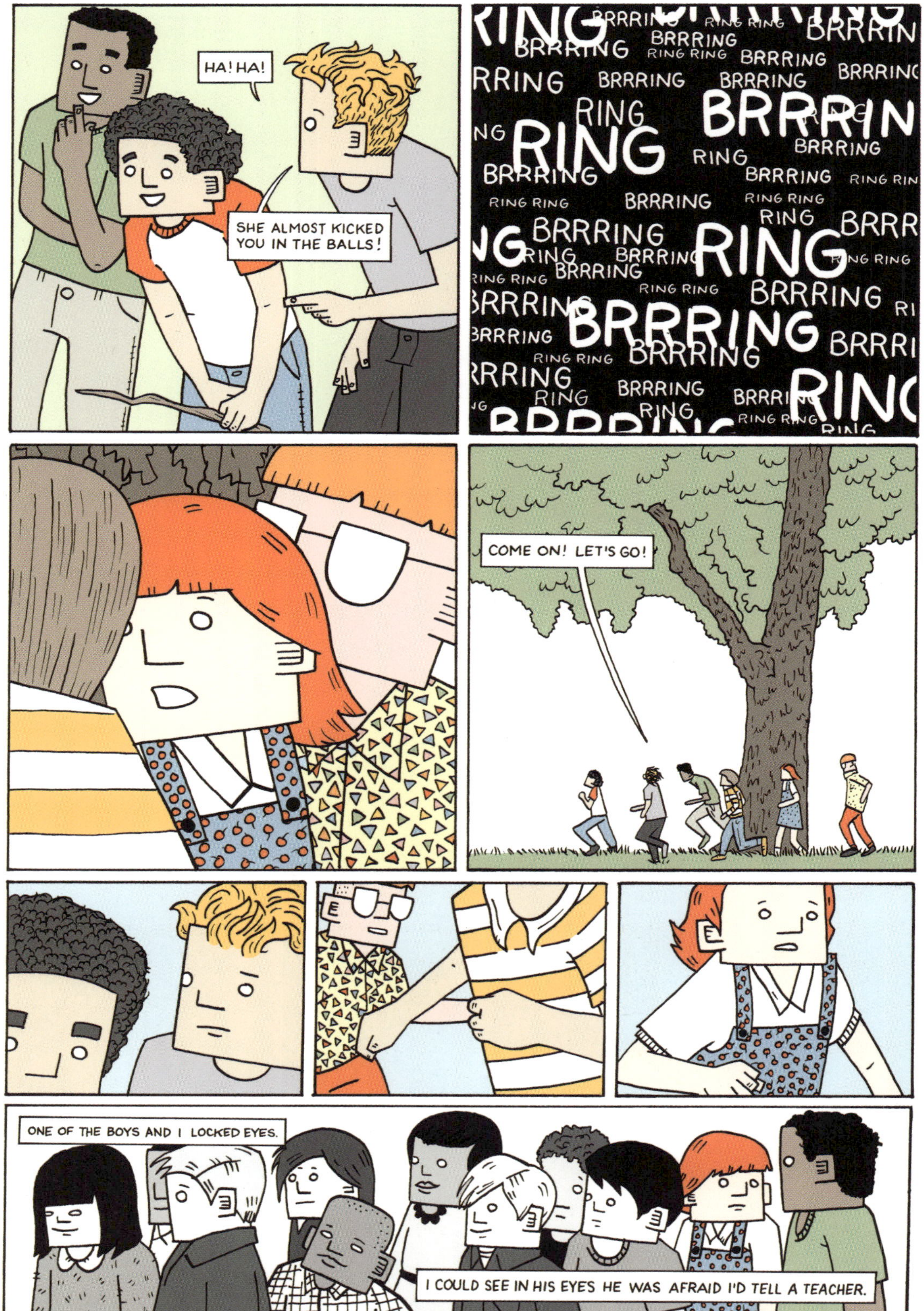
HA! HA!
SHE ALMOST KICKED YOU IN THE BALLS!
BRRRING BRRRING RING RING BRRRING RING RING BRRRING
BRRRING BRRRING BRRRING
RING BRRRING
RING BRRRING RING
BRRRING BRRRING RING RING
RING RING BRRRING RING RING RING
BRRRING RING BRRRING
RING RING BRRRING RING RING
RING RING BRRRING
BRRRING
BRRRING RING RING BRRRING
RING BRRRING BRRRING
RING RING RING RING
COME ON! LET'S GO!
ONE OF THE BOYS AND I LOCKED EYES.
I COULD SEE IN HIS EYES HE WAS AFRAID I'D TELL A TEACHER.

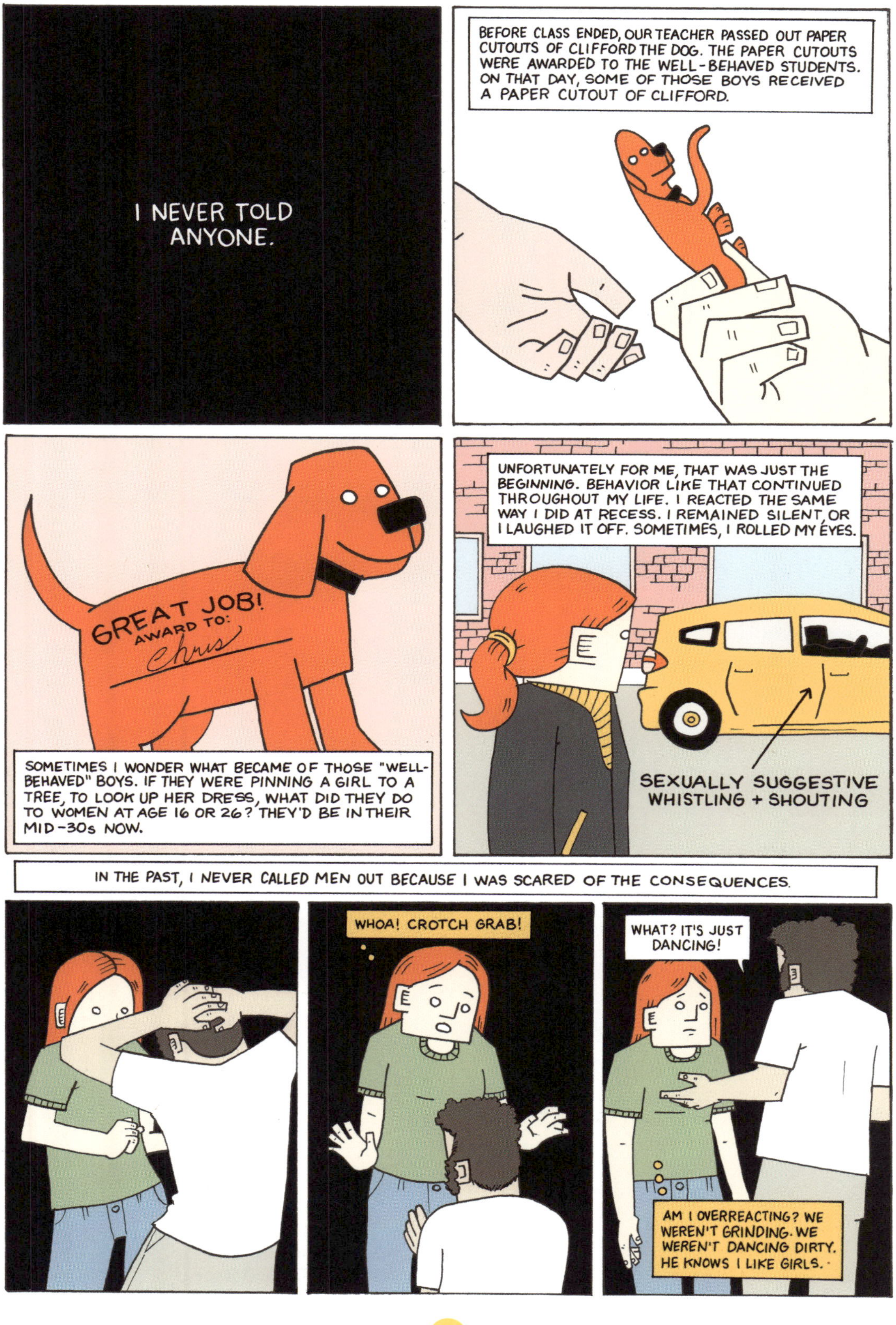
I NEVER TOLD ANYONE.
BEFORE CLASS ENDED, OUR TEACHER PASSED OUT PAPER CUTOUTS OF CLIFFORD THE DOG. THE PAPER CUTOUTS WERE AWARDED TO THE WELL-BEHAVED STUDENTS. ON THAT DAY, SOME OF THOSE BOYS RECEIVED A PAPER CUTOUT OF CLIFFORD.
GREAT JOB!
AWARD TO:
Chris
SOMETIMES I WONDER WHAT BECAME OF THOSE "WELL-BEHAVED" BOYS. IF THEY WERE PINNING A GIRL TO A TREE, TO LOOK UP HER DRESS, WHAT DID THEY DO TO WOMEN AT AGE 16 OR 26? THEY'D BE IN THEIR MID-30s NOW.
UNFORTUNATELY FOR ME, THAT WAS JUST THE BEGINNING. BEHAVIOR LIKE THAT CONTINUED THROUGHOUT MY LIFE. I REACTED THE SAME WAY I DID AT RECESS. I REMAINED SILENT, OR I LAUGHED IT OFF. SOMETIMES, I ROLLED MY EYES.
SEXUALLY SUGGESTIVE WHISTLING + SHOUTING
IN THE PAST, I NEVER CALLED MEN OUT BECAUSE I WAS SCARED OF THE CONSEQUENCES.
WHOA! CROTCH GRAB!
WHAT? IT'S JUST DANCING!
AM I OVERREACTING? WE WEREN'T GRINDING. WE WEREN'T DANCING DIRTY. HE KNOWS I LIKE GIRLS.

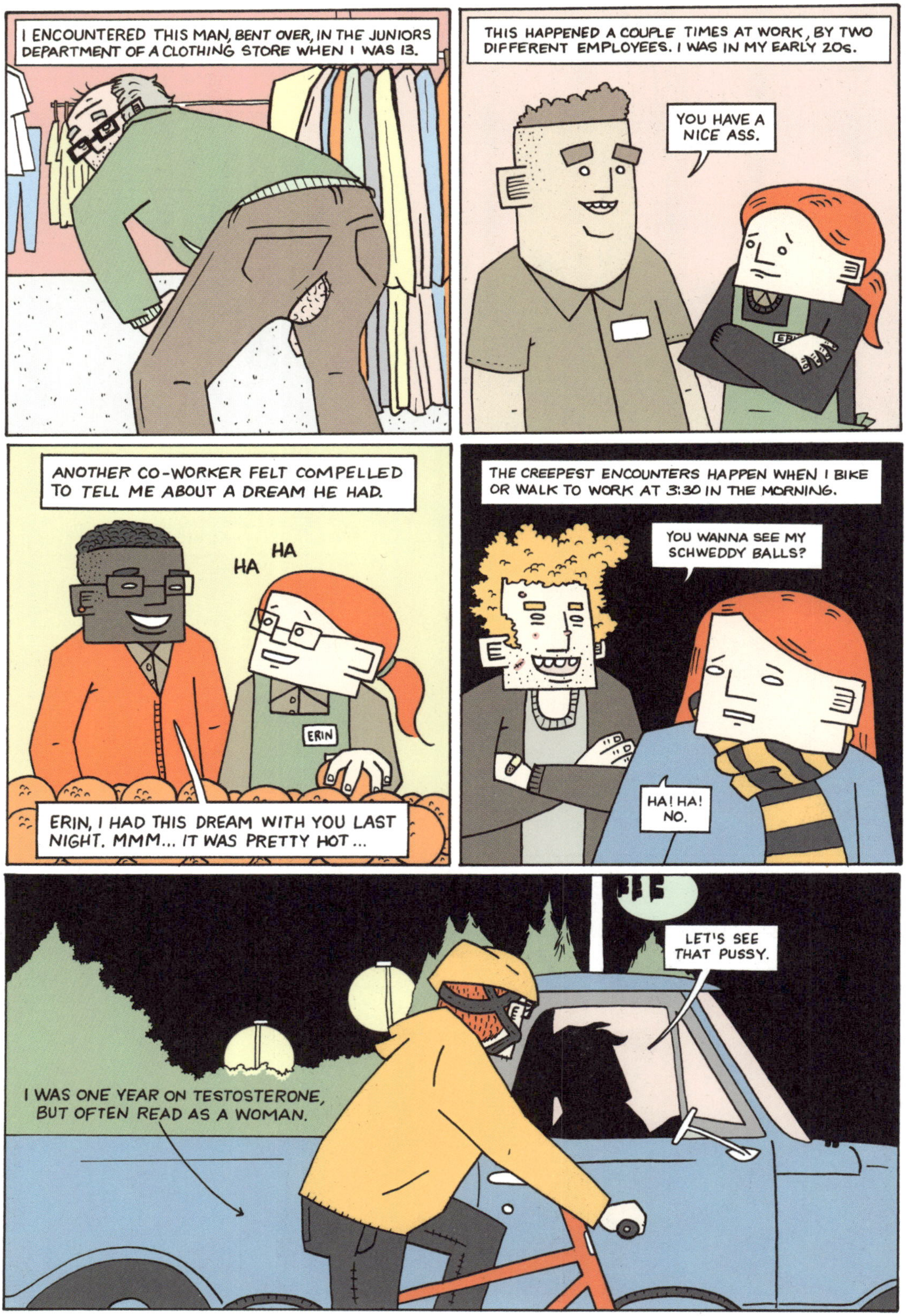
I ENCOUNTERED THIS MAN, BENT OVER, IN THE JUNIORS DEPARTMENT OF A CLOTHING STORE WHEN I WAS 13.
THIS HAPPENED A COUPLE TIMES AT WORK, BY TWO DIFFERENT EMPLOYEES. I WAS IN MY EARLY 20s.
YOU HAVE A NICE ASS.
ANOTHER CO-WORKER FELT COMPELLED TO TELL ME ABOUT A DREAM HE HAD.
HA HA
ERIN
ERIN, I HAD THIS DREAM WITH YOU LAST NIGHT. MMM... IT WAS PRETTY HOT...
THE CREEPEST ENCOUNTERS HAPPEN WHEN I BIKE OR WALK TO WORK AT 3:30 IN THE MORNING.
YOU WANNA SEE MY SCHWEDDY BALLS?
HA! HA! NO.
LET'S SEE THAT PUSSY.
I WAS ONE YEAR ON TESTOSTERONE, BUT OFTEN READ AS A WOMAN.

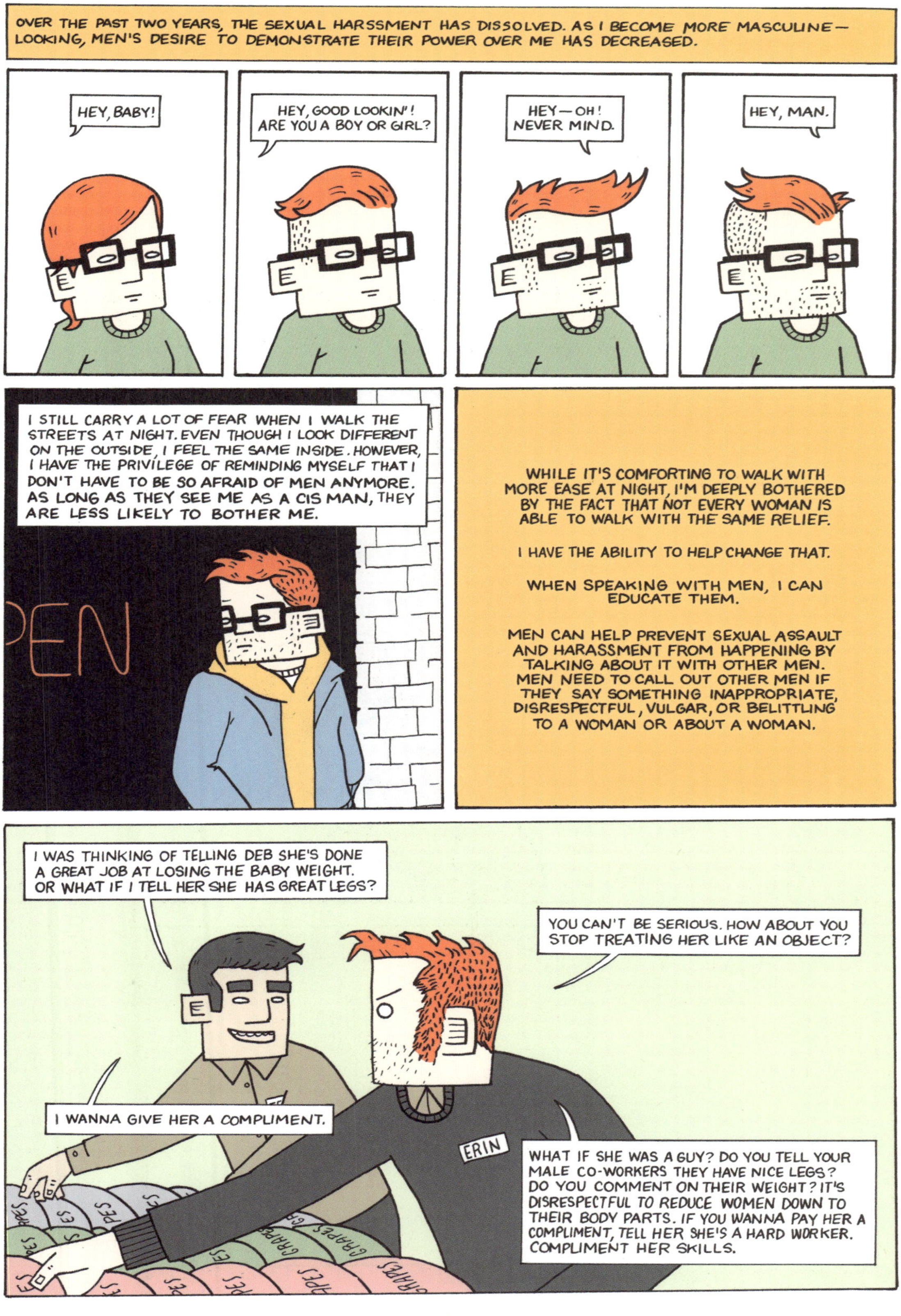
OVER THE PAST TWO YEARS, THE SEXUAL HARSSMENT HAS DISSOLVED. AS I BECOME MORE MASCULINE—LOOKING, MEN'S DESIRE TO DEMONSTRATE THEIR POWER OVER ME HAS DECREASED.
HEY, BABY!
HEY, GOOD LOOKIN'! ARE YOU A BOY OR GIRL?
HEY—OH! NEVER MIND.
HEY, MAN.
I STILL CARRY A LOT OF FEAR WHEN I WALK THE STREETS AT NIGHT. EVEN THOUGH I LOOK DIFFERENT ON THE OUTSIDE, I FEEL THE SAME INSIDE. HOWEVER, I HAVE THE PRIVILEGE OF REMINDING MYSELF THAT I DON'T HAVE TO BE SO AFRAID OF MEN ANYMORE. AS LONG AS THEY SEE ME AS A CIS MAN, THEY ARE LESS LIKELY TO BOTHER ME.
PEN
WHILE IT'S COMFORTING TO WALK WITH MORE EASE AT NIGHT, I'M DEEPLY BOTHERED BY THE FACT THAT NOT EVERY WOMAN IS ABLE TO WALK WITH THE SAME RELIEF.
I HAVE THE ABILITY TO HELP CHANGE THAT.
WHEN SPEAKING WITH MEN, I CAN EDUCATE THEM.
MEN CAN HELP PREVENT SEXUAL ASSAULT AND HARASSMENT FROM HAPPENING BY TALKING ABOUT IT WITH OTHER MEN. MEN NEED TO CALL OUT OTHER MEN IF THEY SAY SOMETHING INAPPROPRIATE, DISRESPECTFUL, VULGAR, OR BELITTLING TO A WOMAN OR ABOUT A WOMAN.
I WAS THINKING OF TELLING DEB SHE'S DONE A GREAT JOB AT LOSING THE BABY WEIGHT. OR WHAT IF I TELL HER SHE HAS GREAT LEGS?
YOU CAN'T BE SERIOUS. HOW ABOUT YOU STOP TREATING HER LIKE AN OBJECT?
I WANNA GIVE HER A COMPLIMENT.
ERIN
WHAT IF SHE WAS A GUY? DO YOU TELL YOUR MALE CO-WORKERS THEY HAVE NICE LEGS? DO YOU COMMENT ON THEIR WEIGHT? IT'S DISRESPECTFUL TO REDUCE WOMEN DOWN TO THEIR BODY PARTS. IF YOU WANNA PAY HER A COMPLIMENT, TELL HER SHE'S A HARD WORKER. COMPLIMENT HER SKILLS.
GRAPES

ACKNOWLEDGMENTS

THANK YOU, CHRIS STAROS, LEIGH WALTON, CHRIS ROSS, ZAC BOONE, GIL LAZCANO AND EVERYONE AT TOP SHELF AND IDW WHO HELPED EDIT, PROOFREAD AND PUT THIS BOOK TOGETHER. BIG THANKS TO BRETT WARNOCK FOR YOUR ENCOURAGEMENT, GUIDANCE, AND MENTORSHIP. THANKS, MOM, DAD, LAUREN, AND ANDREA FOR YOUR CONTINUED SUPPORT AND FOR ALLOWING ME TO PUT YOU IN THESE COMICS. TO JONATHON FOR ALWAYS BEING THERE FOR ME, FOR OFFERING ADVICE, ASSISTING WHEN I HAD QUESTIONS, AND ALWAYS PUSHING ME. BOBBY, THANK YOU FOR YOUR PATIENCE WHEN I HAD TO WORK LONG HOURS, FOR MOTIVATING ME, FOR YOUR SUGGESTIONS, AND FOR OFFERING TO INK OR EDIT WHEN I STRESSED ABOUT DEADLINES.

DEAR READER,

THANK YOU FOR READING! I REALLY APPRECIATE YOUR INTEREST AND SUPPORT.

YOURS TRULY,
ERIN

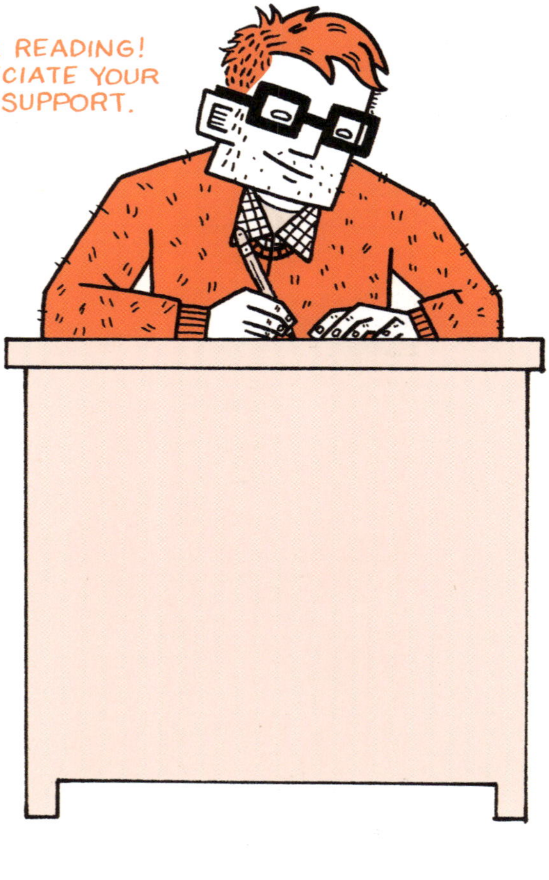